MONEY FOR MINISTRIES

MONEY FOR MINISTRIES

Wesley K. Willmer, Editor

VICTOR BOOKS

A DIVISION OF SCRIPTURE PRESS PUBLICATIONS INC.
USA CANADA ENGLAND

Recommended Dewey Decimal Classification: 254.8
Suggested Subject Heading: FUND-RAISING

Library of Congress Catalog Card Number: 88-62839
ISBN: 0-89693-562-0

Cover Designer: *Gary Gnidovik*

CONTENTS

Foreword *Norman L. Edwards*   9

Introduction *Wesley K. Willmer*   11

SECTION I. THE POWER AND RESPONSIBILITY
          OF THE DONOR   13

1. Considering a Godly Perspective in Providing Money
   for Ministries
   Wesley K. Willmer   15

2. God's Call for Responsible Giving
   Gordon K. Moyes   25

3. On Becoming a Strategic Steward
   J. Alan Youngren   35

4. My Personal Style of Giving
   Anonymous   49

5. Above Reproach: The Measure of Credibility
   Arthur C. Borden   64

6. How To Have More Money To Give
   Ronald W. Blue   76

7. Lifestyle Stewardship
   Lawrence W. O'Nan   84

SECTION II. THE RESPONSIBILITY OF THE CHURCH
           AND PARACHURCH ORGANIZATION   95

8. The Role of Stewardship in the Local Church
   Edward J. Hales   97

9. Guidelines for Organizations To Develop
   a Christian Philosophy of Fund-Raising
   John F. Walvoord   106

10. How Much Is Enough?
    Eugene B. Habecker   117

11. Integrating Faith into an Organization's
    Fund-Raising Practices
    Jerry E. White   133

12. The Electronic Church: Its Role in Christian Fund-Raising
    David W. Clark   140

13. Using the Bible as a Guide for Fund-Raising Costs
    Holmes M. Bryan, Jr.   148

14. Fund-Raising Constraints: Law and Ethics
    George R. Grange II   159

SECTION III. THE EVANGELICAL FUND-RAISER'S
              CHALLENGE   173

15. Servanthood: The Fund-Raiser's Call
    David L. McKenna   175

16. Developing Lifelong Relationships with Donors
    J. David Schmidt   185

17. Preserving the Person in the Fund-Raising Process
    D. Bruce Lockerbie   199

18. A Witnessing/Work Perspective on Fund-Raising:
    The Zacchaeus Factor
    R. Wayne Clugston   208

19. George Mueller and the Quest for Biblical Balance
    in Fund-Raising
    James C. Killion   220

20. Strategic Planning: Spirit Driven or Market Driven?
    Larry F. Johnston   233

21. The Spiritual Life and Ministry of Christian Fund-Raisers
    Charles W. Spicer, Jr.   248

22. Raising Personal Support
    H. Andrew Read   259

SECTION IV. THE CLIMATE IN EVANGELICAL
             FUND-RAISING   269

23. Heresies in Evangelical Fund-Raising: A Theologian's
    Perspective
    Carl F.H. Henry   271

24. What the Public Thinks about Evangelical Fund-Raising
    Paul H. Virts and George Gallup, Jr.   282

25. The Evangelical Donor Talks Back
    James F. Engel   295

26. Ethical Attitudes and Beliefs of Evangelical Fund-Raisers
    Linda A. Keener   307

27. Historical Perspectives on Evangelical Fund-Raising
    Lawrence M. Weber   315

28. Does It Pay To Pray?
    Melvin E. Lorentzen   322

29. No Competition in the Kingdom
    Gordon D. Loux   332

SECTION V. A BIBLIOGRAPHY OF FUNDING
                  THE EVANGELICAL ENTERPRISE   343

30. A Bibliography of Funding the Evangelical Enterprise
    Janis W. Sokoloski   345

NOTES   365

Foreword

The publication of this volume is the culmination of many years of prayerful concern about the way in which Christians go about raising and giving funds for their many causes and enterprises. I have had the privilege of watching the thought and effort behind this book evolve over a period of years—both as a close friend of the editor, as the president of the Christian Stewardship Council, and as a board member of the Evangelical Council for Financial Accountability.

The concern for the deficiency of a theology to guide the giving and asking practices of evangelicals was expressed by Wes Willmer almost five years before the publishing date and more than three years before the electronic media scandals of 1987. No one anticipated that Christian fund-raising practices would be front-page news for most of that year.

While most fund-raisers were trying to anticipate the possible impact of major U.S. tax reform on charitable giving, there were some who still believed that the advancement of the kingdom was not in the hands of the Congress or the Internal Revenue Service.

For over twenty-five years the Christian Stewardship Council has required every member to subscribe to a nine-point Code of Ethical Pursuit. In the late 1970s, evangelical Christians voiced a deep concern for receiving and managing God's funds in a way that would be above reproach by donors, skeptical unbelievers, and the government. Out of these concerns was born the Evangelical Council for Financial Accountability (ECFA).

In March of 1987, the conference "Funding the Christian Challenge" was jointly sponsored by the Christian Stewardship Council and the Billy Graham Center. Conference Chairman Wesley Willmer initiated and organized this event to heighten awareness of these concerns and as preparation for publishing portions of this book. This book would have never succeeded had it not been for the strong conviction and commitment of Dr. Willmer.

I see this as a significant step in making the necessary tools available for evangelicals to mature in their practices of giving and asking. It is reassuring to know that God will fulfill His eternal purposes through His faithful followers who give in response to their understandings of the teachings of Scripture and with joy for all that God through Christ has done for them.

Norman L. Edwards, President
Christian Stewardship Council, 1984–1988

Introduction

Evangelicalism has often been regarded as a cultural mastodon that somehow survived the advent of modern civilization. As the fastest growing and most visible and ambitious segment of American Protestantism, evangelicals represent 20 percent of the American population. More ministries, more money, and more methods exist than ever before, and out of this activity results a real void—a serious deficiency of a biblically based theology of stewardship to guide the giver and the asker in funding the evangelical challenge.

The purpose of this book is to provide practical, yet scholarly and well-thought-out benchmarks to guide both givers and askers in developing and implementing a theology of the funding process. The authors represent a balance of laymen, theologians, fund-raisers, pastors, and educators—all givers and serious about their faith.

John R.W. Stott in his book, *The Message of the Sermon on the Mount*, points out a critical point about the passage, "Do not be like them" (Matthew 6:8). Stott writes, "The followers of Jesus are to be different—different from both the nominal church and the secular world, different from both the religious and the irreligious." This publication builds on that concern and challenges evangelicals to be unique and consistent in following God's direction in their giving and asking for funds. *Money for Ministries* attempts to provide both theoretical and practical guidance in stewardship for those desiring to live within God's perspective.

The book is divided into five distinct sections: (1) The Power and Responsibility of the Donor, (2) The Responsibility of the Church and Parachurch Organization, (3) The Evangelical Fund-Raiser's Challenge, (4) The Climate in Evangelical Fund-Raising, and (5) A Bibliography of Funding the Evangelical Enterprise. Each section has integrity as a unit within itself, and each in turn contributes to the total work. Many of the individual chapters also can be used for individual or group study such as Sunday School classes, or for college or seminary reading.

An undertaking such as this results from the cooperation and support of many people. I am indebted to many individuals and organizations that uniquely contributed to the completion of this publication. Initial encouragement and acceptance of the vision for the book came from Wes Willis and Mark Sweeney followed by capable production and editorial assistance from Greg Clouse and Carole Streeter, all of Victor Books. Georgia Douglass of Douglass Editorial Service provided data input and editorial assistance.

Financial backing for various portions of this project came from three foundations and their representatives: The Lilly Endowment, Inc. (Charles A. Johnson), The Glenmede Trust (Martin Trimble), and The Maclellan Foundation (Hugh O. Maclellan, Sr.).

The Christian Stewardship Council and the Billy Graham Center graciously agreed to cosponsor the conference, "Funding the Christian Challenge," which provided a springboard for much of the thinking for this publication. Other cooperating agencies of the conference included the Association of Institutional Development Officers, Christian Education; the Canadian Council of Christian Charities; the Christian Booksellers Association; the Christian College Coalition; the Christian Ministries Management Association; Christianity Today, Inc.; the Development Association for Christian Institutions; the Evangelical Council for Financial Accountability; the National Association of Evangelicals; the NAE Stewardship Commission; and National Religious Broadcasters.

Encouragement and direction for the book was provided by J. David Schmidt, J. David Schmidt and Associates; Bobbi Denslow, Moody Bible Institute; Jane Halteman, Christian Stewardship Council; Norman Edwards, Screen Communications; Stanley Thompson, Free Methodist Foundation; Jack Richardson, Billy Graham Evangelistic Association; Joel Carpenter, Institute for the Study of American Evangelicals, Billy Graham Center, and the board of directors of the Christian Stewardship Council. And finally, my wife, Sharon, and three children, Stephen, Kristell, and Brian.

It is my prayer that because of this publication individual believers will be encouraged and God's eternal kingdom will be furthered as others come to a saving knowledge of His grace.

Wesley K. Willmer
Wheaton, Illinois
1989

The
Power and Responsibility
of the Donor

(1)
CONSIDERING A GODLY
PERSPECTIVE IN PROVIDING
MONEY FOR MINISTRIES

WESLEY K. WILLMER

We live in a day of much need, many requests, and plenty of wealth. Funding evangelical ministries is big business—many give and many ask. Unfortunately, the process of giving and asking tends to be more happenstance than directed. When givers and askers don't realize that they should be working together, tension results and God's kingdom suffers.

At the core of the problem is confusion about defining, understanding, and applying a godly, biblically based theology of stewardship. There is little teaching on the why and how of giving and asking, and the impact the two activities have on each other. If the giver and asker can become more like-minded in understanding the process, God's kingdom will ultimately benefit.

This chapter is a general framework providing guidance to both givers and askers who are seeking a godly perspective on funding the evangelical enterprise. It is divided into three sections: (1) keeping God's kingdom in perspective, (2) the giver's responsibility, and (3) the fund-raiser's approach. It is up to us as individuals to apply these principles to the particular causes we represent or support.

KEEPING GOD'S KINGDOM IN PERSPECTIVE

In our fast-paced and self-oriented society, it is easy to lose perspective of whose world we are in, whose money we are spending, whose organizations we are dealing with, and how we are approaching our everyday interactions with our money. At the heart of God-pleasing practices in the giving and asking of funds is the ability to view the world, man, and human relationships from God's perspective. This perspective is best presented by answering four questions: Whose money? Whose givers? Whose work? and Whose fund-raisers?

● Whose money? At the conference on *Funding the Christian Challenge*, Gordon MacDonald, then president of InterVarsity Christian Fellowship, said, "One of the greatest missing teachings in the American church today is the reminder to men and women that nothing we have belongs to us."[1] This is a very uncomfortable theology in America because of our unquestioning acceptance of the concept of private ownership—that we have the right to own our possessions. Understanding ownership from God's perspective is quite different, however, and is a central issue in developing a godly perspective in the giving and asking of funds. Legally, ownership is determined on the basis of possession of title, conquest, purchase, or one's own labor. For the Christian, however, there is a spiritual dimension in which we look at possessions from God's perspective. We have been given material means to use, but not to own.

Jesus certainly addressed the topic of money and possessions in His teachings. He did not denounce money, nor material possessions. In the Synoptic Gospels, one verse in six discusses the correct way to handle possessions. Sixteen of the parables deal with possessions.

Money is clearly a primary resource devised by the world, but used by God to enable us to distribute possessions to those in need. This is an important concept to keep in mind, whether we are giving or asking for funds. It is easy for fund-raisers and ministry leaders to get caught up in a their-money-for-our-ministry mentality. Whether giving or asking, we need to go back to the fundamental fact that God is the source of all resources. Psalm 24:1 tells us that God owns everything. It is impossible for a ministry to ask for our money if we don't have any. If our money belongs to God, all they can ask us for is God's money. The decision becomes ours as to whether we will distribute that money according to the suggestion made to us. Money is not ours to possess, but to distribute as good stewards.

I have heard Christians say, "I can't talk to people about money, because what they do with their money is between them and God." In reflecting on the tavern owner who gave D.L. Moody $20,000, Moody said, "The devil's had it long enough—it's now God's turn."

From a godly perspective, our responsibility is to recognize that all resources are God's; when we respond to a giving opportunity, we are releasing God's money to supply the need.

Evangelical fund-raisers are *not* responsible for whether or not people give. They *are* responsible for challenging potential givers to consider what they might do. That is what Paul was telling Timothy in 1 Timothy 6:17-21. We often think these verses have to do with our being generous. They don't; they teach us about our responsibility to enable others to be generous.

Giving involves more than money. When the beggar at the Jerusalem temple asked Peter and John for money, Peter said, "Silver and gold I do not have, but what I have I give you" (Acts 3:6). And the beggar was healed. The theme of many portions of Scripture is, "What I have I give to you."

Imagine the prayer support, the personal talents and skills, and the other gifts that can be given. We must never forget that we all have much to give. A good reminder of this is in Carl F.H. Henry's *Such As I Have*,[2] where he portrays scenarios on giving, most of them offerings of deep dedication, but only a few involving money.

As we become aware that all the resources of the world belong to God, we realize our responsibility to be good stewards in distributing the resources entrusted to us. Both givers and fund-raisers should acknowledge these concepts of divine ownership and human stewardship as fundamental to their activities.

● Whose givers? Mankind is made in the image of God. Because we are created by Him, we have value to God for who we are, not for what we may have achieved.

Many fund-raising programs begin with the assumption that people give out of "identifiable self-interest." On the other hand, a godly perspective suggests people should give for reasons of love, vision, compassion, and stewardship. Organizations seeking a godly perspective have a special obligation to encourage this higher, spiritual motivation of donors. Accepting money from people without caring about them or their involvement with the organization runs counter to God's perspective of valuing people. The fund-raising process can actually desensitize givers into responding from wrong motives.

From modern marketing principles we can draw an underlying principle for ethical marketing that is helpful to our thinking. The marketing process is an exchange of value, not stealing or coercion.

When a fund-raiser approaches a person about giving money, whether through letters, on the phone, or in person, it should never be a question of using gimmicks, or figuring out how to get at them and their money. It should always be an exchange of values. As I look at the New Testament, one thing I see over and over again in the passages about giving is relationships—often long-term relationships. If I had to describe in one word this exchange process, it would be *relationships*, a valued personal link between the giver and the asker, with what God is doing in the world.

As Chuck Colson, the chairman of the board of Prison Fellowship Ministries, states:

> I believe an organization should get to know their donors and develop a relationship with them. It's not right to take money from people without caring about their spiritual life and their involvement with us. . . . We feel a responsibility to a donor to encourage him and help him spiritually. We think we should be teaching our donors and involving them in the ministry, so that they really understand what it is we believe and why we believe it.[1]

● Whose work? In light of the answers to the first two questions, it becomes apparent that providing money for ministries is God's work and that He has provided all that is necessary to accomplish His work (Exodus 25:2). It is He who works in people's hearts and motivates them to give. *Ora et labora,* prayer and work, reflects the necessary balance between dependence on God's blessing and the fund-raiser's responsibility for his own efforts. This was graphically illustrated as Nehemiah rebuilt the Jerusalem wall. He was confident that his God would deliver the people, yet he instructed half of his servants to carry on the work while the other half served as guards (Nehemiah 4).

Faith, prayer, and dependence on God are not substitutes for effort, caution, and reason. On the contrary, rightful dependence on God demands that we engage in certain necessary human efforts. Claiming that God is capable of accomplishing His purposes without them, or that we can do His work without Him, is to ignore the needed balance between prayer and work.

When we realize that God works through people, programs, and organizations, our giving and asking practices come into harmony with each other, the tension is eased, and ministry flourishes.

• Whose fund-raisers? The fourth principle speaks more specifically to the fund-raiser seeking to implement a godly perspective of funding kingdom work. Some may argue that fund-raisers don't fit at all, but it seems clear in the scriptural accounts that certain people became responsible for seeking money. If this is God's world and He owns everything, then fund-raisers are "workers in His vineyard," stewards to care for the resources God has loaned to each of us.

With this perspective in mind, the fund-raiser's attitude needs to be, "God, show us the way," not, "We can do it." The fund-raiser must not sit on his hands when God calls him to move. Surely the rallying call should be, " 'Not by might nor by power, but by My Spirit,' says the Lord Almighty" (Zechariah 4:6).

Fund-raisers and other leaders in a work should set the pace. The commitment of the people will usually rise no higher than that of the leadership (1 Chronicles 29:3, 6). This means leaders must be involved in giving time, talents, and resources.

It is possible that carefully planned fund-raising schemes actually hinder God's work, and that pleas for money actually block God's channels of support. If fund-raising is not done with God's perspective in view, it may have a long-term negative effect.

How often do you hear fund-raisers talk about prayer as a resource? Many have more faith in the mailing list than in the prayers of their constituents. If churches and organizations are God's, shouldn't we be trying to develop an attitude of daily prayer in the homes of constituents? The priorities of fund-raisers should be governed by whose they are, and not by the particular organization to which they are attached.

THE GIVER'S RESPONSIBILITY
In this day of relentless appeals and requests for funds, each of us as financial supporters must realize the inherent power we possess to hold people and organizations accountable for their programs and activities.

• What should motivate us to give? At the core of the issues affecting givers is the personal motivation for giving. Obviously, we all give for different reasons—to get something in return, to give something that is needed, to pay a debt, to avoid taxes, or to express religious convictions.

While it is often assumed that donors respond to noble causes and creative ideas, more often than not, we give because of sentiment, guilt, or social pressure. Christians should be motivated to give for biblical reasons as prompted by the Holy Spirit. If this is to happen, fund-raising appeals must be biblical and must never exploit the call or gift of God in order to achieve a fiscal end. As Chuck Colson says, "I have a real problem with Christianity that appeals to the egocentric culture, because to me it's cheap grace."[4] The giver has a responsibility to ignore appeals that play on egos.

In his book *Mega Gifts*, Jerold Panas points out that people don't give because there is a need. They give to heroic, exciting programs rather than to needy institutions.[5] As Harold Seymour says, "The cause must catch the eye, warm the heart, and stir the mind."[6]

Each of us has to decide what motivates our giving. The easy way generally is to go with the flow of the appeals. The more difficult way—and higher calling—is to put time and energy into getting good information and then being open to God's leading. (Chapter 3 develops this topic further.)

• Why should we give? The most obvious reason is that God commands us to give as a part of His plan and order for our lives. In 1 Timothy 6:17 we are instructed, "Command those who are rich in this present world not to be arrogant nor to put their hope in wealth, which is so uncertain, but to put their hope in God, who richly provides us with everything for our enjoyment."

We are to do good, to be rich in good deeds, and to be generous and willing to share. In this way we will lay up treasures for ourselves as a firm foundation for the coming age, for giving is a spiritual issue with immediate and eternal consequences.

Jesus asked the rich young ruler to give because of what it was going to do for him (Luke 18). The primary benefit is always to the giver (Philippians 4:17-20). No one is too poor to give to something. As people minister to you, you should give to them.

A third reason is that giving and receiving are part of the life of fellowship. Giving is a form of fellowship (2 Corinthians 8-9) and without sharing, the believer is off balance. As we give, a change will take place inside us, our relationship to others and to God will change. We are called to be stewards of God's resources, because this is God's plan and order for our lives (1 Corinthians 4:2).

– We are to give cheerfully. "Each man should give what he has decided in his heart to give, not reluctantly or under compulsion, for God loves a cheerful giver" (2 Corinthians 9:7).

– We are to give liberally. "Give, and it will be given to you. A good measure, pressed down, shaken together and running over, will be poured into your lap. For with the measure you use, it will be measured to you" (Luke 6:38).

– We are to give sacrificially. "They gave as much as they were able, and even beyond their ability" (2 Corinthians 8:3).

– We are to give proportionately (Deuteronomy 16:17; 2 Corinthians 8:12); proportionate to need, as in the example of the cup of cold water in Matthew 10:42; proportionate to resource, as in the illustration of the two copper coins in Mark 12:42; and proportionate to both need and resource, as in the story of the five loaves and two fish in John 6.

– We are to give systematically. "On the first day of every week, each one of you should set aside a sum of money in keeping with his income" (1 Corinthians 16:2).

Jesus said, "For where your treasure is, there your heart will be also" (Matthew 6:21). The story of the rich young ruler in Luke 18 is a good example of money being a heart issue that involves the whole person. When money is mentioned in the Scripture, it involves the response of the total person.

THE FUND-RAISER'S APPROACH

From the Bible we can draw numerous principles for developing a customized fund-raising philosophy and practice. Donors should also know these principles, because they have a responsibility to hold accountable fund-raisers and the organizations they represent.

• Work within existing relationships. Accounts of fund-raising in the Bible most often occur in the context of existing ministry relationships—that of "partners" or "fellow workers" (Philippians 1:5; 4:3). Commonsense marketing focuses on those who have an interest in the cause and are most likely to develop a relationship. Our first priority is to communicate with those who are already in the fold— friends loyal to the organization. A good relationship requires effective communication and that involves the total person—the emotions, the intellect, and the will. The money people bring to an organization is exchanged for a "relationship"—a valued personal link with what God is doing in the world through the fund-raiser—through the leaders of the organization, its employees, and its constituents.

• Emphasize opportunity, not just need. The fund-raiser's focus should be on providing prospective donors opportunities to show concern and support for the ministry or organization, and not on begging for support because of need. The Apostle Paul's attitude was that giving was not to be done because of critical need, "We can't get along without you and your support," but rather, "Here is an opportunity for you to join in partnership to see the work advanced." (See Philippians 4:10-13.)

In light of divine ownership and human stewardship, the responsibility of the fund-raiser is to present opportunities for people to distribute their resources. It is never a question of figuring out how to get their money.

• Seek involvement and commitment. The fund-raiser should seek more than token giving—rather, a person's involvement and commitment (Philippians 4:14-16). The reference is to assistance "again and again," and speaks to developing repeat donors, loyal and faithful supporters—lifelong friends. Programs and efforts should focus on developing long-term relationships with supporters who are involved and committed to what the organization is doing. Communication should encourage people to respond out of their total being because giving involves both the mind and the heart.

• Realize the giver is more important than the gift. The fund-raiser who understands the value God places on people knows that the gift is secondary to concern for the individual. This means that fund-raising activities should never be manipulative. Manipulation must be "out" and service "in." Giving must be combined with a relationship in which the donor and donee grow together. Never should a potential donor be viewed as an "expendable name" on a list—or as someone to be pressured for gifts.

• Recognize there will be spiritual blessing. Giving is an activity which is pleasing to God and results in spiritual blessing to the donor (Philippians 4:17-19). Fund-raising activity has a higher calling beyond "collecting the dollars and running." The donor receives a benefit and reaps spiritual blessing as a result of the interactions.

When people are helped to give worthily, spiritual blessing follows (1 Chronicles 29:9). The fund-raiser provides opportunities for people to participate in what God is doing in the world and to exercise their gifts. The focus needs to be on facilitating the giver's interest in enhancing a particular ministry.

• Realize that donors are giving up a piece of their treasure. As Matthew 6:21 tells us, "For where your treasure is, there your heart will be also." One of the most important steps toward building a relationship is getting a first gift. Once a gift is given, it should be treated as if it were a piece of a person's heart. Therefore, proper acknowledgment of the gift, disclosure of its use, and reports of future plans are essential.

• Know why the donor gives. "Any enterprise is built with wise planning, becomes stronger through common sense, and profits wonderfully by keeping abreast of the facts" (Proverbs 24:3-4, TLB). Fund-raisers should know their constituents empirically, for who they are, why they give, etc. A healthy relationship requires communication which involves listening as much as sending messages. A consistent method of researching and knowing your donors is essential. This may be a basic mailed survey, a simple phone sample, or focus groups. Whatever the method, the data is essential—because communication is a two-way process between the giver and the asker.

• Never exploit sacred trust, manipulate a person, hide costs, or avoid reporting failures. In Mark 12:38-40 we read, "Watch out for the teachers of the law . . . they devour widows' houses . . . such men will be punished most severely."

Requests for funds should never exploit our sacred trust relationship with our constituents. Correspondence that begins, "God told me to contact you," or an appeal that concludes, "Unless you give now, our ministry will end," is no better than the scribes' long robes, long walks, and long prayers. The responsibility of fund-raisers is to present the case accurately and enthusiastically—not manipulatively—and then leave the results to God.

Fund-raising management should not hide costs or avoid reporting failures. Potential donors deserve to know what percentage of a gift goes directly to ministry and what goes to administrative costs. Donors have a right to know how their gifts relate to the goals for which the money was raised. Full disclosure is essential to honest communication and long-term relations.

FAITH, RELATIONSHIPS, AND SERVICE

I try to integrate these principles into my everyday work by applying them to three concepts: faith, relationships, and service. Presuming the assumptions of divine ownership and human stewardship, my daily activities reflect this perspective, and prayer becomes an important component of my work. (Recognizing that it is God who works in people's hearts motivating them to give,\I believe it is my responsibility to pray for them and ask God to work in their hearts.

My focus in raising funds is to develop lifelong relationships between the constituency and the organization. All communications (publications, phone, mail, personal calls) become an effort to build relationships of honesty and integrity.(I avoid manipulative techniques, despite pressures to reach a particular goal.) This endeavor is a sacred trust that must be taken seriously. My role, then, is one of service to facilitate these relationships—to provide giving opportunities, to assist people in wise estate planning, and to offer counsel on total giving. Through these services, God's people are enabled to work together in providing sufficient funds for ministries.)

WESLEY K. WILLMER has been active in evangelical fund-raising for over 17 years. He has held administrative positions at several Christian colleges, taught regularly, and been involved in consulting with numerous evangelical organizations. In 1987 he initiated and chaired the national conference, Funding the Christian Challenge: Seeking Godly Ways in the Asking and Giving of Funds, which attracted 600 people representing 400 organizations.

Dr. Willmer has authored and edited books in fund-raising, plus more than a dozen articles for professional journals. In 1986 the Council for Advancement and Support of Education (CASE) selected him from among its 14,000 individual members at more than 2,800 institutions to receive its annual award for significant contributions in research and writing. He is on the board of the Christian Stewardship Council.

(2)
GOD'S CALL FOR
RESPONSIBLE GIVING

GORDON K. MOYES

One of my sons keeps homing pigeons. The pigeons were born and raised in the confinement of coops. But it is the nature of pigeons to fly free, and eventually the day came for them to be released. It takes a great act of faith to release birds that once were featherless and bare in your hands. My son opened the coops and watched as they circled in the sky, coming down, not to reenter their coops, but to sit on the rooftops, the fences, and the trees.

From every vantage point the pigeons watched as I considered ways of recapturing them and placing them back in their coops. I thought of large fine nets strung between long poles, of setting bird traps, of climbing roofs to frighten the birds down, and so forth. While I was thinking of more sophisticated and complex methods to recapture the pigeons, my son simply scattered some food inside the coop, and they all flew in!

He gave, and the birds returned.

I was spending my efforts on structures, strategies, and systems. Stewardship is not a matter of strategies to get, but of remembering to give. God calls us to give responsibly and places much significance on our stewardship.

GIVING

Jesus understood the seduction of things and the liberation that comes through a right handling of the things we possess. That is the reason 16 of His 38 parables were concerned with how we handle our money and possessions. One out of every 10 verses in the Gospels (288 in all) deals directly with how we gain, save, and use our possessions. It is said that the Bible has some 500 verses about prayer, some 500 verses about faith, and some 2,000 verses on how we acquire and use our money and possessions. Our stewardship is one of the great tests of our spirituality.

Paul taught the young church, "The Lord Jesus Himself said, 'It is more blessed to give than to receive' " (Acts 20:35); other Scriptures indicate how giving provides us with freedom and blessing. Let me amplify this in three areas: giving denies materialism its illusion, giving denies acquisitiveness its seductiveness, and giving denies greed its pleasure.

● I was driving down a tollway, nearing the tollgates, when I was passed by a red Ferarri. But at the tollgate I was able to read the bumper sticker: "He who has the most toys when he dies wins." Right? Wrong! I have conducted funeral services for more than a thousand people, and I have never seen a hearse followed by a U-Haul trailer. You cannot take it with you.

Materialism, though an illusion, gives a feeling of permanence to a transient generation. Materialism is the ultimate misuse of God's gifts. Stewardship is using God's gifts. Our giving places our living into perspective and breaks the illusion of materialism. This particular difficulty is in part a result of our current self-oriented culture.

● When we learn to give, we free ourselves from the seductiveness of acquisitiveness. By nature we are hoarders, and our primal insecurities demand that we gather more and more things, as if ultimate security lays in piles of possessions. Jesus told of a successful man whose whole life was spent in acquiring more and more symbols of success. He built bigger and bigger barns to store his hoard, saying to himself:

"You have plenty of good things laid up for many years. Take life easy; eat, drink, and be merry."

But God said to him, "You fool! This very night your life will be demanded from you. Then who will get what you have prepared for yourself?" This is how it will be with anyone who stores up things for himself but is not rich toward God (Luke 12:19-21).

In the ruins of Pompeii, archaeologists found the body of a man who, instead of fleeing from the ashes of Mt. Vesuvius, had waited to gather his gold. He suffocated while reaching out for gold coins that had fallen from the bag clutched in his bony fingers. It had stopped him from fleeing and cost him his life. Jesus said, "What good is it for a man to gain the whole world, yet forfeit his soul?" (Mark 8:36)

Time magazine of December 1, 1986 featured an article entitled "Going after the Crooks," which described Wall Street inside traders who deal in multibillion dollar takeovers of U.S. companies. It spoke of Ivan Boesky, who earlier had been described as one of the great American financiers. Although worth $200 million,

> no amount of money seemed to convince him he had arrived. He wanted so much to be accepted, and he thought money was the only way. Last week Boesky spent much of his time folding up his ambitious social and personal commitments . . . far more painful was his decision to leave the many prominent groups that had given him a measure of social status, including his power as trustee of the American Ballet Theatre and finance director of the National Jewish Coalition. Boesky often gave lavishly to charities but irritated some fund-raisers with his hard bargaining for control and recognition. "There are givers and users. He is a user," said one.

Boesky did not have his money—his money had Boesky. He had never learned to give and so deny acquisitiveness its seduction.

• A third principle is that those who gain do so because of the pleasure in greed. The Scriptures never hide the fact that pleasures exist in sin for a time, but God's Word turns people to the longer view of the lasting values.

The satisfying of immediate hungers is a sign of our age—instant food, instant coffee, instant mashed potatoes, fast food, fast cars, fast sex, drugs, alcohol, nicotine, gratification—now!

But the quick fix is followed by despair and hunger until the next quick fix. When a person learns to deny himself, and to give himself and what he possesses, he discovers lasting joy. Giving denies greed its short-term pleasure, choosing instead lasting satisfaction.

Paul said, "For the love of money is the root of all kinds of evil.

Some people, eager for money, have wandered from the faith and pierced themselves with many griefs" (1 Timothy 6:10).

Each of these three areas are concerns that Christians must continually guard against in order to take a positive approach to responsible giving.

WHAT IS RESPONSIBLE GIVING?

Our theme goes deeper than just giving; it stresses responsible giving. Giving responsibly is our response to the calls about us—our sensitivity to the needs of the world. Responsible giving calls us to face the reality of poverty, and to confront the need of ministry and the cost of opportunity.

Poverty in Third World countries assails us from television and magazines, as we see pictures of children with thin legs and bloated bellies. But poverty is real in the United States, in the inner cities and the rural areas. A 1984 Gallup Poll discovered that 23 percent of adults always have difficulty meeting their monthly payments and another 27 percent frequently have difficulty meeting their commitments; so about half the adult population of the U.S. cannot make their monthly commitments without a serious struggle.

Christians give to relieve poverty. From the very first days of the church, giving to aid the widows and orphans became a practice. We are called not only to words of salvation, but also to deeds of service. I am encouraged by the many evangelical relief programs that take this concern seriously.

Every one of us knows the need that exists for an expanded ministry in the name of Christ: in worship, health, welfare, education, mission, witness, and proclamation.

There is no shortage of locally based grassroots opportunities for Christians to get involved in. Human needs of every shape can be met through the ministry of Christ, as individual Christians and local congregations take up such projects as:

● supporting children in underdeveloped countries

● constructing fresh-water wells in places such as Haiti or India

● building homes for the poor or delivering food to shut-ins and older persons

● involving themselves personally to work in hospitals, prisons, children's homes, or inner-city missions

- supporting local hospice or AIDS programs, hunger and poverty relief, literacy programs
- assisting in fund-raising efforts to support such tasks.

Faced with the reality of poverty, the need of ministry, and the cost of opportunity, the mission I represent, Wesley Central Mission in Sydney, uses many ways to fund our work. No one method dominates. My congregation is responsible for the largest Christian welfare ministry among the poor undertaken by any one church in the world. Each year we fund it by raising about $1 million by direct mail, $1 million through wills and estates, $0.5 million through auxiliaries and fund-raising groups, $0.5 million through the sales in our shops of secondhand clothing, $0.5 million through corporate donations, $0.5 million through television and radio programs, $0.5 million from the sale of orange juice from a citrus orchard we run, $0.5 million through sales of video and audio tapes, and so on, reaching a budget of $43 million for this year.

Throughout my ministry, I have given leadership to the raising of about $150 million to enable a local church to complete its ministry. By God's grace and the people's faithfulness, we are meeting the reality of poverty, the needs of ministry, and the cost of opportunity.

Rarely have we been given large donations. Once, a businessman became impressed with the earnestness of our ministry and sent me a check for $5,000. He was so overjoyed with my response and delight, that he sent a second for $95,000! That remains to this day as our largest single gift.

GOD'S CONCERN FOR RESPONSIBLE GIVING

"God so loved the world that He gave His one and only Son" (John 3:16; see also Romans 8:32 and 2 Corinthians 9:15). The giving of His Son was the ultimate gift of many that God in His grace bestows on us. "For you know the grace of our Lord Jesus Christ, that though He was rich, yet for your sakes He became poor, so that you through His poverty might become rich" (2 Corinthians 8:9). The Lord Jesus, like "every good and perfect gift, is from above" (James 1:17). But what other gifts does God give?

The satisfaction that comes from honest labor is one gift mentioned in Scripture:

That every man may eat and drink, and find satisfaction in all his toil—this is the gift of God. . . . Moreover, when God gives any man wealth and possessions, and enables him to enjoy them, to accept his lot and be happy in his work—this is a gift of God" (Ecclesiastes 3:13; 5:19).

Salvation is another gift of God mentioned in Scripture:

But the gift is not like the trespass. For if the many died by the trespass of the one man, how much more did God's grace and the gift that came by the grace of the one man, Jesus Christ, overflow to the many! Again, the gift of God is not like the result of the one man's sin: The judgment followed one sin and brought condemnation, but the gift followed many trespasses and brought justification. For if, by the trespass of the one man, death reigned through that one man, how much more will those who receive God's abundant provision of grace and of the gift of righteousness reign in life through the one man, Jesus Christ (Romans 5:15-17).

For it is by grace you have been saved, through faith—and this not from yourselves, it is the gift of God (Ephesians 2:8).

Eternal life is another gift of God mentioned in John's record of Jesus' encounter with the woman at the well:

Jesus answered her, "If you knew the gift of God and who it is that asks you for a drink, you would have asked Him and He would have given you living water. . . . Whoever drinks the water I give him will never thirst. Indeed, [it] will become in him a spring of water welling up to eternal life" (John 4:10, 14).

For the wages of sin is death, but the gift of God is eternal life in Christ Jesus our Lord (Romans 6:23).

The Holy Spirit is another gift given by God: "You will receive the gift of the Holy Spirit" (Acts 2:38; 10:45). And through the Holy Spirit, we are given additional gifts and graces—charismata—that equip us for our Christian witness, worship, and work. These gifts and graces are necessary to complete the challenge ahead of us, and God gives us the resources we require. "He who did not spare His own Son, but gave Him up for us all—how will He not also, along with Him, graciously give us all things?" (Romans 8:32)

We in turn are to give of ourselves wholeheartedly: "Therefore, I urge you, brothers, in view of God's mercy, to offer your bodies as living sacrifices, holy and pleasing to God—which is your spiritual worship" (Romans 12:1).

God desires our offerings. The comments Jesus made about sacrifices were not about making an offering, but about people who put restrictions on their offerings (Matthew 23:18-19). Our responsibility is to give to God our offerings without strings attached.

Our tithes and offerings are God's by right, for the firstfruits belong to Him. Tithing is God's key to your successful personal finances. Tithing puts God first, makes you budget in discipline, involves your family as a team, frees you from the great dollar hang-up, proves the reality of your faith, and releases the promises of God.

A tithe of everything from the land, whether grain from the soil or fruit from the trees, belongs to the Lord; it is holy to the Lord. If a man redeems any of his tithe, he must add a fifth of the value to it. The entire tithe of the herd and flock—every tenth animal that passes under the shepherd's rod—will be holy to the Lord (Leviticus 27:30-32).

Christians live under grace and, therefore, their tithing is not a legal requirement but a response of grace to God. Jesus Himself fulfilled the Old Testament Law including tithing, but He never revised the law *downward*. Christians are expected to tithe and then give offerings as they respond to the needs about.

God owns everything. When billionaire Howard Hughes died, naked and terrified of flies, someone asked how much he left. The answer, of course, was, "All of it!" The ultimate measure of a man's wealth is how much he is worth when he has lost everything. Naked we come into this world and naked we depart. Our wealth consists not in the abundance of our possessions, but in who we are as children of God. How we must remember, "The earth is the Lord's, and everything in it, the world, and all who live in it" (Psalm 24:1). We may possess things, but God owns them.

A friend of mine, the managing director of one of the largest chemical companies in the southern hemisphere, recalls how from 1960 he led the way in providing for shorter working hours, and better conditions and wages. Once a year he would send with every pay slip a letter that said, "We do not wish to preach to you, but we want you to know that we believe this business has prospered because, having faith in God, we seek to serve to the best of our ability. It may not be always easy to believe that it is more blessed to give than receive, but this is just as true today as when Jesus first told it to His disciples. It is because we know something of the joy of Christian giving that we now desire to increase your wages by 10 percent. We make only one request, that you refrain from thanking us. If you find it in your heart to do so, you should thank God from whom every good gift comes."

Our prayers are based on the promises of God. "I am the Lord, the God of all mankind. Is anything too hard for Me?" (Jeremiah 32:27) God promises resources to those who pray in faith. "Therefore I tell you, whatever you ask for in prayer, believe that you have received it, and it will be yours" (Mark 11:24).

"This is the assurance we have in approaching God: that if we ask anything according to His will, He hears us. And if we know that He hears us—whatever we ask—we know that we have what we asked of Him" (1 John 5:14-15). That fruit of our prayer is powerful in its effect. He gives us power to become.

The formula "$e = mc^2$" is known by college students but understood by very few people. Most of us know it had something to do with Einstein and was the formula that led to the release of enormous power and to the atomic and nuclear eras. It was the key to the discovery of a new thrust in power.

In funding Christian enterprises, "e" stands for every, "m" stands for member, "c" stands for commitment, and the "2" stands for the effort multiplied by itself. The fruit of that kind of prayerful effort is powerful in its effects. "If you believe, you will receive whatever you ask for in prayer" (Matthew 21:22).

GOD'S CALL FOR RESPONSIBLE GIVING

We have to be sure of God's call to us. God called Isaiah, and he was sure of that call (Isaiah 6:1-10). God called Jeremiah and he was sure of that call (Jeremiah 1:4-10). God confirmed His call on the life of Jesus at His baptism, in the temptations, and at the Mount of Transfiguration.

We must live certain of His call, and confident in His resources: When God calls, we can trust Him to provide the resources. "Is anything too hard for the Lord?" (Genesis 18:14) His resources are infinite, "For every animal of the forest is mine, and the cattle on a thousand hills" (Psalm 50:10).

Responsible giving or stewardship is not man's way of raising money, but God's way of raising people. He is at work making us to be the people He wants us to be through how we give. A fund-raising campaign may be the church's most significant spiritual teaching. An emphasis on stewardship is not something to be left to a special Sunday of the year, like the church's mission, witness, education, and worship, it must be part of the fabric of its life.

The church's budget is not a list of its expenses, but a record of its vision. It is not a list of bills to be met but a program of ministry to be achieved. Responsible giving is to be expected. Christian donors must realize that the pastor, fund-raiser, or Christian executive concerned with fund-raising has a responsibility to teach stewardship of God-given resources. "Command them to do good, to be rich in good deeds, and to be generous and willing to share. In this way they will lay up treasure for themselves as a firm foundation for the coming age, so that they may take hold of the life that is truly life" (1 Timothy 6:18-19).

We are indebted to God. First Corinthians 6:19 underscores the Christian's dependence and indebtedness to God. "Do you not know that your body is a temple of the Holy Spirit, who is in you, whom you have received from God? You are not your own; you were bought at a price." Jesus commanded, "Store up for yourselves treasures in heaven, where moth and rust do not destroy, and where thieves do not break in and steal" (Matthew 6:20).

God rewards our faithfulness. We must never give because of the expectation of a return. That is a faithless prosperity doctrine that abuses the promises of God. To give knowing that God blesses the giver is an act of Christian knowledge. But to give in order to induce God to bless us further is an act of unchristian blackmail.

Those of us who give know that we receive more than we have ever given. St. Francis of Assisi put it succinctly: "For it is in giving that we receive." The miser never experiences it. The widow gives her mite and receives joyfully everyday. "Give, and it will be given to you. A good measure, pressed down, shaken together and running over, will be poured into your lap. For with the measure you use, it will be measured to you" (Luke 6:38).

God is able to make all grace abound to you, so that in all things at all times, having all that you need, you will abound in every good work. As it is written: "He has scattered abroad His gifts to the poor; His righteousness endures forever." Now He who supplies seed to the sower and bread for food will also supply and increase your store of seed and will enlarge the harvest of your righteousness. You will be made rich in every way so that you can be generous on every occasion, and through us your generosity will result in thanksgiving to God (2 Corinthians 9:8-11).

We who would fund the Christian enterprise by our responsible giving must be like the Macedonian Christians, who gave

as much as they were able, and even beyond their ability. Entirely on their own, they urgently pleaded with us for the privilege of sharing in this service to the saints. And they did not do as we expected, but they gave themselves first to the Lord and then to us in keeping with God's will (2 Corinthians 8:3-5).

GORDON K. MOYES serves as the superintendent of the Wesley Central Mission (Sydney), Australia's largest Christian welfare service which conducts 45 services of worship a week and cares for people in 55 centers. The mission has recently completed an $80-million building expansion program and has a $200-million mid-city building in progress. Dr. Moyes has preached throughout Australia and in 20 countries, and lectured in colleges and seminaries throughout the world. An author of more than 30 books and booklets, he also edits the national award-winning magazine Impact, with a readership of 60,000. He is a TV and radio program host and has scripted 37 half-hour documentary films made in five countries and sold internationally.

Dr. Moyes lectures in business management and is a member of 25 boards and committees. He is chairman and director of a number of companies in film production, general insurance, publishing, public and private hospitals, medical ethics and research.

(3)
ON BECOMING A
STRATEGIC STEWARD

J. ALAN YOUNGREN

We Americans thrive on buzzwords, and beyond question, *strategy* is *the* buzzword of the '80s. Doing a seminar or workshop? Want to fill the seats? Then somehow get the words *strategy* or *strategic* into the title. Or, if you want someone to accomplish some particular task for you, give that person a strategy for doing it. Who would throw away a perfectly good strategy?

You would think that this constant emphasis on strategy would push us to be strategic about our Christian giving, but it doesn't work that way. Most of us in the evangelical community had our giving habits well established before the decade of strategy.

The majority of us have giving habits closer to personal indulgence than to strategy. We soon discover that immediate gratification can be obtained from giving, if we work it right. We learn to give to television personalities who fire right back to us programs we enjoy immensely. We're not really making a gift but an exchange, a business transaction—the program for the gift.

Television also teaches us how to brush flies from the eyes of African children with a $10 bill. We soon learn that we hit as many flies with a ten as we could with a hundred-dollar bill, so we do it ten times, get ten thrills instead of one, and blow 10 to 20 percent of our gift on processing costs sustained by the agencies receiving our gifts, who have to process those small gifts.

We don't place our money as an investment in the work of God's kingdom nearly so much as we spray it as a quick antidote. The fun of spray-giving greatly outranks the responsibility of careful stewardship.

The late A.W. Tozer was wise to our ways. He asserted, "Tender-hearted saints think with their feelings and pour out consecrated wealth indiscriminately."¹ Nationally known fund-raising consultant Robert Sharpe is more specific in his assessment of Christian donors. He finds they come in four varieties: impulsive—70 percent; habitual—20 percent; thoughtful—7 percent, and careful—3 percent, with an unfortunate distribution among the categories.

Most certainly, people reading this book will not fall into the first two categories above. In fact, most readers will be wanting to know what's involved in moving from "thoughtful" to "careful."

We need to become strategic about our stewardship. A strategy can be defined as "a plan or method for obtaining a specific goal or objective." And, of course, to be effectively strategic we must have the right objectives. There are five areas in which we need sound objectives. In this chapter we will examine each of them.

Area I: Why Are You Giving?
          Objective: To give for truly biblical reasons . . . out of truly biblical motives

Area II: How Much Are You Giving?
          Objective: To give as freely as God would have you give, but to determine that level of giving in advance, so that you can *plan* your giving

Area III: How Are You Giving? That is, how are you going about the exercise of your stewardship responsibilities?
          Objective: To handle your giving in a godly and careful manner

Area IV: To What Are You Giving? That is, which of dozens of categories of ministry around the world will you support?
          Objective: To define your interests and identify six to ten interests you can fully support on a continuing basis

Area V: To Whom Are You Giving? That is, which of many organizations devoted to the mission task categories you have chosen will become your representative in that work?

Objective: To identify the organizations which best combine commitment, effectiveness, and efficiency in delivering work in your areas of interest

WHY ARE YOU GIVING?

Believers are told to give out of heartfelt thanks, glad obedience, and real concern. A good passage of Scripture to consult on this is 2 Corinthians 8:7-15.

> But just as you excel in everything—in faith, in speech, in knowledge, in complete earnestness and in your love for us—see that you also excel in this grace of giving.
>
> I am not commanding you, but I want to test the sincerity of your love by comparing it with the earnestness of others. For you know the grace of our Lord Jesus Christ, that though He was rich, yet for your sakes He became poor, so that you through His poverty might become rich.
>
> And here is my advice about what is best for you in this matter: Last year you were the first not only to give but also to have the desire to do so. Now finish the work, so that your eager willingness to do it may be matched by your completion of it, according to your means. For if the willingness is there, the gift is acceptable according to what one has, not according to what he does not have.
>
> Our desire is not that others might be relieved while you are hard pressed, but that there might be equality. At the present time your plenty will supply what they need, so that in turn their plenty will supply what you need. Then there will be equality, as it is written: "He that gathered much did not have too much, and he that gathered little did not have too little."

When we begin to give instead out of some legalistic need to perform as Christians, we are well on the way toward frustration and defeat in our stewardship. Before long this attitude can lead to carelessness in giving, then reduction in giving and, finally, defeat in other areas of our spiritual lives.

HOW MUCH ARE YOU GIVING?

Every steward who wishes to be strategic in the exercise of his stewardship duties should begin by deciding what portion of his income he will return to God. To the extent that this giving strains his financial equilibrium—and it should—he will tend to find it difficult to maintain a positive and aggressive attitude toward his stewardship responsibilities. Certainly he must draw on the resources of his relationship with God to offset the personal and family wear and tear of "giving until it hurts." But he should also recognize another resource. The manner in which he goes about the accumulation of the monies he will give can affect his attitude.

The first decision, then, is the percentage of income which will be given. Whether this percentage is five or ten or twenty or fifty, it should be a determined figure, based on the income the steward is currently receiving.

Once that figure is determined, the challenge is to accumulate the money and then enjoy giving it away. As the reader may well know from his own experience, once one is behind in giving, it is harder to catch up than it was to stay paid up. And once you're really behind, meeting your goals becomes close to impossible—unless, of course, the portion you have determined to give is not a financial challenge to you.

What can the Christian steward do to make accumulation a pillar of his giving program rather than a pitfall, a joy rather than a burden? First, he should eliminate the two most common and harmful mistakes Christians make in readying money for giving—giving from what is left, and tying dispersal to income.

● Do not give out of what is left. Historical record indicates that the primary principle guiding stewardship in the early church was that of firstfruits. The key to firstfruits giving is that the first money set aside from income is that portion going to the Lord's work. The idea is to "live on the rest" after God's portion is gone, rather than giving to God whatever is left after you have maintained yourself "in the manner to which you have become accustomed." The latter approach is the way most Christians manage accumulation, and is their first big mistake. The firstfruits approach to accumulation is also an effective means of maintaining a positive attitude toward stewardship responsibilities. If you live on the rest, you will have to tailor your lifestyle and "needs" to available dollars so that you do not consume what you originally intended for God's work.

• Do not tie accumulation to dispersal. Many people believe they should set aside (accumulate) and give (disperse) their stewardship monies the same way a baseball player in the middle of a double play should catch and then throw the ball—all in one motion.

I do not have to give away today what I set aside today. Many people have been pressed into feeling that their stewardship monies are burning a hole in their pockets by an overzealous reading of Paul's admonition in 2 Corinthians 8:11, where he urges them to "complete" or "finish" the work of providing for the saints at Jerusalem. Such zealots often translate this admonition, "Do it immediately." Be assured, however, that any group deserving support is going to be operating on an annual budget. In this context, "immediately" becomes any time within the operating year. When you are concerned that monies be distributed as soon as they are received, you increase your vulnerability to three specific stewardship problems:

– Dilution of effect, due to breaking up of a large gift into smaller monthly (or other) units.

– The size of the gift being determined by circumstance. If, to avoid dilution of effect, you decide that your total gift to one organization will be everything set aside in one period (say, one month) then the size of that gift is determined by circumstance, i.e., the amount available from that period, and not determined by careful, prayerful decision-making on your part.

– Getting rid of it. When a steward has money on hand and believes it should go out immediately, but doesn't have any specific recipient, this error is ready to happen. Eighteen hundred years ago, the *Didache*, a significant second-century Christian document, wisely advised believers, "Let thy alms sweat in thy hand until thou knowest to whom thou givest." That advice is equally good today.

It is possible, however, to make this matter seem simpler than it is. Accumulation and dispersal do need to be coordinated. Also, there is no ideal or single best accumulation procedure. This is because stewards (like other people) receive their income in a variety of patterns. Some receive a fixed amount at regular intervals—weekly, biweekly, or monthly. Others receive varying amounts at these same regular intervals. And still others receive varying amounts at sporadic intervals. The steward must suit his accumulation procedure to his income pattern.

Nevertheless, one particular technique is sure to help anyone—set aside stewardship money at the time you put your income in the bank, before it gets mixed with the rest of your money. The simplest and most helpful manner of doing this is to set up a separate checking account for stewardship monies only. The predominant value of the separate account is psychological. Most stewards will find that because this money is thus separated from the rest of their holdings, it is gone—they will no longer so much as think of using it for their personal needs and wants.

This tactic has significant potential for making stewardship a positive and enjoyable experience. Some stewards will even find that the separate account affords a freedom akin to giving away somebody else's money, without short-circuiting the joy of sharing.

If you do not establish a separate account, at least keep some continuing written record of how much stewardship money is accumulating in your regular bank account. This technical separation of funds will help accomplish the goal of taking the Lord's portion "off the top," rather than giving to God from "what is left."

If you wonder why I make such an issue of setting aside firstfruits in a disciplinary manner, let me offer the following suggestion. If accumulating your stewardship monies annually is easy for you, or if sending off an occasional check consistently adds up at year's end to what you wanted to give, it is possible that you should challenge yourself to give at a level of your income that would require sacrifice and continual effort on your part. Accumulation requires this kind of effort only when you have a truly challenging goal for how much you will give.

HOW ARE YOU GIVING?

Prudent accumulation is dominated by one or two principles. Actually giving the money, however, involves many more considerations. In accumulating money you are only preparing to have an effect; with dispersing the money, you are actually having that effect, with each organization you are supporting. The wise steward wants to manage every aspect of making each gift.

The wise steward not only seeks to support the most effective and efficient workers, he also seeks to make those workers more effective and efficient through his support of them.

The wise steward will therefore avoid two serious problems which plague Christian stewardship today. The first of these we'll term "dilution of effect," the direct result of the proliferation of small gifts. The logical approach to combating this problem is the obvious one: give fewer, but larger gifts. As Harold Seymour points out in his classic, *Designs for Fund-Raising,* the average donor has the "mental room" to maintain an active interest in the work of approximately six organizations.[2] If we evangelical donors could restrain our acceptances to six, then we would be giving six significant gifts to organizations we know well.

Unfortunately, it seems we can hardly refuse any appeal for funds. The result is meager individual gifts. The average gift to a Christian cause is under $10. This "spraying" of gifts prevents the donor from making a real impact anywhere, makes it virtually impossible for the donor to keep track of the multiplicity of organizations he supports, and syphons off as much as a fifth of these small gifts to processing costs.

Many donors don't realize that processing costs are multiplied many times by small gifts. The cost of receiving and processing a gift doesn't vary with the size of the gift, because the processing procedure is the same regardless of size: a gift must be entered in a number of records and deposited in the bank, and the donor sent a receipt. This means that the recipient organization pays as much to process a $10 gift as it pays to process a $100 gift. Consequently, processing takes ten times the bite out of ten gifts of $10 each as it does out of one gift of $100. The wise steward accumulates all the money he will give to a single organization or project and sends it all at once.

The key to coordinating the accumulation and dispersal lies in planning. In planned dispersal, you begin your stewardship year (usually corresponding to the calendar year) by listing your proposed gifts, noting the order in which you will make them and the size of each.

Quite naturally, a list of your gifts from the previous year probably dominates this new list. Perhaps you are a steward newly convinced of the value of truly knowing those to whom you give and have just finished gathering information about potential recipients; or perhaps you are a steward experienced in these matters and thoroughly committed to a list of six to ten recipients. Whatever your situation, you should accumulate funds until you have enough for the first gift on your list, and then make that gift. In this way you will give systematically to every organization on your list, adopting the giving order from the previous year, if it still reflects your commitment.

If you cannot accurately forecast your income, the resulting difficulty lies not in compiling your list, but in determining the size of each gift. For those who have this difficulty but still want to use a dispersal list in order to give money uniformly over a twelve-month period, here are three approaches to the problem:

• Prioritize the list. In other words, list your recipients in order of importance, putting the organization to which you are most committed first (probably your church), and maintain that pattern. Then put an amount next to each name on the list—an amount representing what you will give that recipient if your income for the year turns out to be close to your estimate. What you are then saying to yourself is, "I am not going to give organizations lower on the list anything until I have accumulated X dollars for organization number one, Y dollars for number two, etc."

• Delay sending any gifts until you can quite accurately estimate your income for the year (but don't delay putting money aside).

• Send donations to your entire list quarterly or semiannually. This is the least commendable alternative, but it may fit your need.

Finally, let's talk about the long view—maintaining commitment. Only the best stewards have given more than a passing thought to the matter of the continuity and consistency of their support of chosen recipients. But this is a strategic matter that warrants attention and discussion.

The candidates for your support should be obliged by you to furnish the information you need to select them. If you choose to support them, they tacitly take on the added obligation to keep you informed. But from the time they gain a place on your stewardship list, you have an obligation to them too, as long as they continue to merit your support.

The essence of this obligation can be summed up in the word *commitment.* You ought to feel committed to your recipients as long as they work responsibly in the areas of ministry in which you are involved. And it is important to realize that your commitment is a very real part of your support. They need to know they can count on you. You maintain your commitment—and demonstrate it—by two means: *consistency* and *continuity.*

Consistency involves timing, a determinant factor in successful cash-flow management within the organizations you support. Your annual gift (remember that a single gift per year is the easiest on their processing capacities) should reach the recipient at the same time each year—within the same month. The more an organization's support comes from committed donors making predictable gifts, the more efficient that organization can be. And you help maintain that efficiency when you inform them of any change in your annual gift. So if you decide to alter the amount, timing, or frequency of a gift, advise the recipient with a note mailed separately, or enclosed with the gift.

Continuity means an uninterrupted flow of support—in real dollars—at an established level. This involves caring for two additional provisions:

– Inflation adjustments. Handling adjustments for inflation can be simple. Assign to each of your recipients a percentage of your total giving, and as your income increases, their percentage of it increases accordingly. If your income is fixed or unchanged, no increase in size of gifts is called for. Conversely, if your income increases dramatically, nothing in your commitment requires that your present recipients receive a share of the complete increase. Only an inflation adjustment is in order.

– A share in your estate. The principle here is definitely not that money should continue flowing indefinitely to your recipients in fixed amounts and at fixed intervals. The recipients should, instead, be granted a portion of your estate, to be distributed, if possible, in single lump sums.

As I end this portion of the chapter, you may be wondering about all those earnest letters coming from folks you support, carrying news of an unexpected crisis or opportunity, and asking for a special gift. What about the planning for such "emergencies"? At the risk of sounding cynical, I offer two responses.

First, if these crisis/opportunity messages didn't work so well, you wouldn't receive so many of them. Don't be part of the reason they work. Assume they are meant for someone else. Notice how many coincide nicely with the end of the sender's fiscal year.

Second, if you truly want to give to such a need, take the money from what you would spend on your next vacation, not from another organization on your list.

TO WHAT ARE YOU GIVING?

Without a careful defining of your stewardship interests and then a focusing of those interests, you will find it impossible to limit yourself to six to ten recipients, or you will select recipients at random.

Some readers may be alarmed by this emphasis on their interests in giving, rather than on God's will. But I believe that the two are related, not opposed. God gives you these interests as stimulants to your concern. As such, they encourage you to give. In fact, it is a tribute to God's love and thoughtfulness that He directs our steward-ship by giving us interests in varying areas of the work of the Great Commission. If we follow and develop these interests, they can add to our joy in giving.

In approaching the defining of your interests, take time to sit down—with your spouse, if you are married—and think about them carefully. Identify your interests clearly, and think about them long enough to discover which ones matter most—and therefore have priority. Or, here's another approach to getting started. Without doing any previous reflection, sit down and begin to pray about Christian work and Christian workers anywhere and everywhere. The activities and groups that enter your prayers most quickly are valuable indications of your true interests.

Thanks be to God that He has given one person a strong interest in Africa and another in China; that someone is primarily interested in home missions and another in telling the Word to primitive "unreached" peoples; that one person has a passion for church plant-ing and another for evangelism. All the work must be done, and a variety of interests is primary insurance that it will be done.

Out of a feeling that people everywhere are in real need, particu-larly spiritual need, some stewards support the organizations they find most effective and efficient. Other people's highest priority is the support of a particular individual or individuals. They often develop a strong allegiance in this sort of situation, supporting whatever organization that individual is with at the time.'

Stewardship interests can be grouped into three general categories: geographical, cultural, and functional. Bear in mind, however, that these are not a set of mutually exclusive categories leading to an exhaustive list of interests. Rather, they are a series of alternative perspectives.

In order to stimulate your thinking about your interests, following are three lists that flesh out the categories mentioned above, but are by no means exhaustive:

● Cultural—people in particular cultural situations or people comprising particular cultural groups
  - the poor and culturally disadvantaged
  - peoples of particular world religions and sects
  - people in various racially based subcultures within our society
  - "unreached" peoples living in primitive areas of the world
  - people in other Western nations
  - people of Communist bloc nations
  - people of other developed nations
  - people of developing nations
  - students
  - foreign students studying in the United States
  - armed forces personnel
  - children
  - businessmen and women
  - housewives
  - people in a particular industry or profession
  - athletes

● Geographical
  - home missions (USA or Canada)
  - Central and South America
  - Europe
  - the Middle East
  - Africa
  - Asia
  - Australia

● Functional
  - evangelism
  - church planting
  - literature
  - translation
  - relief and development
  - medicine
  - service and support (transportation, technology, coordination and cooperation)

– education (Christian schools and colleges, literary training, counseling).

One important caution before you begin—do not attempt to identify every interest you can uncover, but limit yourself to your strongest preferences. Most stewards, taking stock in this manner, will identify somewhere between six and ten interests (including their own church); the ideal is in this range. If the number of interests you put together doesn't fall within this range, remember that it is better to have fewer than six than to try to maintain more than ten.

Unless you can devote most or all of your time to your stewardship, you should limit yourself to this number, because this is as many as you can effectively keep up with. The key word here is *effectively*. Keep in mind that thorough stewardship is a time-consuming matter. As you read earlier, you need to select your recipients on the basis of thorough knowledge, which means obtaining answers to detailed questions, not simply looking over the limited information that gift-seeking organizations will send you.

Finally, remember that each of your annual gifts should be large enough to be meaningful to you. Each should be a real stimulus to your continued concern for the group receiving that gift. Supporting too many organizations means sending out a plethora of smaller gifts that will probably diminish your sense of purpose.

In saying this, I am not suggesting that you toss out your current list of recipients and begin again. I am, however, advocating what may be a rather significant change in your approach to deciding who will receive your money. You should go from a subjective viewpoint (determined completely by your interests) to an objective viewpoint (determined by your assessment of which organizations will best serve your interests). Accomplishing this change means obtaining the best information you can acquire.

TO WHOM ARE YOU GIVING?
This fifth question brings us to a premise which is the fulcrum of this chapter: namely, that avowedly evangelical Christian organizations vary significantly in the degree to which they are worthy to receive support. The heaviest demand on the wise steward is in placing stewardship monies as an investment, with due diligence. Abuses in raising funds are everywhere, and the wise steward will be deter-

mined to be supportive of only the most worthy groups.

In our book *Your Money, Their Ministry* (Eerdmans, 1981) Edward J. Hales and I put abuses into three categories. Purportedly evangelical organizations raise funds for ministry, and then fail to deliver on their promises to accomplish the work because:

- they won't—fraudulent intent
- they can't—inability, especially administrative incompetence
- they aren't who they say they are—doctrinal misrepresentation.

The wise steward differs fundamentally from the other donors by recognizing that the most persuasive fund-raiser is not necessarily the most effective at ministry. There is no necessary correlation between the ability to minister and the ability to raise funds to minister. For this reason the wise steward refuses to make giving decisions on the basis of any information he receives at the initiation of any fund-raiser. Instead he acquires his own very specific information from a variety of reference sources he or she may consult and from the organizations themselves.

The sources reflect a two-step procedure in selecting gift recipients. The first step is *identification* (finding a usable number of candidate organizations in the field of each of your stewardship interests). The second step is *evaluation* of each of the groups you have identified. Again referring to what we said above about ministering and fund-raising, it is much better that you find the organizations than that they find you.

What you're looking for in the first step, identification, is *legitimacy*. In any group or community, there are those who live by the standards and mores of the group, and those who don't. Does a given organization belong to an association made up of its peers? And does that association have among its membership requirements maintenance of certain standards? There are sources from which you can answer these two questions. Does a given group belong to the Evangelical Council for Financial Accountability (ECFA)? If so, it likely isn't a group that wants to hide in the shadows on the outskirts of the community.

In the second step, evaluation, you the wise steward go on the offensive. You contact the organizations which have become candidates for your support. In a letter of inquiry you might ask the candidate for five specific responses, as follows:

– its doctrinal statement

– its statement of purpose and some information of successful past fulfillment of these purposes

– a complete list of its officers and board of directors

– its most recent financial statement, and if possible, the two previous fiscal year statements; plus the auditor's cover letter if the statements have been audited

– a statement of key future plans for its program: special projects and, especially, permanent projects.

As a result of this information, and your evaluation process, you should be able to make well-informed decisions as to the credibility of the candidates you decide to support. (See chapter 5 for a further explanation on determining the credibility of the organization.)

Use the power and influence you have as a donor and write inquiries to organizations you are serious about supporting. You will gain information, and you will send them the message that only the worthy groups deserve to prosper.

J. ALAN YOUNGREN earned an M.B.A. degree at the Columbia University Graduate School of Business with the intention of using large-corporate business experience as final preparation for serving Christian organizations. He spent seven years marketing items sold in supermarkets.

In 1970 Mr. Youngren began consulting organizations within Christian enterprise, for-profit and not-for-profit, working with them to strengthen their communication of themselves, their products, and their services. In 1981, he co-authored with Edward J. Hales a book entitled Your Money, Their Ministry *(Eerdmans), a study of Christian giving from the donor's point of view. In 1986 he began publishing a magazine,* Christian Management Review, *with the purpose to bring together management personnel in all areas of Christian enterprise. The magazine recently received the National Religious Broadcaster's 1988 Magazine Award for Excellence.*

(4)
MY PERSONAL STYLE
OF GIVING

ANONYMOUS

As one who gives as anonymously as possible, I write this chapter similarly, not to create mysterious intrigue—or to distance fundraisers or the IRS—but simply because I believe that is how God would have it.

This is my stewardship autobiography—a story that began in my late teens when I came to know Christ as Saviour and Lord of my life. Today I am a retired corporation executive whom God, in His mercy and providence, has blessed with material wealth and challenged with a responsibility to distribute those assets for His glory and according to His will. As Christians, each of us is called to be a faithful steward of whatever God has entrusted to us, and I pray that much of what I say will help you and encourage you to make God-honoring stewardship decisions. I want you to experience, as I have, the joy of being a cheerful giver!

I will be speaking for both my wife and myself. We have been married over 45 years, so I can scarcely think back to a time when a stewardship decision was not made with my partner. I write from the perspective of a married man; for the most part, however, the same principles should apply to a single person entrusted with much or little.

Having a common purse has influenced all areas of our finances, but most particularly our stewardship. We have never had "her" money and "my" money. The common purse led us to common stewardship, and we have always planned and worked together in our giving. To be practical and for tax purposes, we have sometimes separated what we owned as it became valuable as an estate, but in our thinking, it always remained together. I grieve for men and women whose life partners are not sympathetic with their desires to be good stewards.

God's Word is the authority and basis for our giving. Many passages speak directly to stewardship and have greatly influenced us. My wife and I take for ourselves again and again David's prayer.

O Lord God . . . praise Your name for ever and ever! Yours is the mighty power and glory and victory and majesty. Everything in the heavens and earth is Yours, O Lord, and this is Your kingdom. We adore You as being in control of everything. Riches and honor come from You alone, and You are the Ruler of all mankind; Your hand controls power and might, and it is at Your discretion that men are made great and given strength.

O our God, we thank You and praise Your glorious name, but who am I and who are my people that we should be permitted to give anything to You? Everything we have comes from You, and we only give You what is Yours already! For we are here for but a moment, strangers in the land as our fathers were before us; our days on earth are like a shadow, gone so soon, without a trace.

O Lord our God, all of this material that we have gathered . . . comes from You! It all belongs to You! I know, my God, that You test men to see if they are good; for You enjoy good men. I have done all this with good motives . . . willingly and joyously (1 Chronicles 29:10-17, TLB).

A copy of this prayer lies under the glass top of our desk, where we can see it and read it silently or aloud as we attempt to serve the Lord as stewards of time and resources.

Stewardship is a duty, as our Lord said in His discussion with the Pharisees about their tithing (Matthew 23:23). Accepting this fact is foundational. What we also recognize is that the principle of tithing laid down in the Old Testament amounted to a good deal more than 10 percent of income, because multiple tithes were involved.

More than a duty, stewardship is also an expression of the fruit of Christ's life by the Holy Spirit within us: "The fruit of the Spirit is love, joy, peace, patience, kindness, goodness, faithfulness, gentleness and self-control" (Galatians 5:22). Notice that each one can relate in some way to giving.

In addition, generosity is evidence of being led by the Lord. *The Living Bible* paraphrases Luke 11:41, "Purity is best demonstrated by generosity." The generosity spoken of is not a means to purity, but a result of a life made pure through Christ's gift of salvation to us. This does not mean that generosity is the only evidence of purity, but it is a significant evidence.

There should be no misers among God's people. William Wordsworth's poem on the King's College chapel ceiling at Cambridge speaks to this:

Give all thou canst; high Heaven rejects the lore
Of nicely calculated less or more.

Contrast the person who "nicely" calculates, ever so grudgingly, what he should give against the cheerful giver whom God loves (2 Corinthians 9:7).

My wife and I have been challenged by studies of Bible words translated "single-mindedness," "simplicity," "liberality," "sincerity," and "generosity"—all of which come from the same Greek root (see Matthew 6:22; Luke 11:34; Romans 12:8; 2 Corinthians 8:2; 9:11, 13; 11:3; Ephesians 6:5; Colossians 3:22). By fitting them together and forming a scriptural model for motivation and efforts of giving, we have established our life's focus in this regard.

Besides these and other passages from God's Word, friends and family have been major influences in our attempts at good stewardship. An early boss of mine was a great steward. My father-in-law was a missionary and had very little, but he gave faithfully. My senior partner demonstrated stewardship as he was just beginning a fledgling business and there was little to give. A professor who had a meager salary was the person who encouraged my wife and me to have a common purse. Each of these people demonstrated a love for the Lord and His work that was manifested through their gifts.

As a result of how we have tried to apply what we have learned from the Bible, from others, and from experience, we have established the following principles for our stewardship decisions. I admit that some of these ideas are personal preferences, but perhaps they will help you as you seek to be a faithful steward.

TAKE THE INITIATIVE AND DEVELOP A PLAN

Many people come to my wife and me requesting financial support for their ministries. We want to be open to all who come, but we really prefer to take the initiative, seeking out those places where we should be putting the Lord's money, and then devising a stewardship plan. My wife and I currently have the responsibility of distributing just under $1 million a year. We believe that taking the initiative helps us keep a balance that we might not have otherwise. We don't want to be swayed by the influences that inevitably come into play when a fund-raising proposal is presented.

First Corinthians 14:40 says, "Everything should be done in a fitting and orderly way." So once a year, we plan and budget. Setting aside a specific time for mulling over requests and making decisions is absolutely imperative. The fall works best for us; we try to finish in October or November, but sometimes are delayed until December. If someone comes to us with a request at another time of the year, we hold the recommendation until October.

Being orderly guards against impulsive giving. We take time to think through requests, reading over the proposals, discussing and praying about them. We sometimes counsel with one or more of our adult children, with close friends, or others with whom we are involved in stewardship thinking and actions. We then make our decision. Some commitments are for the coming year, and some are for two or three years.

When we have reacted impulsively to presentations in the past, we have often been disappointed when we came to our regular planning time, realizing that we would not have ranked that stewardship matter as high on the list as we would have other ministries. Then we have come up short and found ourselves unable to fill needs that we otherwise would have, because there just was not enough money to go around.

Organizations headquartered domestically get more exposure, and we sometimes feel that those who have personal contacts with us urge us to make commitments on the basis of those personal contacts. Christians on the cutting edge of missions, particularly those in the unreached areas or in the growing church overseas, do not have such opportunities. Being systematic in our giving, planning and making decisions once a year, helps us keep a balance rather than being pressured by fund-raisers who contact us.

We appreciate the time, work, and money invested in organized fund-raising programs and departments, but we try not to be swayed—or annoyed—when it appears to us to be overdone. I am more prone to be annoyed than my wife, and so she helps me keep a balance so that I do not react negatively to the substance of the proposal or project being presented for our stewardship consideration.

Occasionally friends, sometimes those who are CEOs of organizations, institutions, or missions, are offended when we say no to their request for funds. We regret this, but we are giving to the Lord and not to the fund-raiser, even though he might be a close friend, and we don't always feel led to put funds into a particular organization or project.

CHOOSE A SPECIALTY

We have contributed to many different types of ministries and are interested in all areas of God's work that we have been led into, but we have found it best to find a specialty. Ours happens to be training overseas nationals; yours may be some other. We plan for most of our annual giving to be to specific, cutting-edge projects to advance the cause of Christ, particularly overseas. Our interest is focused on a number of missions, schools, and special groups that work with nationals; we can personally write to them and specifically pray for them, and involve others in doing so, also.

I mentioned earlier that for those who are on our support list, particularly individuals, we keep a small reserve for emergency needs, such as health problems, travel requirements, automobile accidents, etc. These emergency funds are almost always used at the end of the year; if they aren't, we allocate them to specific projects to "clear out the decks." Individuals do not receive the bulk of our support, but we do help 35 to 40 individuals, in addition to another 35 to 40 who are receiving scholarships administered through various block funds given in the past or through our family foundation.

When we give to individuals, such as young people from the United States or Canada who are training to go overseas or nationals training to return to their homelands, we make a pact with them upfront. We agree to assist them financially, but they are responsible to keep their word. If what they promise to do is not carried out within a specified time (varying according to the circumstances and individuals involved), then they are obligated to repay the funds as soon as possible. Sometimes we have had to say that this means 10 percent of their gross income, or $100 a month, whichever is greater, for these young people cannot treat the gift as a pot largess that they can dip into but not have any real responsibility for. If something causes them to go back on their word, we have to accept the fact that they are accountable to the Lord. We did what we felt God would have us do, but we are not collection agents. We leave it with the Lord for the Holy Spirit to deal with them. Our responsibility is summed up in Christ's words to Peter recorded in John 21:19, "Follow Me," and we try to live by that command as best we can.

One thing my wife and I have had to learn after we give a gift is not to be either impressed by gratitude or offended by the lack of it. What we gave was the Lord's. We are to be faithful in our stewardship, ask God to bless the funds, and recognize that the expression of thankfulness is the responsibility of the individual.

We are increasingly convinced that the words in Romans 1:21 speak of root sins that are evidenced in unthankfulness: "For although they knew God, they neither glorified Him as God nor gave thanks to Him." We become concerned for those who do not express gratitude. It's not that we want to be thanked; it's just that we care about them.

STRETCH THE COMMITMENTS AND MULTIPLY THE GIVING

We extend ourselves financially. Some people cannot understand this, because they don't know the details of how we have to balance the cash flow. The in-and-out cash must be planned very carefully because we stretch our finances when we make our commitments.

As a young couple years ago, my wife and I attended a missions meeting where we learned of a need of $100 for a missionary who was being sent out. We had $100—that's all we had—and we put it in the pot. That $100 was earmarked for a refrigerator that we needed ourselves, but we gave it anyway. Within a week or so we received a gift to pay for that refrigerator from someone who knew nothing about our giving to the missionary. From that time about 45 years ago, we have continued to extend ourselves in our stewardship commitments. We want to do so, for it keeps us amazed at His provision. We are afraid not to be stretched financially, for it keeps us humbly trusting in His mercy and power.

There have been times when we have wondered whether or not to buy something—for instance, just how much money should be put into decorating a house? Or, how much should be spent on furniture? But here the controlling principle has been the utility of what we plan to buy. We ask these questions: What is going to be the use of this item? How will it forward our representation of the cause of Christ? Will it make us more effective as we live for Christ? Each of us as Christians must answer these questions, with God's leading and His wisdom.

One challenge in our stewardship planning is to try to multiply the giving—not only to make our dollars go farther but also to extend to others the joys of giving. I will elaborate on a few of the ways we have found to do this—tax incentives, matching gifts, wise use of our assets, and involving friends and family.

Giving simply in order to get tax breaks is pointless. Tax deductions never really give you more money; you'd be further ahead to keep the money and pay taxes on it.

Gifts to individuals are not tax deductible, but we have increasingly done more of this type of giving, even though there are no tax benefits. In some cases, however, when we do make large gifts to individuals, we place a few stipulations on the gift. We ask the recipients, when they become able to do so, to give the same amount we gave to them to some part of God's work, either as a cash gift or as an estate gift. Usually, if the gift is a significant amount, we request that they set it aside in a revocable trust and then designate that this asset (or a specified portion of it) be given to a ministry upon which we and they agree. This action does not create a taxable event for them at the time and is dependent solely on their keeping their word. We do adjust the amount to be given by them so that the charitable deduction that accrues to the person or the estate leaves them on either an after-adjusted basis without incremental interest cost or on a present value basis practically without interest costs. In this way, as a businessman, I can serve the Lord faithfully and share the blessing with these others too.

Loaning money is part of our overall stewardship planning. When loaning money to people in financial distress or need, we do not charge interest, even knowing that noninterest-bearing loans under the current tax regulations are not financially beneficial (because of the imputed interest application). This practice of not charging interest is, however, a biblical principle binding on us when we are helping someone in need, but it does not apply to purely business or investment transactions.

We carefully consider tax advantages, however, when they will enable us to multiply our giving. They can help us have more money to give to the Lord's work in other ways. Taking advantage of tax breaks whenever we can does not aggrandize ourselves but is a prime consideration in wise giving, though it is never a motivation.

We like to do matching giving. For example, we recently heard that a missionary friend in Latin America needs an automobile. We have some funds set aside for emergencies, and we could go into those funds and probably buy the car totally ourselves. But it is much better to include others in on the joy of giving, and to see that extra money is put into the Lord's work that otherwise might not. So we'll probably challenge supporting churches or individuals by sharing this need with them and letting them contribute on some kind of matching basis.

The boss that I spoke of earlier taught me about matching gifts. He almost always gave to projects, saying, "Yes, I'll take the *last* $5,000"—or $50,000, or $100,000, whatever the amount. He helped establish a number of organizations that are today leading evangelical ministries, and through matching gifts he allowed the blessings of giving to be shared by others.

These types of matching-gift challenges don't spur us on to haphazard giving. When someone comes to us and says, "Here's a matching deal. If you'll do this, we'll get this," it may or may not influence us in what we do. We aren't motivated as though we were in some athletic contest, but rather by sound and careful judgment which we have brought before the Lord in our thinking and careful planning.

Deciding on the use of our assets has been a difficult area for us. We have wondered if we should give away the principal that we have, which is mostly in stock, the value of which has grown since we purchased it many years ago. We came to the conclusion that stewardship and investment decisions require essentially the same kind of thinking and transactions. So we decided to invest not with an objective to build up our asset values for their own sakes or for personal aggrandizement, but with the purpose of investing for the Lord's work, which will count for all eternity.

That is not to say that we had in our minds the thought, "If we keep this, it will grow in worth, and then we can do more for the Lord." Some of the stock units that we have given in past years would have later multiplied monetarily 20 or 30 times. Our attitude has been to pray, "The money is Yours, Lord. We have done the best we know how to do. Now it is Yours to act or not to act." When the values of our investments went down in a bear stock market, we prayed similarly, "Lord, the money is Yours. You have to decide, and we leave it in Your hands."

At times instead of giving a block grant for specific projects to a mission or school, we have given the equivalent investment yield of that grant. This method accomplishes as much for the recipient as our giving a full block grant, because the organization would have invested it themselves and would have benefited from only the interest anyway.

Sometimes with a venture such as a new church or a parachurch organization, a great deal of money is required. The amount can vary and ought to be dispersed in stages. I learned this principle while working as a business assistant to the man I mentioned earlier who launched, or helped to launch, a number of major parachurch organizations in our country. Dispersing funds in stages provides a discipline for those directing the venture itself—as distinct from the fund-raising process—to accomplish the necessary planning, organizing, training, and operating of the project, while encouraging communication with their governing board and involved stewards in a timely manner.

In an existing church or parachurch ministry, my wife and I make it a practice not to give over 3 or 4 percent of the budget for operating expenses (including the missions budget, if we are giving to a church) and not over 10 percent of the budget for a capital drive.

In a capital budget for a mission or a Christian higher education institution, we keep our capital contribution in some kind of balance with the giving of the directors or trustees. The total given by all the directors or trustees needs to be in balance with the amount that is donated by the public who is served.

We have never taken part in general fund-raising, that is, going out and raising funds for any particular work or letting our names be used to pressure others to give. In fact, we have agreed with some of our friends who have also been blessed financially that we do not send people with requests to them, and they do not send them to us. So when folks come to us quoting someone else as having sent them, I know that cannot be true. Many times, however, we share with these friends our own interests, and they do the same with us.

Working with other people, especially our younger friends and family members, multiplies giving and provides them growth in stewardship experiences, encouraging them to continue those thrusts. For example, sometimes instead of selling a piece of real estate to a young Christian friend, we have sold it at a bargain, or even given it, to a mission. Our friend would then buy that real estate from the mission, realizing the stewardship that was involved. Often we have seen this so involve them in the work of that mission that they became earnest stewards for that same organization themselves.

Another way to extend our giving has been to set up scholarships named for friends, particularly older friends. Their families and friends in turn become involved in contributing to and praying for the recipients of such scholarships. As these scholars graduate and return to their countries to serve—or go out from this country as missionaries—a bond has been established, and the recipients find themselves blessed with avid supporters in prayer and financial backing.

TAKE THE TIME AND GET OUT AND GO

Good stewardship takes time—time to pray, to think, to research, to write, to talk with individuals, and to encourage others to see them. It is a discreet type of work, often hard work. For example, with a number of the scholarships my wife and I have established, we have not personally been involved because of our preference for anonymity. But we have followed those for whom scholarships have been named to be in touch with the recipients. We ask them to learn about the students' successes and failures, their needs and aspirations, so that we can pray with them for these scholarship recipients.

The job of handling the paperwork on my desk takes hours and hours. But time is also necessary to be alone with the Lord and to be together, my life partner and I, to pray over and think about the matters of our stewardship.

One of the best ways to get a vision (and a blessing) of God's work is to go and see it. It takes time, but going to see what is happening, whether or not we support that particular effort, is invaluable. We have been fortunate to have been able to take a number of trips overseas, but we are not interested in travel for travel's sake. There are many places and people to see and only travel allows these opportunities, but our travel has been enhanced by learning firsthand what God has been doing, both now and in the past. Firsthand exposure to a ministry and the people directly involved in it gives insights otherwise impossible to attain. Bonds of friendship result from such visits, and add great joy and extra dimensions to our prayer and financial support.

Having those involved in God's work in our home is another good way of learning what is going on and gives us an opportunity for prayer and fellowship. The telephone and computer have also provided access to many missionaries. We have appreciated the use of the electronic mailbox system that has provided contact for us to some areas.

ANONYMITY WITH ACCOUNTABILITY

My wife and I prefer to be as anonymous as possible in our giving. Obviously, when we make a matching gift commitment with someone, that person knows it. Or, if we provide a home for a pastor or help a Christian couple in special need, there are a few people who must know about our gifts. But we attempt to keep our giving between us and the Lord.

Sometimes we have been disappointed when fund-raisers at an institution we have given to go out and use our names to pressure others. I don't appreciate that tactic; we don't want our name used in that way.

We are fully disclosed, however, in the sense of being accountable. We provide an audit trail so that the IRS can check our finances at any time. Paul's words about the "brother who [was] praised by all the churches" (2 Corinthians 8:18) fit here, in terms about our being open to those to whom we make commitments and to those who have a right to audit what we do.

Receiving from organizations and individuals accurate and full accounts of the projects and ministries we support is a real satisfaction, for it is often difficult for us to obtain complete information on administrative costs assigned to projects or ministries. In the end, we simply come to the Lord and say, "We have done the best we know how to do. Those in the organization are responsible to You. This is in Your hands." Inadequate reporting or excessive overhead, however, does influence our future stewardship decisions with these ministries.

What about the so-called "failures"? For example, my life partner and I have been involved with several Christian camps through the years. Some have had to close. People have said to us, "Well, that's money down the drain." But that's not so! There may have been mismanagement. There may have been failures of leadership. But if it was used effectively for some time, if there have been young people won to Christ—even one, then it was money well spent.

We are always impressed by those who come to us for funds, when they are themselves extended financially. On the other hand, we are unimpressed when we learn, for instance, that a school's faculty is constantly agitating for higher salaries, when we know that their compensation is far above many missionaries we support. We wonder if that is a place where we want to put the money entrusted to us, if they are not being extended themselves in the work of Christ.

GIVING TO THOSE WHO HAVE MINISTERED TO US

We have a special responsibility to those who have ministered to us spiritually, pastors particularly, but also some friends who have been like pastors to us. Galatians 6:6 says, "Anyone who receives instruction in the word must share all good things with his instructor" (see Romans 15:27 and 2 Corinthians 8—9). In accordance with this principle, we have for years sent nondeductible gifts to our pastors. Sometimes we have sent money for them to use for a vacation. Does a pastor need a sabbatical but the church can't handle it financially? Then we have stepped in. Is there a home need? The block of funds we have set aside to encourage our pastors can be used for this.

Here are a couple of specific examples. A former pastor moved into a situation in which he could not possibly survive with the amount of salary he was receiving. We stepped in, paid up the mortgage for his home, and then gave that refinanced note to a mission. With very modest payments, he is now paying the mission for that house. He has a sense of giving to the mission, but in reality is paying off his mortgage. He was not given an outright gift, but he can afford this arrangement and is buying a home, gaining on the principal month by month.

Another pastor friend needed an addition to his home. After a careful look at his budget, analyzing what his young family's needs would be, we came up with an arrangement. We gave an amount equal to 17 percent of the present value of the house to be used for the addition. A simple land trust was set up that stated that at the death of himself and his wife, 17 percent of the market value at that time would go into a specifically named area of God's work. The pastor and his family are enjoying the addition to their home, and in the future the Lord's work will receive the original 17 percent we gave, plus a portion of a return on that investment through the increase in the market value of the home.

A WORD ABOUT ENDOWMENTS

At the risk of offending some people, especially some fund-raisers, I want to interject a few comments on my personal perceptions of giving to endowments. Over the years my wife and I have contributed to ministry endowments, but we have come to have less regard for them, believing that almost every organization ought to be totally dependent on the generation it is serving and not on endowments. Knowing there is a pot of money in endowment tends to lead some people to preoccupation with how much this or that group within an institution or mission can get out of it. In addition, the organization tends to slip away from acknowledging the Lord as its true and constant Source of supply. As it loses its accountability to its stewards, its focus as a cutting edge for the outreach of the Gospel can become blurred.

I am speaking of endowments that would underwrite the general operations of a mission or a Christian school, whether a Bible school or college or university, particularly endowments for its regular undergraduate and graduate programs. Our disappointment over some endowment funds should not cloud the fact that one valid place for them is to pay for the maintenance, repair, and upkeep of buildings.

Another valid place for endowments is scholarships or the underwriting of specific projects, such as a special collection of materials by a group of authors that will be used on an ongoing basis for years to come.

Now, instead of giving to endowments at any mission or school, we prefer to give block amounts, sometimes over several years, through a family foundation. The foundation has enabled our children to be active in stewardship, and together we have greater involvement in the use of the funds. My wife and I have commitments from our children that if in the future they sense that the foundation is not fulfilling the purposes we have intended, it will be dissolved, and the total principal be given away, to be used up within a few years in the outreach of the Gospel, and not go into any organization's endowment.

IN CONCLUSION

So, my Christian friend, is any of my giving history applicable to your stewardship? For instance, I hope you can see the importance of systematically taking time and initiative in making decisions about your giving. Become as personally involved as possible in the ministries you support. Don't allow your support to end after you have written your check. In some cases you can visit those you support; more often you can write. But always you can pray.

Be creative in the handling of your stewardship so that you multiply your giving, whether the gift be time, money, hospitality, effort, or whatever. Try to stretch your finances as far as possible when making your commitments. Enjoy seeing the growth in your life and in those you encourage to become involved as a result of giving. Share the privilege of giving by involving others, and the outcome will be more money, more prayer, more blessings, and more joy—for everyone!

But, most important, put God in charge of your stewardship. Let Him lead you in your own adventure of giving, in accordance with His Word and through the guidance of His Spirit.

My wife and I rejoice every time we take a group of envelopes containing checks that are ready to be mailed, place our hands on them—as was done with the Old Testament sacrifices—and pray and dedicate them to the Lord for His use. We did this when the children were young, at our dinner table during our family worship, and we do it now, sometimes just the two of us and sometimes with our adult children when they are at our home.

With loving, grateful hearts, may we each humbly acknowledge that, after all, our meager offerings—whether a mite or a million—are but mere pittances compared to the gift of Him who gave us His all.

(5)
ABOVE REPROACH:
THE MEASURE OF
CREDIBILITY

ARTHUR C. BORDEN

There is an old adage that goes something like this: "You can fool some of the people some of the time, but you can't fool all the people all the time." Fooling people, whether all of them or some of them, is an unfortunate fact of life. We weep with the widow who withdraws her savings to pay ten times too much for roof repair. We are angered upon hearing of an employer who convinces immigrants to work below minimum wage. Gross examples of trickery move us because they test our idea of credibility.

In our society we take steps—even legal ones—to protect people from less-than-credible others. But when it comes to charitable giving, our tendency is to assume (and ideally we should be able to do so) that the groups we give our money to are above reproach. We naively give little care to insuring that the organizations are credible. As Christians we sometimes are squeamish about raising credibility questions. After all, if we question a person's credibility, aren't we judging, and doesn't the Bible say that we should not judge?

This chapter focuses on credibility—on what donors can do to ensure that the organizations they give to are credible.

THERE IS NO SUCH THING AS INSTANT CREDIBILITY

The dictionary defines *credibility* as "the quality or power of inspiring belief." Having credibility means being trustworthy and responsible, indicating a favorable estimate of character reliability, reputation, and good name. To be credible is to offer reasonable grounds for being believed.

Credibility cannot be bought, borrowed, or stolen. It must be earned, built up. Except for the rarest of exceptions, it never happens instantaneously. It is achieved over a period of time but can be destroyed overnight. It is established much more easily than reestablished.

As Christians our idea of credibility comes from the belief in an omnipresent and almighty God whose presence provides just reason for ethical and moral behavior. A holy and righteous God watches how we live when no one else is looking.

We serve a credible God who sent us a credible Son with a credible message. Did you ever stop to think where the credibility comes from in the Gospel message? The word *gospel* in the Greek is derived from the root words which mean "a perfectly delivered heavenly message." Its credibility comes from the consistency of the message found in Scripture and the consistency of God's character.

What is also striking is the consistency of the results when people believe. The same words of Scripture read by people of different cultures and ages produces *precisely* the same results of peace, joy, hope, and security of eternal life in every person, in every culture, in every era in history. This divine track record is what gives us the sense of believability and trustworthiness in the Gospel.

History has also shown that any and all of the world's societies run better in an environment permeated with trustworthiness, believability, and confidence or credibility. Governments must exercise confidence in each other's monetary systems, borders, and so on. Businesses must have faith and trust that products will be produced and shipped as promised. A transportation system is based on a system of trust in the pilot, or the other driver. From police and fire protection to families and households, credibility is of paramount importance for life to run smoothly.

Jesus' ministry gave evidence that He was the Messiah, the Christ. His miracles and teachings demonstrated conclusively that He was the Son of God. In his eye-witness account of Jesus, John points out that the signs and teachings recorded "are written that you may believe that Jesus is the Christ, the Son of God, and that by believing you may have life in His name" (John 20:31).

Jesus knew that He, the Son of God, had to be credible. He

invited Thomas to put his finger where the nails had been so Thomas would believe.

To inquire, then, about the operation and program of an organization or Christian leader so that credibility can be verified is an appropriate way to demonstrate our concern for God's work.

DONORS HAVE A RESPONSIBILITY
TO DO THEIR HOMEWORK

Most donors have been hesitant to recognize their responsibility to investigate the management of a ministry before contributing. Often they assume that if the organization is Christian and its leaders are Christians, it must be responsibly doing a good job. Unfortunately, that is not always the case. When we give we need to recognize that we are stewards and that our gifts must be *given* wisely, as well as *spent* wisely. Too many donors believe that if they give to a ministry that misuses their funds, they are in no way accountable for that misuse.

Recognizing the responsibility of the donor does not take away any of the responsibility of the ministry. But too often blame for problems is put on the organization and little, if any, placed on the donor. Let's face it—if donors were perceptive and demanded accountability, most ministries would at least try to do their duty. The main reason ministries get away with misuse of funds is that donors do not hold them accountable.

The donor is responsible to know the ministry he is supporting. That means much more than knowing about a ministry. A donor should begin by asking questions which will lead to an understanding of the ministry:

 – What does it do?
 – How does it do it?
 – How long has it been in this particular ministry?
 – What do others think about the way in which it is carrying out its mission?
 – Does it concentrate on one thing or does it do many things?
 – Does it provide services directly to the beneficiaries or does it assist others in providing the services?
 – Does the donor agree with what it teaches, with what is being done, and with the way the work is being carried out?

Donors should never try to force an organization to create a special ministry for the sake of a gift. Every donor has a right to restrict his or her gifts for a particular aspect of the organization's ministry, but should not be unreasonable in the restrictions put on a gift. The purpose for donor questions is to get information and to act on it. The organization should be driven by the vision of the leadership, including the board, and guided by its stated purpose. If this is so, a donor can then respond in good conscience and support that vision and program.

Getting the answers to questions is not difficult, but it does take time and effort. The first place to seek information is from the organization itself. Request literature and other material from a ministry and review it thoroughly. The following are things to look for.

• History of the ministry. If it is an older, established ministry, it obviously has a track record. Many effective ministries have a short history. They have been formed by people who sensed a need and decided to do something, and frequently these organizations or agencies are still under the leadership of the founders. These younger ministries often have an enthusiasm and sense of mission that has been lost by older ministries. On the other hand, many of the older, established ministries are still in existence because they have performed well for a long period of time.

• Statement of purpose. Statements of purpose, often called mission statements, are becoming more common in Christian organizations. Those who don't have one published can certainly put something together for you; however, you can definitely give higher regard to organizations whose statements of purpose and doctrine are printed. This tells you they are accustomed to providing such information.

It is in a statement of purpose that an organization can most accurately and meaningfully define itself. Its leaders may tell you why the organization exists, what they are determined to accomplish and, in broad strokes, how they are going about it. Or they may provide a statement so brief and so general that it neither defines their goals nor limits their fund-raising categories in any way. The unworthies don't want to define themselves in any way that would later limit what they can tell you they are doing.

Your analysis of the statement of purpose should have three steps. First, taking everything it says at face value, read through the statement to confirm that the organization's work has enough in common with your stewardship goals to warrant your further interest. Second, read everything else they send you. Third, critically reread the statement of purpose in the light of all the material they have furnished you. Do any of the assertions in their statement of purpose seem like mere window dressing? Do they talk of great ministry, but actually concentrate on the "hot button" activities that appeal so strongly to the masses of donors? Do they talk passionately about certain work, and then turn around and hand the money to someone else to actually do the work, someone they do not name and who is, therefore, not subject to investigation? These procedures are more common than you may think.

• Doctrinal statement. If you think you're going to make hair-splitting theological distinctions between various candidate organizations on the basis of their doctrinal statements, you're in for a letdown. Most organizations realize that the overwhelming majority of persons requesting doctrinal statements are evangelicals. Therefore, when you ask for one, they will almost universally assume you are an evangelical. If their statement is one that they know you will be comfortable with, they'll send you a copy. If not, they simply won't send it.

Being pegged by such a request will work to your advantage. An evangelical organization will perceive you as having strong donor potential, and a nonevangelical organization will see you as an unlikely donor.

Some ministries have a broad base and do not have to be very specific in their doctrinal position. This is true for certain social agencies, literature ministries, evangelistic associations, and certain other types of ministries. A relief agency, for example, can work with many churches because the service it provides need not be restricted by a denominational position.

On the other hand, church-planting ministries, some literature ministries, and many educational and teaching ministries require more narrow doctrinal positions. Regardless of the importance of doctrinal outlook to the purpose of an organization, the donor should understand what the ministry stands for and should be able to enthusiastically endorse the position that it holds.

• The listing of the board of directors. Many mission organizations, with presumably significant work going on all over the world—and mass mailings reaching you regularly—can apparently recruit only the relatives of the leader to serve on the board. Why is this? Occasionally, it is because the work is actually so ineffectual that no one of reputation will associate his or her name with the group. Much more often it is that all others are being carefully excluded from the board, because this organization is a family business. The people running such groups are determined to keep the affairs of their operation a totally private matter—and usually for the very reasons you might suspect.

Even more common than the family board is the board comprised entirely of employees of the organization—a situation that can also be used to guarantee secrecy. The Evangelical Council for Financial Accountability (ECFA), the Better Business Bureau (BBB), and the National Charities Information Bureau (NCIB) have established guidelines on this matter. The ECFA limits employee members to 49 percent of the board or less. The BBB is much more stringent at 20 percent, and the NCIB permits only 1 staff person on board.

You should also look for balance on the board—geographical balance, balance of talents, and balance in their ties to the organization.

• Financial statements. Much progress has been made recently in the area of financial accountability. The traditions of accounting itself and the Federal Accounting Standards Board are on the side of the donor. In brief, here is what you're looking for:

– First, you want to determine that you have received a complete financial statement, that each of the three parts is there—a balance sheet, a revenue and expense statement, and a statement of changes in fund balances (compared to the previous year).

– Next comes the matter of the audit of this statement or statements. Is the statement in your hands an audited statement? Audited by a certified public accountant? How do you know? Is the auditor's cover letter included with the statement? It had better be, for you have no way of being sure the financial statement you hold is an audited one except with the accompanying letter from the CPA who audited it. In that letter the CPA must attest to his use of "generally accepted auditing standards" and to the "fairness" of the statement in relation to "generally accepted accounting principles." Then he must render one of three possible opinions on the financial statement as audited:

unqualified (referred to as "clean")—the CPA's unqualified attestation that the documents examined "present fairly the financial position of the organization"
qualified
adverse—states that the documents examined "do not present fairly the financial position of the organization."
  – Finally, did you get the three years' worth of statements you asked for? Or did they just send you their latest because the previous ones were unfavorable or not audited?
  • Statement of future plans. Unfortunately, too many organizations never think about this element of ministry, or haven't thought enough about it to have a statement. The absence of a statement of future plans is not necessarily a negative indicator; but its existence is a very positive sign.
  Ask yourself two questions about each project or undertaking in their statement. First, what do you think of the individual worth of each new goal or project? Would this activity alone be a valuable ministry? Second, does this new activity complement and advance the group's present purposes, as outlined in their statement of purpose? Organizations with long-range plans tend to be serious about the stewardship of present and future resources.

OTHER SOURCES OF INFORMATION

The local church should be an invaluable source of information for donors, but unfortunately it often is not, because the church has not been asking questions either. However, the pastoral staff or the missions committee is frequently aware of ministries with problems and of ministries that should not be supported. If the donor has any questions, the local church should be contacted to find out what is known about a ministry.
  The local ministerial association is another source of information, especially about community based organizations.
  A number of national Christian associations can provide information, such as:
  • Evangelical Council for Financial Accountability (ECFA)
  • Evangelical Foreign Missions Association (EFMA)
  • Interdenominational Foreign Missions Association (IFMA)
  • National Religious Broadcasters (NRB)

- Christian Camping International (CCI)
- Christian Ministries Management Association (CMMA)
- Christian Stewardship Council (CSC)
- International Union of Gospel Missions (IUGM)
- National Association of Evangelicals (NAE)
- Association of Church Missions Committees (ACMC)
- Association of North American Missions (ANAM)

In addition, two secular agencies, the Philanthropic Advisory Service of the Council of Better Business Bureaus (PAS) and the National Charities Information Bureau (NCIB) may have information to help in evaluating certain ministries.

A word of caution is in order: simply because an organization is not affiliated with or reported on by any of these agencies does not mean that it is not worthy of support. On the other hand, affiliation with one of these agencies is not the sole criteria in determining whether or not to support a ministry. All of these are just aids in making stewardship decisions.

Some of the agencies, such as the Evangelical Council for Financial Accountability, produce reports on ministries and indicate whether they meet certain standards. If a ministry does not meet the particular standards of one of the agencies, the donor should find out why and then make a determination. For example, a different kind of accounting method may not meet an agency's standards, but that does not necessarily imply wrongful practices on the part of the ministry.

THE ORGANIZATION HAS A RESPONSIBILITY TO MANAGE EFFICIENTLY

Just as the donor has the responsibility to ask questions, the organization has a responsibility to respond to them. Clearly written mission statements, doctrinal statements, program information, and financial reports should be readily obtainable. If any of the information is confusing, incomplete, or unclear, additional questions should be asked and properly answered before contributing.

Donor inquiry about staff support is wise and necessary. Is the staff responsible for raising their own support or are they salaried? What are the guidelines for determining the amount of support or salaries? Because most organizations have traditionally kept salaries confidential, even within the organization, disclosure of actual salaries might be difficult to obtain. As a general rule, the salaries of Christian leaders are modest. Refusal to reveal salaries is probably not a reason not to support a Christian ministry, especially if the donor is confident about other aspects.

The overall use of funds should be a concern. How much of the money is going to the actual programs of the ministry, how much to fund-raising, and how much to management? Keep in mind that fund-raising and management expenses can be too low as well as too high. If an organization is raising millions of dollars and has no fund-raising expenses, it may not be properly accounting for its use of funds.

Fund-raising is a legitimate expense. After all, it is a means in which ministries communicate with donors about their needs and their programs. Some organizations, such as churches, have low fund-raising expenses; but new or less interesting ministries may be worthy of support, even though their fund-raising expenses may exceed 30 percent of their budgets.

Management expenses are very important. If a ministry has very low or no management expenses, it might be well to ask, "Who's minding the store?" Good management requires making certain that those raising the funds and those carrying out the program have the resources that they need to do the best job. Bad management does not make for an effective ministry.

GIVE TO CREDITABLE APPEALS

As a donor, you can become aware of needs of a particular ministry in several ways. Each method has certain advantages and some problems. Here are a few suggestions:

• Door-to-door visitation. If someone knocks on your door and is requesting funds for a ministry that you have never heard of, the best policy is to refuse to give them anything. Any conscientious Christian is aware of numerous organizations that need his or her support, and there is no reason to feel guilty for not giving to an unknown ministry or cause. If the person is asking for support for a ministry that you know about, make certain that the person is authorized to solicit support for that group. Con men and women often use the names of well-known groups to get money. The best policy is not to give to anyone who knocks on your door whom you do not know and who is not from your community. If you do give, give only a token amount. If you want to contribute more, get more information and give at a later date. Do not give to help someone earn a trip overseas or a scholarship to some school. Instead, help your own children or those of some worthy family in your church.

• Appeals to a church. Naturally you should be able to trust those whom the leadership in your church present to you as worthy recipients of your largess. Even here, there is danger of being duped. Occasionally, leaders of a local church are taken in by someone raising money for a desperate need, where the money never gets to where it is supposed to go. Often the solicitor presents himself as being associated with an organization whose name is similar to a legitimate agency.

• Telephone solicitation. This type of solicitation is increasing. Commitments should be made only to ministries that you know; if you do not know the ministry, request information in writing. No appeal is so urgent that you need to respond by giving to a stranger. Most responsible organizations will contact only those individuals who have had some previous contact with the ministry. Under all circumstances, be very cautious about giving a credit card number to anyone.

• Radio and TV appeals. Carefully consider what type of broadcast ministry you want to support. One criteria to guide you is whether the program ministers to you. If you are receiving some benefit that you are not likely to receive from your church, you may want to respond to one or more of these ministries.

• Space advertisements in magazines and newspapers. Advertisements are used for certain types of ministries. The advertisements usually tell of a need, but give little information about the organization. If the organization is unknown to you, it may be wise to use the coupon to get more information before making a contribution.

• Mail. This is probably the most common type of appeal, and it gives the ministry an opportunity to tell more about itself than some of the other types of appeals. It also gives the donor an opportunity to take time to prayerfully consider his or her response to such an appeal. Any direct-mail appeal should tell you enough about the organization and the need so that you know how your gift will be used. An appeal that is based purely on emotional phrases and is unclear as to how the funds will be used, does not deserve your response. A number of gimmicks can be used in this type of appeal, but not all of them are bad, for it often takes something special to get our attention, since most of us receive so much of this type of mail. Take time to carefully read the appeal, disregarding the gimmicks, and consider the appeal and the organization on its merits and on the basis of how you think God wants you to use the money that He has entrusted to your care.

SUMMARY

Credibility is a prerequisite for effective ministry. It always has been and always will be. Without it, leaders falter and eventually lose their way. Supporters lose faith in the organization and support dies.

Credibility is one of those qualities God expects of us—it is not an option. The credibility of an organization will rise only as high as the personal ethics of the organization's leaders.

The good news is that most Christian ministries are run by honest, well-intentioned people who desire to serve the Lord. They are responding to what they believe is the call of God. Very few leaders in Christian ministries try to take advantage of the public or intentionally misuse contributions.

Many Christian organizations are as well run as any business in America, and their executives are concerned about getting the best use from the resources that have been provided to them by donors.

But some leaders of Christian ministries are so busy trying to carry out their mission that they do not take the time and effort to put in proper management and financial controls for effectiveness and efficiency. You, as a donor, are providing a service to them and the rest of the Christian community by asking probing questions and requiring complete answers. This lets the leaders know that you are concerned with how your gifts are being used, and this same concern will encourage them to continually strive to improve their ministries and do a credible job.

Ask questions, become informed, and give liberally and regularly to those ministries that are doing a good work well.

ARTHUR C. BORDEN is the president and chief executive officer of the Evangelical Council for Financial Accountability (ECFA). He received his bache-

lor of arts degree from The King's College and master of theology degree from Dallas Theological Seminary.

Prior to assuming his position with ECFA, Mr. Borden was the director of marketing and church relations for The Genesis Project. Other previous vocations include serving as a missionary in Venezuela with Orinoco River Mission, executive secretary for Central America and Venezuela with the United Bible Society, and the special Washington representative for the Departments of Health and Social Services of the Puerto Rican government. For seven years he served as the secretary for church relations for the American Bible Society.

(6)
HOW TO HAVE
MORE MONEY
TO GIVE

RONALD W. BLUE

Several years ago I visited with a professional person who at age 54 was looking to accomplish several significant financial goals during the balance of his life. He wanted to retire within ten years with enough financial resources to be able to devote his full time to Christian service; he wanted to be totally out of debt as soon as possible; and he wanted to continue to give a fairly significant amount of money to the Lord's work. I asked him to dream a bit about his financial situation and tell me what he would really like to do. He indicated that his heart's desire was to be able to give away at least $1 million during his lifetime.

With his income at $85,000 per year and his net worth at less than $1 million, that goal did not seem to him to be reasonable. After we prepared a financial plan for him, however, he was able to see that it was possible to give away over $1 million during the next five years, be totally out of debt, and have enough financial resources accumulated to devote full time to Christian service. At that time it was just a plan, but today those goals have essentially been accomplished. The man has retired recently, having given away almost $1 million over five years.

In contrast is another professional person I met with recently. He earns over $100,000 per year and is a deeply committed Christian. He, however, is giving less than $2,000 per year. An analysis of his financial situation shows him to be deeply in debt; it is very unlikely that he will increase his giving significantly in the near future.

76

It has been my experience in working with Christians of all economic levels that the second man is far more characteristic of evangelical Christians than the first one. Both men have a strong desire to give of their financial resources, and yet only one is doing so significantly.

According to an article in the May 1986 *Moody Monthly* entitled "Planned Giving: Legalism or Love?" the average giving of evangelical Christians is 2.5 percent of adjusted gross income. My experience over the last 20 years of working with Christians and non-Christians alike in the area of tax planning, investment planning, and financial planning is that while the Christian will give significantly more than the non-Christian, his giving rarely approaches a tithe.

I have had the good fortune over the last several years to work with approximately 500 couples across the country who not only desire to give generously but are doing so. The question logically arises, "Why do most Christians who desire to give more find it so difficult even to tithe?" I believe the answer to that question is both economic and spiritual.

THE ISSUE OF ECONOMIC UNCERTAINTY
Americans today live with a tremendous amount of economic uncertainty. The Third World owes our government and our banks billions and billions of dollars and is, in most cases, unable to repay according to the terms of the original agreements. Oil prices fluctuate dramatically on a day-to-day basis. The dollar rises and declines against foreign currencies in a seemingly uncontrolled fashion. The stock market suffered the biggest crash in history as recently as 1987. Sections of the country have been devastated economically, principally in the Southwest and the Midwestern farming states. The national debt is growing at the rate of $200 billion a year and is very close to $3 trillion total. Consumer debt is at a record high.

Today we are faced with as much economic uncertainty as we have ever seen. As a consequence, we are continually asking ourselves, "Will I ever be able to accumulate enough to have financial security, and if so, will it continue to be enough?" The next question quickly follows, "How much is enough?" Because of the uncertainty, financial decision-making on a day-to-day basis tends to be extremely difficult.

THE ISSUE OF LIFESTYLE

The leader of a large worldwide evangelical organization once asked me what a major donor would look like. My response was that if the person looks as if he can give large sums of money by where he lives, what kind of car he drives, or the country clubs he belongs to, the chances are very good that he is unable to give significantly. If someone were to spend $50,000 per year on his lifestyle, he would have to earn the $50,000 plus the taxes on his gross income, plus any giving that he was going to do, in order to have the $50,000 left to spend on his lifestyle. The major barrier to significant giving is the lifestyle that the evangelical community has adopted. Most of us do not realize the real cost associated with lifestyle.

BIBLICAL MODEL OF FINANCIAL MANAGEMENT

I do not believe that God calls us to either poverty or luxury. Between those extremes an appropriate lifestyle is possible. A biblical model of personal financial management begins with the understanding that it is God who provides for our needs. There is no correlation between how hard we work and how much we make. Scripture makes it clear that we are to work; but the amount of income we make is in God's hands, and He will meet our needs. "In vain you rise early and stay up late, toiling for food to eat—for He grants sleep to those He loves" (Psalm 127:2). A physician may work three days a week and make ten times what a missionary makes who works into the evening and on weekends to accomplish his task. Life is full of seeming inequities. Yet, tremendous freedom results when we accept the fact that our responsibility is to work heartily and to trust God for income, then to live within that God-given income. "Whatever you do, work at it with all your heart, as working for the Lord, not for men" (Colossians 3:23).

There are four basic biblical commandments regarding the use of our income. In addition to these four commandments, there is a principle regarding the use of the excess and a fifth commandment regarding attitude.

• We are commanded to give to the Lord's work. Proverbs 3:9-10 says, "Honor the Lord with your wealth, with the firstfruits of all your crops." First Corinthians 16:2 says, "On the first day of every week, each one of you should set aside a sum of money in keeping with his income, saving it up, so that when I come no collections will have to be made."

• We are commanded to pay taxes. Romans 13:7 says, "Give everyone what you owe him: If you owe taxes, pay taxes; if revenue, then revenue; if respect, then respect; if honor, then honor." Jesus Himself said in Matthew 22:21, "Give to Caesar what is Caesar's, and to God what is God's."

• We are commanded to pay our debts. Psalm 37:21 says, "The wicked borrow and do not repay, but the righteous give generously."

• We are commanded to provide for our family. First Timothy 5:8 says, "If anyone does not provide for his relatives, and especially for his immediate family, he has denied the faith and is worse than an unbeliever."

Therefore, if we believe God provides our income and that He has determined what is the appropriate income for us, we then should prioritize the use of this income to give to His work, pay taxes, and repay debts. The balance left is the amount available to be saved and set aside for the future, and to support our family in a lifestyle we believe God would have us adopt.

What has happened is that many Christians have adopted a desirable lifestyle as their number-one priority and giving to the Lord's work as the fourth or fifth priority. The reasoning often goes like this: "I would like to give, but by the time I pay my taxes, pay my debt, and provide for my family, there is just not enough left over to tithe, let alone give above the tithe." In reality, what has happened is that lifestyle has become the first priority and the biblical priorities have been ignored.

WHY CHRISTIANS DO NOT GIVE

I believe the reason Christians do not give as they realistically could can be summed up in three primary statements: They don't know how much they *can* give and still meet the other objectives they have; they don't give as much as they could because they don't *plan* to give; they don't give as much as they could because they don't know *how* to give.

• Christians don't know how much can be given. The confusion about an appropriate Christian lifestyle and the current economic instability results in confusion as to how much we can reasonably give as good stewards of God's resources and still meet the legitimate short-term and long-term needs of our families. If long-term goals are established, a plan is set to achieve those goals, and then a decision is made to fund the giving objectives, more giving will take place. And, if a limit is set on accumulation, then there can be significantly more giving.

Many Christians continue to accumulate because they have never established finish lines. They may have "arrived" but not yet know it. For example, if the long-term goals of a family are to fund the children's college education, to be totally out of debt, and to be financially independent by the time the husband is 65, then an amount can be established for each one of these goals. Once these goals have been met, the accumulation need not continue.

Often when desirable financial accumulation has been reached, it is impossible to know it because a goal was never defined. The mere exercise of setting long-term financial goals and of analyzing how close those goals are to being reached will, in most cases, free up additional financial resources for giving.

● Christians don't plan to give. The second reason that many Christians do not give as much as they could is that they never develop a plan for giving. Giving too often is responsive rather than proactive. There are always more alternative uses for money than money available, whether in regard to an individual, a family, a business, or a government. Therefore, unless the use of financial resources is well planned, money tends to be spent on the most pressing need at the moment. Because giving is rarely seen as a high priority, there is very little money available for it.

It has been my experience that when a family plans to give, whether a tithe or a greater amount, and follows that plan, they will tend to give substantially more than the family that gives out of the excess, for there rarely is any excess.

The professional person mentioned in the first paragraph of this chapter had the ability to give significant sums of money, but he was not aware of that ability. He had never quantified his goals, and had never given significant amounts according to a predetermined plan. He had always given 15 percent of his income, but was well able to give 50 percent or more through planning. Giving without a plan is like planting a garden without knowing what we want to produce. We will be far more successful if we plan what we want to grow and follow that plan, rather than just scatter various seeds haphazardly.

• Christians don't know how to give. The third reason many Christians do not give to their potential is that they do not know the techniques of giving.

Recently my firm met with a family who had had their estate planning documents prepared by an outstanding law firm. Their projected estate tax liability upon the death of both of them, however, was tens of millions of dollars. Even though this firm was well qualified to give tax-planning advice, they had forgotten to ask the simple question, "Do you have any charitable giving desires?" This family desired to leave *all* of their estate to evangelical causes, and when we asked them that question, it was very simple to do their estate planning and reduce the estate tax liability to zero merely by giving it all away through a private foundation.

For those who are serious about charitable giving, there are many techniques available to help in long-term financial planning. But in order for those techniques to be of value, the potential donor must be aware of them; not all financial counsel is unbiased or qualified in the area of charitable giving.

CONCLUSION

The bottom line of charitable giving is that it should be a spiritual rather than an economic decision. Economically, charitable giving never pays. It may reduce taxes, but it always costs something in terms of cash flow given up or net worth reduced. Therefore, those Christians who give significantly will do so only because of an eternal rather than a temporal perspective. As the martyred Christian missionary Jim Elliot said, "He is no fool who gives up what he cannot keep in order to gain what he cannot lose."

I believe there are three levels of charitable giving—the "should give" level, the "could give" level, and the "would give" level.

The "should give" level is giving out of the firstfruits in obedience to our Lord's commands throughout Scripture.

The "could give" level is the amount of resources you could give up by merely making a decision to do so. For example, it might be a savings account, a stock investment, shares of a business owned, clothing, or a vacation. It is not a faith promise because that means pledging the unseen; whereas in this case, it is merely a matter of deciding what you can and will give. This level of giving will be achieved only if a financial plan is in place that allows you to see what you have available to give.

The "would give" level has to do with future increase of resource. If a financial plan is in place, and if God increases resources through higher income or reduced expenses, a commitment can be made to give out of the excess.

Whether we give now or at death is a question that also needs to be addressed. My own view is that at death we have no choice because we are leaving it all anyway, and so in reality we are not giving up anything. Additionally, I agree with the good advice in this little rhyme:

> Do your givin'
> while you're livin'
> so you're knowin'
> where it's goin'.

God is able to take the resources you entrust to Him now and build for eternity. To some extent, the way you spend eternity depends on how you use God's resources entrusted to you today. Matthew 25:21 says, "His master replied, 'Well done, good and faithful servant! You have been faithful with a few things; I will put you in charge of many things. Come and share your master's happiness!' "

God has entrusted certain financial resources to each of us and has given certain commandments as to the priority uses of those resources. We are commanded to give, to pay our taxes, to pay our debts, and to provide for our families. However, the guiding principle of money management is another commandment found in Hebrews 13:5: "Keep your lives free from the love of money and be content with what you have, because God has said, 'Never will I leave you; never will I forsake you.' " We are to manage His resources to accomplish His purposes and to be content in so doing. We can give more—not by having greater incomes, but by managing in accordance with biblical principles and priorities the resources God has already entrusted to us.

RONALD W. BLUE, a certified public accountant and managing partner of Ronald Blue & Co., received his master of business administration degree from Indiana University. Convinced that Christians would better handle their personal finances if they were counseled with the highest technical expertise and from a biblical perspective, he founded Ronald Blue & Co. in 1979. Ronald Blue & Co. is a firm of financial analysts, CPAs, and attorneys who provide professional services to individuals in the areas of tax planning, charitable gifting, investment planning, estate planning, family budgeting, and more. The company serves clients nationwide and is headquartered in Atlanta with branch offices in Indianapolis and Orlando.

Mr. Blue is the author of Master Your Money: A Step-By-Step Plan for Financial Freedom (Nelson).

(7)
LIFESTYLE STEWARDSHIP

LAWRENCE W. O'NAN

When I think of giving, I often think of the patriarch Moses. I am sure the major question that he asked upon receiving the Ten Commandments from the Lord was the timeless question that is often asked by leaders when God directs them to carry out a major ministry task, "What about funding?"

We know that God provided for the needs of His people as they spent 40 years wandering in the wilderness; but I am sure Moses often wondered how he was going to fund the journey. Our challenge is the same as Moses faced—he had to believe God for miracles. We as contributors must work with diligence and trust God for His resources to fund His endeavors.

Travel with me back to 1947, to a small church in the western hills of Colorado. A young pastor had a challenge—ministry to people in a rural community. That pastor was my father. Little did I know as a three-year-old child that my pennies were helping to mold a ministry for the future. The little church was built in cooperation with many in the community.

Members of the little community church gave money to buy the bricks for the church building while others laid those bricks; and, thus, the church became a reality. At the dedication of the church, my father mentioned that the only missing piece in the church plan was a bell for the belfry. One lady heard of this need, and decided to do something about it.

She wrote to a man in California named Ben Alexander, who

---

hosted a national radio program called "Heart's Desire of America." She asked for a church bell for the little community church in Colorado. Ben Alexander was impressed with the lady's unusual request and invited the people across America who listened to the "Heart's Desire of America" program to participate by sending one penny to help meet this request.

In the weeks that followed, 224,581 people chose to send one penny to help provide a church bell for the belfry. Yes, a few people violated the "one penny" rule—some sent pennies for their dogs, their cats, in memory of their loved ones, etc.

People got involved when a need was shared. One person's desire stimulated others to take action. Giving comes from the heart. Giving involves our emotions. And giving involves our will.

Unfortunately, we now seem to view giving to God's cause as a response to the competition for our dollar. When we understand biblical giving, we allow God to lead us to give in the way that would honor Him.

If we understand our role as Christian stewards, we will no longer need to scratch our heads and ask, "How can we give more?" Instead of viewing participation in God's work as an interruption to life, we will see it as a means to truly living.

But the role of the steward has not been taught from the pulpit in the last few decades. As a result, we become confused and often feel that we are participating in God's work, when in fact we may be simply playing around with our Christian responsibility. We need to apply true biblical giving and then watch God stimulate our hearts.

Giving money results in tremendous blessing. But many people today do not realize the reciprocal response that God provides to His children as a result of their giving from their heart.

Money is not filthy lucre. Rather, it is an item of exchange which God has provided to enable us to carry out His work. Our participation through giving is ministry which helps to touch the lives of people.

If we are going to be successful in releasing time, talent, and resources for the furtherance of the Gospel, we first need to examine the spiritual principles of God's Word as they relate to stewardship. When these key principles are understood, they release in us a new attitude toward giving.[1]

GIVING . . . AND OUR NEED

Today our culture has confused needs, wants, and desires. Let's define what a need is. A *need* is a lack of an item essential to survival. We think of food, clothing, shelter, and things of this nature as needs.

A *want*, on the other hand, is a craving for something that often makes us focus our total attention on that objective. Wants carried to their extreme often become obsessions, and we end up reacting impulsively rather than with control, wisdom, and understanding in seeking God's will and timing.

God has promised to supply our needs. He has not promised to supply all our wants; but as a loving Father, He often makes provision for our wants as well. There is a subtle difference between the two. A need is based on God's promised provision, and a want is based much more on our own self-centeredness.

Ministries as well as individuals can confuse needs and wants. Could it be that some worthy groups are becoming obsessed with their own dreams and self-centeredness? God wants to provide what they need, and He may, out of His own sovereign will, provide their wants as well.

Genuine need stimulates our giving. When we hear of a genuine need, our hearts cry to participate in helping to resolve the problem. I am fearful that many Christian organizations today are lumping wants in the context of needs and begging for them to be met when, in fact, God has said, "Wait and see what I will do."

GIVING . . . AND OUR CULTURE

We live in a fast-paced society in the United States. Many other cultures look at us as being very materialistic and self-centered. Our culture influences our definition of needs and wants. Many people "need" a five-bedroom house with a pool in the backyard, a recreation room in the basement, and three cars in the garage. This orientation grows more from the culture than from meeting the basics of life.

Materialism has been preached from the rooftops: our television sets, our magazines, and our newspapers reflect a society that has it all—or at least wants to.

A few years ago, I was asked to participate in teaching a seminary study on giving. When I picked up the catalog, I was impressed to see three or four courses focusing on biblical stewardship. But then I found out that the only course to actually be offered was the two-week class I would be teaching. The others had been canceled or postponed.

Most pastors have not been trained in stewardship and they are hesitant to discuss such a private matter from the pulpit. Their salary is coming from that same group of people, and they would not want to be viewed as being "money hungry." Also, many pastors themselves are more concerned with their need to get rather than their need to give. And with this preoccupation on getting, they do not want to infringe on their people's lifestyles.

A perception in our culture is that there is not enough money, not enough time, and not enough talent to carry out the need of ministry. A few years ago, the world was thrown into a chaotic confusion. The Middle East had oil, and the rest of the world wanted that oil. There was a crisis. We were running out of oil.

But were we running out of oil? No. The core problem was a matter of imbalance, greed, and selfishness. Competition had created an environment where we thought we needed to get something before someone else got it. An interesting observation about all this was that the American society ended up wanting more than the rest of the world.

There are sufficient resources for the world to be sustained and to live productively. But because of sin, people are greedy and selfish. We have alienated ourselves from working in harmony with each other.

GOD HAS A PLAN

The problem we face is not new. God's plan for man was established in the Garden of Eden as a pattern for us to live by. God gave His very nature and heart to man. He gave man the authority to manage on His behalf, to oversee the many wonders of His creation.

• God's plan is based on timelessness. We cannot imagine living outside of time, but God can. God gave us, however, the gift of time so we would have a frame of reference.

• God's plan is built around truth. What God says and does can be trusted. He does not change. He is steadfast. He is firm. He is consistent. He is loyal. He is faithful. Truth flows from His very Being.

• God's plan is built on giving. The Bible is a record of God in action. He is the giver: God gave, and the heavens and the earth were formed; God gave life to Adam, and He gave him a beautiful mate; even after Adam and Eve disobeyed, He gave them clothing, shelter, and protection—He met their every need.

• God's plan is also characterized by agape love. Deuteronomy 7:7-8 defines why God brought the Children of Israel out of the land of Egypt. His love for them motivated Him to act. Moses explained His love to the generation of people who were heading to the Promised Land:

> The Lord did not set His affection on you and choose you because you were more numerous than other peoples, for you were the fewest of all peoples. But it was because the Lord loved you and kept the oath He swore to your forefathers that He brought you out with a mighty hand and redeemed you from the land of slavery, from the power of Pharaoh king of Egypt.

God's love today says, "I love you no matter what you do or what you don't do. I love you so much that I gave you My only Son."

• God's plan produces peace. When God's plan is implemented, the result is peace of heart to those who believe. If you watch tonight's newscast, you will see chaos, hate, confusion, bitterness, and strife, the very opposite of what God has planned for man. In the midst of our confusing world, Jesus is ready to give us peace.

THE ENEMY'S PLAN

But in contrast to God's plan, let's briefly look at the enemy's plan:

• Satan's plan emphasizes getting. You find this in the Garden of Eden. Satan established the ploy of "get what you can while you can." He motivated Eve's greed to reach out and touch the fruit. Adam was equally stimulated because of his greed.

• Satan's plan appeals to sensual response. We find so often that if it looks good, or smells good, or tastes good, despite whether it is good for us or not, we desire what we see and touch.

• Satan's plan fosters covetousness. His plan results in an unhealthy passion for self-gratification. He knows that our craving for pleasure can result in unhealthy competition, envy, and strife. He desires to separate mankind, not unify us.

These two basic plans govern our actions today. Whose plan are we following, Satan's or God's?

GIVING . . . AND GOD'S PERSPECTIVE

If we accept God's plan and understand His view of giving, we will be more effective stewards and will influence the lives of others in a dramatic way. Scripture is full of practical illustrations of giving.

In my study of Scripture, I find five principles concerning biblical giving:

• God, our Father, owns an infinite supply of everything that we or anyone else could ever need, want, or desire. Simply put: *my Father owns it all.*

One of my favorite passages in Scripture is the account of King David offering a prayer of thanksgiving to God for the people's contributions toward building the temple. He prayed: "Yours, O Lord, is the greatness and the power and the glory and the majesty and the splendor, for everything in heaven and earth is Yours. Yours, O Lord, is the kingdom; You are exalted as head over all" (1 Chronicles 29:11).

David summarized his thoughts in Psalm 24:1 when he said, "The earth is the Lord's and everything in it, the world, and all who live in it."

Yes, our Father owns it all! Nothing that we now possess is ours. Everything is His. He is the owner. He will maintain that right and authority throughout all eternity.

• God has a hilarious time circulating His wealth and resources and wants His children to share in this pleasure. Simply put: *my Father wants me to give hilariously.*

God is an hilarious giver. *Hilaros* is a Greek word, meaning "to cause to shine like the sun." As God has made His very nature to give like the sun gives off heat and light, so He plans for us to give as He gives.

In 2 Corinthians 9:7, we find that famous verse, "God loves a cheerful giver." The word "cheerful" is from the Greek word *hilaros*. He wants us to enjoy the process and give because we were designed to do so, not because we were obligated to do so.

Hilarity also has a degree of laughter and enjoyment, and giving should never be done begrudgingly or out of necessity. It should come from the depths of our heart, because we want to participate.

• It pleases God when His children ask for and then diligently seek some of their inheritance so that they can give it to others. In other words, *my Father wants me to ask.*

Have you ever thought about how important asking is? So often we have not because we ask not. God knows our needs, but He is wanting us to bring our needs, wants, and desires before Him. We need to tell Him how we feel and ask Him to be involved in our lives. He wants us to ask.

Yes, there will be times when He will say no. In those cases, He knows it is not to our best interest for a yes answer at that time. But a no in God's economy is for our protection, not for our abuse. Our Father wants us to ask.

• If we sow according to God's principles, we will reap and will always have an abundance to help others as well as to meet our own needs. Very simply: *what we sow, we will reap.*

God's Word has an abundance of excellent illustrations concerning the farming process. As we sow, we will reap the results of our harvest. In order to have an effective harvest, we must focus on the harvest. In other words, do not plant it and forget it, remain committed to the end—keep our focus on the end result and sow the right seed with generosity—what we sow is what we are going to reap in a multiplied form!

No farmer ever plants one seed of corn and prays for only one kernel to be the result of his labor. He diligently works acres of ground and seeds that ground with the best, so that the end result will be a multiplied harvest.

But there is a negative contained in this principle. If we choose to sow hatred, discord, irritability, and distrust, we can expect to reap what we sowed. The law of the harvest returns to the harvester what he sows. What we sow, we will reap.

• Our giving can begin to reflect the resources of our Heavenly Father's household, not merely be limited to our earthly resources. Very simply put: *We can draw from our Father's resources.*

A few years ago I learned a valuable lesson about God's supply as I was introduced to bank "ready tellers." With my access code, all I need to do to receive a cash advance is use the authority of my bank. Now, even in a town hundreds or thousands of miles from my place of residence, I have the ability to draw on resources because of the authority the bank has given to me.

Likewise, God wants us, as His children, to draw on His resources. Unfortunately, many people feel they are limited in resources, not realizing that God wants them to give what they have—their time, talents, and treasure—so they can receive more from Him to give away.

You see, God cannot fill a full vessel. He already gave us everything pertaining to life and godliness. The only way we can receive more from God is to distribute what we have. Only then will God give us more from His abundant resources. We need to give in order to receive these resources.

GIVING . . . WHERE THE RUBBER MEETS THE ROAD
There are seven steps that you can take as you begin an adventure in giving.

● Give yourself and your possessions to God. As an act of your will, have you turned your life over to Him? Have you said, "Lord, I relinquish all my rights"? God chooses to work only through a person who has turned over the control of his life to Him. Write down all of your possessions and then sign them over to God. Let Him become the head manager of everything.

● Recognize that God is your total and final supply of all that you need. It is because of God's continuous gifts to us that we live and have our being. Your income and long-range investments cannot make you happy. Your family and friends cannot provide you with genuine joy. God and only God is your total and final supply of all that you need.

● Count on Him by faith to empower you with the Holy Spirit. I'm not talking about a big emotional encounter with the Holy Spirit; you need not feel some emotional high. I'm talking about a simple prayer of faith when you say, "God, by faith I am asking You to empower me with Your Holy Spirit and let Your life flow through me." And then, by faith, count on God to do just that.[2]

● Begin to give according to His directions. Watch for opportunities to give your time, talents, and treasure. Give to the needs of others so God can resupply what He has already given to you.

• Thank and praise God for the privilege you have in distributing His wealth and resources. The key to successful living is in thanking and praising God. Praise turns on the power of heaven.

• Expect results. Look for the returns from your giving. As you give, God will return to you what you have given at the point of your need. Jesus said, "Give, and it will be given to you. A good measure, pressed down, shaken together and running over, will be poured into your lap. For with the measure you use, it will be measured to you" (Luke 6:38).

• Give again and again and again. Only as we are continuing to give from what He gives to us, can we keep the pipeline open that touches the lives of others.

Developing giving skills takes practice. In order to practice, you will need to use your skills and talents that God has already given to you. You will need to effectively manage your finances so that you will have sufficient resources to give as God leads you to give to others for their provision.

You will need to manage your time, for wasting time is like wasting money. You may not always be able to provide the dollars that someone needs, but your time can be a tremendous help and blessing of far greater worth than the resources you might give.

CONCLUSION

The way in which we choose to give our time, talents, and treasure is a reflection of our character. The way in which we manage our money tells the world more about us than our words will ever express. The way we manage our time and talents tells the world how serious we are about our commitment to God and His kingdom.

Are you a thermometer or a thermostat? A thermometer only reports on the surrounding temperature. It has no ability to change its circumstances. It merely tells what currently is reality. A thermostat, on the other hand, not only reports the temperature but also triggers action that changes circumstances. A thermostat helps to regulate its environment.

The steward who is not actively or aggressively distributing time, talents, and treasure is missing out on the opportunity to change his environment through changing people's lives.

The best place to learn effective stewardship is through money management. Our money actually becomes our teacher. Giving money today teaches us more about the principles of God's economy than any other item we might give. You see, money is tangible—you can see it, you can feel it, you can experience its power and influence.

God has provided us with a medium of exchange so we can give and receive more effectively and efficiently. God uses money to teach us to trust Him. As we see God work through our money management, we can better understand how He also works through our management of other items in our stewardship inventory.

The amount we give is not the issue. The issue is that we are giving. As we learn the secret of giving, I am convinced God will provide the resources, manpower, time, harmony and unity to carry out His work in His way. Let's begin to truly give!

LAWRENCE W. O'NAN is a 1966 graduate of the University of Colorado. Prior to joining the Management Development Associates consulting firm in 1984, he and his wife, Pat, served over eighteen years on the full-time staff of Campus Crusade for Christ. During this time, he dedicated thirteen years to giving leadership to numerous development thrusts and was privileged to oversee the raising of more than $150 million for evangelism and discipleship.

Mr. O'Nan is a frequent speaker in the United States and abroad in lifestyle stewardship and consults with Christian organizations in areas of management and major gifts strategy design and implementation. He is the author of Giving Yourself Away *and coauthor of* The Organization Stewardship Inventory, The Personal Stewardship Inventory, *and* The Success Factors Inventory.

The
Responsibility of the Church and
Parachurch Organization

(8)
THE ROLE OF STEWARDSHIP
IN THE
LOCAL CHURCH

EDWARD J. HALES

If offering plates could talk, what tales they could tell us. All week long they sit quietly in the treasurer's office or under the podium, waiting for a few brief moments of service on Sundays. Each hand that passes along the offering plate represents a unique life journey, lifestyle, set of problems, ideals, values, and approach to giving.

One hundred years ago it was not uncommon for people, at moments of unusual spiritual tenderness, to drop a watch or piece of jewelry into the offering plates. Fifty years ago, nearly all of the offerings taken in local churches (deposited in offering plates) were paper currency and coins.

In a typical evangelical church, today's offering plates collect most of the tithes and offerings from God's people in the form of checks, drawn on banks. They contain only a handful of bills and even less change.

While the look of the collection has changed over the years, the offering still represents a significant moment of transaction between a person and God, with the local church being the channel for giving.

This chapter focuses on the crucial role such transactions play in funding the evangelical enterprise.

THE CHURCH—A LIVING FORCE FOR GOD
The church is an organism, a body whose parts are people. It is a body with purpose, for "under His direction the whole body is fitted

together perfectly and each part in its own special way helps the other parts, so that the whole body is healthy and growing and full of love" (Ephesians 4:16, TLB).

In his book *Body Life*, Ray Stedman summarizes the influences and impressions of the church—some good and some bad:

The word "church" conjures up many widely differing images. To some the church is nothing but a snooty religious country club with traditional rituals as sacred as those at a fox hunt. To others the church is a political action group, a pressure block of do-gooders, waging battle against social ills. Some see the church as a kind of nonsegregated waiting room for people expecting to take the next bus for heaven. Some view it as a kind of low calorie dessert for any who want something nice that won't hurt their public image. To many, the church is kind of a water boy to the game of life or a religious democracy trying to legislate morals for the rest of the world.

Nevertheless, despite its many weaknesses and its tragic sins the church has been, in every century since its inception, the most powerful force for good on the face of the earth. It has been light in the midst of the darkness so dense it could be felt. It has been salt in society, retarding the spread of moral corruption and adding zest and flavor to human life.[1]

Within the local church we recognize that everyone has a gift from God, and is potentially useful. Not only are we unique, but we are also interdependent in that we should each desire to help the other members.

Since our purpose in this chapter is to deal primarily with the financial stewardship program, we will not deal further with the possibilities of the development of the individual's gifts and service except to indicate that total stewardship development must not be seen as simply a matter of fund-raising. As the members of the body are developed spiritually to assume their responsibility in the total use of their time, abilities, and treasures, the enhancement of the financial program will inevitably follow. The church that desires to develop its stewardship program should consider the following principles for its financial program.

THE LOCAL CHURCH HAS A CRUCIAL ROLE

The advent and phenomenal growth of parachurch ministries has created numerous additional channels through which evangelicals can participate in God's work. Nevertheless, it is a truism to say that from now until the day when Christ comes, the local church will continue to be the principal and priority vehicle through which Christian stewardship is taught and habits of good discipleship are nurtured.

The success of the local church in teaching stewardship is essential to the well-being of the entire mission effort. Insuring that people understand what it means when the offering plate goes through their row is critical not only to the effectiveness of that local church but in the overall outreach and providing money for ministries.

If the church is to be a living force for good, it will need to be organized to meet the needs in its own body, community, and beyond. Obviously, the pastor plays a key role in this. In Phillips' paraphrase of 1 Peter 5:2-3 we read,

I urge you then to see that the flock of God is properly cared for; accept the responsibility of looking after them willingly, and not because you feel you can't get out of it. Doing your work not for what you can make, but because you are concerned about their well-being. You should aim not at being little tin gods but an example of Christian living in the eyes of the flock committed to your charge.

The Apostle Paul wrote in his Epistle to the Ephesians,

Consequently, you are no longer foreigners and aliens, but fellow citizens with God's people and members of God's household, built on the foundation of the apostles and prophets, with Christ Jesus Himself as the chief cornerstone. In Him the whole building is joined together and rises to become a holy temple in the Lord. . . . From Him the whole body grows and builds itself up in love as each part does its work (2:19-22; 4:16).

The local church thrives when pastors, elders, deacons, and mobilized laity each do their biblical part—including giving.

THERE ARE OBSTACLES TO OVERCOME

There are certain obstacles to stewardship being understood and practiced at a local church level. They are known to all of us but they are worth repeating here.

● North American culture continues to put an incredible burden on society and particularly on Christians. The escalation of the race for more comfortable lifestyles and the prevailing belief that "you can have it all" is creating excessive pressure on homes to have two wage earners who are both high performers in the workplace. What was once men's responsibility—to be the providers—is now nearly equally shared by women, who are increasingly a major part of the work force.

Sacrificial giving, or even the act of giving on a regular basis, is too often unacceptable to us. Our comfort-driven society and our own selfish natures do not readily make room for such biblical values as "you gain your life by losing it."

● A lack of clear biblical teaching about stewardship. Too often in our local churches, pastors trot out sermons on stewardship just prior to a building program and then not again for ten years. Unfortunately, pastors and lay leaders have done too little to assist Christians in establishing positive attitudes and patterns for giving. Rather than making stewardship part of the overall fabric of the teaching in the church, they relegate it to an occasional sermon or Sunday School lesson to "help the people think clearly" when it comes to making decisions about putting up buildings or adding staff.

Little wonder, then, that Christians today succumb to cultural pressure and their own natural inclinations and continue to escalate their lifestyles and pursue comfort at the same rate as the people who don't know Christ. Numerous surveys show that the majority of evangelicals give substantially less than an Old Testament standard of 10 percent of their annual income.

● The church's failure to capture the imagination of Christians in the pew. When was the last time you sat in church and heard a stirring report about how God used the giving of people from that church? Rarely, if ever, are results reported, other than in statistical charts.

In an overreaction to the parachurch method of generating funds for projects, local churches rarely creatively package a need for their people to support. As a result, a staleness sets into the process;

because we fail to stir their hearts frequently enough, we don't cultivate sensitive hearts in our people.
• Lack of good methodology. People today need compelling reasons to give. No longer can we bank on loyalty alone to ensure that
people will give. In today's world, people need clear teaching and
mechanisms for giving that fit where they are in life. Whether the
mechanism is providing offering envelopes or estate planning, our
methodology must match the different passages people in the pew
will go through in a lifetime.

These obstacles are real and press in to various degrees on every
local church which has a concern for God's work. Overcoming them
is a critical first step if we are to see stewardship thrive among our
people.

WAYS TO STRENGTHEN THE LOCAL CHURCH STEWARDSHIP EFFORTS

There are many ways to strengthen the local church's stewardship
efforts. A few suggestions are given here.
• Build a worthy budget. Budgeting is a part of most church work
today. But there is a big difference between a budget and a *worthy*
budget.

A well-planned budget is an invaluable tool in raising the level of
giving. The budget will outline the funding for a unified budget and
will enable the congregation to see each part of the ministry in
proportionate relationship to the other parts.

A budget should not be merely a revision of the budget of the
previous year. As many people and groups as possible should participate in the various stages of budget building. The important question
to ask throughout every stage is, "What should we be doing?" rather
than "What's the inflation rate?" or "What did we do last year?"

There are three concepts to be kept in mind during the budget
process. First, a budget is the projection of need. As indicated above,
each department of the ministry seeks to determine what it should be
doing within the year ahead. Second, the budget is the expectation
of a response. Careful consideration needs to be given to the anticipated level of response to the program of the church based on good
stewardship practices on the part of the people. Third, a budget is
not a limitation of potential. The budget becomes the authorized

spending guide, but this does not mean that having achieved a budget figure indicated, the church has reached its full potential to give.

• Give missions high priority. Each church should give careful thought to its role in the worldwide missions ministry. One of the common concerns in teaching stewardship, especially to new believers, is the feeling that "we cannot give to others when we have so many needs of our own." As the church helps individuals mature, they discover the great potential in God's provision for them as they are faithful in their financial stewardship. In this sense the church needs to model a similar understanding of God's provision by being willing to give away from its own local program as the demonstration of its belief that God will, indeed, provide.

• Know the performance potential. Careful study should be given to the participation and performance of giving units and should help to dispel the common myth that "our people are already doing all that they can do." It would be well to determine the community per capita—per household income and establish the potential if each unit were to tithe its income to the local church.

Where the financial program of a church is weak, the chances are that other areas of the church's life are also. The congregation which is "poor" when it has within itself resources to be otherwise, is in a real sense failing to measure up to the demands made upon it by its Lord and Savior Jesus Christ![2]

• Use the Christian education department. An annual emphasis on stewardship in a sermon may be a giant step for some, but in the long run it is not going to be effective, especially if the church is growing. A more strategic response is needed. The Christian education department in most churches is ideally suited for this effort.

In addition to periodic sermons prepared by the pastor, and occasional testimonies from people wrestling with giving, regular teaching can be provided through Christian education. Videotape series, special classes, and small groups are ideal to communicate stewardship truths in ways people can readily grasp at their pace and convenience.

Parents can be shown how to teach young children and teenagers principles of stewardship. People can be taught how to build a balanced family budget, how to save money, how to plan for retirement, how to give away their estate at their death, how to follow biblical guidelines yet provide for a family, and how to respond in a culture that views materialism as its god.

Numerous videotapes and seminar resources are available through the Christian education department to enhance the overall understanding and practice of the congregation in matters of stewardship.

Everyone involved in the work of the Gospel has a vital stake in ensuring strong local churches. In a publication outlining various Christian service opportunities, the service agency Intercristo has stated:

The New Testament is full of the importance of the local church in the life of the believer—the growth of the individual in the local fellowship, his selection for ministry, his dedication to the work, and a continuing support of the individual in his work by the body of believers. The local church is at the center of God's plan to redeem the world. And it should be at the center of all our plans.

• Present stewardship from the pulpit. Paul speaks to ministers as "servants of Christ . . . entrusted with the secret things of God." One of these divine secrets committed to God's servants is stewardship truth. To be a minister of Jesus Christ, a local pastor must proclaim what the Bible teaches on stewardship for "it is required that those who have been given a trust must prove faithful" (1 Corinthians 4:1-2).

It has been well stated that "a call to preach is a call to prepare to preach." He who feels the burden to preach on stewardship should also feel the burden of preparing himself adequately. The minister's preparation should embrace a thorough acquaintance with the Bible's treatment of stewardship and the kindred subjects of tithing and giving. It should also include acquaintance with books on the subject.

In presenting stewardship truths from the pulpit, pastors need to keep the following in mind:

• Deal with people where they are. Earlier in this chapter we discussed the role of culture as an obstacle in helping people be good stewards of their funds. Before preaching a sermon on stewardship,

103

take time to review the giving patterns of your people. The results may surprise you. Preach to where people are—the struggles in which they find themselves. Don't assume people have a biblical understanding of how to make money, use money, and save money. Remember that money is a major force in this culture, influencing every aspect of life. Because of that, people need help, practical handles, and good biblical exegesis on what Scripture has to say about money.

• Call people to action. Decisions about how to disperse money differently, or to begin regular tithing are easily put off in most North American households. The effective sermon will challenge people to take action and provide a way for them to do so. In matters of stewardship it is not simply enough to "let people decide on their own." By its very nature, the issue of stewardship needs a tremendous amount of biblical support and rationale, followed up by practical means of expression. If people aren't provided with the latter, the former is an exercise in futility.

• Make use of positive role models. Nothing can be more relevant and meaningful to a person struggling with stewardship questions than to hear how a fellow traveler has wrestled with the same issues and come to a conclusion. On a regular basis, make use of live testimonies from people in the congregation on how they manage their money and how God fits into that process, on how they make their decisions about purchases and about funding missions, and what their position is on sacrificial giving. Such living testimonies give credence to sermons and show real-life application of biblical truths.

• Challenge your people. There is no substitute for faithful giving by the leadership of a church; from *that platform of credibility*, they can then challenge others to do the same. We are not talking about flaunting works before men, but about the authority which comes when leadership is doing what it asks its people to do. When this is in place, leadership can then enlist church attenders. This can be done through a stewardship program in which every member's home is visited by trained leaders who explain the ministry of the church both at home and abroad. Opportunity is then given to make financial commitment to the Lord's work through the church.

Evangelical churches have been hesitant to conduct an effort of this sort in the past. It has been equated with the problem of "pledging" or "fund-raising" and thought not to be a spiritual exercise. In recent years the "faith promise" has come into vogue among evangelical churches, as a means for increasing missions giving.

Because churches that have used the program have had an increase in giving, it has been assumed that it is the object of the program—missions—that is the reason. But churches that have not had a systematic program of education and commitment will always benefit when such a program is initiated. If the phrase "faith promise" seems to be more acceptable with evangelical churches, then let this type of concerted effort be used for the total church program.

IN CONCLUSION

To fully understand the role of stewardship at the local church level, we need to accept the local church as having a primary position in the plan of God. If we truly believe this, stewardship will not be regarded as something we add to the church as an optional program or appendage but rather as the authentic and expected response of people to God's plan. Some of what we call "stewardship" can be held out and examined, but most of it flows through the everyday activity of the church and is an integral part of its life, growth, and ministry.

As the church provides effective training and practice in the area of stewardship, the whole kingdom enterprise is benefited. The suggestions in this chapter call for diligent effort and consistent application, but the end result is well worth the time and attention given.

EDWARD J. HALES is executive director of the Christian Stewardship Council. Prior to this he was pastor of the First Baptist Church of Portland, Maine. He received his training at the Moody Bible Institute, Gordon College, and Wheaton College.

Pastor Hales has served many years in the field of stewardship, including six years as the Director of Field Services for the National Association of Evangelicals (NAE), and has written and produced a number of stewardship materials. He coauthored with J. Alan Youngren Your Money/Their Ministry (Eerdmans). He speaks on stewardship, church administration, and missions in conferences, seminars, and denominational meetings throughout the United States.

(9)
GUIDELINES FOR ORGANIZATIONS TO DEVELOP A CHRISTIAN PHILOSOPHY OF FUND-RAISING

JOHN F. WALVOORD

Christian leaders discover early in their careers that their organizations prosper largely in proportion to financial support. But they also discover that many feel any emphasis on money is a concession to materialism. The Scriptures are often cited that condemn the love of money as counterproductive to spiritual values, such as when Paul states that, "The love of money is a root of all kinds of evil" and that a "man of God" should "flee from all this and pursue righteousness, godliness, faith, love, endurance and gentleness" (1 Timothy 6:10-11); or Christ's statement, "You cannot serve both God and money" (Matthew 6:24).

Despite these references, Scripture provides limited direction about fund-raising. Abraham did pay to Melchizedek a tithe of all his possessions, though there is no record why he did so. Also, under the Law, Jews were required to bring various tithes and offerings to the priest. It is estimated that in all they gave more than 20 percent of their income.

In the New Testament, Christ and His disciples apparently financed their operation by gifts from interested friends. There is no record that Christ ever promoted fund-raising as such. Obviously in biblical times there were no formal schools, missionary societies, or other organizations such as we have today. Churches in the New Testament supported their own work. There were exceptions to be sure. Paul commended the Philippian church for helping in his financial support (Philippians 4:10-19), but apparently Paul did not require that they send him gifts. Moreover, the Philippian church was the only church that supported him (v. 15).

If there is no real parallel in the early church to the situations that exist today, how can Christian organizations determine the parameters of proper solicitation of funds for their support? The road of investigation soon points to the matter of balancing faith and works as far as securing funds is concerned.

DETERMINE THE BALANCE OF FAITH AND WORKS

The theology involved in faith and works for a Christian or a Christian organization is obviously an integral part of any system of faith. Christian salvation is related entirely to faith in Jesus Christ, in contrast to the work of keeping the Law (Romans 3:21-26). On the other hand, faith alone without works is declared by James to be dead (James 2:15-17). By this it is clear that real faith will produce works even though works are not a condition of salvation. Works are rather the fruit of the work of the Spirit in the heart of the believer and as such constitute an evidence of eternal life.

The balance of faith and works is an essential part of every practical approach to life. Obviously some are trying to accomplish by works what only God can do. On the other hand, there is also a tendency to trust God for things that God has committed us to do.

Prayer should have a supreme place in the life of a Christian. In our prayers we can take our needs to God and expect Him to work on our behalf. Prayer, however, is not a basis for excusing ourselves from doing what God has enabled us to do.

The conflict between prayer and human effort was one of the problems I faced when I first became responsible for fund-raising at Dallas Seminary in 1945. The theory was that if we were worthy and were faithful in prayer, no fund-raising activity would be necessary. However, the seminary was badly in debt and had overdue salaries which amounted to more than two years of its budget. Prayer had been faithful and the school was worthy of support, but somehow the money had not come in.

In attempting to find the causal factor in this, I soon determined the problem was that we had not communicated what we were doing; we had not shared our needs with our constituency. After sending out a letter approximately every six weeks for several months, the flow of income for the first time in the history of the organization began to equal its budget. While only God could move a donor to give, it was our obligation and our duty to place in the donor's hands the information needed to make an intelligent choice about whether to support the institution. From that point more than 40 years ago, I had the joy of seeing the seminary properly funded and its annual budget go from $50,000 to $11,000,000.

Of course it was necessary for us to pray. I do not believe any work of God or any individual life prospers without prayer, but on the other hand, writing a letter, keeping people informed, was something we could do. We should not expect God to disseminate information that we can give out through our own effort.

Publicity sent out should recognize the important place of prayer and challenge individuals and churches to remember a work and its prayer needs, whether they are material or spiritual. Though prayer in itself is not sufficient to accomplish God's work, it is an indispensable element without which a Christian work cannot prosper. Accordingly, information about a Christian organization should not be directed simply to fund-raising but also to creating prayer support and interest in the organization's ministry.

In my early struggles to arrive at a philosophy of fund-raising, I gradually came to see that there are three great essentials in supporting a Christian cause. First, it must be worth supporting financially. Second, it must be worth supporting in prayer. Third, the organization must communicate effectively with its constituency, informing them about what the organization is accomplishing. On the one hand, we should ask God to do what only He can do, that is, guide donors and enable them to give and to pray. On the other hand, we should give information and be a part of the communicating process so that people would not have to give blindly to work about which they know nothing. Simply put, policies concerning fund-raising must be in line with the Word of God.

Essential to every system of theology is the fact that God blesses communication. This is how the Gospel is brought to the world. Individuals must bring the truth and challenge people to believe. When this is carried on, supported by prayer, God will bless it and cause people to come to Christ.

The inadequacy of prayer by itself can be seen in relating this to the extension of the Gospel. If prayer were all that is needed, sending out missionaries would not be necessary. Instead, prayer groups could be organized at home and somehow the heathen would come to Christ. Historically, however, this has never worked. People have never found a Christian community that did not have contact in one way or another with the Christian Gospel. Someone must communicate to them their need of the salvation that God has provided. God's method is to preach the Gospel and to give out information. Likewise, in support of a Christian organization, information must be disseminated, and people must be alerted to what is being accomplished and what their share in this work might be. God blesses this approach, as demonstrated in many organizations.

AFFIRM YOUR RIGHT TO SOLICIT FUNDS

In approaching a philosophy of fund-raising, not only does the Bible support effective communication, but it is also clear that in most situations it is wrong not to give out information concerning the work. In the case of Paul addressing the Corinthian church about the need of saints in Jerusalem, the apostle wrote in 1 Corinthians 16:1-3 that they should take collections at Corinth for the Lord's people, collecting it on the first day of the week and saving it up so that there would be no collections after Paul arrived. Paul stated that he would send the gifts to Jerusalem with letters of introduction for the men whom the Corinthian church approved and, if necessary, Paul would go with them.

If solicitation of funds is biblically approved and even required for certain situations, how can an institution be guided as to how such activity should be carried out? In attempting to answer this question, we should give careful thought concerning the method and wording of such solicitation.

Obviously some Christian organizations go far beyond the biblical pattern. A familiar approach is to have frequent crises which reveal that they desperately need support. Not only is such a practice questionable but it also does not produce support, as people get tired of going through one crisis after another. Christian organizations do have genuine crises such as the end of a fiscal year, or some other point in time where an accounting is required, but crises should not be contrived. Not only should communications which are sent out in the mail be carefully worded, but the searching questions should be.

"Is the communication the truth? Will a reader get an accurate understanding of the need for support in prayer and funds?" The appeal may be made as attractive as it is possible, and should always be in good taste and face the reality that not everyone who receives the communication will be in a position to help.

The Bible definitely teaches that gifts should be directed by the Holy Spirit. Not every individual will be led of the Lord to give to a specific work. No Christian is able to support every worthy work and it is necessary to establish priorities in a personal stewardship program based on such facts as the individual has at his disposal.

Appeals should not attempt to create guilt on the part of the recipients if they do not support a particular work. The appeals should rather be on the basis that the organization is doing a good work which deserves the support of the Lord's people in prayer and gifts.

Often in conferences on funding, there is some concession to the idea that fund-raising has an inherently evil quality. This is not what the Bible teaches. The Bible is full of references to money, and Christ Himself emphasized stewardship of material things again and again. In the Gospel of Luke, for instance, He discussed money in chapters 2, 3, 5–7, 9–12, 16, and 18–21. There should be no apology in presenting stewardship as a duty of Christians in teaching the Scriptures themselves or in publications about an organization's financial needs.

Paul's example in 1 Corinthians 16 supports the idea that solicitation of funds under certain circumstances is justified. Both the Old and New Testaments have much to say about stewardship as a part of the Christian's duty and privilege. In 2 Corinthians 8–9, Paul gives an extensive discourse on how we should give with generosity, cheerfully, and according to God's direction. Though solicitation of prayer and gifts should be done in a proper way, it is contrary to Scripture to apologize for dealing with money, for it is an integral part of any Christian organization.

BE SURE THE ORGANIZATION IS WORTHY OF FINANCIAL AND PRAYER SUPPORT

In the triad mentioned earlier, three essential questions were asked, namely, Is an organization worth supporting? Is it worthy of prayer?

and Is it communicating effectively? Obviously the question of whether a work is worthy of financial and prayer support is most important in any fund-raising philosophy. Unfortunately, some large Christian enterprises which have received substantial support have demonstrated themselves to be unworthy of that support.

Accordingly, in fund-raising there must be honesty in presenting needs and honesty in reporting what the organization is accomplishing. Obviously, an audited finanical statement should be supplied to donors. Reports of prayer support and accomplishments of the organizations should be fairly communicated.

One of the problems facing every Christian organization is whether it should go into debt. Some organizations make a point of not going in debt and paying cash for everything. The scriptural basis for avoiding debt should be carefully understood. The statement is made that we should not owe any man anything but to love one another (Romans 13:8). This has been construed by some to mean that an organization or an individual can have no debts and that a Christian organization should operate on a no-debt principle.

Christian organizations, of course, have a perfect right to do this, but in doing so they should realize that they are not following a law of Scripture. In the Greek language there are two tenses, the present tense, which we have in English, and the aorist tense which is not in English. The difference is that the present tense speaks of continued action and the aorist tense speaks of an action that is finished. For instance in Romans 13:8 if it had said, "Owe no man anything" and used the aorist tense it would mean that we should never owe anybody anything under any circumstances. Actually the verb is in the present tense which means, "Do not keep on owing." The *New International Version* expresses it, "Let no debt remain outstanding." In other words we should not incur debts we cannot pay. The very fact that the command is in the present tense indicates it is proper under certain circumstances to go into debt.

The debt problem faces organizations much the same as it faces individuals. It is poor judgment for an individual or an organization to spend more in its current expenses than it is receiving. But to pay cash for a building or, in the case of an individual, to purchase a home, is very difficult. If there is a debt incurred which can be retired on a reasonable schedule, it would be in keeping with what is commanded in Romans 13:8.

DEVELOP A DEFINED CONSTITUENCY AND EFFECTIVE COMMUNICATION PLAN

In a local church a pastor can communicate directly the financial situation of the church. The congregation can observe what is done with their funds. Even then, it is advisable to issue a monthly statement indicating what their financial situation is. No expensive promotion through the mail is necessary.

For an institution which is national or international in its scope, it is obvious that friends and donors cannot see from week to week what is being accomplished. Under these circumstances it is necessary to communicate by mail. One of the effective means is to issue letters at reasonable time intervals which bring the individual up to date on what is occurring and at the same time report the financial situation. This has proved in practice to be an effective way in securing support.

In addition to letter-writing, news bulletins can give more general information about what is happening in the organization in the discharge of its duties.

If an organization has a denominational constituency, its support should come from those who are part of that group. If the organization is interdenominational, however, it has to create its own constituency. This should be much larger than those who support the work financially. A way to accomplish this is through other effective means of communication which may include spiritual ministry to them not directly related to fund-raising. Some organizations have a radio or television program accomplishing this. A magazine can be created as an effective means of providing spiritual nourishment to the constituency. For instance, Dallas Seminary publishes *Kindred Spirit*, a quarterly magazine containing inspirational articles. Only about 15 percent of those on the mailing list actually support the seminary financially. But the larger constituency is essential to prayer support and the goodwill of individuals who know about the seminary. In a similar way other organizations today frequently have an effective magazine printed in attractive style which will do its work in not only acquainting people with the work of the organization but even more important will minister to them spiritually.

Some organizations secure mailing lists of various kinds and appeal immediately to them as donors. Our experience at Dallas Seminary has been that this is not an effective program. Rather, a ministry-centered publication should be sent for a period of time. This may include information about the organization, its history, goals, and accomplishments. Only after a period of ministering to them do we present them with an opportunity to make a donation.

Using a procurred mailing list to solicit funds often receives only a 1 percent response. An approach where they are given information before they are expected to either pray or give may result in a greater response. In approaching the whole matter of promotion of an institution, fund-raising should be only one aspect of the communication plan. There should be a genuine interest in ministering to those who minister to the organization either by prayer or gifts.

REALIZE ALL DONORS DO NOT HAVE TO BE TREATED ALIKE

One of the cliches often heard in fund-raising discussions is the idea that all donors must be treated alike. This, however, is not practical nor necessarily biblical. It is impossible, for instance, personally to write everyone on the mailing list of a large organization and use first-class mail. If the list is large the cost becomes prohibitive. On the other hand, if mail is second or third class, often people of means will never see the communication. In many offices only first-class mail is passed on to the executive or official. Accordingly, there must be consideration of what is practical from a standpoint of cost in giving out information. In some cases, it is desirable to use a first-class letter or even a personal call. The goal of such contact should always be to inform and challenge the person, not necessarily to press for a contribution. Regardless of their strata in giving potential, donors should not be confronted with the concept that if they do not make a contribution they are somehow out of the will of God. A better approach is to challenge them with what is being done, asking if it is possible for them to participate.

STEWARDSHIP OF LIFE, MONEY, AND FUND-RAISING

The matter of stewardship in financial things is only part of the total picture presented in the Bible. Actually, Christians are required to practice stewardship of life as well as of money. This concept of stewardship should be applied to organizations as well.

113

The Bible obviously teaches that those who have received the gift of salvation have been bought by the sacrifice of Christ and owe their life to God. Accordingly, the very first step must be to recognize stewardship of life. Money is only one aspect of stewardship. The ultimate question is whether one is fulfilling a stewardship in life. First Corinthians 6:20 states that we are bought with a price. Therefore, we owe God everything.

In addition to stewardship of life there is stewardship of money. According to Hebrews 13:16, the sacrifices mentioned include sharing with others. Hebrews 13:15-16 states, "Through Jesus, therefore, let us continually offer to God a sacrifice of praise—the fruit of lips that confess His name. And do not forget to do good and to share with others, for with such sacrifices God is pleased." Though our first step in stewardship should be to present our bodies to the Lord as living sacrifices (Romans 12:1-2), God is also interested in our praising Him, doing good, and sharing with others. This involves a stewardship of money. It is stated that God is well pleased with such sacrifices, and the term is exactly the same as when God said Christ was well pleasing to Him.

One of the basic problems in the Lord's work today is that there are so few who really adopt a biblical basis for stewardship. Many people give emotionally and respond to an appeal that happens to touch their hearts. There are few Christians, however, who give systematically and from a biblical standpoint.

In keeping with the Old Testament, a good place to start is a tithe, though the New Testament does not mention this. In fact, the New Testament has a much higher standard. According to 2 Corinthians 8 and 9, Christians should give in keeping with how God has blessed them. If in the Old Testament Israel was required to give more than 20 percent of their income, how much more should Christians strive to give in light of their abundant blessings. It should be very obvious that the Bible offers a program of stewardship that requires sacrifice.

Just as the individual is charged with a stewardship of life and of money in his personal life. and commitment, so a Christian fundraiser should be doing his work as a servant of God who is seeking to maintain, support, and further a work which God is using to His glory. Those who are in charge of fund-raising should come back to basic principles, first facing the fact that the Bible supports solicitation of funds for worthy causes. The method of such solicitation must be carefully scrutinized. God honors proper communication whether it is the preaching of the Gospel or whether it is informing people about a Christian organization. People should be challenged to support their local churches as well as missionary work around the world. They should be challenged to alleviate famine especially in relationship to the Christian church. Christian organizations sometimes need to build hospitals as a means of getting the Gospel to a needy people. Schools are necessary to prepare leaders as well as lay people.

In fulfilling the stewardship of fund-raising, there should be clear-sighted understanding of principles that govern it. Currently, there is a problem in some missionary organizations which require candidates for the mission field to raise their own funds by solicitation. Once the missionary is on the field, however, sometimes the stand is taken that the mission is not responsible for communicating special needs on the field such as famine or a need for a church building or a hospital. If a missionary goes to the field on the basis of a solicitation, it should be a matter of concern to a mission to disseminate information concerning specific financial needs on the field.

Accordingly, in our modern world the faith principle should be reexamined and faced with scriptural truth that information is sometimes necessary to encourage the people of God to do what they should do. Some mission boards are discovering that they can greatly extend their work by having an effective means of communication to their supporters about the needs on the field and the need for new missionaries to go to the field.

In conclusion, it may be restated that in a biblical philosophy of stewardship there is stewardship of life, stewardship of money, and stewardship of fund-raising. These are God-given responsibilities. Those of us who are related to Christian organizations should respond in keeping with what is right, asking God to give us integrity and help in our work. Those engaged in fund-raising for Christian work are sometimes unsung heroes. Their ministry may be absolutely essential to the life and well-being of the organization in its outreach for God. On the one hand, one must depend on prayer as the needs of the present and the future are faced. On the other hand, clear insight into what God expects us to do is demanded as we seek to serve the Lord.

115

John F. Walvoord

JOHN F. WALVOORD, chancellor of Dallas Theological Seminary in Dallas, Texas, is recognized as one of the leading conservative evangelical theologians in America. In the past he has been a pastor, a professor of systematic theology, and a seminary president, and currently has an extensive ministry in Bible conferences. Dr. Walvoord is a specialist in the field of biblical eschatology. He is the author of a number of books and contributor to numerous published symposiums, reference works, and Christian magazines. From 1952-85 he served as the editor of Bibliotheca Sacra and continues as a regular contributor.

Dr. Walvoord has received degrees from Wheaton College (B.A. and D.D.), Texas Christian University (A.M.), Dallas Theological Seminary (Th.B., Th.M., and Th.D.), and Liberty Baptist Seminary (Litt.D.).

(10)
HOW MUCH
IS ENOUGH?

EUGENE B. HABECKER

Is it possible in our growth-oriented, success-rewarded society to have too much? This is a critical issue that Christians and their institutions must address. Colleges confront it when they consider the number of buildings, the size of endowments, and the enrollment of students; churches face it in regard to the size of the staff, the number of members, and the facility and programs; adults are concerned about the size of their homes, the amount of their savings and life insurance, and their type of lifestyle; businesses deal with the size of their plants, the quantity of products produced, and the cost of services rendered. Eventually some decision has to be made on this issue at a variety of levels: Just how much *is* enough?

Even as Christians, much of our desire for visible growth is the result of a secular mind-set. Whether we like it or not, Charles Darwin has greatly influenced Christian thinking in this regard. Jeremy Rifkin in his book, *Algeny,* reviews the many ways social Darwinism has become an influence. Rifkin argues persuasively that Charles Darwin, doing nothing more than reflecting the social and economic structure of nineteenth-century England, proceeded to rephrase that social structure in the form of a scientific-sounding theory explaining man's relationship to nature. As Rifkin notes,

Darwin dressed up nature with an English personality, ascribed to nature English motivations and drives, and even provided nature with an English marketplace and the English form of government. Like others who preceded him in history, Darwin borrowed from the popular culture the appropriate metaphors and then transposed them to nature, projecting a new cosmology that was remarkably similar in detail to the day-to-day life he was accustomed to.[1]

The basic tenet of "Darwin's theory of the origin and development of species centered on the survival of the fittest."[2] Expressed as a "natural" principle, "in the struggle for survival, nature ensures that the strong will triumph and the weak will perish."[3] Translated into internecine competition between Christian organizations, many work overtime to develop organizational strength so that they will be the most fit of the survivors. John White puts the issue quite succinctly:

Expansion is unthinkingly accepted among Western Christians as something good and desirable in itself. And by expansion I do not mean the spread of the Gospel, but the growth of particular institutions. Expanding organizations come into conflict over money, territory, and workers. At times mature thinking prevails, and there is cooperation and collaboration. But equally often, conflict results in the kind of competitiveness I have already described, which is not the less fierce for being described in pious cliches as "a matter for prayer."

So the operation gets bigger. If smaller groups get crowded out, maybe that proves that God has lost interest in them. They should have had more "faith." Just as in laissez faire capitalism so in the Christianizing industry, the law of the survival of the fittest must be the law of God Himself.

As new organizations come into being, the finances of older groups are threatened. It may be that a denominational missionary society finds funds are flowing to an upstart interdenominational society. Or again, a well-established interdenominational society discovers that its constituency is now more interested in newer groups.

Obviously some Christian groups feel the pinch more than others. Some denominational missions have large reserves of capital. Wherever the pinch is felt most keenly, there the battle rages most fiercely. And a battle it is. Behind the firm handshakes and ecclesiastical jocularity, a struggle for economic survival often rages, nonetheless deadly for being covert.[4]

The modern thinking about colleges, for example, suggests that not all will survive, the obvious inference being that the weak will perish. Many denominational church groups regularly assess their strong and weak churches and determine what should be done to keep strong churches strong and to help the weak. Not many denominational leaders would express sadness at the loss of another denomination, just as not many pastors would lament the fact that more people come to "my" church and fewer to "yours." There is not a shared commitment on the part of Christian organizations to see that each survives and thrives. Rather, the commitment is to see "my" entity grow, at "your" expense if necessary, and to become as large as possible. If "yours" does not survive, maybe it did not deserve to continue.

Many church leaders use as their motivation for growth and expansion that of the salvation of new converts. But as many church groups have learned, it does not follow that "new conversions" will always translate into new members. Church growth and efforts at evangelism are not necessarily directly related.

Another central feature of Darwin's theory of evolution was the ongoing improvement inherent in the process. This concurred with the "Victorian propensity to believe in progress."[5] As Rifkin observes, however, the idea of " 'no limit' to the process of improvement was not held only by Darwin." He quotes French aristocrat Marquis de Condorcet, "No bounds have been fixed to the improvement of human faculties. . . . the perfectability of man is absolutely indefinite."[6] As Darwin saw it, survival of the fittest was the key point to this ongoing improvement or growth: "[There is] . . . one general law, leading to the advancement of all organic beings, namely, multiply, vary, let the strongest live and the weakest die."[7] Darwin observed that "too many organisms" were "competing for too few niches in nature." He went on to observe that "there are only two ways to promote an organism's survival; either compete for the existing . . . niches or find new ones that have yet to be filled."[8]

One can readily notice how organizations reflect these Darwinian principles. In fact, one could almost substitute the word "organization" for Darwin's word "organism" and the practical realities would be the same. His suggested way for survival would closely parallel the classic advice in marketing—find a need and fill it. Competition abounds, and to win, "more" is needed.

My involvement with Christian organizations suggests that social Darwinism is alive and well. In many organizational operations, the pursuit of "more," whether church members or donors, is a primary mission. Organizations throw great resources into the fray, including those great "spiritual" variables such as facilities, tradition, and reputation. Why? Why do Christian organizations appear to follow the best principles of Darwinism in their efforts to grow or expand? Is survival what life is all about? Can this method be condoned by Scripture, or isn't that even a relevant inquiry?

The irony of this "survival of the fittest" competition is that in terms of their religion, not many Christian colleges or other Christian organizations would identify themselves as supporters of Charles Darwin. But, in their operational priorities, Darwin has become one of their best-followed prophets.

Fortunately, Scripture has something to say about this. Biblical thinking proceeds along two distinct lines. In terms of the intangibles of the kingdom, enough is never enough. In terms of tangibles, be on your guard—enough might be too much.

ENOUGH IS NEVER ENOUGH

When I use the term *intangibles,* I have in mind concepts such as spiritual growth and fruit of the Spirit. In these matters, Scripture seems to tell us that enough is never enough. "But grow in the grace and knowledge of our Lord and Saviour Jesus Christ. To Him be glory both now and forever! Amen" (2 Peter 3:18). Luke writes that "Jesus grew in wisdom and stature, and in favor with God and men" (Luke 2:52).

In his letter to the Philippians, Paul must have either anticipated or been confronted with the issue, "How much is enough?" Apparently, some were feeling comfortable with their spirituality and were content to rest at that spiritual level.

Not that I have already obtained all this, or have already been made perfect, but I press on to take hold of that for which

Christ Jesus took hold of me. Brothers, I do not consider myself yet to have taken hold of it. But one thing I do: Forgetting what is behind and straining toward what is ahead, I press on toward the goal to win the prize for which God has called me heavenward in Christ Jesus.

All of us who are mature should take such a view of things. And if on some point you think differently, that too God will make clear to you. Only let us live up to what we have already attained (Philippians 3:12-16).

Paul appears to suggest that we do not have the option to look back at our spiritual curriculum vita and say that enough is enough. Indeed, we are to forget all that and continue to strive "toward what is ahead" . . . in order "to win the prize" for which God has called us. To press home his point, he concludes by saying that those who are mature in the faith will press forward as he does. In other passages Paul goes to considerable length about things Christians ought to be constantly striving for. These passages suggest, then, that in terms of spiritual goals and priorities, enough is never enough, and our pursuit of these goals ought always to be a high priority.

Perhaps this issue is the easiest of the two. But what about tangibles such as money and material possessions? It appears that Scripture suggests limits should be placed on the number of tangibles we possess.

ENOUGH IS ENOUGH

Scripture does not prescribe precise limits to accumulation beyond a certain number of dollars, members, or buildings. A variety of principles, however, give guidance on the matter.

• There are repeated references that suggest that God wants people, and presumably organizations, to accumulate or to deaccumulate only at His command, so that hope and trust will always be in Him. Joshua 11 tells of a huge army "as numerous as the sand on the seashore" being assembled to fend off the vastly outnumbered yet invading Israelites. After telling the people that He would give them victory, God told them to make sure to "hamstring [the enemy's] horses and burn their chariots" (v. 6). Why? Would not the collection of these marvelous instruments of war have done much to aid them in their next encounter? It appears that God wanted the people unequivocably to have their dependence and hope on Him alone. He knew that the Israelites, like ourselves, would depend on tangibles for victories and not on Him, and so this instruction. As John Yoder has observed, "If . . . we forsake our goods to follow Him, we are proclaiming our trust in a Father who knows our needs."[9]

In Joshua 6 through 8, the same principle is expressed differently. Chapter 6, for example, provides the story of the conquest of Jericho with the instruction to "keep away from the devoted things." Achan failed to obey this command, and he and his family paid with their lives. In chapter 8, after the conquest of Ai, and unlike God's previous command, the Lord reversed His instructions to the people, "You may carry off their plunder and livestock for yourselves" (v. 2). The point was clear, deaccumulation or accumulation was to take place only at His command.

At least three times in the Book of Deuteronomy the people were cautioned about the problems associated with accumulation:

> When the Lord your God brings you into the land He swore to your fathers, to Abraham, Isaac and Jacob, to give you—a land with large, flourishing cities you did not build, houses filled with all kinds of good things you did not provide, wells you did not dig, and vineyards and olive groves you did not plant—then when you eat and are satisfied, be careful that you do not forget the Lord, who brought you out of Egypt, out of the land of slavery (Deuteronomy 6:10-12).

> When you have eaten and are satisfied, praise the Lord your God for the good land He has given you. Be careful that you do not forget the Lord your God, failing to observe His commands, His laws and His decrees that I am giving you this day. Otherwise, when you eat and are satisfied, when you build fine houses and settle down, and when your herds and flocks grow large and your silver and gold increase and all you have is multiplied, then your heart will become proud and you will forget the Lord your God, who brought you out of Egypt, out of the land of slavery (Deuteronomy 8:10-14).

There are numerous other examples in Scripture pointing out that excessive accumulation leads to movement away from trust in God. Therefore, accumulation of things ought to take place only with a green light from the Lord. Accumulation ought not always be assumed to be right or necessary. Trust in God and obedience to Him—not accumulation—needs to be our highest priority. This leads to a second obvious observation.

● There can come a point in the accumulation of things when we trust in what we possess and forget about God. In Deuteronomy 31, the prediction was made that a key reason for the people turning away from God would be their thriving in the land of milk and honey.

> When I have brought them into the land flowing with milk and honey, the land I promised on oath to their forefathers, and when they eat their fill and thrive, they will turn to other gods and worship them, rejecting me and breaking my covenant. And when many disasters and difficulties come upon them, this song will testify against them, because it will not be forgotten by their descendants. I know what they are disposed to do, even before I bring them into the land I promised them on oath (Deuteronomy 31:20-21).

Hosea 13:6 underlines this concept, "When I fed them, they were satisfied; when they were satisfied, they became proud; then they forgot me." A point comes when accumulation of things and the experience of "success" resulting from accumulation turns people's hearts away from God.

A key question for the Christian leader in this regard is, "If my ministry's financial strength, if its endowment vanished tomorrow, would I continue to place my trust in God?" God wants that trust, regardless of our financial resources.

In many ways, one of the reasons we accumulate tangibles is to protect us from the unknown. As Cheryl Forbes observes: "Our insurance industry, our pension systems, our Social Security program are all designed to protect us—to give us power over the unknown."[10] To the leader of the Christian organization this is one of the goals of an endowment fund. This self-sufficiency, this security, however, if taken to an extreme, can serve as a substitute for God, as was noted in the Old Testament passages referenced. Jeremy Rifkin makes this interesting point: "God has always been associated with the idea of total self-containment. To be God is to be without need, to be totally self-sufficient and invulnerable."¹¹ While one might quarrel with Rifkin's theology, it is not terribly far from God's concern expressed in Deuteronomy, "When you become sufficient and content, you forget about Me."

● The contentment of the people of God is not to be based on the accumulation of things. As Christians, we should be content because God will never forsake us. We are to be content with what we have, whatever it is, and keep clear of the problems associated with the love of money. Implicit in the concept of contentment is not that we need to deaccumulate—indeed, He says be content. But rather, if we love what we have, then we need to deaccumulate. This, it seems, was the problem with the rich young ruler—he was not prepared to deaccumulate (Mark 10:17-29). He wanted his money to be between him and his love for Jesus; but Jesus said, "It doesn't work that way."

In several different passages, Paul offers a similar message, first about accumulating and contentment.

> But godliness with contentment is great gain. For we brought nothing into the world, and we can take nothing out of it. But if we have food and clothing, we will be content with that. People who want to get rich fall into temptation and a trap and into many foolish and harmful desires that plunge men into ruin and destruction. For the love of money is a root of all kinds of evil. Some people, eager for money, have wandered from the faith and pierced themselves with many griefs (1 Timothy 6:6-10).

Paul, furthermore, predicts the ruin of "some" people, who, "eager for money, have wandered from the faith." Later in that same chapter he instructs Timothy:

> Command those who are rich in this present world not to be arrogant nor to put their hope in wealth, which is so uncertain, but to put their hope in God, who richly provides us with everything for our enjoyment. Command them to do good, to be rich in good deeds, and to be generous and willing to share. In this way they will lay up treasure for themselves as a firm

foundation for the coming age, so that they may take hold of the life that is truly life (vv. 17-19).

Here the instruction is to deaccumulate so that they may "lay up treasure for themselves . . . for the coming age." One of Paul's descriptions of the godless age to come was that people would be "lovers of money" (2 Timothy 3:2). Paul continues this theme of contentment:

I am not saying this because I am in need, for I have learned to be content whatever the circumstances. I know what it is to be in need, and I know what it is to have plenty. I have learned the secret of being content in any and every situation, whether well fed or hungry, whether living in plenty or in want. I can do everything through Him who gives me strength (Philippians 4:11-13).

Here his emphasis is not necessarily on deaccumulation, but on knowing how to enjoy much or a little because money, or circumstances, is not the source of his contentment—Christ is.

● Various references in Scripture illustrate the principle that "enough is enough." In Numbers 26 the story of the census of each of the tribes of Israel was recorded. "The land is to be allotted to them as an inheritance based on the number of names. To a larger group give a larger inheritance, and to a smaller group a smaller one; each is to receive its inheritance according to the number of those listed (vv. 53-54).

Each tribe was not to get the same amount of land. Rather, the land size was based on the number of names in the tribe. This suggests limits as to the amount of inheritance each tribe would be given. It was a way of saying enough would be enough.

This point is made clear in Numbers 27:1-8. The daughters of Zelophehad appealed to Moses for land. They argued that their father died sonless; and because he had only daughters, and since land was assigned to families based on sonship, their family as part of the tribe would not be getting all they were entitled to. In Moses' appeal to God on the issue, God agreed with the women. Here, the concern seems to be that each tribe receive its full and rightful inheritance—and no more or no less.

No inheritance in Israel is to pass from tribe to tribe, for every Israelite shall keep the tribal land inherited from his forefathers. Every daughter who inherits land in any Israelite tribe must marry someone in her father's tribal clan, so that every Israelite will possess the inheritance of his fathers. No inheritance may pass from tribe to tribe, for each Israelite tribe is to keep the land it inherits (Numbers 36:7-9).

One tribe's inheritance was not to grow at the expense of another tribe. Wheeling and dealing for a larger share of another tribe's market was clearly not permitted by God.

Leviticus 23 contains instructions regarding how the people were to harvest their crops. "The Lord said to Moses, 'Speak to the Israelites and say to them: When you enter the land I am going to give you and you reap its harvest, bring to the priest a sheaf of the first grain you harvest' " (vv. 9-10).

Clearly, the people were not to get all they could from their harvest. Enough was enough. In chapter 25, we see instructions concerning the Sabbath. After hearing God's rules, the people inquired as to the logic of such rules, "You may ask, 'What will we eat in the seventh year if we do not plant or harvest our crops?' " (v. 20) Their question was to this effect: "Does following the law of God make sense? Won't we starve?" God's answer was that He was trustworthy and, no, they would not starve. Enough would be enough. God then proceeded to set forth how He would handle their concern:

I will send you such a blessing in the sixth year that the land will yield enough for three years. While you plant during the eighth year, you will eat from the old crop and will continue to eat from it until the harvest of the ninth year comes in (25:21-22).

CONSIDERATIONS
To a large extent Christian organizations of all kinds are heavily influenced in their operational aspects by social Darwinism, e.g., survival of the fittest. Many Christians place great organizational effort on the accumulation of tangibles, something which Scripture

clearly cautions us about, and place not nearly enough emphasis on the pursuit of intangibles—something the Scriptures strongly encourage us to do. If we measure God's blessings by material prosperity, then He has blessed substantially Harvard, Yale, Princeton, and Stanford. As Charles Colson asks, "Is our new property proof of our success? No, I believe that line of thinking is one of the sad delusions of the church. . . . The success of . . . ministry is to be measured not by the size or beauty of its buildings, but by the holy things which happen within them."[12]

Regarding the tendency to declare an accumulation to be the result of the blessing of God, E.M. Bounds cautions:

No amount of money, genius, or culture can move things for God.[13]

An increase of educational facilities and a great increase of money force will be the direct curse to religion if they are not sanctified by more and better praying than we are doing.[14]

The campaign for the twentieth or thirtieth century fund will not help our praying but hinder if we are not careful. Nothing but a specific effort from a praying leadership will avail.[15]

It seems we have reversed what appear to be fairly clear biblical priorities and also mislabeled them. But why?

Christian organizations tend to reward their leaders more for accumulating tangibles than for qualitative growth regarding intangibles. I know of few Christian leaders, for example, who were asked to resign positions for not spending enough time in prayer. But I know of many evangelical leaders who have lost positions because they were not good enough accumulators—whether of students, money, facilities, or church members.

Is it not possible that God might want an organization to remain small—but properly managed—and possess little in terms of facilities or financial resources? From earlier discussions we saw where God specifically instructed the Israelites not to accumulate and not to take advantage of the latest technology to advance His purposes. Was He wrong and are we right? One would think so, given the operating agenda for many Christian organizations.

Leaders of these organizations know how the game is played, and they proceed headily along the road to accumulation of things for their ministries. If a college, enrollment had better increase, the endowment grow, and buildings be put in place. It is nice to know that students are spending more time praying and living out the commands of Scripture by attending to the needs of the elderly—but that won't lead to a raise for a college president or bring him recognition elsewhere, let alone win him attention from the leadership of the "elite" Christian organizations. By setting these tangible expectations for the leader, even if by default, corporate boards implicitly approve operating principles that appear to focus on accumulation.

Many pastors realize their chances for promotion and recognition within their denomination depend on the opportunity to lead the right church. As a result, and without "praying" about it, decisions are made to avoid "serving" in a smaller church in order to optimize their chances for promotion within the denomination. All this is done with the effective use of spiritual sounding language—"God hasn't led me there" or "God has led me to the larger church." Many times our answers as to why we serve where we do amount to nothing more than self-centered, spiritualized lying. Denominational officials play the game in reverse, giving key assignments to pastors who have played the game well in smaller churches. Obviously, one of the significant ways to get the attention of denominational officials is to have rapid church growth and a major successful building program. So the organizational leadership game continues, to reward the accumulation of tangibles.

While some boards and church leaders may be at fault for having misplaced priorities in these areas, the leader—whether a college president, pastor, or other organizational official—has to accept responsibility for this state of affairs. All who follow Christ need to keep priorities and goals biblically based and centered on Christ, regardless of the career impact. Our commitment to Christ ought to mean that we will follow Him, anywhere, anytime, wherever He leads.

He may lead a pastor to the small, out-of-the-way church; He may take a missionary to the jungles of a foreign country; He may lead an educator to be a professor at a small, little-known, Christian liberal arts college. The Christian's responsibility is to obey, and God will provide what is needed. Our sufficiency, after all, does not rest in the tangible assets of an organization but in Christ.

Leaders of Christian organizations often talk about how they would not want to go to a particular Christian college or other organization "because of all the problems there." But that is the point—God is enough! He is the miracle-working God who can take an impossible situation and make it work. We, however, have to give Him the chance to work; perhaps He wants us to be a part of the solution.

APPLICATIONS

How much is enough? What kinds of goals should a leader have in this regard? The Scripture sets no absolute quantitative guideline in terms of tangibles. Alternatively, the Scripture cautions about the problems of overaccumulation, and organizations must be sensitive to these warnings. Too many Christian organizations ignore these kinds of issues, but they must be addressed. Even though Rifkin's comments are written in the context of concerns for biotechnology, they are appropriate here as well.

This does not mean that our lives should barely be lived; that the best course of action is virtual inaction so as not to use any more of the resources than absolutely necessary to merely survive. It does mean that we need to continually ask ourselves how much is enough, and be willing to discipline our appetites so that they remain within the bounds dictated by a sense of fair regard for every other living thing.[16]

As Rifkin further suggests, not only must we keep before us the question of how much is enough, but we also need to continually ask how the accumulation of tangibles will impact kingdom needs and priorities.

• Organizations ought to be generous with whatever tangibles have been accumulated. Many churches might better utilize underused facilities. Churches often hesitate to allow their buildings such uses because "it would bring in the wrong kind of people," itself an incredible irony; or, wanting to prevent property damage, they couch their institutional selfishness in the language of "stewardship for the property the Lord has entrusted to us."

A more radical suggestion, but one that does have precedent in the Scripture, is to tithe organizational income received, whether gift or endowment income. This is probably already being done by many churches, but why shouldn't Christian colleges or other Christian organizations do it also? The most prominent arguments raised in opposition to this principle is that these agencies ought not be giving away money that has been given to them; and, second, most of their budgets are too low now, and if they gave dollars away, they would be in even worse shape. Let me respond to the second argument first.

The reason Scripture commands tithing is not to improve an economic situation but in response to a command of God and the important priority He is in our lives. Individuals are expected to tithe, so why not Christian organizations? Unfortunately, many commands of Scripture seem to become less than practical operatives when applied in an organizational context. Ironically, God's dealings in the Old Testament were used with the Israelites as a corporate entity as much as with individuals.

With regard to the argument against giving away "gift" money, this was precisely the kind of situation faced by the Levites. Because the Lord was their inheritance, they were not given any assignment of land in the Promised Land as were the other tribes. This was a reminder stated several times for them.

> I give to the Levites all the tithes in Israel as their inheritance in return for the work they do while serving at the Tent of Meeting. . . . I give to the Levites as their inheritance the tithes that the Israelites present as an offering to the Lord. That is why I said concerning them: "They will have no inheritance among the Israelites" (Numbers 18:21, 24).

The Levites received the tithe or gifts from the people. But the fact that they were the high priests, the fact that they lived off the offerings of others, did not excuse them from their responsibility to tithe as well. Note verses 25, 26, and 28:

> The Lord said to Moses, "Speak to the Levites and say to them: 'When you receive from the Israelites the tithe I give you as your inheritance, you must present a tenth of that tithe as the Lord's offering. . . . In this way you also will present an offering to the Lord from all the tithes you receive from the Israelites.

From these tithes you must give the Lord's portion to Aaron the priest.' "

What would be the impact on the kingdom if the 10 largest Christian organizations, in terms of endowment, would redistribute 10 percent of their earnings to smaller, struggling, less wealthy, Christian organizations?

• A further recommendation to leaders is to deaccumulate. Most organizations have excess or unneeded books (from library weeding or bookstore inventory), related supplies, and unneeded and out-dated equipment that could be effectively used elsewhere in the kingdom. Some organizations might even want to consider the concept of loaning executive or faculty members to struggling organizations that would benefit from their professional expertise.

• A final recommendation is for leaders to focus on making even more significant investments, both in themselves and in the people who work for the organization in the area of spiritual growth. People need to be encouraged to seek first God's kingdom, and that has got to be expressed as the organization's most important priority. Bounds points in this same direction when he states:

The plea and purpose of the apostles were to put the church to praying. They did not ignore the grace of cheerful giving. They were not ignorant of the place which religious activity and work occupied in the spiritual life; but not one nor all of them, in apostolic estimate or urging, could at all compare in necessity and importance with prayer.[17]

This kind of distinctive must characterize our churches and our Christian organizations, and it is the function of leaders to constant-ly be modeling these priorities and encouraging others to share in them. Our organizations must become known more for these kinds of priorities, rather than for our beautiful buildings, our many members, and our balanced budgets. We have to be more than a Christian club.

God's love constrains us, as evangelical Christians, to be in the business of accumulating intangibles, not buying or building tangi-bles. Christian agencies and organizations will probably not move in these directions unless they are led by men and women of God who are always pointing their people in the direction of asking and seriously addressing the question, "How much is enough?"

Then Moses gave an order and they sent this word throughout the camp: "No man or woman is to make anything else as an offering for the sanctuary." And so the people were restrained from bringing more, because what they already had was more than enough to do all the work (Exodus 36:6-7).

EUGENE B. HABECKER, president of Huntington College, Huntington, Indiana, plays an active role in the college's fund-raising. Over the past six years, gift income to Huntington has exceeded $20 million.

Dr. Habecker is a commissioner and consultant/evaluator for the North Central Association of Colleges and Schools, and serves on a variety of boards, including the National Association of Evangelicals, and the Christian College Coalition. He is active in the Church of the United Brethren in Christ and serves as that denomination's director of education. His most recent publication is The Other Side of Leadership *(Victor Books, 1987). He holds the Ph.D. from the University of Michigan and a J.D. from Temple University.*

(11)
INTEGRATING FAITH
INTO AN ORGANIZATION'S
FUND-RAISING PRACTICES

JERRY E. WHITE

No one can avoid questions of integrity and ethics. You can make rules, but they will not produce men and women of integrity.

Having taught at the Air Force Academy for a number of years, I am familiar with their honor code: "I will not lie, cheat, nor steal, nor tolerate those who do." So simple to say, yet difficult to keep—almost impossible for someone who is not a Christian.

You might wonder why such a fine institution would have a difficult time keeping its own honor code. As I have reflected on that, I feel the problem arises from attempting to impose a Christian ethic on a non-Christian institution. The only way to impose Christian ethics on non-Christian institutions is through law, with extreme penalties imposed when that law is broken. When I was at the Air Force Academy in the '60s, breaking the honor code meant immediate dismissal. At one time 105 students were dismissed.

Even the finest Christian institutions must take great care to hold high standards of integrity. We can go through our mail and find a number of items that would possibly illustrate questionable ethics in fund-raising. Each of us must be responsible for himself before God, coming to grips with what He requires of us.

EXTERNALS REFLECT INTERNALS

The first issue we must face concerning integrating our faith into our organization's fund-raising practices is that the method of fund-raising reflects the character of the organization. This is inescapable. The integrity of those responsible for fund-raising decisions is at stake. As goes our fund-raising, so goes the public perception of our organization. What do they see of us, really? They see our public fund-raising methods. They see our publications. And they see a bit of our ministry. But it is unlikely that more than a few have actual knowledge of what we do or are close participants in our ministry.

Our fund-raising methods reflect not only the character of our organization, but also its values. They reflect who we are. Whatever methods we use ultimately come from the hearts of the leadership. Clearly, we must have money to fulfill our missions. Sometimes that need will cause us to conduct the ministry and make decisions in different ways than if we did not need to solicit funds.

What are some specific questions relating to integrity in fund-raising? Let's consider three that I feel are very important to ask your organization and yourself.

● Why are the funds raised? What is the real need? The need should agree with the purpose and vision of the organization. Even when the need is obvious, we still must examine our motives. Some of us are reluctant to make needs known and ask for money. We find this frequently with our staff. To help them, we have developed a Bible study which focuses on biblical principles of personal fund-raising. Each individual must develop his own convictions based on the Word of God.

● What fund-raising methods are used? What are some dangers? Obviously, there are dangers of deception and misrepresentation. But I think one of the worst dangers is using a method that is out of character with the organization. What are the organization's values? Unless we have clearly enunciated our values, we have no guide for our fund-raising methods. We know, of course, that the end does not justify the means. No matter how worthy the end, we still must evaluate whether the means are right and godly.

We must be men and women of integrity in the way we raise money. There can be no deals. We must not coerce people. And we certainly cannot coerce God.

● Where are the funds spent? Are they really used for the purpose for which they were raised? Are they spent wisely? We all have a responsibility for good stewardship. Also, what is our measure of results? How effective is what we do? Have you ever heard of a

Christian organization closing its doors because its leaders thought, "We aren't really being efficient or effective, and someone else can do this better?" I recently heard of two organizations that merged because their purposes were the same and they felt they could accomplish them better together. Are good budget controls in effect and will they prevent abuses? We have a serious responsibility to direct funds to proper needs and effective purposes, under careful controls.

WE NEED BIBLICAL ETHICS

All of us in Christian ministry want our ethics to be biblical. But what is a biblical system of ethics? I believe this system involves four checkpoints. The first checkpoint is the Bible. We must know and follow what the Scriptures teach. Second, we need the Holy Spirit to guide us. Third, we should receive the counsel of godly men and women. We need to talk to one another, to assess what other people are thinking, to get counsel. It is comparatively easy to sit in our offices with our own organizational committees or executive teams and wrestle with the issues. But we need the counsel of godly men and women whom we respect deeply in the Lord. We must guard against insular thinking. Finally, we must live with our consciences. The Apostle Paul said, "So I strive always to keep my conscience clear before God and man" (Acts 24:16).

In regard to conscience, I like the story of Mark Twain who recalled that when he was a young boy, he used to steal watermelons. He remembered lurking around the corner from a man who was selling melons from a cart. When the man wasn't looking, Twain "ran around and grabbed one and went behind the building. I cut it open, I sank in my teeth, and all of a sudden some strange feeling came over me. I went back to the watermelon cart—and got a ripe one." That is not what Paul is talking about.

Conscience can be seared. Our conscience does not automatically tell us the right things to do until it has been conditioned by the Holy Spirit and the Word of God. Even in Christian work, our consciences can fail us as we "get used" to using techniques, methods, and approaches that do not have the resonance of the Spirit and the renewal of God's Word in our hearts and consciences.

Additionally, what is lawful may not be right in the sight of God. Just because we *can* do something does not mean that we *should*.

How we conduct ourselves in our freedom affects our testimony and our integrity. We are not free, as leaders, to do anything we wish.

"Better a poor man whose walk is blameless than a fool whose lips are perverse. . . . Many a man claims to have unfailing love, but a faithful man who can find? The righteous man leads a blameless life; blessed are his children after him" (Proverbs 19:1; 20:6-7). As you live in integrity, so will your children be blessed. Our personal integrity affects our organization, and even our families.

Here are some specific issues clearly not lawful in God's sight; yet, we must deal with them as we consider ethics and integrity.

● Lying. It is possible for Christians to lie. I have noted it in myself. I have a tendency to cover myself, so I must be careful to speak the truth. Is our appeal—*and every detail in it*—the truth? Is the *packaging* the truth, or are we trying to fake out the recipient under the guise of creativity?

● Cheating. How do you define cheating? The Academy honor code says, "I will not lie, cheat, or steal." Think about that for yourself. When you misrepresent something, is that cheating? When you falsify a minor point in a document, is that cheating? When you don't tell all the truth, is that cheating?

● Stealing. You say, "Well, I don't steal from anyone." Malachi speaks about robbing God (Malachi 6:10). It is possible for us who are responsible for funds to effectively steal from those who give and to steal from God by not using the funds in the way God intends for us to use them.

● Misrepresentation. Saying one thing and doing another. Painting the picture in rosier shades than the reality. Not being quite truthful in what we're communicating.

● Sexual immorality. What does that have to do with fund-raising? Remember, the issue is not integrity only in fund-raising, but integrity in our lives. Sexual immorality is one of the pitfalls that we, as committed men and women, must guard against. All of us are vulnerable.

FALSE IMPRESSIONS

Never allow misrepresentation to creep into any appeal. You will have to guard against it with the greatest care. "We will close our doors if this gift doesn't come in. . . . Thousands will die in such-and-such a country if you do not give. . . . Without your help we could not continue our ministry." Test the truthfulness of every statement you make publicly or to an individual.

We have wrestled with the idea of how to state appeals for money. If we use an illustration or an event that happened in Asia in an appeal, will the donor think the money is going to that specific ministry rather than to The Navigators as an organization? Is it deceitful to use the money on administration? We take great care to phrase our letters so that they will not be misleading.

This touches on the issue of technology in fund-raising. In a *Christian Herald* article, Ron Wilson commented on fund-raising letters:

The government has declared mail fraud illegal. Almost anyone can incorporate a nonprofit group, get a third class mail permit and rent a list of names, including yours, and the abuses of the system by many of those incorporators include collecting funds for programs that don't exist, skimming off an inordinate amount of income for overhead, stretching the truth, not telling all, bending the facts, etc. Manipulating the fears and concerns of innocent people. . . . Christians argue endlessly over the ethics of these techniques. The debate is healthy.[1]

Defenders say they are using God-given technology for the work of the kingdom. Detractors accuse them of deceit, insincerity, and manipulation. Unsure of whom to believe, the public ends up relying on the integrity of the people managing the cause they decide to support. We are those people.

In Hebrews 13:18 we read, "Pray for us. We are sure that we have a clear conscience and desire to live honorably in every way." Misrepresentation may, in the short term, bring in some money; but in the long term, our cause will die.

ENSURE ACCOUNTABILITY

Accountability is not automatic—even among Christians. Unless you as a leader take steps to ensure it, it will not be present in sufficient degree.

A familiar passage of Scripture charges us to be trustworthy stewards. "Now it is required that those who have been given a trust must prove faithful" (1 Corinthians 4:2). In addressing the question of how an organization conducts itself honorably and with integrity, I would like to challenge each of us as individuals to conduct ourselves with integrity, honesty, and honor before God. As it goes in our own hearts, so it will go in our organizations.

Who is accountable for fund-raising and disbursements? In a sense, everyone is accountable, from the clerk who opens the mail to the CEO. But unfortunately, when everyone is accountable, often no one feels accountable. So let's be a bit more specific.

First, the CEO is *ultimately* accountable for all that goes on in that organization. Second is the CEO with his or her executive team; third, the person in the organization responsible for fund-raising, often called the development officer. Fourth, the Board of Directors is accountable. And finally, everyone *is* accountable, in the sense that if they ever see anything that might be questioned in terms of integrity, they must speak up.

Second Corinthians 8 is a passage that can be applied to fund-raisers. In verses 20 and 21, we read, "We want to avoid any criticism of the way we administer this liberal gift. For we are taking pains to do what is right, not only in the eyes of the Lord but also in the eyes of men." The purest heart before God still needs to answer to others, and something which is most honorable before people still needs to be checked with God.

There may be activities in your organization or your life that are perfectly legitimate, yet are looked on negatively because they may have the appearance of wrong or evil. So these need to be brought before God and discussed with your team, praying over the why, the how, the where, and the who, seeking God to guide you in how you live personally and organizationally.

It is virtually impossible to ensure integrity. Yet there are a few things you may be able to do. First, strive to live without deception. I believe it is possible to be totally honest before men and before God. Second, it is important to have an open book to donors. If we fear doing this, we may need to ask, "What do we have to hide?"

As for accountability, I don't think any of us, given the opportunity, would not be tempted in some way to misuse funds. Just think about when you're traveling, when you fill out an expense report, or when you're going to buy a meal. It really makes a difference which account the expenses come from, doesn't it? We think twice if we are spending our personal funds rather than the business expense account funds. We need the accountability of having to write down what we spend and the purpose.

INTEGRITY STARTS WITH THE LEADER

Methods and principles used in fund-raising reflect the character of the organization. The character of the organization is, in turn, a direct reflection of the character and integrity of its leaders. As Christian leaders, each of us should set as a personal goal to be a man or woman of integrity, to have a good conscience before God and men, and to have a clear witness to the world by our personal lives and by the way we operate our ministries.

The leader is responsible. The buck cannot be passed. Consequently, I would urge you never to delegate fund-raising to one person only. Incorporate a system of checks and balances. Remember that people, not organizations, make decisions. We can never dismiss something that does not have a clear, unmistakable mark of godly honor and integrity with the excuse, "I didn't make the decision," or "A committee did it." We must take personal responsibility for fund-raising decisions.

As leaders, we need to examine our own personal lives before God, so that we do lead our organizations by faith, not expediency.

JERRY E. WHITE, general director of The Navigators, is a former professor at the United States Air Force Academy. He holds a bachelor's degree in electrical engineering from the University of Washington, a master's degree in astronautics from the Air Force Institute of Technology, and a doctorate in astronautics from Purdue University. He first came in contact with the Navigators as a student at the University of Washington and maintained close contact throughout his 13 1/2 years of active service in the Air Force. He helped begin Navigator ministries at the Air Force Academy in 1964 and at Purdue in 1966, and was the Navigator's Pacific regional director for 10 years and Executive Director for 3 years.

Dr. White and his wife, Mary, have coauthored several books including Friends and Friendship. Jerry has also written others including Honesty, Morality, and Conscience.

(12)
THE ELECTRONIC CHURCH:
ITS ROLE IN
CHRISTIAN FUND-RAISING

DAVID W. CLARK

Over the past decade, the popular and Christian press have devoted much attention to the "electric" or "electronic church."[1] While there have been some thoughtful analyses of these growing television ministries,[2] for the most part, the popular press has been uncomprehending and stereotypical in their evaluations. This has changed little during the intense media coverage of the Bakker and Swaggart scandals. Some of the "analyses" in the Christian press have likewise taken the form of strident attacks.[3]

A number of charges have been made against the "electronic church." In almost every case, the charges are unsubstantiated by any empirical evidence. As Jeffrey K. Hadden, a well-known sociologist, noted eight years ago:

> The most amazing thing about this debate is that it has been allowed to thrive so long when, in fact, the issue is an empirical one. The research methods of the social sciences are quite capable of providing very substantial insight, if not definitive answers, to this question.[4]

With few exceptions, such as the seminal *Religion and Television* study done in 1984, most critics have tended to be long on evaluation and short on factual data.

It is important to note that what has been called the "electronic church" is, in reality, a highly diverse group of religious broadcasters representing several distinct theological traditions. Critics in the popular press tend to ignore this theological diversity. This may be because the evangelical approach to the proclamation of the Gospel is a common tie which tends to blur the important theological traditions represented. There are, for example, significant differences in the theology of Oral Roberts, Jerry Falwell, and Robert Schuller.

Likewise, there are important differences in the content of these programs. For example, even a cursory content analysis will reveal differences between the two most popular Christian talk shows, *The 700 Club* and *The New PTL Club*. Each is appealing to a different audience with a somewhat distinctive programming approach. Most critics of these programs tend to ignore these important differences in the content and style of such programs.

THE ELECTRONIC CHURCH AND THE LOCAL CHURCH: FRIENDS OR FOES?

The term *electronic church* is, in a sense, a pejorative one which implies that such ministries are intentionally recruiting members away from the local congregation. With few exceptions, this is simply not the case. The majority of these programs, in one way or another, recognize the primacy of the local church and urge their viewers to get involved in a local congregation.[5] Some of these ministries refer the names of thousands of those who telephoned seeking ministry to cooperating local churches for follow-up. Of course, not every local church is interested in or prepared to deal with such referrals who may have severe spiritual and emotional needs.

It is my view that these television ministries, like all parachurch ministries, can justify their existence only on the basis of performing ministry activities whose technical complexity and resource needs are beyond the local congregation. The demands for talent and finances of a daily or weekly television program clearly are beyond the resources of most congregations. Yet, some of the most prominent programs such as Robert Schuller's, Jerry Falwell's, and James Kennedy's are the product of one large local congregation that has attracted a national audience and developed a national support base.

But these pastors are not attempting to establish branches of their own congregation in a community; rather, they are usually seeking to support the existing local churches. National television ministries cannot take the place of the local congregation and dare not try. Their role must be that of strengthening, helping, and cooperating with the local church.

The primary criticism leveled at television ministries is that they are drawing attendance and financial support away from the local church. Martin Marty has called them an "invisible religion . . . which threatens to replace the living congregation with a far-flung clientele of devotees to this or that evangelist or entertainer."[6] Yet, I am not aware of any significant empirical research which substantiates this charge.

On the contrary, the 1984 Annenberg-Gallup study, "Religion and Television," demonstrated that "watching religious programs goes hand in hand with both attendance at and financial contributions to the local church."[7] The viewers of these programs simply do not see them as competing with their local church. TV programs and church are "complementary and mutually reinforcing activities rather than as substitutes for one another."[8]

The same study found significant high positive correlations between giving to religious television ministries and attending and supporting the local church. Since correlation is not causation, we cannot say unequivocally that one action caused the other. But this research does establish that involvement with religious television ministries is likely to be related to involvement with the local church rather than mutually exclusive, as some have charged.

Christian Broadcasting Network (CBN) research throws additional light on this relationship. In a 1983 donor study, they found that 86 percent of their donors gave to the local church, 57 percent gave to health organizations, 53 percent gave to missions, 44 percent gave to world hunger, and 25 percent gave to educational institutions.[9] In short, those giving to support The 700 Club are also very actively involved in supporting other ministries.

Another line of research conducted at CBN over the years, shows that at least some donors move from supporting CBN to supporting the local church or other ministries. A study of former donors found that unaided, 18 percent said they had redirected their support to the local church. When asked to indicate levels of agreement with possible reasons for not continuing their support, 57 percent strongly agreed that their "first commitment is to give to the local church,"

142

and 13 percent strongly agreed that other ministries deserved their support more.[10] The picture that emerges is of a donor base that is discerning and active in redirecting their support.

There is also some evidence from research that giving to TV ministries is not done at the expense of other parachurch ministries or charities. In the 1980 Gallup study, "The Christian Marketplace," religious television ranked fifth behind churches, health organizations, the United Way, and missions as the first choice of donors. When asked which organizations they had given to more than once per year, Christian radio and TV tied for seventh place."[11] The public does not appear to give television ministries a very high priority in their giving, in comparison with other ministries and charities.

FUNDING FOR TELEVISION IS ALWAYS FROM THE VIEWER
The Annenberg-Gallup study also contains important information on the frequency of appeals for funds and the amounts requested on prominent religious television programs. Compared to the television programs produced by the mainline denominations, the television ministries are making far more frequent requests and asking for larger amounts of support.

There have, undeniably, been some excesses in the number of appeals on some programs. Billy Graham has cautioned: "There is a danger when TV preachers begin to beg too frequently and too fervently. Money is a means; it must never be the message."[12] We must wonder what impression is given by some programs to the sincere viewer seeking to find God. A few seem to be almost endless appeals to stave off crises and stay on the air. No doubt, many of these appeals are based on authentic financial crises. Still, broadcasters must remind themselves of those in the audience who tune in with the simple plea, "We would see Jesus."

Ideally, no fund appeals of any kind would need to be made in a religious program. But, in reality, all television programming is ultimately funded by the viewers. Programs on the commercial networks are paid for by the advertising which, in turn, is paid for by those viewers who buy the products advertised. Public television is funded by the federal government with tax money as well as by individual and corporate donors. Similarly, religious television must be funded by the viewers who voluntarily support the programs.

THE FOUNDER SYNDROME AND RELIGIOUS TELEVISION
Religious television programs are usually the product of a very specific vision given to the founder. Often this individual has experienced a certain amount of rejection from the religious establishment for his innovative thinking. In the case of television ministry, the mainline religious establishment has yet to launch a viable national television program. This role has instead been assumed by a small group of spiritual entrepreneurs who have had the vision and ability to develop programs and build the large donor infrastructure capable of funding the high costs of television ministry.

Each of these major television ministries reflects the personality of the founder to a lesser or greater degree. This is only natural and typical of any organization in which the founder continues to exercise control. As the founder moves away from active leadership, the organization is somewhat freer to develop its own identity. Since television ministries are relatively young organizations, most continue to be led by founders and continue to reflect the idiosyncratic strengths and weaknesses of that individual.

One characteristic of these young organizations is the occasional inclusion of a founder's family members within the structure of an organization. This should not be anymore surprising than the tendency to include family members in a family-founded business. If they are competent, trustworthy, and spiritually committed to the mission of the ministry, I see no logical or biblical reason to exclude them from participation or even leadership in the organization. For most parachurch organizations, the participation of family members has proven to be minimal beyond one generation.

SOURCES OF ACCOUNTABILITY IN THE
ELECTRONIC CHURCH
Because of the idiosyncratic nature of these parachurch television ministries and the frequent lack of a more traditional form of church governance, the charge has been made that they lack accountability to their constituencies. While it is true that many lack formal accountability to an ecclesiastical hierarchy, there are, nevertheless, several sources of formal and informal accountability which affect television evangelists. Proverbs 23:7 says that as a man "thinks in his heart, so is he."

• On the *intrapersonal* level, those who would be the bearers of God's good news stand accountable before God for their ministry. Their private lives should match their media image. They must be men and women of deep personal spirituality who spend time daily before God and in the Word. Their personal lives must fulfill the scriptural requirements of spiritual leaders (1 Timothy 3:3). If this ceases to be the case, they have an ethical obligation to seek spiritual counsel from those who can discipline and help them.

• On the *interpersonal* level, those who lead television ministries must have among their coworkers and friends some who will fearlessly "speak truth in love." Ideally, these individuals should be protected from the threat of job loss. My own experience in a parachurch ministry is that, while not many individuals are accorded the interpersonal accountability role, there are always some Nathans who have earned special credibility within an organization and can have great influence on a leader. They must be prepared to insist that "the show not go on."

Another source of interpersonal influence is other leaders in similar ministries. There is more interaction and influence at this level than most people realize. Also, the role of self-regulatory groups such as Evangelical Council for Financial Accountability and the National Religious Broadcasters' Ethical and Financial Integrity Commission (EFICOM) should not be underestimated as a source of influence toward accountability.

The governing board of an organization is also a source of accountability. The role of the board is, to some degree, prescribed by the law affecting nonprofit organizations. Moreover, a board has the duty to see that the organization is in compliance with the 501(C)(3) requirements of the Internal Revenue Code. There is some recent evidence that the IRS intends to monitor this compliance more carefully.

Typically, boards give wide latitude to the founder of an organization. There is ample evidence in the *PTL* scandal that the directors failed to function as a duly consulted governing board. Had they done so, the scandal might have been avoided. Boards must be made of deeply committed Christian leaders who represent a variety of professional viewpoints, but who share the common vision of the organization.

• *Donors* to television ministries exercise a very powerful demand for accountability from these ministries. Their letters, telephone calls, and personal visits provide constant feedback. Moreover, unlike most parachurch ministries, the leaders of these ministries are seen by their donors on a daily or weekly basis. The television audience is seen today by many mass communication researchers as active, inquiring, discerning, and one which will not long abide that which it disapproves of or dislikes. Likewise, viewers who support television ministries are attracted and held by what they see. Decline in support to television ministries begins first with a decline in viewing.

The rapid feedback provided by donor response can be both a help and a detriment to a television ministry. It points to the tension these ministries feel between providing content which meets the spiritual needs of the donor base, and addressing the spiritual needs of those in the audience who will never be donors.

• The *secular media* also represent a source of accountability for the major television ministries. Unlike most parachurch ministries, these television ministries are the frequent focus of the secular media. I believe this is due, in part, to their rapid growth and high visibility, and also to the fact that the secular media understand the enormous power of television to confer status on people and ideas and to set an agenda of what issues the public will think about. Thus, they see these television ministries as competitors for an audience.

The function which the secular media have assumed is that of surveillance. They see themselves as the self-appointed societal institution charged with the responsibility of focusing on any event or person which may seem unusual or improper. The media select such events by an unwritten criterion; thus, to some extent, they are unaccountable for their own actions. It is clear from several recent surveys of the press that the gatekeepers and reporters who lead the secular media have attitudes and beliefs significantly different from those of the public they serve. This is particularly true about religious and moral beliefs. Thus, it is not surprising that their coverage of television ministries is sometimes hostile and often filled with equivocations. More important, perhaps, is the apparent lack of understanding the secular press has of the work of Christian ministries. But the secular press has an undeniably important role to fulfill in making these ministries accountable.

DAVID W. CLARK currently heads a marketing research and consulting firm, Communication Analysts, Inc. From November 1987 to June 1988 he served as the federal bankruptcy trustee for Heritage, USA which was in Chapter 11. Previously he was vice president of marketing for the Christian Broadcasting Network, after having been the network's director of research and the dean of the School of Communication at CBN University.

Dr. Clark earned the B.A. from Evangel College, the M.Div. from Northern Baptist Seminary, and the M.A. and Ph.D. from the University of Iowa. He has consulted widely with broadcasting, banking, and other organizations on strategic market planning, and has written numerous articles on communication. A former pastor and professor, he continues to preach and teach in the U.S. and abroad.

(13)
USING THE BIBLE
AS A GUIDE FOR
FUND-RAISING COSTS

HOLMES M. BRYAN, JR.

The Bible teaches primarily through principles and examples, and usually does not give us instructions on what to do moment by moment in our lives; but these principles are complete enough to show Christians how to live in a godly manner. The concern of this chapter is to learn how these biblical principles and examples can be applied to financial development and, more specifically, to methods of determining fund-raising costs.

As we study this topic, we can't expect to find Bible references so specific as to give an exact amount at which an organization is to keep its costs. As far as is known, God didn't tell Paul not to write 2 Corinthians 8 and 9 unless he could guarantee at least a four-to-one return on investment.

Knowing this limitation, we can examine some scriptural examples of fund-raising costs and, more importantly, some principles that relate to fund-raising costs, hoping to provide good guidelines for Christian organizations.

RELIEF OF THE SAINTS AT JERUSALEM

The first New Testament example of fund-raising is for the relief of the saints at Jerusalem (2 Corinthians 8–9). This is probably the most familiar passage in the Bible concerning fund-raising. But does it teach anything about costs?

The only costs immediately obvious that Paul incurred were ink, parchment, his time, and perhaps the cost of a courier. There were, however, other costs. Paul sent Titus along to Corinth with two unnamed "brethren" for the expressed purpose of collecting the gifts being prepared by the church there (2 Corinthians 8:16-24). These "field reps" would have incurred expenses including travel, lodging, and food as they traveled to Corinth, stayed there, and then traveled with the gift to Jerusalem.

The primary purpose of sending these representatives was to make sure that the gifts were prepared in advance, generous, and not grudgingly given" (2 Corinthians 9:3-5). The expenses incurred could indeed be considered fund-raising costs.

The main principle to be learned from this Scripture is that fund-raising costs are legitimate. What this passage does not tell us is whether these costs were taken from the gift being collected or from another source. Based on other verses (such as Luke 10:4-8 and Matthew 10:9-11), the costs were probably borne by individuals within the church at Corinth and by others along the way, with nothing being taken from the gift itself. Also, it is not known what the costs were in relation to the size of the gift. Perhaps there is a reason that this was not revealed, and that will be considered later in this chapter.

One additional principle relating to fund-raising costs stands out in these two chapters. Second Corinthians 8:20-21 says, "We want to avoid any criticism of the way we administer this liberal gift. For we are taking pains to do what is right, not only in the eyes of the Lord but also in the eyes of men."

It was not enough for Paul to say only that they were taking pains to do what was right in the eyes of the Lord. God is omniscient and knows our hearts. People, however, need to demand more proof of honesty. Paul handled this with the church at Corinth by sending not one but three persons to handle the collection of the gifts, taking care to give credentials concerning the character of each (2 Corinthians 8:16-23).

Similarly, there is a need for Christian organizations and individuals to go out of their way to provide proof of their integrity to their donors. Knowing that their own motives are right before the Lord is not enough. This is especially true in the area of fund-raising where it is sometimes easy to give the appearance of evil by the way fund-raising is accomplished.

How can it be ascertained that our fund-raising expenses are right in the eyes of men? Following Paul's example, it would be advisable to include more than one person in the process. Having to justify your budget to some other objective person, preferably someone who understands development, is one of the best ways to accomplish this. It is also good fiscal policy.

PAUL'S PERSONAL SUPPORT

In 1 Corinthians 9, Paul defends his right to receive support from the church at Corinth. Here, the Scripture will be examined first, and then the principles learned will be related to fund-raising costs. Paul asks sixteen rhetorical questions in those verses to prove his point.

In verses 4 through 6, Paul points to the other apostles as examples. They all eat and drink, some take their wives along on their ministry assignments, and they refrain from working at some other job to fund their ministry.

Paul uses several examples in verse 7 to show that it is customary to pay for services. Here he is positioning his ministry as a service to them. Verses 8 through 10 are Paul's interpretation of an Old Testament law that gives credence to the fact that he should receive support.

Verses 11 and 12 indicate that others are receiving *material* support from the church at Corinth because of the *spiritual* service to them. It was already a common practice for ministers like Paul to receive support. Similarly, verse 13 indicates that it was common practice for Old Testament priests to receive their support from those to whom they ministered.

Finally, in verse 14 Paul concludes his defense with his strongest argument, that "the Lord directed those who proclaim the Gospel to get their living from the Gospel."

Although this Scripture is primarily concerned with the proper funding of ministry and not the expenses of fund-raising, the principles learned therein can be applied to fund-raising costs. The argument that it is customary to pay for services rendered is probably the most obvious principle related to fund-raising. Simply stated, it is proper for those who benefit from the service of fund-raising to pay for the costs associated with raising those funds.

Additionally, these verses seem to indicate that it is customary for the provider of services or producer of a product to be paid out of the product or service itself. The vinedresser was paid out of the produce grown (v. 7); the shepherd out of the flock he tended (v. 7); the ox out of the grain he was threshing (v. 9); and the priests out of the sacrifices and contributions made by the people (v. 13). Verse 10 adds, "When the plowman plows and the thresher threshes, they go out to do so in the hopes of sharing in the harvest."

Applying this principle to fund-raising costs, it becomes obvious that the practice of taking the cost of raising the funds out of the funds themselves is appropriate. Or stated another way, the development office should raise funds in hopes of sharing in the results.

Paul's strongest argument for personal support (v. 14) not only supports this conclusion but adds a new dimension. What does Jesus Christ have to say about the funding of ministry, and what principles therein can we apply to fund-raising costs?

FUNDING THE DISCIPLES AS EVANGELISTS

First Corinthians 9:14 refers to the Lord's instructions to His disciples, as He was preparing them to go and preach to Israel that "the kingdom of heaven is at hand." Although Christ had a "support team" to fund His ministry (Luke 8:1-3), He gave some specific direction to the disciples concerning how they would fund their ministries. These directions are found in Matthew 10:9-11 and Luke 10:4-8. Since the passages are essentially the same, only the one in Matthew will be scrutinized closely.

Do not take along any gold or silver or copper in your belts; take no bag for the journey, or extra tunic, or sandals or a staff; for the worker is worth his keep. Whatever town or village you enter, search for some worthy person there and stay at his house until you leave (Matthew 10:9-11).

Jesus instructed them not to raise money from one group of people in order to have a ministry to another group. However, they were to receive support (in this case, in the form of food and shelter) from those to whom they were ministering. The principle here is that the worker is worthy to receive support from those to whom he is ministering.

A worthy worker is one who is doing the job he was sent to do, in this case, preaching. It stands to reason that by performing his job well, he will be able to more easily fund his work. In this sense, the cost of ministry is inseparable from the cost of fund-raising. Fund-raising is actually part of the cost of getting the Gospel out, not a separate overhead item.

Fund-raising, in fact, is a ministry to those from whom funds are being raised. Scripture backs this up elsewhere. Paul admonishes Timothy to "command [those who are rich] to do good, to be rich in good deeds, and to be generous and willing to share" (1 Timothy 6:18). As a ministry to the rich, Timothy was to "command" them to give.

Teaching stewardship is not only a ministry but a legitimate cost of fund-raising. In his letter to the Corinthians, Paul taught the principles of stewardship as a part of the process of raising funds for the saints in Jerusalem.

The method of fund-raising taught by Christ was followed by the apostles to finance their ministries. Paul's primary practice was the same, but he departed from this in two ways: tentmaking and receiving support from those to whom he was not currently ministering.

TENTMAKING

The only place tentmaking is mentioned as a means of supporting ministry is when Luke writes of Paul staying with Priscilla and Aquila: "because he was a tentmaker as they were, he stayed and worked with them" (Acts 18:3). Paul had just arrived in Corinth from Athens, where he had been only a short time. Prior to that he had been in Berea, a city in Macedonia, but was run out by the same Jews who had run him out of Thessalonica. It's important to note that Timothy and Silas, who had been traveling with Paul, stayed in Berea when Paul left for Athens (17:13-14).

Paul gave instructions to those who had escorted him to Athens to have Timothy and Silas come to him as soon as possible (v. 15). They finally caught up with him at Corinth (18:5). It is inferred in verse 5 that Paul ceased making tents to support himself at this time and "devoted himself exclusively to preaching."

This detail is pointed out in order to show that Paul spent only a short time in tentmaking. Just how short a time is not revealed, but it was certainly not for the entire eighteen months that Paul stayed in Corinth.

The remainder of his time in Corinth, Paul received support from the churches in Macedonia. "And when I was with you and needed something, I was not a burden to anyone, for the brothers who came from Macedonia supplied what I needed. I have kept myself from being a burden to you in any way, and will continue to do so" (2 Corinthians 11:9).

We know that the church in Macedonia supported Paul, not just Timothy and Silas, because of Paul's thank-you letter to the church at Philippi, one of the churches of Macedonia: "Moreover, as you Philippians know, in the early days of your acquaintance with the Gospel, when I set out from Macedonia, not one church shared with me in the matter of giving and receiving, except you only" (Philippians 4:15).

Paul's next stop "after departing from Macedonia" was Athens and then Corinth. Corinth was, in fact, Paul's last stop on this journey before returning to Israel (Acts 18:18-22). Therefore, the ministry being supported by the Philippian church mentioned in his letter to the Philippians was his ministry at Corinth.

Tentmaking and receiving support from a church other than the one to whom he was ministering was obviously a departure from the norm for Paul. The only other place that it is recorded that Paul departed from the norm was at Ephesus. In Acts 20:34, Paul states, "These hands of mine have supplied my own needs and the needs of my companions."

Understanding why Paul did this will bring some important principles to light that can be applied to fund-raising costs. The answer is found in 1 Corinthians 9, where Paul defends his right to receive support from the church at Corinth. In verse 15, he explains that he doesn't want their support, now or ever, because he doesn't want anyone to "deprive [him] of this boast."

His "boast" is explained in 2 Corinthians 11 where it is again coupled with the fact that he did not receive support from Corinth.

As surely as the truth of Christ is in me, nobody in the regions of Achaia will stop this boasting of mine. Why? Because I do not love you? God knows I do! And I will keep on doing what I am doing in order to cut the ground from under those who want an opportunity to be considered equal with us in the things they boast about. For such men are false apostles, deceitful workmen, masquerading as apostles of Christ (2 Corinthians 11:9-13).

By not accepting support from the church at Corinth, which would have been his normal procedure, Paul set himself apart from the false apostles who were receiving support from them. "That in preaching the Gospel I may offer it free of charge" (1 Corinthians 9:18). Paul reasoned correctly that because he was receiving no material gain by preaching the true Gospel, they would believe this Gospel over the false gospel being preached by the false apostles.

Profit-making activity, such as tentmaking, is a Scripture-sanctioned means of raising funds for ministry. However, it is not the preferred method, at least not for Paul, who ceased making tents as soon as support arrived from Macedonia.

The primary principle to be learned from all this is that the Christian organization may need to cease doing what it knows to be acceptable in God's eyes, if that is causing a brother to stumble. In fact, 1 Corinthians 9 is Paul's example of how he ceased doing what Christ sanctioned—receiving support from Corinth, because it might have caused them to believe false apostles. It immediately follows his exhortation in chapter 8 concerning the eating of meat sacrificed to idols.

There are times when a Christian organization will not be able to raise funds from those to whom it is ministering. Sometimes this will be because the process of raising funds may cause them to stumble. But, more than likely, it will be for some other reason. A common one will be that the people to whom the organization is ministering don't have the means to support the ministry, as with children, students, the poor, etc.

As these Scriptures have been examined, it seems the priority for fund-raising methods for the Christian organization would be in this order:

- Raise funds from those to whom it is ministering.
- Raise funds from other Christians.
- Use profit-making activities to raise funds.

Paul's raising of funds from the church at Corinth for the support of the saints at Jerusalem is an example of the second method.

There may be other times when the principle of not causing a brother to stumble should help in determining proper fund-raising costs. The application of this principle is broad in the kingdom.

THE FARMER

"The hardworking farmer should be the first to receive a share of the crops" (2 Timothy 2:6). This is the third of three metaphors that Paul uses in the second chapter to instruct Timothy concerning his duties as a teacher.

In this particular passage, the farmer is the teacher. The crops are the fruits of the labor of faith. Paul is telling Timothy that as a teacher he ought to be (or some translations say "must be") the first one to receive the spiritual benefits of faith in Christ. Paul indicates that Timothy should be "first" or before those he will be teaching. The principle here is that it is necessary for one who teaches spiritual things to have first experienced spiritual fruit and blessings in his own life.

Paul may also have been referring to remuneration when he said "a share of the crops." Paul has certainly said this elsewhere in his writing, such as in 1 Timothy 5:17 and 1 Corinthians 9:1-14. But here in 2 Timothy 2, because of the context of verse 2, "The things you have heard me say in the presence of many witnesses entrust to reliable men who will also be qualified to teach others," Paul is probably describing to Timothy why he needs to have a fruitful ministry before he can teach others how to instruct believers.

Although the context is spiritual, the principle certainly should apply to remuneration. It is obvious that a farmer ought to receive his share of the crops as payment for raising those crops. The principle here was best stated by Jesus Christ in Matthew 10:10: "The worker is worth his keep." The same principle should also apply to fund-raising costs. In fact, the principle is universal.

Examining the illustration of the farmer in detail should help us to understand possible applications of this principle to fund-raising costs. Here are several examples of possible situations the farmer might face. The following assumptions are made in each example:

- The farmer is raising corn.
- The farmer needs the equivalent of 100 bushels of corn per year to provide for himself and his family.

155

• The farmer needs an additional 50 bushels of corn per year as seed corn for the following year.

• The farmer is hardworking as described in 2 Timothy 2:6.

Example 1: In an average year, the farmer harvests 750 bushels of corn. At a total cost of 150 bushels (or 20 percent), this leaves 600 bushels profit and a 5:1 income to expense ratio.

Example 2: In one year, because of exceptionally good weather, the farmer harvests 1,500 bushels of corn. At a total cost of 150 bushels (or 10 percent), this leaves 1,350 bushels profit and a 10:1 income to expense ratio. That's not a bad year!

Example 3: In another year, because of drought, the farmer harvests only 200 bushels of corn. At a total cost of 150 bushels (or 75 percent), this leaves 50 bushels profit and a 1.33:1 income to expense ratio. That's not a very good year, but at least the farmer has enough to provide for his family and has seed corn for next year.

Remember that there is an assumption that the farmer is "hardworking." He is putting in the same amount of effort each year in cultivation of the corn. The variation in production is dictated primarily by external circumstances.

Assuming that the farmer is paid based on a percentage of the total production, we see that he will be overpaid in one year and underpaid in another. In reality, it may be that the average year so seldom occurs that he is usually being overpaid or underpaid.

To relate this illustration to development, simply replace the farmer with a development director, and the bushels of corn with thousands of dollars. The field being cultivated represents the donors and the landowner is like the president of a Christian nonprofit organization. Although the analogy is simplistic, the principles derived are still valid.

One obvious principle is that it is impractical to base a budget on ratios, percentages, or averages. Although these calculations should be known and watched, there are too many other variables that are more important in determining development budgets: organizational need, cause concept, external public relations, and makeup of the donor base, to name a few.

Ratios and percentages should be used to help determine norms for future planning, to measure trends in program effectiveness from year to year and as an indicator of possible problems with a program. However, a more important number to all, including donors, is the bottom line, or profit, because profit translates to ministry effectiveness.

To illustrate this, assume that there are two farmers working under similar circumstances. Farmer 1 harvests 750 bushels of corn at a cost of 150 bushels (or 20 percent) for a profit of 600 bushels and a 5:1 income-to-expense ratio. Farmer 2 harvests 1,000 bushels of corn at a cost of 300 bushels (or 30 percent) for a profit of 700 bushels and a 3.3:1 income-to-expense ratio.

Just looking at ratios, percentages, and total costs, Farmer 1 appears to be the farmer of choice. His expenses are lower, both in terms of total costs and as a percent of income. His income to expense ratio is much better than Farmer 2. But look at profit! Farmer 2 provided 100 bushels more profit. The landowner for these two farmers should be more pleased with Farmer 2 simply because there was more money left over for him.

Should this not also be true in Christian fund-raising? If more money is available for getting the Gospel out, the means of measuring of costs of fund-raising diminishes in significance greatly. This is not to suggest that there should be no concern for how funds are raised. However, it is to suggest that ratios, percentages, and average costs should be insignificant in determining development budgets when compared to the more strategic measure—profit.

More important than whether fund-raising costs are low is the question of how the organization is using what is left after costs. The results being achieved are ultimately more important. In a recent article in *Fund-Raising Management* magazine, Jerry Huntsinger had the following to say on this issue:

> I used to be in favor of a ceiling on fund-raising because I felt it provided controls. But now I wonder. How can you legislate what the fund-raising costs should be for an orthopedic hospital serving crippled children in Calcutta? It's hard enough to raise money for India these days. It's hard to raise money for operating a hospital. And so, if a charity cannot meet the 30 percent fund-raising cost, should it close up the hospital? What if it takes 50 cents to raise $1 for the hospital, or 75 cents to raise $1? If we say that it must take only 30 percent or the crippled children can spend their lives without operations, perhaps we are being a little rigid, to say the least.[1]

Mr. Huntsinger's comments are from a purely logical perspective. How much more meaningful his point is when fulfilling the Great Commission becomes the cause concept! Would the Lord really want the Gospel to be communicated less if the cost of raising the funds began to exceed some arbitrary limit?

CONCLUSIONS

The cost of fund-raising should be viewed as part of the cost of doing ministry. The Christian organization should be able to justify its costs of fund-raising before God *and* men.

According to the examples of Christ and Paul, the priority of prospects for funding a ministry are: those to whom ministry is directed, other Christians, and for-profit activity. And finally, from the hardworking farmer, it is learned that too much emphasis on fund-raising costs expressed as percentages or ratios may be limiting the good efforts that God has called ministries to perform.

HOLMES M. BRYAN, JR., graduated from Louisiana Tech University in Ruston, Louisiana, earning a bachelor of science in civil engineering. Currently, Mr. Bryan is internal development consultant for Campus Crusade for Christ which includes responsibilities for creating and modeling of development programs of many of its U.S. and international ministries as well as new central development programs. Previous experience with Campus Crusade for Christ includes director of foundation relations, director of development systems, director of current giving, and director of development.

Mr. Bryan lectures at national conferences on topics including fund-raising from foundations and development systems and services.

(14)
FUND-RAISING CONSTRAINTS:
LAW AND ETHICS

GEORGE R. GRANGE II

"When a country is rebellious it has many rulers" (Proverbs 28:2). Cloaked in constitutional euphemisms of "personal freedom" and "rights of privacy," we are a people who glory in rebellion. Ironically, rebellion eventually causes the growth of the very civil authority it seeks to disregard. The outworking of this truth is obvious at many levels. The lack of self-restraint invites social restraint. At an organizational level, the lack of self-regulation creates a vacuum that will be filled by civil regulation. The more persistent and widespread the lack of self-restraint, the more pervasive the imposition of Caesar's authority. This proliferation of civil authority is inversely related to the effectiveness of self-control at all levels.

This may partly explain the gale-force winds of media scrutiny, public criticism, Congressional inquiry, and new governmental controls that buffeted the evangelical enterprise in 1987. Curiously, these winds were not externally generated. Rather they were the necessary—indeed desirable—inrushings of external restraint into the ethical vacuum created by self-indulgence, carelessness, pride, and blatant disregard for moral probity.

But the purpose of this chapter is not to vindicate the proliferation of government regulations, not to trumpet doom nor advocate battening the hatches. Rather it is to address the questions voiced by concerned executives and directors of the overwhelming majority of the 366,000 Section 501(c)(3) tax-exempt organizations which have every intention of acting responsibly, but need to know who are the existing Caesars regulating their funding activities, what is required to comply, and what are the tools of responsible self-government.

HISTORICAL PERSPECTIVE

First, a brief historical perspective is necessary. Nonprofits, and particularly religious nonprofits, have enjoyed unparalleled autonomy until the last 50 years. Until 1940 there were few Caesars exercising authority over churches or other religious organizations. On the taxing front, the practice of exempting religious organizations can be traced back to the British Statute of Charitable Uses of 1601.[1] In this country, tax exemption for charitable organizations dates back to 1894,[2] even predating the creation of the federal taxing authority under the sixteenth Amendment.[3]

Regarding civil liability, the British doctrine of charitable immunity was adopted at the founding of this nation as part of the common law, and provided virtual blanket immunity from typical tort and contractural liability for all churches and other charities.[4] Moreover, a century ago religious organizations benefited in common with all society from the absence of legal requirements. Life, not to mention daily commerce, was rather simple and uncluttered—no zoning restrictions, no historic preservation laws, no security regulations, no employment discrimination statutes, no court-created clergy malpractice duties. But the legal landscape had lost the pristine simplicity of the Ten Commandments and the Golden Rule. Today many regard it as a severely overgrown thicket. This transition from historic unregulation to ultraregulation is equally discernible in the religious fund-raising arena.

The extent of this transition is suggested by Alexis de Tocqueville's perceptive observation in 1840 that while organized religion was less powerful in the U.S. than in other nations and in other eras, its influence was more lasting: "It restricts itself to its own resources, but of these no man can deprive it; its circle is limited, but it pervades it and holds it under undisputed control."[5]

Much has changed in the last century and a half. No longer is it true that religious control is "undisputed" within its circle of influence. Forces within, as well as forces without, have arisen to aggressively challenge religion's claim of authority, authenticity, and finality. But most pertinent is the dramatic departure from parochial funding sources. Organized religion no longer categorically "restricts itself to its own resources."

When de Tocqueville penned his observation, most of organized religion was still carried on in and through the local churches. There were no multimillion-dollar parachurch ministries; no national and international televangelists; even the YMCA movement was still 11 years from birth, the Salvation Army 40 years off, and the American Red Cross, 41 years distant.[6] The resources of religion were primarily the tithes and offerings of local congregations. Because of the accountability inherent in membership funding, there was little need for external controls on either the collection or expenditure of these resources.

Today that has changed dramatically. Because much of organized religion today no longer "restricts itself to its own resources" in the traditional parochial sense, its accountability for, access to, and use of these resources is no longer unquestioned either. The advent of computerized letters, laser-jet printers, and twentieth-century telecommunications gives new meaning to John Wesley's oft-quoted burden for world evangelization. Not only is the "world the parish" for many evangelical organizations that take seriously the Great Commission, but pocketbooks throughout this global parish are often within the assigned territory of their fund-raisers.

BOUNDARIES FOR FUND-RAISING

The intensifying competition for charitable funds and the erosion of self-regulation have drawn numerous "Caesars" at local, state, and federal levels to begin setting new boundaries.

● Common law fraud and trust doctrines. Among the first of these boundaries are the common law trust and fraud doctrines, which provide that funds received by churches and other charitable organizations must be used for the public purposes for which they are raised and not diverted to private purposes.[7] Under the Trust Doctrine a state attorney general, for example, may initiate court intervention where there is evidence that a religious entity is misappropriating funds or diverting them from public to private purposes.[8]

Fraud is a criminal offense deeply embedded in the common law, and is equally applicable to businesses and charities. Fraud is misrepresentation with the intention of inducing others to detrimentally rely on that misinformation.⁹ Today, in most states these laws have been codified and are finding even more active use as a regulatory control device for fraud and misuse of charitable funds.¹⁰

• Securities laws. The next major restriction of charitable solicitation activity was incidental. The federal securities laws and so-called state "blue sky laws" were spawned in the 1930s to curb notorious securities abuses. Subsequently, they often found application by creative state regulators confronted with naive, inept, if not outright fraudulent abuses by churches and other religious organizations in issuing bonds, notes, and other fund-raising devices.¹¹

• Charitable solicitation laws. The most direct and significant response to real or perceived fund-raising abuses has been the proliferation of charitable solicitation laws at both the state and local levels. In the past 20 years, 33 states and the District of Columbia have adopted some form of charitable solicitation legislation to regulate fund-raising activity by any charity seeking funds from the residents of that state through any means whatsoever—radio, television, telephone, letters, or personal contact.¹² Consequently, any charity engaged in nationwide fund-raising must either register under or establish an exemption from the laws of 33 jurisdictions. Unfortunately, there is nonuniformity among the states in these statutes. Most state charitable solicitation laws require both initial and annual registration. Exemptions for churches soliciting solely from their members is provided in many states, while fewer states extend the exemption to all religious organizations with IRS 501(c)(3) status. Where exemptions are available, they are usually not automatic but must be applied for.

Perhaps the most controversial aspect of these laws, at least from a legal vantage point, is the attempt by several states to establish ceilings for acceptable fund-raising and administrative expenses. Many of these provisions have been successfully challenged on constitutional grounds.¹³

Efforts to bring uniformity among the states culminated in the National Association of Attorney Generals endorsing in December 1986 a model charitable solicitation law which is under active consideration by a number of states.¹⁴

In addition to state charitable solicitation laws, numerous cities and local municipalities have adopted similar ordinances. No comprehensive summary of these ordinances has been compiled. Typically, they must therefore be discovered on a jurisdiction-by-jurisdiction basis.[15]

These laws seek to control charitable abuses and fraud primarily by means of registration and disclosure. Often the disclosure required is largely duplicative of information required on the annual federal tax filing for tax-exempt organizations, IRS Form 990. This layering of registration and disclosure requirements on top of existing trust duties and fraud liability theories demonstrates an erosion of public confidence in the willingness or ability of these organizations to make ethical and nonself-serving choices unprodded.

FEDERAL REGULATION OF RELIGIOUS ORGANIZATIONS

Congress, always galvanized by nationally publicized abuses, has considered at least a dozen bills to regulate charitable fund-raising. Beginning with the Van Deerlin Bill introduced in the 93rd Congress in 1974, Congress has looked at ways to curb charitable abuses by various federal disclosure laws.[16] It was not until 1979, however, following the Pallottine Fathers scandal,[17] that significant momentum began to build in Congress for such legislation. Most of this support coalesced around the Wilson Bill.[18]

Substantial public support for some kind of federal action grew in response to the national repugnance at learning that only $1 million of some $20 million raised by this Catholic charity actually went to help the needy individuals so graphically displayed in its fund-raising literature. Perhaps only the growth of the self-regulation movement deflated, at least temporarily, the momentum for federal fund-raising regulation. Thus, the Wilson Bill never came to a vote.

● Recent legislative activity. Federal legislative activity which has been largely dormant in the charitable area for the last eight years was kindled again in the 100th Congress, primarily because of several high-profile abuses which were prominently scrutinized and displayed by the media during 1987. From heavenly hostage fund-raising campaigns to seven-figure salaries and jet-set lifestyles of prominent television evangelists; from the revelation of secret listening devices for fabricating words of knowledge during religious healing services, to the disclosed role of nonprofits as part of the Iranian-Contra connection in channeling millions of dollars of Contra aid, the public and Congress were fed for months on religious and nonprofit news-

burgers. This gave Congress all the nourishment it needed to focus its hearing spotlight on nonprofits. The result has been more legislative scrutiny of nonprofits than in any Congress for 20 years. Witness the following cavalcade of developments.

• Revenue Act of 1987. The 100th Congress proposed new charitable solicitation legislation (HR 2942) which was subsequently incorporated into the recently enacted Revenue Act of 1987.[19] Thus with little discussion or debate, and ferried by the need for a fiscal 1988 budget, federal regulation is now added to the labyrinth of charitable solicitation control.

• House Ways and Means Oversight Subcommittee. The House Ways and Means Oversight Subcommittee was unusually active as well during the 100th Congress, holding hearings on political and lobbying activities by nonprofits; on unrelated business income activities, and creative entrepreneurship of nonprofits; and on fund-raising and operational activities by televangelists.[20] At the televangelist hearing, the issue of self-regulation and its effectiveness again emerged as perhaps the single most important buffer between charitable entities and new federal regulations. Chairman Pickle and some members of his committee seemed ready to give religious fund-raisers, specifically televangelists, a further window of opportunity to get their act together and demonstrate the effectiveness of self-regulation.

• House Postal Subcommittee. On other federal regulatory fronts, the House Postal Subcommittee has reentered the charitable regulatory scene with inquiry into the mailing activities of prominent religious broadcasters.[21]

• Internal Revenue Service. Other legal considerations at the federal level affecting evangelical organizations in their search for funds arise from various regulations of the Internal Revenue Service, the Federal Trade Commission, and the Federal Communications Commission. The Internal Revenue Service collects the most comprehensive information on the fund-raising activities of nonprofits through the annual Form 990. Since 1969, this has been a mandatory filing for all tax-exempt organizations except churches and certain smaller organizations. This reporting discloses comprehensive financial information including a breakdown of fund-raising and administrative expenses. It also discloses on a confidential basis the names of substantial contributors and highly compensated employees. There have been repeated efforts in recent years to expand the disclosures required by Form 990 and to implement a meaningful IRS audit program in response to unsatisfactory or questionable disclosures.

A significant development in the Revenue Act of 1987 as noted above is the requirement that tax-exempt organizations themselves maintain for public inspection their three most recent 990 reports. Given the practical difficulty of obtaining these reports from the IRS (even though theoretically they are publically available) this new requirement should substantially increase public accessibility to this information.

Under its unrelated business income tax regulations, the IRS regulates and taxes certain fund-raising activities of tax-exempt organizations that are determined to be derived from a trade or business regularly carried on by the organization and that are not substantially related to the organization's tax-exempt functions.[22] The IRS has been particularly active in monitoring creative entrepreneurial activities by tax exempts.[23]

The IRS also has regulations where gifts to charities involve an exchange for goods or services. Thus, if a taxpayer makes a payment to a church or other religious organization and in return receives or expects to receive an economic benefit, then the payment does not constitute a deductible charitable contribution up to the fair market value of the contribution received.[24] Examples of payments to churches or religious organizations that do not qualify as deductible contributions include: payments to a church for use of facilities for a wedding, tuition payments to parochial schools, payments to a religious home to care for a relative of the donor, and payments for the purchase of raffle tickets.

The IRS, through the Tax Reform Act of 1984, imposed new requirements on donors and tax-exempt organizations where noncash gifts are involved. The donor must secure a qualified appraisal and complete certain additional tax forms in making gifts of property to charities in excess of $5,000 per year, and the recipient charities in turn must complete and submit additional tax returns if that property is transferred within two years of receipt.[25]

Through its detailed and often convoluted regulations prescribing the proper tax treatment of various forms of gift annuities and trusts, the IRS exercises a heavy hand on the throttle of deferred-giving programs. For example, the use of typical deferred-giving devices, such as charitable remainder unitrusts, can trigger the private foundation rules and the corresponding limitations and excise taxes on self-dealing, jeopardizing investments, and other prohibited transactions.[26]

• Other federal agencies. The Federal Trade Commission has authority to investigate and regulate unfair trade practices—a term that has been interpreted broadly enough to bring certain nonprofit practices under its scrutiny.[27] Similarly, the Federal Communications Commission (FCC), in the context of its control of the nation's airwaves, has on occasion investigated the use of those airwaves by religious entities for fund-raising purposes. Most publicized was the FCC's inquiry into the solicitation of the Heritage Village and Missionary Church (PTL Network), which was accused, though never convicted, of diverting to other uses funds raised for specific charitable and religious purposes.[28] This is commonly referred to as "bait and switch" fund-raising: soliciting funds on the basis of an emotionally appealing project with the intention of using only a small portion of those funds for that purpose and applying the remainder to other projects.

ETHICAL CONSIDERATIONS AFFECTING
FUND-RAISING PRACTICES

The law provides external restraints; ethics furnishes internal guidance. Ethics could be defined as the system of morals and values guiding personal choices when all external restraints are removed. Chuck Colson is accurate in his prophetic insight that "[never] before in the history of Western Civilization has the public square been so devoid of transcendent values."[29] However, for followers of Christ, it need not and must not be so.

The public square affords the humble and ardent follower of Christ an ideal setting for engaging in a rigorous, self-denying, and no-compromise exercise of translating transcendent values into such practical choices as stewarding our resources rather than selfishly possessing, preferring others rather than self, seeing true leadership as servanthood by seeking at all times to advance the interests of others, denying greed in order to be generous, becoming of no reputation in order to advance the interest of others, using things to love people rather than using people to love things, and adopting a reverse Madison Avenue ethic of promising less and delivering more than advertised. In sum, ethical considerations present one of the most strategic opportunities for Christians to shine by living like Christ in a wicked and perverse generation.

ETHICS OF INDIVIDUAL FINANCIAL INTEGRITY

The remainder of this chapter focuses on two principal channels for expressing moral convictions in ethical choices: the individual and the corporate. Individual integrity must be the bedrock if corporate and societal ethics are to be solid and dependable. Collegial coercion, like legal restraint, can temporarily control conduct as long as the pressure is maintained, but it rarely changes belief. Unless personal integrity is rooted in that which is transcendent, efforts to establish cohesive corporate integrity will tend to fly apart from the center. For the follower of Christ, those transcendent values are to be found in revelation of God's love, holiness, and ultimate judgment. But how do these values translate into personal financial integrity?

Perhaps no single word summarizes the ethics of financial integrity better than *accountability*. Accountability suggests the biblical concept of *stewardship*, but it places the emphasis on the important element of *giving an account*. This implies that there is both a standard by which actions and attitudes may be measured and a time of measuring. Accountability arises whenever one becomes a fiduciary; that is, whenever one receives assets to be managed not for personal benefit, but for the benefit of others. Interesting is the similarity between the legal mandate and the scriptural mandate in determining the standards by which faithful stewardship will be evaluated. The law clearly establishes two legal standards: the duty of loyalty and the duty of care.[10]

• The duty of loyalty requires the avoidance of all conflicts of interest and personal benefit in the management of entrusted funds, and further requires that these funds be managed exclusively for the benefit of others. In the case of a religious organization, the beneficiaries for whom the funds are managed are typically the general public at large or some denominated subgroup of the general public. In the context of a Christian organization, the duty of loyalty would require a fiduciary to disclose and avoid conflicts of interest, to refrain from voting on matters involving personal interest (e.g., salary questions or royalty agreements for books authored by officers or trustees, etc.), and to avoid all personal benefit from the entrusted funds (except reasonable compensation for services rendered).

• The duty of care requires a fiduciary to exercise reasonable and prudent care (typically, the same care a reasonable man would exercise in his own financial affairs) in managing and administering the entrusted funds. For example, the duty of care would prohibit a fiduciary from investing entrusted funds in risky investments or from failing to properly conserve the entity's assets or funds from theft, misapplication, or other losses. These two duties give expression to an ethics of personal financial integrity, as well as form the foundation for an ethics of corporate financial integrity.

ETHICS OF CORPORATE FINANCIAL INTEGRITY

Undoubtedly, many elements of corporate financial integrity could be identified but five basic elements of effective corporate accountability are identified and discussed below.[11] Whatever the criteria, however, they will be of little meaning unless there is a vehicle effectively enforcing those standards. The most effective vehicle is one representing a community of shared values. For that reason, in an increasingly pluralistic society, self-policing is inherently more effective than purely legal enforcement mechanisms.

Effective peer-enforced accountability tends to foster a desire for integrity and informed awareness, out of which consistent compliance will tend to spring more naturally. Government regulation, on the other hand, tends to foster a we/they mentality and an attitude of minimal compliance and maximum avoidance.[12]

Assuming an effective self-policing mechanism is in place, the following five elements of corporate financial integrity and accountability can be implemented.

• Meaningful disclosure. First, accountability requires meaningful disclosure. To be meaningful, disclosure must be accurate, timely, and to the proper constituency. Such disclosure requires an outside audit in most cases. Though certified audits are generally not required by the IRS or by any other governmental standard imposed on nonprofits (except for schools and entities receiving certain government funding), they have become normative in the business community as an essential ingredient of financial accountability and responsibility.

• Meaningful budget process. Perhaps the single most important tool in implementing accountability, next to a full disclosure policy, is a meaningful budget process. In simplest terms, a budget is the organization's plan of action translated into dollars projected over the course of the next accounting period. It is the organization's blueprint for the coming months or years, expressed in monetary terms. It should project, in detailed income and expense categories, the *realistic* goals and objectives of the organization.

This means that the organization must know what its goals are before it can properly prepare a budget. Obviously, if an organization is fuzzy regarding its goals, meaningful financial planning will be equally elusive. Therefore, monetary projection of goals is the first function of the budget.

The second budget function is to provide a tool to monitor the financial activities of the organization throughout the year. When properly used, the budget will provide a barometer which will alert the operating and executive officers, as well as the board, if their financial goals are not being satisfied.

Third, an effective budget process is also a principal protection against the charges of misdirection of funds for private benefit. In other words, if all disbursements of the organization's funds are made in strict accordance with the budget, and the budget is properly scrutinized and reviewed by the appropriate officials and governing board, then the opportunity for inadvertent or deliberate misappropriation is greatly reduced.

• Effective internal controls. Internal controls are the procedures used by an organization to receive, maintain, and disburse its cash and other assets. Effective control procedures recognize and adequately deal with two corrosive influences: the corrosive influence in the world (moth, thief, and rust, etc.) and the corrosive influence of man's heart. Because of the former, assets not properly administered tend to depreciate and dissipate. Because of the latter influence resources tend to be stolen, pilfered, casually borrowed, or applied for personal benefit. Comprehensive internal control procedures which include safeguarding assets, detecting fraud, proving accuracies, improving spending efficiencies, maintaining a businesslike separation of various financial responsibilities,—etc., are beyond the scope of this chapter, but there are excellent resources available."

• Effective accounting system. In addition to adequate internal controls, an effective accounting system should be set up by a knowledgeable accountant or CPA which results in financial statements that are:

– easily comprehensible by the average person;

– concise so as not to lose the average reader in obscure detail;

– all-inclusive about the activities of the organization;

– provided with adequate reference points for comparison, such as budget comparisons and comparisons with prior years' operations;

– prepared on a timely basis; and

– explaining in comprehensive footnotes items which are not self-interpreting or unusual transactions, or which involve related party dealings. The accounting system both internal and external should be reviewed annually by the organization's outside auditor.

• Annual audit. An audit is a series of procedures followed by an experienced professional accountant to test, on a selective basis, transactions as well as internal control procedures to form an opinion on the fairness and accuracies of the financial statements for that period of time.

One of the most helpful results of an audit is the auditor's Management Letter which is typically produced with every audit but is separate from the audit opinion. The Management Letter should be requested from auditors who do not routinely provide one, and should be sent directly to an audit committee composed of members of the board who are not staff and are not involved at all in handling of the money. The purpose of this separation of function is to achieve the greatest possible objectivity from the auditor in conducting his audit as well as to achieve a greater accountability in implementing the auditor's recommendations.

With these procedures in place, especially when springing from a solid foundation of personal integrity and when enforced by active self-policing organizations, Christian fund-raising should demonstrate meaningful financial accountability. If such steps are conscientiously and expeditiously taken, perhaps the vacuumlike pressure now building to impose external controls can be sufficiently reduced, thus avoiding an even greater crisis and the governmental restraints that would predictably follow.

GEORGE R. "CHIP" GRANGE II is managing partner of Gammon & Grange, a Washington, D.C. law firm specializing in communications and nonprofit law. He has devoted his legal career to working with nonprofit organizations both professionally and as a volunteer member of the Boards of the Christian Legal Society, Christian Ministries Management Association, and the Evangelical Council for Financial Accountability. Currently Gammon & Grange advises 80 nonprofit corporations, including churches, parachurch organizations, and other religious and educational tax-exempt organizations in all areas of legal compliance.

Mr. Grange's law firm is pioneering the concept of preventive lawyering with nonprofit organizations and has developed and implemented the only comprehensive legal audit for nonprofit organizations. He and his wife, Kathy, and their four children live in Gaithersburg, Maryland.

The
Evangelical Fund-Raiser's
Challenge

(15)
SERVANTHOOD:
THE
FUND-RAISER'S CALL

DAVID L. McKENNA

No one can be a president in Christian higher education for almost 30 years without being a fund-raiser. So, I am to be counted as a colleague in fund-raising. I share in the successes and failures, the exhilaration and exhaustion, the praise and loneliness, the ministry and profession.

Consider my dilemma as a fund-raiser when I reported that we just announced the receipt of a signed and sealed will totalling $6.16 million—the largest gift we have received—and then struggled for perspective when a faculty member grumbled that the money was not yet in hand.

Or, the circumstances in which donors were honored at the dedication of a fully funded and endowed building, and then a donor-sponsored student forum raised the question, "Do we treat the major donor better than we treat the little giver?"

DISTORTED IMAGES

Honesty requires that we recognize the perceived contradiction when we deal with the subject of fund-raising and servanthood. Let's face it: servanthood is not the general public image of the fund-raiser's role and ministry.

I asked ten successful fund-raisers to answer the question, What one word do you think describes the public perception of a fund-raiser among evangelical Christians? The word *beggar* came in first, with *hustler* not far behind. One respondent cheated on the one-word answer with a vivid, two-word description, *Suede shoes.* Keep in mind that these are the words of friends, not enemies. No wonder someone said, "When it comes to fund-raisers, there are pros and cons." The sad fact is that the distorted image continues to be reinforced by isolated but repeated shabby incidents that come to public attention.

The fund-raiser's public image can be distorted by the signals that are sent as well as by images that are created. An editorial column appeared in our newspaper with a title that included the phrase "fences of the heart." The writer took to task the First United Methodist Church of Houston, Texas for erecting a $150,000 wrought-iron fence around its property to keep out "street people." No matter that one of the ministers had been slain and a part of the building set on fire; no matter that the porch of the church was used for drinking and drugs, pimping and prostitution; no matter that the pastor tried to explain the church's leadership in urban ministries for the needy and its $1 million budget for missions; no matter that he announced a $100,000 fund-raising project specifically for the street people. Worst of all, no matter that the columnist wrote his article from random news clippings without checking the facts. For millions of readers, a wrought-iron fence became the symbol for "fences of the heart."

SMEARED REPUTATIONS

It's tough to be a servant when your reputation is smeared. Dare I suggest that irreparable damage is done to our public reputation each time a tearjerking, trinket-offering, ministry-ending, death-threatening tactic is used by religious fund-raisers? Take, for instance, Oral Roberts' hysterical "Give or I die" appeal in the spring of 1987, which became the public laughingstock. A cartoon on the editorial page of the *Arizona Republic,* two days after the Roberts' telecast, depicts Christ dying on the cross with Richard Roberts on one hand and Oral on the other. Waving his arms toward the television camera, Richard is pleading, "Give to my daddy. . . ." On the other side, Oral is sweating and intoning, " . . . or I die." The caption at the top of the cartoon reads, "And He was crucified between two thieves." A cartoon in the Lexington *Herald-Leader* showed Oral in the belfry of a church being held hostage by God, the terrorist!

Who can blame Mike Royko for using Oral's antics as fodder for his nationally syndicated column. With an irreverent tongue-in-cheek, Royko urged people not to give in response to Oral's life-and-death plea. Instead, he envisioned a great spiritual revival beginning on March 31st after Oral dropped dead. According to Royko, then even agnostics and atheists would know that God means business.

QUESTIONED ETHICS

It's tough to be a servant when our ethics are questioned. Whatever we do is watched. Whether we like it or not, the media will be quick to report the number of Christian organizations that are being investigated for alleged violations of Evangelical Council for Financial Accountability (ECFA) standards, but will fail to pick up the annual report of World Relief that shows administrative overhead dropping to 12 percent or to commend the Church of the Nazarene for its resolution on a matching-gift policy that is a strong ethical and biblical witness. Perhaps we need a well-publicized award to honor organizations that are models for Christian leadership in fund-raising, financial management, and effective ministry.

WEAK THEOLOGY

It's tough to be a servant when our theology is weak. Coming even closer to home, let me suggest that the servant role of the fund-raiser is further threatened by the serious deficiency of a biblical theology of stewardship among evangelical Christians, especially in affluent America. Although biblical stewardship engages the whole of life, money is the special gift which triggers and informs our response to the lordship of Jesus Christ. How do you work as a servant in fund-raising when secular self-interest has been sanctified among Christians? The temptation is to play the game by the rules of self-interest and justify the secular means by spiritual ends.

LACK OF RESPECT

It's tough to be a servant when our work is misunderstood. Let's face it. We live with misunderstanding of our fund-raiser's role within the institutions where we work. Whether the institution is ecclesiastical, educational, medical, missions, communications, or another kind of ministry, many trustees or directors do not understand fund-raising and many professionals who perform the service functions supported by fund-raising do not care. Like constituents of a politician, they only ask, "What have you done for me lately?" Again, we need recognition for fund-raisers who are models of servanthood, not just for the sake of our profession, but for our institutions as well.

It's tough to be a servant when our role is not recognized. Fund-raising has developed into an occupation with high expectations but without the criteria for a profession. By definition, a profession is a career which requires advanced, formal, and specialized education with standards for self-regulation and titles of deference, such as doctor or reverend or letters of credential, such as Ph.D., J.D., or C.P.A. Fund-raising is a semiprofession with experiential learning reinforced by periodic seminars, self-regulated without teeth, and entitled by whatever label gets a foot in the door. Perhaps the next step for developing maturity in the profession is to create the curriculum, the code, and the credentials for the qualified fund-raiser.

No wonder, then, that fund-raising tends to be a profession whose members struggle with self-esteem, face exhaustion, and either drop out or move on with high frequency. To be a ministering servant in such a setting is a miracle of grace itself. Pogo would say, "We are faced with insurmountable opportunities." Jesus, however, would remind us, "I came not to be served, but to serve, and give My life a ransom for many." If ever there was a time when servanthood could be demonstrated, it is now in the ministry of fund-raising.

Jesus' Parable of the Talents is a unique guide for our thoughts.

[For the kingdom of God] will be like a man going on a journey, who called his servants and entrusted his property to them. To one he gave five talents of money, to another two talents, and to another one talent, each according to his ability. Then he went on his journey. The man who had received the five talents went at once and put his money to work and gained five more. . . .

After a long time the master of those servants returned and settled accounts with them. The man who had received the five talents brought the other five. "Master," he said, "you entrusted me with five talents. See I have gained five more." His master replied, "Well done, good and faithful servant! You have been faithful with a few things; I will put you in charge of many things. Come and share your master's happiness" (Matthew 25:14-16, 19-21).

Servanthood, not unlike fund-raising, is a role that is often misunderstood and easily distorted. Therefore, we are in for some surprises as we explore the elements of trust, risk, accountability, and reward for the person whom Jesus calls to be His servant.

THE TRUST OF A SERVANT

To be a servant is to manage that which we do not own. Servanthood is more than a role; it is a relationship. No one can read the Parable of the Talents without confronting three fundamental truths about the biblical theology of servanthood.

Truth: The servant owns nothing.

Truth: God trusts His servants with everything.

Truth: God's servants give total loyalty to their Master.

What a privilege! Owning nothing but entrusted with everything, we are called by God to be His choice servants with the responsibility for managing all His resources.

What are those resources? The Scriptures make it clear that God has entrusted us with His Creation, His Law, His Gospel, and His Grace. For each, we are called to be His servants and His stewards— two terms that are inseparable in the teachings of Jesus. Our stewardship task is well defined. We must preserve His Creation, including our material resources, obey His Law, and proclaim the Gospel of His Grace. Paul saw proclaiming the "mystery of the Gospel" of Jesus Christ (Ephesians 6:19) as his highest order of stewardship. Have you ever thought about it? The matter of money is directly connected with the mystery of the Gospel. We often quote Paul's warning to Timothy, "The love of money is the root of all kinds of evil" (1 Timothy 6:10). There is another side to the equation. The Parable of the Talents teaches us that use of money is a test of whether or not God can trust us with the stewardship of His Gospel.

Servanthood, then, is our trust. Jesus' concept of servanthood is a radical departure from the Greek idea of servanthood. Plato equated a servant with a slave in a contemptible profession motivated by self-interest. Servanthood took on positive meaning only as a free man gave himself in blind obedience to the state. From this comes the idea of a "civil servant." The Old Testament rescues servanthood from the Greek idea of self-interest or submission to the state. While still seeing a servant as a person who has a duty to perform or merit to be earned, the New Testament shifts the focus toward serving others.

The biblical image of a servant comes to full maturity when Jesus leaves the honored seat at the Passover Feast, strips off the symbols of His position, wraps a towel around His waist, and washes the feet of His disciples. Imagine God waiting tables and washing our feet. Peter's protest tells us how reluctant we are to accept that role for Jesus or ourselves. Servanthood is a complete reversal of the motives that drive us. In an era when secular prophets tell us that radical self-interest is the dominant force shaping American character, we who are called to be the servants of Jesus Christ must be identified as anomalies in the system, because we are willing to sacrifice ourselves in the service of others. Why? Because of grace. As Jesus Christ gave Himself for us, we give ourselves for others. Hence, we understand Paul's definition of the servant as a "love slave"—totally obedient to God, totally given to others. Gratitude is the basis for our giving. Particularly in the field of fund-raising, where motives and means can be turned into the ends of self-interest, we are called to be love slaves of Jesus Christ. If the Spirit of Christ and the stewardship of the Gospel inspire our work, our public image will be as servants, not beggars.

THE RISK OF THE SERVANT

Jesus expects His servants to be creative risk-takers with His resources. The Parable of the Talents tells us about a man who entrusted money to his servants. When the master returned home, he called his servants to him in order to settle accounts with them, to find out how much each man had gained by trading.

Servants are usually considered managers, not investors. But stewardship is more than conserving the resources that God has entrusted to us. Money tests our faith as well as our love, for Jesus has other expectations. The media, the Internal Revenue Service, and the

Evangelical Council for Financial Accountability (ECFA) are not alone in asking how much of the donor's dollars are spent on promotion and administration. Beyond that, however, Jesus wants to know how effective His servants have been in multiplying His dollars through investment.

A dilemma confronts us. How do we balance the creative risk-venture of faith with the stewardship principle of counting the cost before we build the tower? I confronted this question while writing an article for the *Christianity Today* Institute on the subject, "Financing the Great Commission." In His command, "Therefore go and make disciples of all nations" (Matthew 28:19), Jesus identifies the resources that are required for the fulfillment of the Great Commission—time, space, people, knowledge, and energy. He does not mention money, and for good reason. Jesus knows of our tendency to substitute institutional programs for incarnational people and finances for faith. Particularly, He wants us to remember that people are the primary resource for fulfilling the Great Commission. Here we have another stewardship test. Are we multiplying our money through investments in people who are fulfilling the Great Commission? More and more, I am responding to our donors with reports on the multiplication of their investment in the lives and ministries of our students. Admittedly, seminary students are ready examples of invested dollars, but I would ask the same question of any ministry in which I was engaged in fund-raising. To multiply our ministry through people with the goal of world evangelization is the risk venture to which Jesus still calls His servants.

May I add the hard fact that the servant who takes a creative risk is also open to failure? At one time or another, every fund-raiser has received that classical response from a prospective donor, "I have *nothing but praise* for your proposal." It's tough to be a servant who takes a risk in a success-oriented society. Yet, from the secular world we are learning that leaders are people who live with both success and failure. For them, it is not a matter of winning or losing; it is a matter of winning or learning. Harry Truman was asked, "What do you do when you make a decision that is a mistake?" He answered, "I make another one." In his own way, he was anticipating the response of Mother Theresa when she was asked, "How can you go out into the streets of Calcutta among the sick and dying every morning with the knowledge that you can never catch up with the need?" She answered, "The Lord doesn't call us to be successful. He only asks that we be faithful." Our call to servanthood in the ministry of fund-raising is the call to be faithful, even at a risk.

THE ACCOUNTABILITY OF A SERVANT

To be a servant is to be accountable for that which we will not use. Our accountability is *personal.* Biblical servanthood is not so spiritual that the principles of good management are cancelled. Jesus refutes such a notion in the Parable of the Talents when He calls the servant to accountability. "Well done, good and faithful servant!" is a full-fledged performance appraisal. On a moment's notice the faithful servant is expected to answer for the quality of performance, the integrity of person, and the consistency of process. In other words, we are accountable for our motives, our means, and our ends in fund-raising. Personal integrity is the test of our motive; moral consistency is the test of our means; and quality performance is the test of our ends. To fail any one of these tests is to fail our trust as servants. When I asked the ten fund-raisers in my informal survey for one word to describe why fund-raisers fail, they were almost unanimous in the answer: "Unworthy."

Our accountability is *communal.* Jesus leaves His servants with the responsibility for all His household. "Economics" is a strong biblical word that means "to manage the household." We sometimes forget that we are accountable for more than the dollars we raise. Dollars are not the bottom line for the fund-raiser who is a servant of God. Our accountability is to the household of God—beginning with our donors, extending to our institutions, embracing the body of Christ, and reaching to our publics. In my weekly radio commentary, I invoked this principle in an appeal to Oral Roberts, calling him to account as a brother in Christ and a colleague in fund-raising. Assuming that we are brothers, the press has asked me what I think about Oral's tactics, and some prospective donors have chided me because my style lacks the urgency of a life-and-death drama.

Our accountability is *eternal.* Note that the Parable of the Talents says nothing about the ends to which the master's resources were used. Jesus saves that question for the vision of the Final Judgment that immediately follows. In this convicting scene we see the highest level of accountability that we have as servants of God, stewards of

His resources, and managers of His household. At the Final Judgment, the division will come over the question of caring for people who suffer from hunger, thirst, loneliness, nakedness, sickness, and imprisonment. Those who suffer are special members of the household of God for whom we are responsible. Time and time again, Jesus reinforced the truth that He holds us personally responsible for the use of our money to relieve suffering. Whether it is the Rich Young Man, the Rich Man and Lazarus, the Rich Fool, or the Good Samaritan, we cannot ignore the fact that we who have money and we who raise money are accountable for its ministry as well as its management.

THE REWARD OF THE SERVANT

To be a servant is to be satisfied with that for which we may not be praised. When we think of the Parable of the Talents, we put the emphasis on the Lord's commendation, "Well done, good and faithful servant." We need nothing more. If as fund-raisers we can hear these words, we will have our reward. But the parable teaches us that God has a bonus for His servants. If we are good, faithful, and effective in our stewardship, we are honored with increased responsibility and the inner sense of joy.

All of us who are in Christian fund-raising are deacons who wait on tables. Yet, we must not forget that we are stewards of the Gospel as well as stewards of money. If we are faithful in our primary task, God will give us the power and the privilege of stewarding the mystery of the Gospel as well.

I cannot forget a man who was a genius of immense wealth, but whose only friend was alcohol. He didn't have a charitable bone in his body when he handwrote a $500,000 gift for our Christian university. Although the steps were small, we edged forward in our conversations to bits and pieces of spiritual things and God made it easy for me to love him. Then one day his secretary called me to say, "The boss hasn't been the same man since he made that gift." He gave us a farewell on his yacht when God called us to a new ministry. The cruise included a side trip past the home of his former wife who had left him because of alcohol. As he blew the horn and waved, he gave me a greater gift than a half-million dollars when he said, "I've been off the juice for two weeks now." I knew what he meant. In his own way, he wanted me to know that he was searching for salvation.

How naturally that memory fits into the other bonus that God reserves for His faithful servants. As in the Parable of the Talents, Jesus extends the invitation to His servant, "Come and share your master's happiness." What an honor! Fund-raisers cannot expect much praise for their work. If we fail, we are criticized; if we succeed, we are only doing our job. Jesus understands the unsung role of His servants. Therefore, He reserves His personal joy for those who are faithful. Joy is the intrinsic glow of satisfaction in knowing that you have been faithful to your calling whether anyone else recognizes it or not.

Our task is one of the most difficult in the world: to manage what we do not own, to risk that from which we will not profit, to account for what we will not use, and be satisfied with that for which we may not be praised.

But what of joy? Our high calling is to be trusted servants of Jesus Christ in the ministry of fund-raising. But there is more. If we are faithful to our trust, His joy is our joy.

To be a trusted servant of the Lord Jesus Christ in the ministry of fund-raising is quite enough.

DAVID L. McKENNA currently serves as the president of Asbury Theological Seminary in Wilmore, Kentucky. Earlier presidencies include Spring Arbor College and Seattle Pacific University. He has earned a B.A. degree from Western Michigan University, a M.Div. from Asbury Theological Seminary, an M.A. and Ph.D. from the University of Michigan, plus has been given several honorary doctorates. He has served in the field of higher education for over 35 years, which qualifies him well as a college consultant in accreditation, finance, curriculum, development, long-range planning, presidential search, and evaluation.

Dr. McKenna is a frequent speaker at conferences, churches, and seminars, and the author of several books, including The Whisper of Grace *(Word),* MegaTruth *(Here's Life), and* Communicators Commentaries *on Mark and Job (Word).*

(16)
DEVELOPING
LIFELONG RELATIONSHIPS
WITH DONORS

J. DAVID SCHMIDT

"Beans this week, Dear." With that pronouncement on a Monday morning, my dad the pastor would send an important message to my mom and family. The "freewill" tithes and offerings given by the church people the day before had been a little thin. Money would be a little tight the next week.

Dad's words set in motion certain austerity measures. Mom would buy one roast or ham early in the week, then stretch it over several meals. My 50-cent allowance would be cut to 20. And my dad and I would wait one more week to get our hair cut.

As a young boy growing up in the home of an evangelical pastor and his wife supported on freewill offerings, such austerity measures rarely fazed our family. It was just part of what it meant to be in God's work in the church. Besides, God was always faithful through the giving of His people. We never missed a meal and our needs were always met.

In reflecting on those days, I have come to rediscover something I sensed as a boy—the austerity measures we occasionally took *never* impacted the relationships my parents had with people in the congregation. The quality of their ministry didn't fluctuate a millimeter even when the income did.

Dad would keep on preparing new sermons. Mom kept on being a friend to board members' wives. Dad would visit the sick, produce his radio broadcasts, and run the church whether things were tight or not. They served the widows who tithed from their Social Security checks, the businessmen who did not give regularly, the farmer who would tithe with eggs and meat.

My folks took a higher road and a longer view, committing them-selves to build relationships with people *not* on the basis of their financial performance or net worth, but on the basis of their *personal* worth. The lesson in relationship-building was clear—the rich and poor were treated evenhandedly. Mom and Dad ministered to people whether they were faithful in giving or not.

Unfortunately, it appears that a disturbing amount of evangelical fund-raising today operates on an entirely different value system. Marrying God's eternal value of preaching the Gospel with a secular value of "at any price," we see a kind of Christopaganism emerging in how some evangelical fund-raisers handle relationships.

The growing pressure on development personnel to meet a budget and deliver a healthy bottom line seems to be felt increasingly at the donor level. Pressure on the donor, even if it makes that donor uncomfortable, is not viewed by some as of great consequence. After all, "Donors are expendable. We can always replace them if they quit giving. Besides, if someone isn't offended by our mail, it's not effective."

We have built our Christian organizations on thousands of shallow relationships (which are pressed frequently and hard), and a handful of major supporters (whom we take good care of). It is a far cry from the evenhanded approach to relationships which characterized the ministry of my dad and mom.

In our well-intentioned desire to meet needs, we have devalued our relationships with supporters by relating to them on the basis of their giving performance. "Donor lists numbering in the thousands and even millions require this," you argue. "It is good stewardship to segment and relate to people based on their giving ability." And there is the heart of the problem. *We have set up stewardship as a higher value than love for God's people.*

In our mad dash to be productive stewards, building biblical rela-tionships with supporters increasingly seems to be a second or third priority.

What follows is a *call* to a radical rethinking of our relationships with supporters. It is not a call to the "real offenders somewhere else." It is a call to all of us who are raising funds for mission work, churches, colleges, and denominations. We are long overdue to rethink how we can bring glory to God and also demonstrate His love in our relationships.

If we are going to take seriously God's call to love our neighbors as ourselves, we will need to rethink our motivation and our methodology.

On the pages that follow we will rediscover the beauty of God's model for relationships; we'll look at how Western culture affects our relationships; and last we'll apply God's Word to learn how to develop lifelong relationships with those we serve.

A FRIENDLY GOD SET THE PATTERN FOR RELATIONSHIPS

Relationships are God's idea for mankind. The Holy Scriptures are one cohesive account of how God relates to us. Genesis 2:18 gives us our first clue as to God's divine plan for relationships. "It is not good for the man to be alone. I will make a helper suitable for him."

From the beginning God was sending us a message: There is very little room for Lone Rangers in the kingdom. God longs to be invited to participate in our relationships with each other, and He expects relationships to be a crucial element in executing His will.

As Christians, we believe we are made in the image of God. This idea that it was not good for man to be alone reflects the very character of God Himself who is a friendly but jealous God, who longs for friendship with His Creation.

When we are alone, we are isolated, cut off from others. This sense of aloneness and isolation was termed "not good" in God's eyes. God saw that He had to provide a way for man to not be alone, to prevent isolation. God created in Adam and Eve a model of relationship so that one with another, we could do the will of God, be fruitful and multiply, and fill the earth and subdue it. God was a part of Adam and Eve's relationship. Apparently, His walks in the Garden in the cool of the day were a part of His routine. He wanted to be with His Creation.

This first model yields some key insights about relationships: they provide for personal and spiritual growth; they make us able to subdue the earth and be fruitful; they are a crucial part of how we fulfill the will of God in our lives; God wants to be a part of every relationship.

From the first relationship described in Genesis, through the closing book in Scripture, throughout history to today, God has related to *every* person in *every* culture with loving-kindness, trustworthiness, faithfulness, justice, forgiveness, purity, dependability, and omniscience. God brings these and other changeless character traits into every relationship He has with man. This constancy gives us great security and also signals an important value—if this God lives within us, we too can and should demonstrate these same character traits in our relationships—including those with donors.

If Adam and Eve were God's first relationship example, His ultimate and best demonstration of what it means to have a proper relationship came in His Son, Jesus Christ. First John 4:8 makes it clear that the *initiative* to build a relationship between God and man came from God, not man. "This is how God showed His love among us: He sent His one and only Son into the world that we might live through Him. . . . We love because He first loved us" (1 John 4:9, 19).

In Colossians 1:21, we read, "Once you were alienated from God and were enemies in your minds because of your evil behavior. But now He has reconciled you by Christ's physical body through death to present you holy in His sight, without blemish and free from accusation." By sending Jesus Christ to pay the penalty for rebellion, God provided a way for Creation to be reconciled to Himself. Through faith and repentance mankind could be redeemed from his hopeless situation. In His sacrificial death at Calvary and triumph over death, Jesus Christ made it possible for all mankind to *relate* to their Creator.

What Jesus Christ did at Calvary offers us hope that we can renew our relationships with one another. If a relationship with God can be restored through Jesus, then surely the power that raised Christ from the dead can empower us to overcome deficiencies in how we relate to each other. Here is the exciting and key truth: God desires a perfect relationship with us and desires for us to have perfect relationships with each other. He was willing to pay a high price to make that possible.

The Gospels graphically picture Jesus modeling how we should relate to each other. He came to give, not to receive. "I have come that they may have life and have it to the full" (John 10:10.) And He said, "I am the good shepherd, I know My sheep and My sheep know Me—just as the Father knows Me and I know the Father—and

I lay down My life for the sheep" (John 10:14). Jesus modeled a sacrificial approach to relationships. In feeding the 5,000 by the Sea of Galilee, providing sight for the blind, healing of the demon-possessed son, Jesus gave with no thought of receiving anything but glory for the Father in return.

After Jesus' death, resurrection, and ascension, God provided a counselor, the Holy Spirit, to teach us all things and remind us of everything Jesus had said (John 14:26).

Consider then God's handiwork: His consistency in relating to all mankind the same way; a perfect pattern for relating to each other in Jesus Christ; the Holy Spirit always present with us to teach us how to relate day to day.

This divine model for relationships is a crucial starting point for us as we seek to develop and maintain God-honoring relationships with our supporters.

In life, we define ourselves in terms of relationship: I'm married to . . . I work for . . . I attend church with . . . I voted for. . . . In our deepest being, we are relational. We need each other. Our lives are a complex weave of relationships, running the gamut from casual to intimate.

In his book, *We Need Each Other*, Dr. Guy Greenfield contends that everyone has a need for intimacy.[1] He suggests that our relationships move from shallow to intimate. "Most people operate on several levels simultaneously, depending upon the who, what, where, and why of their contacts with a variety of people. Also, as one moves from the shallower to the deeper levels, the number of people one relates to becomes smaller." As we move deeper in our relationships, we find satisfaction does not come with superficial relating. Greenfield says that only at the deeper levels of relating will Christians discover the necessary power, will, and strength for living the Christian ethic.

Greenfield's idea that we need deeper relationships for truly Christian living could present a profound dilemma for Christian fundraisers. When you have a mailing list of 100,000 names, or even 5,000, the idea of strengthening relationships other than through mass media seems absurd. But how do we decide how we will proceed with donors?

First, intimacy with every donor is not necessary for effective fundraising. There are many low-involvement donors who desire only a superficial relationship with an organization. They may want to keep the number of transactions between them and the organization to a minimum.

Secondly, intimacy with every donor would be impossible to manage. Most development personnel and budgets can barely keep up with those donors who do want to have a deeper relationship with the organization let alone cultivate relationships with others.

Third, donors are offended by false intimacy, which they sense is just one more *method* to get them to give.

So, how do we usually respond to this volume of superficial relationships? Our patterns tend to be predictable. We continue to relate to our supporters in proven ways which raise funds. We fall back on the familiar approach of relating to people on the basis of their giving performance. People who respond to urgent appeals keep getting them. Major donors get preferential treatment. If people give faithfully each month, we seek to "cross-utilize" them by soliciting "special" gifts. We send more mail and often call that "building a relationship."

We must find balance. We must be responsive to those showing interest and concern, but maintain a pure heart and loving action. Our goal should be to value the person as much or more than their gift. In his book, *The Person Reborn*, Paul Tournier says that humanity moves between the two poles of simplicity and complexity.[2] He goes on to say that only a very few manage to combine both tendencies and, in his view, "a lively Christian faith is the best precondition for the accomplishment of this miracle because it gives both profound understanding and simplicity of heart." Taking Paul Tournier to heart, the best way to discover balance in who we relate to, how deeply and why, will be best determined in the context of a close friendship with God.

The fact is we cannot maintain intimate relationships with thousands of people, nor should we. But on the other hand, we must not throw up our hands and say, "Therefore, I will do nothing to strengthen existing and future relationships in workable and manageable ways that honor God and show love."

Western culture creates difficult choices for us. Consider the following cultural pressures which strain godly relationships:

• Bigger is better. "Grow your mailing list even if you have a lot of low-involvement supporters."

- Quicker is better. "Go for the quick one-time gift. We're in fund-raising, not here to educate our supporters."
- Absolute values cannot be known or agreed on. "Some passages of Scripture simply can't be applied to our situation."
- Waste is a part of life. "Donors are expendable. If they're offended by our practices, so be it. There's more where they came from."
- The bottom line is everything. "Ample income to meet needs and growth is of higher priority than how we get there."

These negative values are, to be sure, offset by positive Western values. While the Western world retains a disproportionate amount of the world's wealth, it also contains a disproportionate amount of charities (330,000 plus at last count). Our volunteerism and charitable giving for nonprofit causes exceeds all other cultures combined. But one problem in Christian fund-raising is the marriage of Western performance values with biblical mandates. We end up with a kind of Christopaganism which taints our motivation.

It is usually the major donors who get the special attention and private dinners with our organization's president, not the widows who give five dollars faithfully each month out of their social security checks. When was the last time you saw an organization honor a widow who pledged $10 a month? We assign value to people based on the size and frequency of their gifts.

In Christian fund-raising, we *say* relationships are key. But often our definition of what a good relationship is tends to be one-sided. *We send* twelve direct-mail appeals a year. *We send* four to six newsletters. *We send* invitations to special events. *We make* personal phone calls, if giving levels warrant it. *We send* thank-you notes with return envelopes in them, seeking a return gift. Most of what we do in terms of relationship building tends to be on our terms—a means to an end. If we send this appeal or this premium, then the donor will give us some money.

What a contrast to Jesus, who provided healing and guidance so that people would believe and God be glorified. When we enter into a relationship with donors, is it also for their good, so that they will benefit? So that their faith will be strengthened and God will get the glory?

We need a different approach—one that exemplifies God's evenhanded character; one patterned after Christ, who values people for who they *are*, not for what they do.

Here, then, is the radical call for us to rethink our fund-raising relationships. It is a call for proper motivation expressed in proper methodology.

Love must be sincere, hate what is evil, cling to what is good. Be devoted to one another in brotherly love. Honor one another above yourselves.

Rejoice with those who rejoice; mourn with those who mourn. Live in harmony with one another. Do not be proud, but be willing to associate with people of low position. Do not be conceited (Romans 12:9-10, 15-16).

Therefore, as God's chosen people, holy and dearly loved, clothe yourselves with compassion, kindness, humility, gentleness, and patience. Bear with each other and forgive whatever grievances you may have against one another. Forgive as the Lord forgave you. And over all these virtues put on love, which binds them all together in perfect unity (Colossians 3:12-14).

The common themes in these passages are right heart and right action. What brings damage to our personal relationships are the *same* things that bring damage to our relationships with supporters. Failure to be trustworthy, forgiving, transparent, dependable, accessible, or honest will impact negatively on our relationships with donors. Somehow in fund-raising we want to view our relationships with donors as different. How can you have these biblical qualities of relationship with 25,000? It comes back to motivations that please God and actions that show love to His people.

THREE STEPS TOWARD BETTER RELATIONSHIPS
WITH SUPPORTERS

Out of a right heart will come right motivation. Out of right motivation, then, will come right methodology. But right methodology is not easily achieved, even if our hearts and motivations are right. It is easy to say, "Look what we do for you, donors—we give you all of this information. We help you distribute wealth God has given you. We call you. We send you receipts. We even pray for you at our staff meeting. Your gifts will allow us to win the world for Christ by the year 2000. Your gifts allow us to go where you can't and meet these great needs in society."

We have a responsibility to God and people to go deeper than "doing more" for our supporters. What we as fund-raisers do affects people internally. We are either hardening their hearts or eliciting a spirit-directed response. We are encouraging either obedience or disobedience. If we really believe this, we'll take steps to insure that our relationships with supporters are genuine, honest, and respectable, no matter what size gift they give or how often they give it. Here, then, are three significant steps we can take to build lifelong biblical relationships with supporters.

• We need to get out of wrong relationship with some of our supporters. Jesus said that if a hand or foot offends us we should cut it off. This was a graphic call to remove ourselves from *any* relationship which would distract us from serving God fully. Is it possible that we are in some "adulterous" relationships with supporters? What if, through our name-acquisition activities and our manipulative cultivation of supporters, we have actually drawn around us people who, while they occasionally send us checks, are *not* the people God intends to support our organizations?

We excuse 10 percent or less response rates in direct mail as normative. The low response rates could be indicators of wrong relationships instead of "just the way direct mail is." The convoluted support bases in most of our Christian organizations will likely never be sorted out unless we take steps to purge them of the uninvolved and uninterested. We need to do our best to clearly communicate our organization's work and needs—then let God be responsible to lead the ones *He chooses* to support us. This laissez-faire approach could free us to not play Holy Spirit, and actually result in the right people providing Spirit-led gifts in right portions to meet our needs. We need to ask God to send us the right people; we need to give people opportunity to *grow* into their commitment, rather than the heavy-handed "urgent opportunity" approach so characteristic of donor prospecting.

Believing God is in perfect control, we should not fear the consequences of purifying our donor bases. God will surely provide the supporters necessary to do His complete will for our organizations. In keeping with His character, God promises to supply all of our needs so that we may meet the needs of others.

- We need to strengthen our existing relationships. There are many ways to do this. When we send donors multiple appeals each year and bombard them with information, we create one-sided relationships. One-sided communication is not the way to build long-term relationships in fund-raising. How much better to take the time to listen to our supporters through research and small group meetings to determine who they are and what their concerns are for our organization. How much stronger we would be to have their insights on our organization's agenda. Too often, we mainstream people into our appeal system right after a banquet or their first contact with us, never giving them time to build their understanding. Consider the long-term positive impact if, for example, a denomination provided its local churches with a plan to educate visitors and new members as to the vision of the denomination.

It has been clearly proven that people move through certain phases on their way to commitment. As they become aware of us, an understanding is built. Then they become involved with us, and eventually committed. While that process might occur in one evening at a dinner, through a visit to a church, or a mail transaction, the likelihood is that it will take multiple contacts. Some relief agencies have missed this idea by a country mile. Through persuasive and emotional appeals, they gain a surge of one-time donors who eventually fall away after one or two gifts. They go for the quick hit now and pay the results later with high attrition rates and an inability to generate a second gift. We could fault their development strategy. We should fault their relationship strategy.

In our press for more income, we often seek to upgrade people at a rate faster than their commitment allows. Relationships cannot be rushed, and when we try, we pay the consequences of shortened or halfhearted involvement of donors.

- Besides exercising a sense of timing, there are several things we can do to strengthen existing relationships.

—We can honor the giver. Proverbs 24:15 says, "Do not lie in wait like an outlaw against a righteous man's house." God expects us to treat all donors with dignity. Too frequently, badgering appeals which coerce people to give "before the devil grabs the money" or which send people to the post office for unnecessary certified mail only serve to irritate the thoughtful and sensitive supporter.

—We can exercise care as to how the gifts we receive are used.

—We can seek the will of God about our ministries. When we try to extract from our donors the means to expand our ministries faster and beyond what God has led us to do, we can count on strained and broken relationships with people *in step with* God who won't respond to our pressure. Staying in the will of God will prevent this (Proverbs 24:3).

—We can strengthen our relationships with supporters by relating to them *without regard* to how frequently or how much they give. While we should be *responsive* to people who show *any size* of growing commitment to our work, we need to call into question the select treatment of major donors. A notion exists in our work that "well-to-do people expect to be treated differently." Yet, Jesus approached and asked a lifestyle change from the rich young ruler (Mark 10:17-31).

—We can provide personal time for any faithful donor. Why is it that those who give substantially to our organizations get to go fishing with the organization's president? What organization do *you* know that invites *faithful small* donors to the private reception with the guest speaker before a special event? Perhaps a mission organization could encourage its donors—regardless of their gift potential—to go along on a work trip to one of its outreaches. In James 2:1-4 we read,

> Don't show favoritism. Suppose a man comes into your meeting wearing a gold ring and fine clothes, and a poor man in shabby clothes also comes in. If you show special attention to the man wearing fine clothes and say, "Here's a good seat for you" but say to the poor man, "You stand there," or "Sit on the floor by my feet," have you not discriminated among yourselves and become judges with evil thoughts?

• We can strengthen our relationships with supporters by teaching stewardship. There is a difference between a denomination *having* a stewardship department, on the one hand, and aggressively and strategically equipping pastors to teach stewardship principles from the pulpit, on the other. There is an appalling lack of clear biblical teaching on stewardship in our churches today. Usually, if it does get addressed it is just prior to a building campaign. Our supporters need to hear God's truth on stewardship long before a building campaign or when ready to do estate planning. Teaching stewardship should be our primary task as denominations, parachurch organizations, missions, colleges, or consultants. Out of clear biblical teaching on the subject will flow understanding and response.

Jesus once pointed out to the disciples a poor widow who gave two small copper coins worth only a fraction of a penny. "This poor widow has put more into the treasury than all the others. They all gave out of their wealth; but she, out of her poverty put in everything—all she had to live on" (Mark 12:43-44). Her *sacrificial* commitment came from her *deep* understanding of God's economy. We would do a great service to our supporters to challenge them to give sacrificially.

• We can strengthen our relationships by not boring our constituents to death. Have you read your organization's mail lately? Does it give *dynamic* testimony to God's faithfulness and the results of givers' support? Do you report back what happened *after* an appeal and close the loop in the supporters' minds? Do you have an *effective* system for collecting relevant and timely information from the front lines of your ministry? Remember, supporters *want* to see what God is doing, whether it is readily understandable to them or not. We do donors no favors by showing only the victories. We do them even more of a disservice to subject them to lifeless accounts of our ministries.

• We must nurture new relationships differently. People will always move in and out of our personal lives and our organizations. Relationships change. Some become deeper, and others, through changing circumstances or interests, fade away. This is part of the ebb and flow of life. We would do well to accept that the Holy Spirit may lead people at certain times to support *or* cease to support our organization.

When we have opportunity to proactively seek new supporters, how will we do it?

Many denominations today still seek to raise their annual budgets on loyalty which is minimally present in younger constituents and nonexistent in newcomers to their churches. They mainstream new converts with little attention to bringing these new people up to speed. Little wonder many denominations are in fiscal crisis year after year.

The same applies to parachurch organizations as well. Jesus has been nurturing us from the first day we came to Him in faith and repentance. He calls for commitment, at a pace we can handle. This should be our model as well. How much better it would be to begin by educating our supporters; then, at an appropriate time in the future, to inspire and challenge the new supporters. We too often begin with challenging and then move to inspiring and educating. An educated, high-involvement supporter will consistently outlast a low-involvement supporter. Such development of people takes time, but it's worth the wait.

OUR RELATIONSHIPS CAN BE A DWELLING IN WHICH GOD LIVES

The great value of our evangelical organizations is that we provide a way for people to do what is right in the sight of God. We give people opportunities to be involved in God's great agenda of bringing people to Himself and of meeting human needs.

This is a commendable and appropriate agenda which must be protected. We can never deviate from providing a way for people to do what is right. But, in doing that, we must avoid a Christo-paganism which allows for any methodology to go unchecked. We must regularly check our hearts and motivations.

Only God can truly hold us accountable. While our culture says, "Produce, produce, produce," Jesus says, "Love the Lord your God with all your heart and love your neighbor as yourself" (Matthew 12:33). To be obedient, we may need to break off some relationships we have built by manipulative techniques. We may need to strengthen other relationships by getting to know our people—through research, by involving them in decisions, serving them at their point of need, or providing the kind of helpful information about our cause and ministry that they seek. We may need to give people an opportunity to get to know us before we pounce on them for the gift.

Too often organizations have been built on shallow relationships that require an annual infusion of new names and donors to meet the budget and expand. We have a responsibility to ask ourselves if the continuation of this process is detrimental to God's work long-term.

We can rejoice that God has given us a model in Scripture. He did not leave us floundering. We have clear direction for forming healthy relationships. Let us reaffirm our commitment to God's way of doing things. Let us realign our priorities to better match God's evenhanded treatment of people. Let us not be easily swayed by the cultural pressures of productivity, self-sufficiency, and fulfillment. Let us explore new ways to involve people in our ministries. Let us never abandon our vision but let us at the same time be willing to settle for fewer dollars and smaller ministries, if necessary, because we are obedient to Christ. Let us really love people and show it by our actions (1 John 3:18).

God said to Jeremiah, "Call to Me and I will tell you great and unsearchable things you do not know" (33:3). Let us take the long view of our relationships with people. This long view may mean less money short-term. It may mean we cannot fund the expansionary tendencies of our board of directors or our leaders. It may even cost us our jobs to be obedient to Christ. God doesn't want sacrifices of creative management or saving Him money. He asks us for obedience first.

"Consequently, you are no longer foreigners and aliens, but fellow citizens with God's people and members of God's household, built on the foundation of the apostles and prophets, with Christ Jesus Himself as the chief cornerstone. In Him the whole building is joined together and rises to become a holy temple in the Lord. And in Him you too are being built together to become a dwelling in which God lives by His Spirit" (Ephesians 2:19-22).

Our relationships with supporters are the building in which God lives by His spirit. May we honor Christ and His people as we build them.

J. DAVID SCHMIDT started his own consulting firm in 1977. His firm provides marketing, development, and promotional services to Christian organizations across the country. Schmidt travels extensively in the United States and Canada and has completed mission work trips to Latin America, Asia, and Eastern Europe. He is listed in the 1983 and 1984 editions of Who's Who in the Midwest. Schmidt has authored numerous articles as well as five devotional books for teenagers, which have sold more than 160,000 copies.

Mr. Schmidt is a graduate of Wheaton College in Illinois, with an M.A. in cross-cultural communications.

(17)
PRESERVING THE PERSON IN THE FUND-RAISING PROCESS

D. BRUCE LOCKERBIE

It is a difficult task to think and act like Christians in the business of raising money for God's work—whether the cause is foreign missions, relief agencies, radio and television broadcasts, schools, colleges, and seminaries, urban and campus evangelism, or local churches. Christian fund-raisers know the bottom-line reality, that while a ministry must be baptized in prayer, it is fueled by money. Finding a godly standard by which to do both is not easy.

What makes the task so difficult is that, to our knowledge of *technique* in the fund-raising business, we add the biblical warrants that undergird our work. In this respect, we know too much for our ease of conscience. Most of us have become expert exegetes of those texts exhorting the brethren to "give and it will be given to you" (Luke 6:38).

But stuck just below the surface of our consciousness, like an infected sliver, is our realization that our asking often is questionable. The Apostle James accuses some of his readers of not receiving because "you ask with wrong motives, that you may spend what you get on your pleasures" (James 4:3); as the *King James Version* puts it, some of us "ask amiss."

But such has not been our problem, generally speaking. Few evangelical "ministries" could have claimed not to be receiving. The situation most often is that, in spite of the way we ask (even when we "ask amiss"), we still receive, no matter how questionable and unworthy our appeals.

THE ETERNAL VALUE OF PERSONS

Biblical Christianity is committed to the eternal value of persons. Biblical Christianity is unlike other faiths, religious philosophies, or cults, with their doctrines of ultimate assumption of the individual into some ephemeral oversoul or vast unconsciousness or the state supreme. Biblical Christianity teaches that each individual matters personally, now as well as in eternity. Even the Apostle Paul's metaphor of the body of Christ does nothing but enhance the significance of each individual organ, each functioning member (1 Corinthians 12:12-31). Furthermore, in our eternal, heavenly state, though transformed and glorified, we are still assured of our identity, of knowing even as we are also known (13:12).

But if this is orthodoxy for the hereafter, should it not also pertain equally to the here and now, particularly among fellow believers? Thus, in our concern about raising money for ministries, should not donors and potential donors have a status far above the level of opportunistic strategy and fund-raising tactics?

Donors too are persons. Donors are not mere lists of names or segments of a pyramid; donors are not zip codes or LYBNTYs (Last Year But Not This Year) or other acronyms. Donors are not today's mail—a stack of envelopes to be slit, emptied of their contents, programmed into the computer, then discarded. Donors are individual people, each of them precious to God; each of them, therefore, worthy of our respect.

MAKING THE PERSONAL APPEAL TRULY PERSONAL

How well I remember the first time—sometime in the late 1960s—that I received a *Reader's Digest* sweepstakes letter, complete with personal references to my family, place of residence, automobile, and all imbedded throughout the letter. My children were astonished; I was flabbergasted! Such knowledge was too wonderful for me! I immediately subscribed. Today, I'm somewhat less impressed when the Publishers' Clearing House envelope arrives, in spite of all it presumes to know about me and my family.

But I am utterly underwhelmed when I get appeals from some Christian organizations whose direct mail techniques make it clear that I am nothing more to them than a "Dear Occupant," a carrier route sort, or worse: a nameless shot in the dark. I am further distressed when my family name has been misspelled, especially if that identical misspelling turns up on a series of mailing labels sent by a dozen different special pleaders. Some years ago, a Christian agency fired a development officer, who took its mailing list with him and apparently sold it many times over. For years, I had occasion to reflect on his character every time an appeal addressed to Bruce Tockerbie arrived in my mailbox.

But even when my name is spelled correctly, I am outright offended by the crude tactics employed by some allegedly Christian ministries who, in their all-absorbing rush to raise money, demean my personal worth—by which I mean my God-ordained attributes of will, expression, and reason; and my everyday common sense, which I take to be part of God's gift of common grace.

I refer to those charitable institutions specializing in manipulative devices intended to cajole, wheedle, tease, irritate, humiliate, mortify, or paralyze with guilt by their outrageous fund-raising ventures: Promoting relief work by means of horrific photographs of African waifs with sunken eyes and swollen bellies; underlining their text in crayon to attract my special attention; promising me a fragment of their Holy Ghost-induced, sweat-stained shirt; or calling for a semisanctified version of the patently illegal chain-letter scheme.

Then there are the rip-off artists, assuring me, as does the Reverend Roosevelt Franklin, that for just $14, I can receive "Sister Lulu's Prosperity Package."[2] In spite of the opprobrium such revelations bring to the name of Christ, I for one am gratified by the disclosures made by James Randi concerning Peter Popoff's hidden earpiece[3], and by CBS News' Bob Sirott concerning W.V. Grant's prior screening of potential subjects for on-camera "miracles." I regard these painful disclosures as a service to the integrity of Christian evangelism and Christian fund-raising.[4]

Such disclosures remind me of a document in my files from my only appearance on *The PTL Club*, as it was then called. This page on *PTL* letterhead is a release handed to guests for their signature just seconds before being called on the set. There was no time to read carefully and comprehend the implications of what was being signed—or signed away. This release reads:

I hereby grant Heritage Village Church and Missionary Fellowship, Inc., a/k/a/ *PTL* Television Network, a/k/a Jim Bakker, whose headquarters are Charlotte, North Carolina, all rights to use my participation on the *PTL* Club, in part or in full, audio or video, or both.

So far, so good, you might say; merely an official release indemnifying *PTL* from having to pay any residual fee for the taped rerun of a program. But read on:

as well as all monies sent in my behalf to *PTL* in any way that will be useful in promoting the Gospel of Jesus Christ or helpful to the *PTL* Television Network.[5]

I was handed my copy of this release, glanced at it, and said, "You'll have to give me a moment to consider"—then walked onto the set for my interview. The assistant in the green room attempted to retrieve the release form, but I was already being introduced. After the program, nothing was said, and I came home with the form. It has remained in my files until now.

What this form apparently means is that, for years, guests signed this release, then went before the camera and told about the suffering and needy around the world. As a result, viewers were touched to contribute. But when their envelopes arrived in Charlotte, no matter to whom they were addressed, the release entitled *PTL* to claim the funds.

In fairness, I know of one instance in which *PTL* directed the mailing of gifts to a prominent guest's relief agency headquarters—resulting in a blizzard of mail to that local post office—and later also presented a check to the agency president. But that appears to have been an exceptional instance. More often, the formality of a last-moment release, itself a sleazy ruse, made sure that any funds would accrue to *PTL's* coffers.

No matter how seemingly worthy the motive for asking, no matter how allegedly honorable the cause, these unwholesome methods parallel the wiles of Satan the deceiver, first manifest in the Garden. There we find Eve seduced by the serpent's *insinuation* of God's faithlessness, *contradiction* of God's stipulations for obedience, *prevarication* of God's judgment, and *rationalization* of her own willfulness (Genesis 3). But it all takes the form of *equivocation*, the art of saying one thing while meaning quite another. So by "helpful to the *PTL*

Television Network," we now know, the management and board of *PTL* meant something quite other than may have been implied.

Shame on us for not having called them to account far sooner! Shame on us for having allowed ourselves to be manipulated by greedy and carnal profiteers!

Manipulation is one of the ugliest words in our profession. Its definition is "to control or play upon by artful, unfair, or insidious means to one's own advantage." Manipulation is all around us: sensationalism in advertising, negative peer pressure, sexual taunts, guilt trips, spiritual ego boosts. May God forgive us all for imitating the subtleties of Satan in our presumed work for Jesus Christ!

A WORD FROM THE LORD

One of those subtleties has long been the lure of tax deductions as a means of encouraging giving. Of course, I am a realist. I know the inclination of my own heart to ask for and receive the receipt to which I am entitled for presentation to the IRS; furthermore, I defend our right to avail ourselves of all legal and ethical means of avoiding excessive taxation, including favorable interpretation of current legislation and regulations concerning charitable contributions. But in the waning weeks of 1986, and again as the tax law changed at the end of 1987, were we not inundated by nervous fundraisers, warning us that the timing of our gift was critical to our own financial welfare?

How refreshing to receive a letter from Dr. Robert A. Seiple, then president of Eastern College and Eastern Baptist Theological Seminary, framing his appeal for support of those two institutions in biblical integrity rather than expedience! Bob Seiple, now president of World Vision, reminded his readers that "there is a word from the Lord" on all such matters:

> The word from the Lord is not confusion. It is not despair. It is not distraction. It is a call for faithfulness and disciplined obedience. It is a request that we continue to do our part, so that He can bless us beyond our wildest imagination.[6]

Sometimes the significance of the person gets lost even in the worthiest of endeavors. Schools, colleges, and seminaries can be guilty of overlooking the individual in pursuit of his dollars. Some months ago, I received both a letter and a call from an institution with which I have had a certain relationship. Over the course of 30 years, my wife and I have contributed irregularly and never more than a modest $25 or so at a time, perhaps a total of $200 in all. In other words, this college, though worthy of support, has never been a priority recipient of our giving. But the letter suggested a pledge of $3,000; the telephone call, part of a phonathon campaign, introduced me to a pleasant but giddy student who assumed we were on a first-name basis, full of "That's neat!" and "Wow!" enthusiasm. For reasons of sentiment, I agreed to send a check in support of the restoration of the building where I taught my first classes; but that check amounted to little more than 3 percent of the college's expectations.

Why? Mostly because I thought the college's initial approach was both impersonal and absurd in our case. How the sum of $3,000 had been chosen, I have no idea. The numbers themselves did not dismay; what troubled my wife and me was the apparent unconcern on the college's part that we had no history to suggest our willingness to move from our current giving level to the college's suggested level. No one who knew us by name called to encourage us to increase our giving from an occasional $25 to a regular $100 or $250. As John Madden might put it, "Bam!" We got hit with the pitch and that was that.

While I wish to make no odious comparison, my undergraduate university—a secular institution with no pretensions to godly concerns—handled its phonathon in a far more informed and personal manner. The young man on the line introduced himself by full name, rather than the loosey-goosey intimacy and anonymity of the Christian college caller. He knew my giving record since 1956, knew my undergraduate and subsequent graduate school activities, and was able to speak intelligently about ways in which my proposed 1987 gift might be applied to further those interests. Was I impressed? Am I proud to be an alumnus of New York University? Will my contribution reflect this pleasure? Do you think I am unique in my reaction?

GIVING SOMETHING IN RETURN

As professing believers, as representatives of Jesus Christ, as advocates for works of love and grace done in His name, we must be scrupulous in putting persons ahead of programs and projects. We who solicit funds or advise those who do, who quote the apostle in quoting our Lord, "It is more blessed to give than to receive" (Acts 20:35), ought to bear the same words in mind. What are we giving back in return to our donors?

Obviously, the first "give-back" ought to be responsible financial accountability, including appropriate recognition of the contribution by letter of acknowledgment and receipt. Second, the donor should be assured that the gift has been properly disbursed—if designated, to the purpose stated; if undesignated, to some immediate necessity or to the general fund or endowment. Third, if at all possible, a representative whose phase of the work closely benefits from the gift—better still, a scholarship recipient himself, a recovering drug user herself, a Bible translator himself—could be asked to write a note of thanks. To any who might complain that such chores take time from the work being done, I offer this sign from a favorite hometown delicatessen: "Our customers aren't an interruption of our work; our customers are the reason for our work." The same truth can apply to donors.

The best example I know of a Christian ministry practicing what it preaches is very close to me personally. My stepfather, George D. Johnston, is executive vice president of Samaritan's Purse and of World Medical Mission, headquartered in Boone, North Carolina. These agencies, founded by Bob Pierce and now headed by Franklin Graham, translate Christian compassion into deeds of love and mercy through money and service to the world's most visibly needy. But George Johnston knows that we all are needy in some manner, even those among us most able to write a check for a large contribution.

So, he makes it his custom to telephone contributors and, after thanking them for their gift, ask what Samaritan's Purse can do for them. I am certain that most of those receiving such a call must be thunderstruck! Imagine, a caller asking what he can give rather than get! The request is usually for prayer concerning some personal need, and George Johnston is able to assure the donor that, at the daily prayer meeting in Boone, someone in the office will pray by name for the donor's need.

A second instance from the same organization. Recently, the board of directors of Samaritan's Purse and World Medical Mission received an unusual report. Rather than the typical balance sheet, the directors were handed a "Humanity Report," the cover page of which bore this quotation by Chuck Swindoll: "Others will not care how much we know until they know how much we care." The report contains a synopsis of several cases of remarkable donor participation: a 99-year-old woman who has literally given all she has to others, a group of orphans in Jamaica who have given generously, and so on. The report also shows how the office staff participates in preserving the personal touch in this exchange of giving and receiving. Yes, statistics are important and necessary, but not to the exclusion of the personal dimension.

May I also add a word about the difference between *giving* and *trading?* In our particular work with Christian schools, Stewardship Consulting Services often find earnest fund-raisers who depend mostly upon transactions rather than donations, trading rather than giving. The auction for raising scholarship money, the celebrity golf tournament, the magazine subscription campaign, the senior class carwash—all these are instances of trading goods and services for income. They do not represent giving.

Constituents of schools relying on such methods often complain of the unending stream of fund-raising gimmicks—what one father called "the Chinese water torture method of raising money." We counsel our clients that it is more blessed to give than to trade! And the same is true of trinkets and fancy premiums given to donors. Let their gifts speak for themselves, and let the recipient beware of trivializing that gift with either a cheap or gaudy token of thanks.

One of the principal biblical texts about giving is 2 Corinthians 9, in which Paul compares donations to seed.

Now he who supplies seed to the sower and bread for food will also supply and increase your store of seed and will enlarge the harvest of your righteousness. You will be made rich in every way so that you can be generous on every occasion, and through us your generosity will result in thanksgiving to God (vv. 10-11).

In this analogy, the Corinthians are promised what they need: seed and crops for their present sustenance and for a future harvest. From that very harvest comes the wherewithal to increase their generosity. Unlike the rich and foolish farmer of Jesus' parable (Luke 12:13-21), the Corinthians are not to expect luxury; their bumper crop is to enable them to "be generous on every occasion." Their generosity, transmitted by Paul to those needy Christians in Jerusalem, will bring the Corinthians the joy of "thanksgiving to God."

In the end, all we can offer those whom we motivate to give to God's work is the promise that others will thank and praise God because of generous and unstinting giving. Thus, the holiness of God and the authority of the biblical record and promise will be upheld. For the glory of God must be the highest priority in preserving the integrity of personhood in Christian fund-raising.

D. BRUCE LOCKERBIE is an educator, author, lecturer, and consultant. Since 1957, he has been at The Stony Brook School, Stony Brook, New York, where he is now Staley Foundation Scholar in Residence. Author and editor of three dozen books, Lockerbie is also a frequent speaker at colleges and seminaries. He is president of Stewardship Consulting Services, an agency working with educational institutions on fund-raising, administrative placement, and faculty development.

A former world-class runner, Mr. Lockerbie now concentrates on improving his golf game. He and his wife, Lory, have three grown children and have entered the era of grandparenthood.

(18)
A WITNESSING/WORK PERSPECTIVE ON FUND-RAISING: THE ZACCHAEUS FACTOR

R. WAYNE CLUGSTON

"Zacchaeus is a son of Abraham too!"

These words are Jesus' final comment about Zacchaeus in Luke 19. They reveal his motives in initiating contact with an unbeliever who became a major donor. And, more than that, found salvation! To bring this change about, Jesus made a "hospitality covenant" with Zacchaeus. It was simple enough: a relational covenant that inspired Zacchaeus to discover the joys and rewards of charity, of genuine relationships, of giving. It introduced a notorious tax collector to new life.

Every Christian fund-raiser knows several individuals who are counterparts of Zacchaeus. Perhaps they are not tax collectors *per se*, but they are known for their financial connections and their indifference to Christianity. Even disdain, perhaps. All too frequently such individuals are neglected by Christian fund-raisers because they are thought to be unapproachable, or because contact with them would be easily misunderstood or perceived as presumptuous.

Questions abound: Should an organization whose mission is Christian accept a major contribution from an unbeliever? On what basis could such a person be motivated to give? Is it possible to expect a genuine relationship to develop? Does it not seem almost certain that the relationship between a Christian fund-raiser and a known unbeliever will be viewed by both as suspect and opportunistic?

Confronted by the risks which these questions represent, the Christian fund-raiser can readily write off the unbeliever as a prospect for giving and for the Gospel. Neglected in such reasoning is the Zacchaeus factor—the fact that "they too are sons of Abraham." This chapter discusses witnessing as an integral part of the Christian fund-raiser's work. Specifically, it explores the nature of a work/witnessing relationship that can be established between a Christian fund-raiser and an unbeliever.

HAVING A WORK/WITNESSING PLAN

Jesus' encounter with Zacchaeus is used as a model in identifying the elements required to make such a relationship effective. His pattern in dealing with Zacchaeus begins with hospitality, moves on to love, and ends in joy. As He unfolds this pattern, His work as teacher and His witness as Lord are beautifully and purposefully integrated. They are one. Thus, His encounter with Zacchaeus is a perfect paradigm for the fund-raiser to use in approaching unbelievers. It shows how witnessing can be incorporated into the work of Christian fund-raising.

It is easy to fall into the trap of seeing witness and work as separate. Work and witness, far from being dichotomous entities, are best understood when they are given shape by human experience rather than by technical definition. An individual's unique personal experience with another can unlock the holistic potential that work and witness hold. This is the basic insight to be gained from Luke's account of the encounter between Jesus and Zacchaeus. It is an essential insight for Christian fund-raisers to grasp and use in initiating relationships with unbelievers.

In approaching unbelievers, then, it is not enough for a Christian fund-raiser to have a work plan; an integrated witnessing plan is also required. Developing an effective witnessing plan is tough because relationship-building where fund-raising is potentially involved is tough, especially when it extends beyond the community of believers. The key to making such relationships productive—the Zacchaeus factor—lies in understanding several paradoxes: the paradox of hospitality, the paradox of love, and the paradox of joy.

Outlined, the Christian fund-raiser's witnessing plan for building relationships with unbelievers looks like this:

• Stage I Relationships—Understanding the paradox of hospitality

- Focusing on caring—seeing hospitality as an expense
- Focusing on celebration—seeing hospitality as a credit
- Stage II Relationships—Understanding the paradox of love
  - Recognizing disobedience—seeing love as a principle of loss
  - Recognizing obedience—seeing love as a principle of gain
- Stage III Relationships—Understanding the paradox of joy
  - Finding faith—seeing joy as risk
  - Finding hope—seeing joy as a bottom-line security

These relationships are developmental, and of course continually dependent on the power of prayer and the work of the Holy Spirit. The Stage I relationship grows as an understanding of the paradox of hospitality is grasped by both individuals. The caring initially shown by the initiator of the relationship is costly, but eventually it can lead to celebration. When it does, it moves from being an expense to being a credit as the receiver of the hospitality—the unbeliever—begins to understand its cost and is able to return caring. In Stage II the loss-gain paradox is pushed to a higher level. The relationship moves from the microcosm of human hospitality to the macrocosm of divine love. When the unbeliever is able to see that God's love swallows up disobedience, he or she has discovered a basis for believing—and for a new relationship. The Stage III relationship is one of joy, unbounded at first as the risk of faith is experienced, but becoming steadily more poignant and focused as the security of hope is known.

Each of these stages is explored more fully in the remainder of this chapter. Specific strategies are included in the discussion of Stage II, since it is the stage which leads to transformation and is the most demanding. In the concluding section, Jesus' use of the Zacchaeus factor is analyzed and implications for the Christian fund-raiser are summarized.

THE PARADOX OF HOSPITALITY

Hospitality as practiced by Jesus in the Gospels requires covenant relationships, not casual relationships. It involves initial caring, of course, but it goes far beyond the level of initial courtesy and concern. The hospitality Jesus extended to unbelievers involved celebration, thus illustrating the paradoxical tension that every Christian witnessing plan must deal with. Jesus' actions showed that He was not only willing to eat lunch with Zacchaeus, He was also prepared to enjoy His luncheon meeting. He was genuinely prepared to celebrate.

The hospitality covenant is difficult to practice. Jesus stressed this fact again and again, and illustrated it most memorably in the story of the prodigal son. At the end of that story the father demonstrates the hospitality covenant beautifully and fully. He cares for his son by welcoming him with a big hug, and then proceeds to celebrate by arranging a feast. The elder brother, on the other hand, struggles with the paradox of hospitality. He seems to care enough to accept the brother's return, but he cannot celebrate.

The initial goal of the Christian fund-raiser's work/witnessing plan is to establish a hospitality covenant with the unbeliever. If it is genuine, both people involved in the relationship will come to see hospitality as an expense and as a credit. As an expense for the Christian fund-raiser, the hospitality covenant with an unbeliever will require time and may involve tolerating harsh language (often purposely exaggerated), sitting at a meal where alcoholic drinks are served, and listening to criticism of Christian organizations. On the other hand, the hospitality covenant is an expense for the unbeliever too. It costs time; it can involve dealing with criticism of personal lifestyle and values; and it can become a guilt trip.

An individual who has millions in assets is likely to have a different interior map of the world than the fund-raiser who is interested in having some of those assets become a charitable contribution. The point is not that the person of finance knows more, necessarily, but that he or she thinks differently.

For this reason, the hospitality covenant cannot be neatly packaged. It requires more than following a set of prearranged steps. Hospitality, if it is to be genuine, must be entered into holistically. It is a relationship of wholeness or it is nothing. Feelings, intellectual perspectives, failures, successes, idiosyncracies, reputation, the intent to ask for a gift, fears, frustrations, the desire to share the Gospel—all have to be acknowledged as legitimate aspects of the hospitality practiced by the Christian fund-raiser. All are part of the Christian fund-raiser's witnessing/work perspective.

Intimacy is a primary goal of the hospitality covenant. Before it can be achieved in a relationship between a Christian fund-raiser and an unbeliever, the Christian will have to be able to deal with difference. Parker Palmer's insight in his book, *The Company of Strangers*, offers an important consideration and guide in this matter: "The essence of hospitality—and of the public life—is that we let our differences, our mutual strangeness, be as they are, while still acknowledging the unity that lies beneath them."[1] He goes on to caution against the tendency to distinguish ourselves by putting down someone else and pointing out that the natural differences between people should become cause for celebration.

Eating together, focusing attention on the other individual in the relationship, listening, being open and public in building the relationship, showing confidence (by ignoring the criticism that comes from others)—all the things Jesus did in practicing the hospitality covenant with Zacchaeus—are important success factors. Possibly, though, the sharing of a meal is most significant. It is both a symbol and a ritual.

Sharing a meal, Jesus taught, symbolizes unity and love. Thus, in His story about the prodigal son, Jesus pointed out that the elder brother, who was out of harmony with his father and brother, could not feast with them. He describes heaven's undivided joy in terms of a marriage feast.

Sharing a meal is also a ritual, a ritual which brings daily renewal and appreciation (whether it is articulated or not) of life and provision. When Jesus, after His resurrection, instructed Peter to "feed My sheep," He was reminding him of ritual as well as symbol. He was not only saying, "Share the Bread of Life" with others, He was saying, "Keep on eating with my people." He was encouraging Peter, first of all, to do what he was able to do in his own strength: to continue the ritual of hospitality. He was also challenging him to do what the Holy Spirit would help him do: to share the presence of Christ as Saviour in the symbol of the hospitality covenant.

A final point. The Christian's primary contribution to the hospitality covenant should focus on spiritual principles. This lesson was taught to me beautifully by the person who hospitably guided me to a knowledge of Christ. He was also my college literature professor and, though he knew the content of Western literature and the content of the Bible thoroughly, he attracted me to them by the principles of his life and witness.

The key to making hospitality work, to making it a covenant relationship, is getting beyond the expense level. It is seeing hospitality as a credit. It is being willing to celebrate the potential that the relationship holds. When this point is reached, the relationship will begin to be driven by creativity, risk, and the unexpected. Growth will occur, and the focus of the work/witnessing relationship will move from Level I concerns involving the paradox of hospitality to the challenges of Level II involving the paradox of love.

THE PARADOX OF LOVE

At Level 1, the witnessing/work plan moves the unbeliever from seeing hospitality as an expense to seeing it as a credit. Similarly, at Level II in the Christian fund-raiser's relationship with the unbeliever the movement is from the loss to the gain side of the ledger. At this point in the relationship the Christian fund-raiser's goal is to make the Gospel clear—to reveal the good news about love.

Divine love is paradoxical in that it demands complete obedience, but at the same time is able to forgive and look beyond disobedience. To begin to understand Christ, love incarnate, it is necessary to see disobedience (self-will) as a principle of loss and to see obedience (submission to the grace of God) as a principle of gain. It is not often that such principles can be effectively "preached" by the Christian fund-raiser, but they can be made apparent through mentoring and teaching.

Laurent Daloz's recent book, *Effective Teaching and Mentoring,* explores the nature of adult development and learning. In an exquisite style, Daloz combines case studies and developmental learning theory with story and biblical perspective. He concludes that teaching and mentoring require, most of all, "a special kind of relationship, a caring stance" in the changing circumstances of another person's life. He insists that the critical question for the relationship-builder is not "What do I know?" but "What is my place in the growth of the person I care for?"[2]

Two key strategies that define the mentor's place and help to focus a relationship on the paradox of love are the strategies of support and challenge. Support gives a relationship boundaries and is expressed through encouragement, accurate listening, and honest self-disclosure. When it is offered openly by the initiator of the relationship, support produces trust and truthfulness. Parker Palmer has observed that support-building activities on the part of a teacher/mentor create "a spirituality of education." To teach, says Palmer, "is to create a space in which obedience to truth is practiced."' He points out that it is not empty space, but neither is it space that is filled with the sounds of authority. It offers both silence and language. It is characterized by hospitable openness.

• Just as support provides space for a relationship to be, challenge pushes it toward becoming. The Christian fund-raiser is likely to be quite adept at using challenge to get an individual to consider a gift, but the potential donor must give equal attention to using relationship-building, to cause the fund-raiser to think afresh.

Daloz offers several key strategies that a mentor can use to challenge growth within a relationship: setting tasks, engaging in discussion, heating up dichotomies, constructing hypotheses, and setting high standards. Each of these can be a stimulator of growth. They are effective because they create a gap between perception and expectation. That is, they force the individuals in the relationship to know and to be known.

Jesus, the divine mentor, used this tension as a relationship-builder often, in contacts with unbelievers and believers. An impressive example is recorded in Mark 6, where Jesus builds group perception and then tests it with high expectation. He sends the disciples out two by two to heal, giving them authority for the task. They return with outstanding reports of victories in the name of Christ. Then, following this experience, they are with Jesus on the mountainside and face a crowd of 5,000 people. When the disciples point out the need for food, Jesus says to them, "You give them something to eat" (v. 37). It is too high an expectation for them—even though they have access to sufficient power to act in the situation; otherwise, Jesus would not say what He does. Although Jesus has to step in and show them, He continues to hold high expectations for His disciples.

When the crowd is gone, Jesus sends the disciples across the lake and goes to a quiet place to pray. Leaving the mountain in the early morning hours, He walks across the lake. Verse 49 describes the expectation He holds for His disciples as He goes. It indicates that He thought they could handle the task of getting across the lake: "He intended to pass them by." But seeing them in trouble, and being a mentor with limitless love, He does not pass them by. He stops to encourage, to help, to give assurance, to say, "It is I."

Jesus' modeling of the perception-expectation tension is helpful for the Christian who is building a relationship with an unbeliever. There comes a point where the hospitality, shared genuinely at Level I of the relationship, must be tested. Hospitality not only creates an environment of support, but it allows challenge to occur in a relationship. Challenge should not be avoided. Indeed, it cannot be avoided in Level II relationship development, because the goal for such encounters is to confront the paradox of God's love.

In a relationship initiated by a Christian fund-raiser with an unbelieving prospective donor, financial matters should not be avoided. Profit and loss concerns, for example, are common denominators in such a relationship and can be explored on several levels. The obvious level involves conversations dealing with quarterly reports, interest rates, Dow Jones stock averages, and the like. But the Christian mentor is always looking for opportunities for higher level discussion in which perception (and belief) can be tested and expectation set.

• Here is one approach that a Christian fund-raiser might use with an unbeliever at this more imaginative level of conversation. It is an approach that takes the familiar human concept of loss, something every person with financial status recognizes, and then uses it metaphorically to prove an understanding of the spiritual concept of love.

Material for a Mentor's Observations

In the beginning, there was a complete world, a world of obedience—where evenings provided space for human creatures to walk with their Creator. But ever since disobedience occurred, there has been a great falling away. When Eden was lost, there was both spatial and spiritual loss.

Spatial loss, not to be understood merely as lost real estate, includes a diminishing of the necessary, nurturing environment that "I-Thou" relationships require. Alien in the vastness of the lost garden, mankind has not since been able to find, nor has culture been able to create, space equivalent to the holy ground of the Garden. As literary critic Northrup Frye observes in his book, *The Great Code*, the area of sacred space shrinks as the biblical story unfolds:

The Garden of Eden was a complete world, a society without crowding and of solitude without loneliness. Abraham's Promised Land was much smaller but still spacious enough for a pastoral economy; Joshua's Promised Land was smaller still. The division of the kingdom and the conquests that followed cut the sacred space down to Judah, then Jerusalem, then the temple, and finally to the holy of holies within the temple. With the sacrilege of Antiochus, the last vestige of sacred space disappears.[4]

Such an insight can bring the purpose of Level II relationship-building into clear focus. It can provide a basis for grasping the significance of Jesus' obedience and love. As Messiah, He was a wanderer with no place to lay His head. As Saviour, He was continually "creating space": making a place for the lost sheep, standing at the door knocking, taking a towel, ripping the curtained veil with resurrection power!

When Jesus' obedience as the Christ is understood, the love of God is seen as gain—as an invitation to a relationship where grace, freedom, and new life are possible. The paradox of love has been penetrated!

THE PARADOX OF JOY

Often the unbeliever will make a gift when the relationship with the Christian fund-raiser becomes well developed at Level II. While it is not ever possible to fully explain why an individual chooses to make a gift to a Christian organization, the person motivated by a Level II relationship with a Christian fund-raiser usually gives out of a sense of joy. Such giving is an indication that the fund-raiser/donor relationship is entering Level III, where the paradox of joy is explored and shared.

In this stage, the unbeliever risks everything to find faith and finds much more—the bottom-line security of an eternal hope in Christ. It is the culmination of a journey involving witness and work which the Christian mentor and the one he or she has come to care for have made together. As is always true with journeys, there has been a sense of direction, a change of perspective, and a transformation. This journey has ended in the "I-Thou" relationship, allowing the journeyer to find, in Martin Buber's words, "something more in his being, something new has grown there of which he did not know

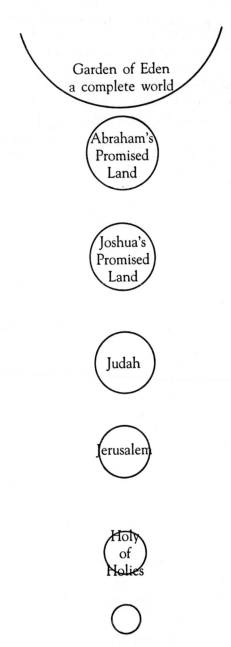

Garden of Eden
a complete world

Abraham's
Promised
Land

Joshua's
Promised
Land

Judah

Jerusalem

Holy
of
Holies

"The Son of Man had
no place to lay His head."

before and for whose origin he lacks any suitable words. . . . Man receives, and what he receives is not content but a presence."[5]

Howard Lowry, a former president of The College of Wooster in Ohio, often told his students about a journey he made into the Carter County caves in Kentucky when he was 14. Traveling with a guide and a few friends, far back in one of the caves he turned a corner and the light from his lantern flashed on a wall containing the names of people who had been there earlier. Among the names, to Howard Lowry's surprise, was his own father's name—carved there many years before.

Relationship-building for the Christian fund-raiser is like journeying into a cave. When the relationship is with an unbeliever, the Christian fund-raiser functions as a mentor, an equipper, a teacher/guide—putting a light into the hand of the other person in the relationship. Work and witness are integrated as the two individuals journey together. They grow and change and seek until, at some turning, there is a transformation: the discovery of the Heavenly Father's name and an acceptance of His eternal love.

Beyond such a turning in the Level III development, joy remains a common bond in the fund-raiser/donor relationship, nurturing a mature respect between two individuals who are not both believers. And the continuing surprise, a major reward of the Zacchaeus factor, is the extent to which joy shapes the Christian's perspective for giving.

This brief analytical outline of Jesus' visit to Jericho, as recorded in Luke 19, illustrates how Jesus built an effective relationship with Zacchaeus. It identifies Jesus' actions and suggests implications which His actions hold for the Christian fund-raiser in developing a witnessing/work perspective which incorporates Jesus' commitment to the Zacchaeus factor.

Scripture	Jesus' Actions	Implications for Christian Fund-raiser
Level I Relationships: Understanding the Paradox of Hospitality		
Crowds came	• His mission was known • Was publicly involved • Projected excitement • Took a positive approach	• Have mission statement • Participate in your community • Be creative/high quality • Be defined by "image," not "stereotype"

218

Zacchaeus hides expectantly	• Was empathetic toward Zacchaeus (probably his sense of alienation, not his short stature, drove him up a tree)	• Be sensitive
"I must stay with you today."	• Made an appointment for lunch	• Be direct
"He has gone to be the guest of a sinner."	• Ignored disapproval of others	• Be confident

Level II Relationships—Understanding the Paradox of Love

"Salvation has come to this house today."	• Jesus gave the gift of love • Zacchaeus accepted the gift of love	• Share the revelation of Christ • Expect a miracle

Level III Relationships—Understanding the Paradox of Joy

"I will give half of my possessions to the poor."	• Zacchaeus finds joy in giving	• Celebrate!
"He too is a son of Abraham."	• Jesus praises Zacchaeus as continuing symbol of hope	

R. WAYNE CLUGSTON has held fund-raising and academic leadership respon-sibilities in Christian higher education for the past fifteen years. Most recently, he served as vice president for academic affairs at Spring Arbor College, Michigan. He has an Ed.D. degree from Seattle University.

Currently, Dr. Clugston is president of Lifelearning and Leadership Institute, Inc., Seattle, Washington, a nationally based educational consulting organization with special expertise in adult learning and curriculum delivery.

(19)
GEORGE MUELLER AND THE
QUEST FOR BIBLICAL BALANCE
IN FUND-RAISING

JAMES C. KILLION

When evangelicals think about fund-raising, they are indebted to George Mueller for having planted many of the philosophical roots that give flower to their thoughts. In fact, one is hard-pressed to find anyone more influential than Mueller, although a worthy companion to Mueller will be introduced later in this chapter.

Church history professors are fond of describing Mueller as a godly man who built and ran orphanages in nineteenth-century England by prayer alone. He never, they say, asked for money or did any of the things one sees in fund-raising today. George Mueller's orphanages had their needs met simply through his intense prayer and life of exemplary faith.

Is that true? Did that really happen just a century ago, far from the biblical land of miracles?

What did George Mueller really do, why did he do it, and how did he do it? Certainly that simple description tucked away in history students' minds is an awesome one. Could it be?

WHO WAS GEORGE MUELLER?

The George Mueller of orphanage fame was a very respectable man, a very cultured man, and a brilliant man. He spoke and wrote and read several foreign languages, spent hours every day studying his Bible—in both the original Greek and Hebrew. At one point it was said that his library consisted of a Hebrew Old Testament, a Greek

New Testament, the best translations available to him, and some lexicons. He claimed no contemporary books on his shelves, for this remarkable man spent his time focused on his work, the study of the Scriptures themselves, and in prayer. He casts an awesome spiritual shadow.

George Mueller was born in 1805 in Prussia (now a part of East Germany) into a family of modest wealth. His father was a tax collector and government official, so George grew up in a home where vast amounts of cash were kept. In fact, by the time he was ten, he was frequently stealing money from his father's tax collections.[1] After those tainted early days, Mueller went into a period of his life that he describes as "days in much sin."[2]

"DAYS IN MUCH SIN"

George Mueller's self-described "days in much sin" began when he was 11 years old and was sent off to school to prepare for the ministry, the career his father planned for him.

In those days the fire from the Lutheran Reformation was dying, and the clergy and the state church were a moneyed, comfortable, and not necessarily spiritual group. George later said that his father wanted him to prepare for ministry because of the comfortable, professional future the ministry would afford.[3]

Things did not go well in his clerical education. He drank heavily, partied, and lived beyond his means. In fact, if you changed the dates and the places, Mueller's lifestyle would sound very much like the drink and drug excesses of today.

When Mueller was just turning 15, he went through the formal time of confirmation. In that process, it was traditional to bring a special offering for the benefit of the church which had provided the ecclesiastical training. George Mueller spent eleven-twelfths of what his father had given him for that offering on a wild, drunken party the night before.[4] The next day Mueller reported to the head cleric with his small offering, saying that it was all his father had sent him. In later years Mueller felt very guilty about his youthful dishonesty, but at the time his conscience seemed not to bother him.[5]

He went on to the university, continued to study for the ministry, and yet had no personal faith. It was a remarkable era in his life. He even did something that once again seems more contemporary;

Mueller records a period in his life where for many days, even a week at a time, he'd go from hotel to hotel, skipping out on his bill after having lived very opulently.⁶

"HE BEGAN A WORK OF GRACE IN ME"

On a Saturday night in November 1825, Mueller went with a former drinking friend to what seems to have been an Anabaptist prayer meeting. There, for the first time in his life, he actually saw people get down on their knees and pray as though they expected there was a God who would hear.⁷

In those days in Germany, it was illegal to preach or read the Bible in public unless you were a clergyman. That group he met with on a crisp November night in 1825 did it anyway. And in that warm, intimate context of fellowship, the Lord began to perform a work of grace in him.

George Mueller did not put his faith in Christ at that meeting, but what started that night, over the next few weeks resulted in personal faith. George Mueller became a changed man, a devout Christian whose perspective was very different from what it had been.

Mueller thought about missionary work after his conversion. And for a time he thought he would go to Bucharest to work among the Jewish people. But a war blocked that move. Then an opportunity arose to go to London.

TO LONDON FOR MISSIONARY WORK

In 1829 George Mueller went to London to do Jewish evangelism, but he became very ill after being in London only six weeks, and was convinced he was going to die. By then Mueller was a great believer in prayer, and so he prayed a lot, expecting soon to be with his Saviour.⁸ He was a new Christian with a tainted past, and he now seemed to be looking for deliverance from this sinful world.

Yet the Lord spared his life, and Mueller spent the summer recuperating in the English countryside. He returned to London, worked for another few months among the Jewish people and then decided that he couldn't work for any man or organization, and that he must work only for the Lord Himself. Mueller reasoned that "a servant of Christ has but one Master."⁹ So he resigned from his mission work among the Jewish people and began looking about for a more permanent ministry. He did some preaching, and on a split congregational vote, ended up pastoring a small congregation in Teignmouth, England. That was in 1830, and Mueller was still only 25.

THE EARLY YEARS IN BRISTOL

In 1832 George Mueller went to Bristol, England where he was to forge a lifetime of ministry. His first work in Bristol was as pastor of a church that funded its expenses with a pew tax. Mueller did not like that system, so instead he installed a box at the back of the church. He said that if the congregation was blessed by his ministry, they should leave something there for his living expenses. They more than made up the money that was lost in the pew tax. In fact, the church had more income that year than in any previous year.

Interestingly, most of the money that found its way into the box did not come from members of that church, but from wealthy relatives and friends of Mueller who knew of his work and his convictions.

THE SCRIPTURAL KNOWLEDGE INSTITUTION

In 1834, Mueller decided to start his own ministry. He called it the Scriptural Knowledge Institution for Home and Abroad. Its stated purpose was to promote the Gospel both in England and around the world.[10]

For two years Mueller did not ask for money, but simply spoke to churches about his ministry. He apparently never made needs known. Instead, he spoke and wrote prolifically about needs that were met in days past and about the trials he had faced until those needs were met. But he refrained from discussion of current, unmet needs.

How consistent was he with that policy? Very! A wealthy person wrote him at one point in this period in his life and said that he had heard of Mueller's work and was burdened for it. He went on to write that since he was inquiring of Mueller—and not being solicited by Mueller—certainly Mueller would be willing to reveal his financial need. Mueller wrote back, saying, in essence: "Yes, I mind. If I tell you, I could be manipulative; you might feel guilt; you might feel

something to give to my need, and so it wouldn't be a gift from God."[11]

The man sent 100 pounds anyway which, he later revealed to Mueller, was what he was intending to send no matter what Mueller's answer had been. Mueller took these kinds of interchanges as clear answers to his prayers.

For two years the Scriptural Knowledge Institution for Home and Abroad wallowed without a ministry focus. It had some income, but not much. (Mueller always did keep a separate fund for himself as opposed to his ministry; he lived fairly comfortably throughout his entire life and apparently never comingled the funds.)

When Mueller discovered the plight of English orphans, he began work on an orphanage which would become one of the main arms of his Scriptural Knowledge Institution.

• The first Mueller orphanage. After collecting funds for about six months, Mueller opened the first orphanage in 1836. At that point he rented quarters on Wilson Street in Bristol. The space was cheap, fairly large, and well located. Right next to the door of the orphanage he placed a box. People in the town would come by and put in money as they heard of his work and felt responsive to the need. Mueller tells us:

> It is quite true that my heart was affected by the deplorable physical condition in which I saw destitute Orphans before I began to care for them; but a higher motive by far actuated me than merely seeking to benefit their health. . . . It is further true, that I had a desire to benefit the Orphans by seeking to educate them; but I aimed at far more than this. . . . Further, when I began the Orphan Work, I aimed at the salvation of the children. . . . Yet even this was not the primary object I had in view; but in carrying on this work, simply through the instrumentality of prayer and faith, without applying to any human being for help, my great desire was that it might be seen that now, in the nineteenth century, God is still the *living* God, and that now, as well as thousands of years ago, He listens to the prayers of His children and helps those who trust in Him."[12]

In reality, George Mueller did something that we are often critical of today. That is, he started his ministry, began raising money, and then found a cause—the orphans. The early years were not good years for the orphans or for George Mueller.

• Times of trial. Here are some entries from George Mueller's diary:

Aug. 18	I have not one penny in hand for the Orphans. . . . Before the day is over, I have received from a sister five pounds.
Aug. 31	I have been waiting on the Lord for means, as the matron's books from the Girls' Orphan House have been bought, and there is no money in hand to advance for housekeeping. But as yet the Lord has not been pleased to send help.
Sept. 5	I am still penniless. My hope is in God; He will provide.
Sept. 8	It has not pleased my Gracious Lord to send me help as yet.
Sept. 10	Monday morning. Neither Saturday nor yesterday had any money come in. It appeared to me now needful to take some steps on account of our need.
Sept. 11	The good Lord in His wisdom still sees it useful to keep us very low.¹³

The dire financial straits continued for a couple of years. George Mueller prayed. No one believed more than Mueller that God would supply. Yet poverty and misery prevailed at the orphanage for years. Slowly things did change. And the growth of Mueller's ministry that his legend is made of followed. What changed?

YEARS OF EXPANDING INFLUENCE

Through George Mueller's "Occasional Papers," "Narratives," plus other printed reports and extensive speaking tours, people increasingly heard about the work he was doing in his Bristol orphanages.

• Publications and speaking tours. George Mueller went on 17 world tours, traveled over 200,000 miles in the days of sailing ships, and visited 42 countries telling the story of his orphanages in Bristol. He continued to pray; he did remain true to his statements that he would not overtly solicit funds; he would not announce needs beforehand; he would not resort to any kind of traditional appeal. He instead wrote and spoke of God's past provision. He faithfully reported to his donors through his published books, through his published testimonies, and through his speaking engagements. He protested angrily when someone suggested it was those means that were alerting people to the need and motivating current income.

• A righteous cause to champion. One must understand that George Mueller was defending God. He was single-handedly attempting to answer the critic who said, "God is not active in our world like He was in the days of the Old and New Testament heroes of the faith."

Was Mueller's ministry supported solely by prayer? Was it a supernatural work of God? There is no simple answer.

• God's grace and man's responsibility. Believers have the tremendous power of prayer available to them, and God hears and answers the prayers of His children. But one cannot demand that God answer, and one cannot necessarily define when and how He has answered. God will do what He will graciously do. On the other hand, how many times do Christians have not because they ask not?

No matter how one evaluates George Mueller, one cannot say that those orphanages ever lacked for funds because he did not ask of the Lord. Balance, hard fought balance, is the Christian's goal.

• The growth of the orphanages in Bristol. By the turn of the century, Mueller's orphanages were five new homes in the countryside. They housed hundreds and hundreds of children. His concept worked.

Since Mueller believed in the work ethic, all of the orphans had a job; some girls blacked boots, others worked in the laundry. All of them learned to sew. All of the girls learned how to manage a household. The boys worked in the fields.

The orphanages in Bristol were a monument to George Mueller's vision and hardworking faith.

NOTEWORTHY FOLLOWERS OF MUELLER'S PRINCIPLES
What about those who followed George Mueller? The concept of "faith giving" didn't stop with Mueller. Perhaps his legend is the greatest, but there are others who followed who also had a very significant influence.

● Hudson Taylor and the China Inland Mission. J. Hudson Taylor and the China Inland Mission are the most noteworthy. In 1865 Taylor, a self-espoused disciple of George Mueller, began the China Inland Mission. In fact, it was the Scriptural Knowledge Institution for Home and Abroad that helped fund the first group of missionaries that Hudson Taylor took with him to China.

Just as George Mueller grew up with a value system and an ambivalence (and, I believe, great psychological anguish) over money based on his youthful stealing, Hudson Taylor also had problems with money. He came from a very wealthy London family and struggled tremendously with the compatibility of wealth and servanthood to Jesus Christ.

Hudson Taylor's struggle over money is perhaps best seen during his years of preparation to be a physician. At one point he was near starvation and would not remind the absentminded doctor who was teaching him medicine that he hadn't paid him in weeks. A good Christian didn't ask for money; he depended on God's provision!

Hudson Taylor did a great work in China. The stories one hears today of what's happened to the church in China despite Communist persecution is in no small part a reflection of the intense discipleship of Hudson Taylor and the CIM missionaries a century ago.

Taylor and the China Inland Mission coined the phrase, "full information, no solicitation." What did they do? They weren't quite as restrictive as Mueller, for if you asked Hudson Taylor what his needs were, he would tell you.

The CIM published a gorgeous magazine, *China's Millions*. In fact, this magazine was every bit as good as the top secular magazines of its day. There, once a month in incredible fidelity, were pictures from halfway around the world from mysterious China.

If you gave to the China Inland Mission, your donation was recorded and published in a book at the end of the year. Like Mueller, CIM used the communication vehicles of its day to talk about the work God was doing.

Did CIM solicit funds? Not in conventional ways. Did they get the message out? Yes. Did they use the best tools of their day? Yes. Is that manipulative? No. But it's not going into a closet and shutting the door to pray, never to mention finances.

● Amy Carmichael. Amy Carmichael, the well-known hymn writer, had a mission in India. She felt allegiance to both George

Mueller and Hudson Taylor, and took Mueller and Taylor to their ultimate theological and philosophical conclusion—mysticism.

GEORGE MUELLER'S WORLDVIEW

If one pursues George Mueller's thinking far enough, mysticism is the inevitable terminus. Mueller, Taylor, and Carmichael built a system of belief and action based not just on their faith in God, but on a view of the world which sees a great conflict between money and ministry.

• The two-story world. George Mueller's worldview which led to his starting of the orphanages in Bristol—the world he saw from his days in study and prayer—was a two-story world.

The upper story is the divine arena—mirrored by Mueller's Bible study and prayer. In the lower story are money and fund-raising. Spiritual things and money do not coexist in the same realm. They are enemies; they are always mutually exclusive; they are inevitably in conflict.

Another way of looking at the situation is to see ministry as a spiritual activity, and fund-raising as a fleshly or evil thing. How do you use evil money to fund righteous ministry without corrupting the ministry? You transfer funds from the lower story to the upper story by a purely spiritual activity—prayer.

Another way of defining this worldview is to say that the spirit and the flesh are in perpetual conflict; that ministry, prayer, godliness, and righteousness reside in the upper realm; and that the flesh, money, commerce, business, and other things of this world are separated in the lower realm.

George Mueller's view of the world was first and best defined by the ancient Greek philosopher Plato.

• Platonic thinking. Plato said that there is the ideal and the real. There is the spiritual and the physical, and they are in perpetual conflict with each other. He described a great, ongoing cosmic battle between the upper and lower stories.

In effect George Mueller said, "I'm going to make sure the upper story wins because I'm not going to go down to the lower story."

There are at least three things wrong with Mueller's view. First, God doesn't see it that way—the Incarnation of Jesus Christ is the greatest proof of that. Second, since God didn't create the world that way, it is not, ultimately, a workable approach. Third, it ironically robs God of His true role as Lord of all Creation.[14]

THE CHRISTIAN AND MONEY

Our life task, not simply as fund-raisers but as Christians, is to merge the two stories into one. The biblical position is that Jesus is Lord of all, and that means money, commerce, and business. It even means the United States Postal Service, as hard to believe as that is.

The Book of Revelation reminds us that God is Lord of all, and that everyone—even the evil one—will acknowledge His lordship one day. Until then, money will be a controversial issue for many Christians and non-Christians because it is so powerful.

Remember how the Pharisees tried to bait Jesus? They wanted to know if they should pay taxes to Rome (a politically volatile question).

Jesus' answer? It's Caesar's money; his picture is on it. So if Caesar wants some of it, give it back to him. The religious leaders didn't expect an easy answer like that; they expected a theological debacle that would entrap Him.

The Apostle Paul wrote instructions to Timothy about the rich and their money. "Command those who are rich in this present world not to be arrogant nor to put their hope in wealth, which is so uncertain, but to put their hope in God, who richly provides us with everything for our enjoyment" (1 Timothy 6:17).

That makes it sound as if money isn't too bad! It sounds like Paul must have believed that God is Lord of all. "Ask them to give." That's what Paul says. Why? Because your need is so great and dramatic? No! The New Testament has a very different emphasis on giving. It doesn't emphasize the benefit to the recipient; it emphasizes the benefit to the giver.

Why should you command a wealthy person to give? "In this way, they will lay up treasure for themselves as a firm foundation for the coming age, so that they may take hold of the life that is truly life" (v. 19).

If you want to benefit someone, help prepare a place for them where thieves aren't going to break in and steal, and moth and rust won't corrupt. Help them send their money ahead by giving to God's work.

As Jesus said, "Where your treasure is, there your *heart* will be also" (Matthew 6:21).

UNITING YOUR WORLD

The Bible does not offer us a split world. Our choice does not become, "Should we stay in our closet and pray, or should we go out and make our needs known?" The answer is that we do both. We bring our world together under the lordship of Jesus Christ.

One of the great dangers of hiring a fund-raising consultant is *not* that he will do something *un*spiritual for you. The great danger is that he *will do something spiritual* for you, and you'll do something unspiritual in response.

A good Christian fund-raising consultant knows how to put together a very biblical program for you, but he might do such a good job that you will think you don't have to pray. But he is not God, and you're not God. Just as your consultant can ask that proverbial lady in Peoria to write a check, God can have her lay down her pen, check unwritten. God alone can motivate her to give.

Your job is to give her the opportunity to give—and to pray that she will. You are to give her the joy and the benefit of having given. You are to help her realize that her gift is important. But you want God to work in her heart to move her to give.

FUND-RAISING AS A MINISTRY

Biblical fund-raising is a ministry. It is not an evil usurper. It is not a thief that comes in to steal good people's hard-earned money. It gives people the opportunity to invest in the Lord's work so that they might be blessed as they glorify and worship God by giving.

Remember what Paul wrote to the Philippians, "Not that I'm looking for a gift, but I am looking for what may be credited to your account." He flips it.[15]

Paul says, "You've been sending me money so I will have some in my account. . . . I'm grateful for that, I needed that . . . but what excites me is that it has been credited to your eternal account." Paul even describes the gifts of God's people as "a fragrant offering, an acceptable sacrifice, pleasing to God."

In Old Testament times, when they offered a sacrifice to God, they put a lamb on the altar and then added certain kinds of herbs and leaves as well so that it would smell good. It was to produce a fragrant aroma, not like death, but like life. Each time a Jew performed that act of faith, God wanted his physical senses to teach him a spiritual lesson through the beautiful smell. God wanted His people to have their noses say, "Ah, that was a good thing to do. It smells so good. How wonderful it is to please God. How wonderful it is to be one of His forgiven children."

God takes as one of the strictest measures of our commitment to Him our ability to part with our most valuable possessions. That was the problem with the rich young man. His money was too important to him.

WHAT DO YOU DO NOW?

Would George Mueller use direct mail? My answer is just a few lines ahead. But before making that judgment, remember this: George Mueller wasn't all right or all wrong. And if you have a sophisticated development program you may not be all right or all wrong either.

You have a very good chance of being right if you learn from George Mueller and add biblical balance to your stewardship program. Mueller was wrong when he expected God to do everything while he *tried* to do nothing. If you're doing everything and expecting God to do little or nothing, then you're out of balance.

In fund-raising, as in all other areas of life, Christians are to strive for balance between faith and works. A proper outlook blends God's role and your role, your belief and your actions, your cognition and your behavior.

When Christians consciously live in a world unified under the lordship of Christ, they can have a stewardship program that honors God, brings Him glory, and provides wonderful benefits not just to those who receive, but, most of all, to those who give.

Yes, George Mueller would have used direct mail today, based on how he used the media of his day. But he would talk in the past tense and only ask you to pray. You have biblical grounds for doing far more.

JAMES C. KILLION received his undergraduate degree in history from the University of Southern California, and his master's degree in theology from Dallas Theological Seminary. He has served the communication and fund-raising needs of religious not-for-profit organizations since 1972.

Mr. Killion is currently the chief creative officer for Killion, McCabe & Associates, a Dallas-based agency serving many historic Christian organizations.

(20)
STRATEGIC PLANNING:
SPIRIT DRIVEN OR
MARKET DRIVEN?

LARRY F. JOHNSTON

As Christian organizations strive for stability and growth in the turbulent operating environment of the '80s and '90s, more and more consideration is being given to the crucial questions addressed in a process known as strategic planning. While strategic planning as a discipline and management process is no newcomer to for-profit organizations in the secular arena, the use of strategic planning for Christian nonprofit organizations is still something of a rarity. It could safely be said that only a relative handful of Christian nonprofit organizations are using strategic planning, with fewer still using the discipline in ways that are truly effective.

The very term *strategic planning* would strike many Christians as being as compatible with a *faith* approach to fund-raising as pork chops are with bar mitzvahs! Cries would no doubt arise in some circles of "leaning on the arm of the flesh" and "relying on our own understanding" rather than "trusting God." Yet are such reactions reasonable? Are management tools truly incompatible with organizations whose operations should be characterized by "a walk of faith"?

This chapter seeks to address the role of strategic planning in Christian organizations, presenting some of its benefits as well as potential perils. With a focus on what drives marketing and fund-raising—rather than on the entire scope of organizational activities generally addressed in strategic planning—an effort will be made to present a model of marketing and fund-raising planning that incorporates the best of both worlds, the realm of faith and the realm of

reason. I hope that the chapter will provoke reflection and evaluation of attitudes and methods prevalent today, and demonstrate that
biblical principles and modern marketing methods are inherently
compatible.

STRATEGIC PLANNING DEFINED

Recognizing that certain terms are "value laden"—especially in the
value-sensitive environment of Christian organizations—it might be
beneficial to begin with some basic definitions of terms and concepts
that will be used throughout this chapter:

strategy—the fundamental logic by which an organization intends
to achieve its objectives

planning—the rational determination of where you want to go and
how you are going to get there

strategic planning—the managerial process of developing and
maintaining a strategic fit between the organization's goals and resources and its changing marketing opportunities[1]

marketing—that function of an organization that can keep in constant touch with the organization's consumers, read their needs, and
build a program of communications to express the organization's
purpose[2]

fund-raising—the process of raising financial support to sustain,
strengthen, or expand the work of an organization[3]

Apparently the processes of strategic planning, strategic marketing, and even "strategic" fund-raising are essentially neutral. That is,
there is nothing inherently good or bad, spiritual or unspiritual,
acceptable or unacceptable about the processes themselves. Any values attributed to these procedures must be derived from the way in
which the procedures are used, not in the procedures themselves.
Stated another way, the problem does not lie in their *intrinsic* value,
but in their *instrumental* value; not *that* they are used, but *how* they
are used.

Within the framework of these definitions, however, distinguish-
ing between two fundamentally different marketing orientations is
important, for doing so will have profound significance for Christian
organizations, both philosophically and practically. The first orientation, which might be called a sales approach, could be described
functionally as *product to market*. Characterized simply as taking what

you have "on the shelf" and selling it, this sales orientation at face value would tend to place little significance on the all-important needs and wants of the consumer (or donor).

A much more viable orientation might be called a *market to product* approach, which seeks to determine exactly what it is that the customer (or donor) wants, and then puts that on the shelf. Or, as the dean of management consultants, Peter Drucker, has so insightfully stated, "The aim of marketing is to make selling superfluous." The underlying assumption is that if an organization does an adequate job of understanding the wants and needs of its customers, and designs programs, products, or services to meet these needs at a reasonable price, little or no selling will be required. Another way of stating the case for the marketing approach is to note that the ease of selling, all other factors being equal, is directly proportionate to the "fit" of the product or program with the customer's needs and wants.

THE SALES APPROACH

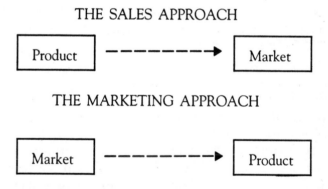

THE MARKETING APPROACH

PROBLEMS WITH BOTH APPROACHES
  • Product to Market. One of the greatest difficulties with a product to market approach is that products, programs, and services are developed by organizations with inadequate consideration being given to the importance of the customer or donor preferences. Numerous and occasionally wildly imaginative schemes have been concocted by visionaries over the years, convinced that because they were personally infatuated with their ideas, others would flock in droves to support them. Not only have such schemes left a bad taste in the mouths of many donors, but they have cast negative shadows over many Christian organizations in the eyes of both supporters and critics alike.

The end results of these approaches are often embarrassing, not only in terms of negative images and public relations liabilities, but also in terms of cost. Valuable time and resources are wasted attempting to promote what is unsellable. A little market research or constituency analysis to determine the desires and priorities of the marketplace would have avoided the waste of funds on products or programs for which there was no market demand.

• Market to Product. This marketing orientation could be called the "find a need and fill it" approach. While almost always the best approach in terms of for-profit marketing of products and services, it can easily lead to a "whatever sells," or "whatever makes money," or "whatever the donors are interested in" trap. For Christian paralocal church organizations in particular, this can be a strong temptation, especially when periods of financial stress tend to distort perspectives and make moral and ethical decisions more difficult. The critical issue for such organizations is clearly not "whatever works," but "What does God want?" A question Dr. Tony Campolo raises about this matter is, "How would this be done if Jesus could have *His* way?"[4]

PIETY OR PROFITABILITY?
Reflecting for a moment on Kotler's definition of strategic planning as "developing and maintaining a strategic fit between an organization's goals and resources and its changing marketing opportunities," one can quickly emphathize with the Christian marketer or fund-raiser. These marketing and fund-raising executives and managers are being measured and evaluated by at least two standards: true piety as measured by biblical precepts, and true profitability as measured by the bottom line. They must balance—and if possible, effectively integrate—what should be a sense of calling from God with the healthy desires or demand of the marketplace.

Before quickly jumping to conclusions, let's look briefly at a humorous but instructive matrix into which most marketing and fund-raising programs and decisions could be placed.

Clarifying some assumptions underlying this conceptual framework might be helpful:

• One can be pious without being profitable. It is easy to be "spiritual" and look with disdain on fund-raising practices and practi-

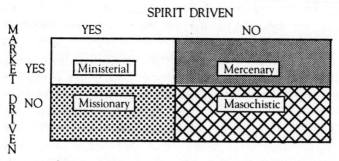

SPIRIT DRIVEN

tioners, as long as we are not the ones who have to raise funds. When confronted with the necessity and personal responsibility of raising funds to sustain a ministry's life-changing and possibly even life-sustaining outreach (humanitarian and relief efforts), it is fascinating to see how quickly the mythical and idealized convictions of some individuals are modified to meet the pragmatic demands of survival in a real world. A famous scientist once said that "the tragedies of science are the slayings of beautiful hypotheses by ugly facts!"[5] So it is with the fund-raising concepts of many "faith" organizations, as they awaken to the intensely competitive realities of the modern marketplace.

● One can be profitable without being pious. It is just as easy to rely wholly on modern marketing, advertising, and fund-raising techniques and leave precious little room for the work of the Holy Spirit in the marketing and fund-raising process. Easier than one might think is the temptation to succumb to what the organization knows will work, whether or not there is any sense of leading by the Holy Spirit. Only those individuals who have not had to "sweat out" making payroll, realizing that the welfare of coworkers' families are depending on their success and that often critical ministry activities are at stake, can easily criticize the tendency to rely on "what works" in terms of modern direct marketing techniques. Yet piety need not be sacrificed for the sake of profitability.

In the *ministerial* quadrant of the matrix, there is both a clear leading of the Lord and a market demand for what the organization is offering to its support markets. This would be the best of both worlds for the Christian marketer, as the task of marketing or fund-raising is facilitated both by the guidance and blessing of the Holy Spirit as well as the eagerness of the support constituency to participate in the program offerings of the organization.

In the *missionary* quadrant there may be strong market demand for what the organization has to offer, yet the presence of God's Spirit in the organization's offering is simply not to be found. Ample evidence abounds, for example, of cult or cultlike teaching today where gross inconsistencies can be found when aligned with God's Word. Yet the apparent growing demand for teaching where style consistently overshadows substance is perhaps merely a sign of the times: "For the time will come when men will not put up with sound doctrine. Instead, to suit their own desires, they will gather around them a great number of teachers to say what their itching ears want to hear" (2 Timothy 4:3-4).

In the *mercenary* quadrant might be a number of organizations in which God continues to bless their evangelistic outreach and continues to change lives, even though their marketing and fund-raising practices have succumbed to manipulative and deceitful practices that give no evidence of being "Spirit driven."

To the poor souls in the *masochistic* quadrant we offer our condolences and consolation. Here are the misguided marketers and fundraisers whose fruitless efforts give no evidence of being either Spirit-driven or market-driven. As noted in my "Diagnostic/Prescriptive Matrix" that follows, the condition of these organizations is often incurable, although unfortunately for our collective miseries, not always fatal!

Johnston's Diagnostic/Prescriptive Matrix for Marketers and Fund-raisers

Position	Prognosis	Prescription
MINISTERIAL	Bright future ahead	Share your secrets with others
MISSIONARY	Short-term struggles, long-term crown	Develop prayer and support group
MERCENARY	Unemployment or promotion (depends on organization!)	Consider repentance or secular employment
MASOCHISTIC	Potentially incurable	Rehabilitation or retirement

PROBLEMS OR PITFALLS

Potential pitfalls for marketers and fund-raisers in Christian organizations can be more easily avoided if we recognize them. Three of these traps could be called Marketing Blind, Marketing Bound, and Marketing Burned.[6]

• Marketing Blind—The Trap of Tradition. Marketing blindness is a condition which results from such a complete identification with traditional religious methods ("information but no solicitation") that we are unable to see the values and benefits of professional marketing, fund-raising, and management practices. Organizations so blinded remind us of the motto of one missionary organization, "75 Years of Tradition Uninterrupted by Progress"!

Adhering to the principle expressed by Hudson Taylor of "moving men's hearts through prayer to God alone," many "faith" ministries refrain from appealing to people directly. Their conviction seems to be, "*Our* way is *Yahweh!*" As a marketing and fund-raising consultant, I am fascinated to observe how the stance of some organizations has ceased to be *sola scriptura* (only the Scriptures for guidance), and has become sola George Mueller. A number of organizations embrace this approach as the only godly way to develop support or raise funds, apparently unaware of other biblical methods of fund-raising no less spiritual than their own.

Others leaning more to the "works" side might dismiss this "faith" approach as theologically engaging but pragmatically insane—a real marketing death wish. Numerous marketing and fund-raising professionals would admit to being fed up with what they feel are appeals to extrabiblical sources of authority rather than to Scripture, and see such appeals based on tradition or the practices of others, such as Taylor and Mueller, as being essentially escape-from-responsibility mechanisms. That is, as long as the validity of the method is denied, there is no need to accept responsibility for the failure to raise adequate funds for an organization or to give to those organizations who raise funds this way.

Amy Carmichael, quoted in John White's book, *The Golden Cow*, notes that there are three scriptural methods for fund-raising: "asking God's people for money, tentmaking (that is, earning your living to support your Christian service) and trusting God to supply by some means known in advance only to Him. A fourth method is not scriptural: professing to walk by faith in God alone and then simultaneously hinting for funds or manipulating people into giving."[7] Advocates in both camps would do well to understand that the first three methods are not mutually exclusive, since Paul used all three. What is important to note is that no single method is essentially superior to another.

• Marketing Bound—The Methods of Madison Avenue. More serious than being marketing blind is being marketing bound. Speaking on "contamination by culture" and how "tools shape the user," Os Guiness writes in *The Gravedigger File*:

> Such is our success today that consumer religion's true believers are the very disciples of Jesus, those who would pride themselves on being the heirs of Martin Luther and the truest sons and daughters of the Reformation. Driven out of the temple two thousand years ago, moneychangers are surfacing in America with all the mystique of a lost tribe of Israel and all the methods of Madison Avenue.
>
> We've done this by cultural assimilation. Consumer religion is an unholy amalgam of convictions and consumption that creates sacramental materialism in the name of Christ. Forget for the moment the wild and ludicrous examples—the vulgar direct mail appeals, the lavish waste of donated funds, the inflated emotional hypes, the crass theologies of success, the self-glorifying building projects, the "holy hardware" and the "Jesus junk." Those are easy to list but really only symptoms. What few people analyze are the forces behind them. They fail to see the powerful undertow of seductive commercial forces in America which are sucking the Gospel down. If consumer religion hadn't already existed, some American entrepreneur would have been glad to invent it.[8]

Also in *The Gravedigger File*, Guiness has the diabolical Deputy Director of the Central Security Council say:

> The state we have reached is critical. The Christian faith has been challenged by new environments before, but never has it faced as massive a threat as it faces from modernization now. No age, no culture, no civilization has ever represented such unmeasurable and unmanageable realities or carried such an

unparalleled capacity to shape the lives of its members. In the spirit of modernity, the spirit of faith does not know what it is up against. It has finally met its match.⁹

So it seems to be with the proliferation of technology available to today's fund-raisers. We now have massive computerized data bases, mind-boggling mailing list segmentation and targeted marketing capabilities, computerized telemarketing equipment, and laser printers that simulate "personalized" P.S.'s in handwriting on direct mail appeals. Available also are demographic and psychographic data to electronically "evaluate" zip code clusters based on probability of response and profitability.

With such intoxicating capabilities, the spirit of faith has indeed met its match in the spirit of modernity. In the pitfall of being marketing bound, some marketers and fund-raisers have become so shaped by the use of these tools and so deafened by the noise of high-speed computer printers that they can no longer hear the "still small voice" of God who longs to get their attention.

• Marketing Burned—Mammon vs. the Master. This is the level at which, through our uncritical identification with and use of modern planning, marketing, and fund-raising methods, we have become badly burned and must live with the consequences. In marketing-burned organizations, we see reliance on methods replacing reliance on our Maker, and reliance on technique fast replacing reliance on the Holy Spirit. These organizations have become so accustomed to *what* works that they have forgotten *who* does the work: "Unless the Lord builds the house, its builders labor in vain" (Psalm 127:1).

Those practicing a sort of methodological idolatry have become guilty of the sin of self-sufficiency. Here marketing and fund-raising practices have been so shaped by the demands of the market and the tools available that service of mammon is outpacing service of the Master.

IS THERE A WAY OUT?

Is there a way to avoid the pitfalls? Are there ways to meet the demands of the market as well as the demands of holiness? Can one engage in strategic planning—whether for marketing of programs or raising of funds—that is both Spirit driven and market driven? Can we begin to deal with the fact that there has been an explosion of marketing knowledge, without a commensurate growth in marketing wisdom?

I believe the answer is clearly yes. But what are the guidelines? How does an organization maintain a steady course in terms of its core mission while at the same time meeting the diverse needs of its supporters? If good marketing is in fact "giving people more and more of what they want and less and less of what they don't want," and good leadership is "not giving them what they want but what they should want," is it possible to reconcile these two?

Before proposing a model that I feel might be helpful, several personal premises should first be stated:

• To honor God, marketing and fund-raising decisions must be congruent with biblical values—honesty, integrity, truthfulness, etc. Note the words "to honor God" rather than "to be successful." It is quite possible to be "successful" in the eyes of the world and fail miserably to honor God.

• There are market demands (the need for personal involvement, participation, belonging, achievement) that represent substantial resource potential and are congruent with biblical values. These can and should be met by Christian organizations in their marketing and fund-raising programs.

• There are market demands that are substantial in terms of resource potential, yet so incongruent with biblical values that they should not be met by Christian organizations (promising blessings and miraculous cures that reduce the act of giving to a misguided "purchase").

• There are programs that are sound in terms of content but not viable in context (good in nature, poor in marketability; sound as a product, poor in a given market). I have in mind many small and worthy organizations involved in a variety of outreaches, but whose "case for support" is so lacking in appeal as to be doomed to limited fund-raising success in a highly competitive and sophisticated marketplace.

• To honor God and be effective in the contemporary marketplace, professional Christian marketers and fund-raisers must strive for an optimum "fit" between value systems—what God wants; market demand—what our constituents want; and the design of our programs and products—what we offer.

Behind these premises are several related convictions: first, that being so heavenly minded that we are of no earthly good is of questionable value to either God or our fellowman. Second, that surviving by prostituting or compromising our values and convictions is unacceptable. Third, that continuing to offer products to nonexistent markets can ultimately be "nonhabit-forming," unless, of course, an organization is well endowed from other sources.

A DIALECTICAL MODEL

To devise programs which have no justification in terms of market needs, or to be a rudderless ship offering to take on passengers regardless of destination as long as the price is right, are two unnecessary and unwise extremes to be avoided at all costs.

A much better approach seeks to design product and program offerings in light of market needs, wants, preferences and demands, but also in light of a clear sense of core mission and biblical values. The following diagram provides a simple means of conceptualizing the process:

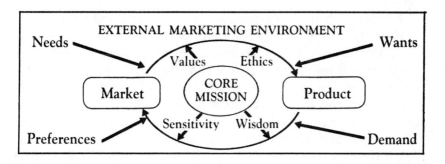

Such a model represents the potential to avoid three "losing" scenarios and to achieve a "win/win" scenario:

● Programs are neither Spirit driven nor market driven = Lose/Lose scenario.

● Programs are Spirit driven but not market driven = Win/Lose scenario. (In this scenario one needs to be big on deferred compensation packages because most of the rewards will be in heaven!)

● Programs are market driven but not Spirit driven = Win/Lose scenario.

• Programs are Spirit driven *and* market driven = Win/Win scenario.

Diagramming this interactive, dialectical planning process in a simple chronological way, the flow would look something like this:

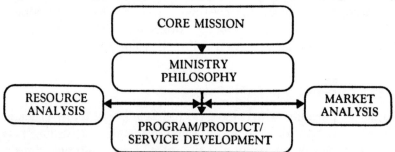

In this flow, one begins with a definition of *Core Mission*, answering such questions as:

• Purpose–Why does our organization exist?

• Programs and Services–What do we provide in light of our stated purpose or reason for being?

• Customer/Client–To whom do we provide these programs and services?

• Scope–Where do we provide these programs and services?[10]

Having addressed the primary and critical question of core mission, the ministry must then articulate the philosophy which will guide its policies and actions both in the marketplace and in·the organization. On completing this statement of ministry philosophy, the ministry can turn its attention to analyzing demand within the marketplace or constituency, assessing the resources available to the organization to deal with these marketing opportunities, then developing the appropriate programs, products, or services to meet these needs within the context of core mission and philosophy.

THE MINISTRY/MARKETING GRID—
IN SEARCH OF THE 9,9 MARKETER

To speak of process, models, and technology is helpful, but failure to address the source of all these—the *people* in our organizations— would be shortsighted and might miss altogether the most critical element in the formula.

An adaptation of the Blake-Mouton Managerial Grid,[11] what I have labeled the Ministry/Marketing Grid, provides more than just a means of assessing our organizations' current ministry and marketing philosophies. It also provides a goal for development professionals and marketers—to achieve outstanding strength in both ministry and marketing, a goal too infrequently embraced in the Christian marketplace.

Ministry/Marketing Grid

Strategic Planning: Spirit Driven or Market Driven? (vertical axis)

| 1,9 Marketing | | 9,9 Marketing |

Prayerful attention is given to ministry concerns, little to marketing.

Strong commitment to marketing is combined with prayerful concern for ministry integrity and effectiveness.

5,5 Marketing

Adequate ministry and marketing take place through satisfactory attention to both.

1,1 Marketing

Minimum effort to meet ministry or marketing concerns

9,1 Marketing

Efficiency in marketing results in ministry concerns interfering to a minimal degree

Low   High

Marketing Concerns

● The 1,1 Marketer. I think we could all agree that there are few organizations that could be characterized by a 1,1 position on the grid. In all likelihood, such ministries would be on the endangered species list if not already extinct. Ineffectiveness in both ministry and marketing, unless endowed by market-insensitive sources of support, is clearly a no-win scenario in today's marketplace.

● The 1,9 Marketer. Although my personal observation is that

245

the number of 1,9 organizations is diminishing (adapting in order to survive in today's marketplace), there are still many ministries, especially small ones, whose commitment is to ministry alone, with little attention given to marketing or fund-raising. My hunch is that unless they wish to remain small—or possibly even join others on the endangered species list—these organizations will be giving increasing attention to the functions of marketing and fund-raising.

• The 5,5 Marketer. A 5,5 position could well be termed "management by mediocrity," a classic case of what it means to be lukewarm. It is in this position that only "adequate" ministry and marketing take place by giving each the attention they require to "get by."

• The 9,1 Marketer. Organizations falling in the 9,1 range of the grid tend toward a very mechanical and, on occasion, even mercenary marketing orientation. In these organizations, relatively few in number, the concern is for bottom-line profitability with ironically little regard for the consequences for those who support the ministry financially. These are the tragic cases of "ministries" functioning like so many for-profit businesses, with donors being mere objects of financial support to further the interests of those in charge, rather than partners and coworkers who give generously and often sacrificially to further the cause of Christ through these organizations.

• The 9,9 Marketer. Here, in my opinion, is the direction in which our energies ought to be channeled. All other positions on the grid represent stark failure, mediocrity, or imbalance. My hope is that a growing number of Christian ministries will rise to accept the challenge of a 9,9 marketing style in which a high commitment to excellence in ministry is matched by a high commitment to excellence in marketing and fund-raising.

To achieve such excellence will require knowledge of God's Word, for there is simply no substitute for the ultimate operations manual. Such excellence will also increasingly require a high level of competency in marketing and its various disciplines—research, planning, communications, advertising, information, and control systems—as the roar of today's advertising and communications engines drown out the subtle, ambiguous, indirect, and poorly focused communications of many Christian ministries.

Yet more than just knowledge, such excellence will require wisdom; for without the wisdom that comes from God alone, our continuing technological advancements and "high tech" strategies are likely to give birth to activities that ultimately are only so much "wood, hay, and stubble."

To achieve such excellence will not be an overnight development. It will take years of research, study, discipline, and a willingness to deal courageously with issues that are often not popular within many Christian organizations. Yet with a world that is desperately hungry for the Good News of Jesus Christ, I wonder if we really have an alternative.

LARRY F. JOHNSTON, president of McConkey/Johnston, Inc., is a well-known development consultant and lecturer working on behalf of nonprofit organizations. He served as campaign coordinator and counsel to the billion-dollar "Here's Life" Campaign of Campus Crusade for Christ. He has also taught at the graduate program of fund-raising management at the University of San Diego. Having consulted internationally with clients in Canada, Europe, and Latin America, he has a special interest in strategic planning and organization development, including the acculturation of development models to fit the needs of different organizational and social cultures.

Mr. Johnston has received a bachelor's degree in foreign languages from the California State University, Fullerton, and has completed course work toward a master of science in organization development at the Graduate School of Business and Management, Pepperdine University.

(21)
THE SPIRITUAL LIFE
AND MINISTRY OF
CHRISTIAN FUND-RAISERS

CHARLES W. SPICER, JR.

A mature spiritual life is critical to the Christian fund-raiser. This maturity results from a deep commitment to the Lord that is determined largely by his devotional life. Because little has been written about the life of a Christian fund-raiser, much of what I have to say is drawn from my own experience.

ARE YOU WHERE GOD REALLY WANTS YOU?

As a Christian fund-raiser, do you look at your work as mere employment, or can you confidently assert that God has called you to the ministry you are in? If you cannot testify to a clear call from God, then I would challenge you to make sure that you are where God really wants you.

When I was a businessman beginning to get involved in missions through my giving, someone challenged me to go to the mission field and check out my investments. My heart was broken at what I experienced and I came back a different man. From that point, I began to evaluate whether God wanted me to remain in the life insurance business or whether there might be something else He was preparing for me. I began to sense the dirt being loosened around my roots as though the Lord were getting ready to transplant me to some other part of His vineyard. The Lord gave me a verse at that time: "Now, Lord, what do I look for? My hope is in you" (Psalm 39:7). Through these words, God was in effect saying to me, "Son, what are you waiting for? Your hope is in Me. Let's get going."

Just hours after I read that promise, He gave me another. It was while I was shaving, preparing to go to my office for a Monday morning sales meeting, that I invited my 13-year-old daughter to come and read aloud to me from God's Word. When she asked, "Where do you want me to start?" I suggested Proverbs, because in my mind's eye I could see instruction for children. She read chapter 15 and then asked, "Do you want me to continue?" I nodded and she began chapter 16: "The preparations of the heart in man, and the answer of the tongue, is from the Lord" (KJV).

What had been happening in my life? For years preparation of my heart had been taking place, from the time I first received Christ as my Saviour until I knew Him as my Lord, and then to the time I experienced a broken heart for the needs of the world. Each period of heart preparation led to another step in His plans for my life.

Eventually I felt God was preparing me for a particular ministry. When I left my business and joined a missionary organization, moving from Maryland to Indiana, I felt so sure that I was where God wanted me to be that there was never a moment's doubt.

The reason I share this personal experience is that I believe it is necessary to know I am in God's will before ever beginning to minister to other people. In order for me to be an effective Christian fund-raiser, I need absolute inner confidence that God is with me and that I am where He wants me to be.

Knowing God's will is vital because life isn't easy, especially in the fund-raising business. There are some rough days, rough months, even rough years. As a matter of fact, when a Christian is doing anything for the Lord, the enemy will cause more problems, disappointments, and heartaches. I'm so thankful that after 20 years in the Lord's work, I can say, "I know God was in my call, and I am where He wants me to be."

It is easy to get sidetracked in the fund-raising business. If you are successful, you will have job opportunities to serve with many organizations. Therefore, you need to know your gifts and calling. Even in the Lord's work, it is possible to become more prominent, earn a little more money, or acquire a few more fringe benefits, because there are plenty of organizations around with tempting offers. For me, however, to move from where the Lord has called me in my work in missions to some other field of Christian service would be to settle for second best for my life. I know where God wants me. The center of His will is where He can bless me. I work harder now than I ever worked when I was in business for myself. After all, now I'm in business for the Lord!

DO YOU HAVE A SERVANT'S ATTITUDE?

Another ingredient in the devotional life of a Christian fund-raiser is servanthood. Do you really believe it is more blessed to give than to receive? I am not talking about just giving dollars and writing out a check. Do you believe this spiritual principle when it involves giving of your time? Giving of your effort? Giving of your prayer life? These are intangibles that are not measured by a check balance; the records are kept by God. As we attempt to serve and to give of ourselves on behalf of other people's needs, we see this spiritual principle at work. And as we develop this sense of servanthood, it eventually becomes our lifestyle.

ARE YOU INVESTING TIME WITH GOD?

Spending time in personal devotions is critical in our walk with the Lord; neglecting these moments of prayer and Bible study leads to wandering from fellowship with Him. I have observed that when problems exist within a Christian home—kids going astray, unhappiness, or persistent agitation—there is a strong probability that the time for personal devotions has been squeezed out.

I believe that time alone with the Lord is basic to our work and most important to consider. God wants to fellowship with us, and we need to individually work out the best time, format, and content of our quiet time with Him.

For me, the best time for personal devotions is in the morning before other things such as the newspaper, TV, and phone calls vie for my attention. If my day does not begin with devotions before I'm off to the office, I come back at night, too exhausted physically and in no mood spiritually to worship the Lord.

I have, therefore, had to structure time for devotions. It's part of my routine, just like getting up, eating, and sleeping. For twenty years I have made personal devotions a discipline of my life. I would not dare do without it.

If possible, I like to spend an hour. But there are times, like when I have to catch an early flight or a late meeting the night before has shortened the night's rest, that I have to adjust to whatever time seems reasonable. A minimum of fifteen minutes is basic, regardless of the circumstances.

We are no deeper in our walk with the Lord than in our prayer life. Prayer results are amazing. I can be terribly perplexed over some issues or pressures in my office, but after five minutes on my knees in the morning with the Lord, suddenly the solution will come into focus. I spread the issues of the day before the Lord and allow Him to give me direction.

Billy Graham has said he reads five Psalms and a chapter from the Book of Proverbs each day, in addition to other Bible reading. Others read a chapter a day or a certain amount of the Word of God. The Gideons have a guideline for reading through the Bible in a year. Radio Bible Class has devotional books, and there are many other helps in this regard. Find something that speaks to your heart, to use when you are at home or in your travels.

To receive specific answers to prayer we need to be specific in our requests. Keep a prayer journal; record when you start praying and then note the date when God answers.

In my office I keep a file of prayer lists and answers to prayer. Reading through it occasionally, I am encouraged as I see how the Lord may have used me in some incident. A definite answer to specific prayer increases our faith and allows us to believe in God for even greater things.

ARE YOU INVESTING IN A PRAYER PARTNER?

Another valuable ingredient in the devotional life of a Christian fund-raiser can be the influence of a prayer partner. There are many examples of prayer partners: Moses and Aaron, Paul and Silas, Moody and Sankey, to name a few. The Bible describes how 1 can put to flight 1,000; but 2 can put to flight 10,000. Multiplication occurs when any two believers on earth agree concerning things. A tremendous release of power results when 2 people agree in prayer. Often my prayer partner's strengths are my weaknesses and my strengths are his weaknesses. Together we both become stronger as we envelop one another in prayer.

One time when my prayer partner and I were experiencing a dry spell and not seeing much happening in our efforts to witness and share Christ with others, we decided to have a time of prayer. As we met, we literally prostrated ourselves on the floor. I don't know how long we were there, but we agonized in prayer. This was not something that we "worked up," but rather something God worked down into our hearts to renew our burden for lost people. When we got up, we knew God had heard our prayers.

I left the next day for a missionary conference in Williamsport, Pennsylvania. I thought my flight from Indianapolis to Pittsburgh would be the time God would seat me next to someone to witness to, but I had no seat partner. In Pittsburgh I had to transfer to another flight. As I was walking up the steps of the small commuter plane, I knew God was going to do something. He had witnessed to my heart that something good was going to happen.

As I looked down the aisle of the plane, my attention was on only one seat. There were other seats, but I knew that was where I was supposed to sit. I turned and introduced myself to a young man from Bucknell University. To my great joy, he was ready to receive Christ.

A missionary on his way to the same conference was seated in front of me. As I disembarked from the plane, he turned to me and acknowledged that he had overheard our conversation. At that moment the thought occurred to me that the missionary could have led that university student to the Lord, but God chose to give me the privilege because I was asking Him for someone that day with whom to share my faith.

Later that afternoon in the missionary conference, I received a phone call from my prayer partner. He said, "Guess what happened in my office?" He went on to tell me how Paul, a friend, had just prayed to receive Christ.

Remember that just the day before we were praying for someone we could share Christ with, and less than 24 hours later, God had allowed us to lead two men to Him.

After receiving the Lord, Paul said that about a year prior to his conversion he had begun to be uncomfortable and convicted—guilt was gnawing at him and a hunger for meaning to life engulfed him. We looked back on our prayer lists and found we had begun to pray for Paul about a year before his conversion. Even when we could not see any outward change, God was speaking to his heart, drawing him to Himself. It took special time of prayer for that breakthrough to Paul's heart.

ARE YOU INVESTING IN AN ACCOUNTABILITY GROUP?
A recent development in the area of prayer partners occurred when a man from my board came and suggested an accountability group. This person sensed a need in my life, not only from a personal standpoint, but from a ministry standpoint. As he and four other men met with me, I asked them the purpose for our meeting.

They responded by saying, "It's to meet your needs—spiritual, physical, and material." They have been invaluable in making me a better-equipped representative of the Lord Jesus. I cannot measure the debt I owe these men who pray for me, take me into their confidence, and develop a relationship of accountability.

To whom do you account on your day-to-day business? Become part of an accountability group and your ministry will be greatly enlarged.

ARE YOU CLAIMING GOD'S WORD?
Psalm 2:8 challenges us to ask for the nations. We can take that same promise and apply it to spiritual things, asking God to add this dimension to our lives. For example, some years ago I recognized that the fruit of the Spirit often was not evident in my life, and asked God to develop this spiritual fruit (Galatians 5:22). Gradually I began to realize, imperceptibly at first, that God was enriching my walk by implanting love, joy, peace, patience, kindness, goodness, faithfulness, gentleness, and self-control.

Ask the Holy Spirit to work through you and develop within you a sensitivity to the needs of others. You will become spiritually aware of hurts in the lives of people wherever you go. God has called us as Christian fund-raisers to a ministry. The Lord works through us, building His church, and our ministry extends beyond simply raising funds for our Christian organizations.

Ask God to do something special in your life. Claim His promises. Ask Him for help in realizing the goals of your own ministry and organization. When they are met, you will not say, "Look what I've done," but rather, "Look what God has done through me."

ARE YOU USING A PERSONAL TRACT?

A personal tract that shares your very own testimony is an excellent way to leave a word of witness. Leave your tract at a restaurant; you may end up tipping a little more than normal because you don't want to detract from the message of the tract. Use it with a service station employee or with the plumber. The opportunities are limited only by your creativity.

I was on a flight from Honolulu to Taipei. As is my custom, I prayed for the Lord to guide me to the person beside whom I would sit. Since my life verse is Psalm 2:8, "Ask of me, and I will make the nations your inheritance, the ends of the earth your possession," it is interesting to me how many times that person I sit by is from another country. Often God brings the nations right next to me as seat companions.

I looked at the man's briefcase and saw a hotel sticker from the Inya Lake Hotel, Rangoon, Burma. Since I had stayed there a couple of times, I had a natural conversation opener. As I talked with this man from Helsinki, Finland, he asked me the nature of my work. My answer bridged to the subject of a changed life and the need for making peace with God.

I asked him where he was in his relationship to God and if he would like to make a decision for the Lord.

He said, "No, not really, but my wife is a believer, and she has people praying for me."

"You know," I said, "we have eight hours on this plane together. Can you think of any better time to discuss these important issues? I would like to help you."

"No," he replied, "I'm just not ready."

"OK, but I'm going to pray for you." I gave him my tract with my testimony and let it go at that. The year was 1984.

As I was taking spiritual inventory in January 1987, evaluating the results of the previous year and my goals for the coming year, one of the things I was complaining to the Lord about was the several hundred dollars I had spent in printing my tract. A number of people had said nice things about it, and I assumed some had been helped, but I could not point to one person who had come to Christ as a result of reading my testimony in the tract.

Two weeks later a letter came to me from Helsinki. The first sentence said, "God told me to write this letter." The writer went on to rehearse the circumstances I have just described relative to our meeting on the plane. In the next paragraph he said, "I want you to know I carried this tract with me in my briefcase and read it many times. About a year ago I made that decision. I prayed to receive Christ. My marriage has been put back together. My wife and I are attending church and we pray together. I know what the abundant life is all about."

The letter came just when I needed to be encouraged in handing out tracts. Praise the Lord! You can enjoy a similar experience. Consider using a tract—it can open up an opportunity for sharing the Gospel. For instance, just say to a waitress, "Take this home and read it. I know you don't have time now, but this will tell you what God has done in my life. He can do the same for you."

I gave my tract to a barber in Erie, Pennsylvania. He was so enthralled with it that he asked for 100 of them to put on his cash register. As his customers came by to pay their bills, he would give them my tract. I never know where some of the seed will fall.

ARE YOU TRUSTING GOD FOR YOUR FAMILY?

I am an only child. I was in business with my dad, and the struggle to leave the business and go into missions was not an easy decision. One of the issues I had to resolve was what would happen when my parents reached the age when they would need me, and I would be 10,000 miles away. After all, the Scriptures say, "Honor your father and mother." How could I resolve this seeming conflict?

The Lord told me He was far better able to take care of my mother and father than I could ever be, even if I lived next door. This promise became reality, and it was wonderful to see the Lord's provision, even during my dad's terminal illness.

The Bible says that you will not leave mother, father, brother, or sister, but that God will give you back a hundredfold. Across the United States and lots of countries around the world, the Lord has given me many mothers, fathers, brothers, and sisters. I cannot even number them all.

I have a "mother" in Great Falls, Montana. If I get within 500 miles of Great Falls and don't visit her, I am in for a scolding. She and her husband pray for me and my ministry and always want to know about the "grandkids." It just so happens they have over a million dollars in a charitable remainder unitrust, but the depth of our relationship did not develop because they had money to invest. While visiting in their home, they told of their deep hurt over the loss of a son. As we shared together from God's Word and prayed, I became an avenue of healing in the loss of that son. Out of our friendship God has brought blessing and fruit.

One benefit in raising funds is friendship with people like these—those in whose homes I feel completely at ease and where I actually become a part of their families.

I was often in the home and church of a pastor friend, and the Lord developed a special bonding of our hearts. I can remember the pastor trusting me enough to ask me to talk with his son. I found the young man sitting outside a grocery store where he was a clerk.

After approaching him, I talked casually and said, "Friend, God has a wonderful plan for your life, and it's not being a clerk in a grocery store."

Today this young man is an executive in a missionary organization. Now, I am sure there were other people who talked with him and prayed for him, but I like to think I had some influence.

Just multiply one opportunity by 365 days a year, and then by the 20 to 30 years God gives you to serve. It is going to be a glorious day when we get to heaven and God pulls back the curtain to show all He's done through our lives. Only God can keep those kinds of records. Isn't it wonderful to think He can use you and me?

Take the initiative in the home where you are visiting. Enter into the burdens of that family. Become a burden-bearer. Feel the heartache of waywardness, of illness, and become serious in your follow-up prayer. It is up to you. Don't wait for somebody else.

ARE YOU TAKING ADVANTAGE OF TRAVELING OPPORTUNITIES?

As fund-raisers, we spend much of our time in hotels, and we can use this opportunity to get work done. I suggest you watch television for news and weather only. Spend time instead reading periodicals and books. Your hotel room can be a place to have a prolonged quiet time that you cannot have at home because of interruptions. Take along some exercise clothes or equipment for working out. Our bodies are temples of the Holy Spirit and must be kept in good condition. Regular exercise will keep you healthier and give you a higher energy level, which can result in more energy to do the Lord's work.

Listen to tapes, such as recordings of Scripture or sermons, when you are driving in your car. Or, carry flash cards with Scripture verses that you can memorize while driving.

Try to be creative in thinking of ways to make your time count. A friend from Houston and I were traveling along a highway in Texas and were amazed to see many dead armadillos on the road. Later, whenever he would see a dead armadillo on the road, my friend was reminded to pray for me.

As part of my responsibilities, I was leading a group up a jungle river in Colombia, South America in a dugout canoe. It was during a difficult time of elections, and all the police had been pulled back into the major cities. Consequently, the remote mountain areas had no protection, and there was the danger that we could be taken as hostages and held by bandits. The nationals discouraged us from traveling upriver to a service we wanted to conduct.

Contrary to what we would normally do, we overruled the advice of the national pastor who was with us. We went and conducted the service, and two people found Christ.

I did not know until sometime later that my Texas friend was on a trip on Interstate 20 and saw an unusual number of dead armadillos the very morning that we were traveling upriver in Colombia. Consequently, he was reminded to pray for me—precisely at the moment I needed it.

My point in relating this story is to encourage you to use your driving time. Take advantage of every moment. Through your prayers enter into the foray of spiritual warfare somewhere around the world.

ARE YOU GIVING YOUR BEST?

God says, "Ask of Me." He wants to give, and so often we have not because we ask not. The embodiment of the Gospel is in giving, for God gave His best—His Son. His Son gave His best—His life. We receive the Son and in turn give to others.

Ours is a ministry of giving. The paradox is that in order to receive, you must give. If you want to have God's blessing, to see financial results in the organization you represent as a fund-raiser, learn to give of yourself. God is the blesser, and what He can do is limitless. Your devotional life can be the proving ground for all God wants to accomplish through your life. And your ministry to others will be an earthly investment that will bring the greatest eternal dividends.

CHARLES W. SPICER, JR. *is the president of Overseas Council for Theological Education and Missions, Inc., of Greenwood, Indiana. He also serves as president of The Stanita Foundation and is a board member of several other charitable organizations. He has authored a book,* Yours for the Asking, *which details lessons learned in communicating his witness both at home and overseas.*

A graduate of Johns Hopkins University, Dr. Spicer holds degrees in political science and business science. He was awarded the Doctor of Divinity by the Madras Bible Seminary, which is affiliated with the Seramphore University in Madras, India. He is a world traveler, having visited more than 100 countries on behalf of the Great Commission.

(22)
RAISING PERSONAL
SUPPORT

H. ANDREW READ

Raising funds personally to support a Christian worker's ministry is a phenomenon that has exploded on the mission scene within the last 35 years, often bringing controversy regarding the biblical basis for such support programs. While the controversy continues, many ministries—new and old alike—are finding it increasingly difficult to add personnel without using this type of fund-development program.

The Bible contains a number of passages that refer to various methods of personal support fund-raising, and because there seems to be no one particular model, there is disagreement on which is best. The focus here is to outline those principles that provide a framework for general application. Principles are distinguished from methods which usually have a tendency to change based on customs and practices throughout history.

A beginning place to examine these principles is to look at biblical patterns of support for people and projects in the Bible. The examples provide a foundation for reviewing personal support fund-raising.

The first mention in Scripture of a follower giving a portion of his possessions to the Lord is Abram, who gave Melchizedek one-tenth of everything he owned because Melchizedek had ministered to him (Genesis 14:20; Hebrews 7:2-6). The point here is the principle of a servant of God receiving a gift from another person because of his ministry. Another example is financing the building of the tabernacle, when Moses was told to go and tell the Israelites to bring the Lord an offering from each man whose heart prompted him (Exodus

25:2-7). Note that this gift was not a tithe, but an offering or contribution.

Later, according to Exodus 35:4-9, the people were told specifically what materials to bring to build the tabernacle. The leaders spoke openly and clearly about the vision, the plan, and the need. Verses 21-29 relate that everyone who was willing and whose heart moved him came and gave an offering on a freewill basis, bringing the offerings every morning, not just at a designated time of formal worship. The Lord provided abundantly—even more than needed—through His people.

The Levites were people "set apart" by God to care for His sanctuary—a special group God had called out to live totally dedicated in His service. They were to be supported by the whole of God's people. The Lord told Aaron, "I give to the Levites all the tithes in Israel as their inheritance in return for the work they do" (Numbers 18:21). This tithe was not only cash but also various articles or material goods, for the Levites had the opportunity to eat from the offerings that were brought to the tabernacle. In other words, their day-to-day living needs were met by all of God's people, and these gifts were given to people called out to be full-time ministers.

Another example from the biblical record that gives us an historical perspective is found in Nehemiah 2:1-8. Nehemiah asked and received the necessary funds from a pagan king to accomplish the Lord's work. This example is one answer to the question that inevitably comes up in any discussion regarding personal support—"Is it proper to approach nonbelievers for support?" This historical evidence shows that a pagan king was asked to support the work of the Lord, and the king responded positively. But this does not give us one clear teaching, for, on the other hand, John, though not instructing Gaius to refuse gifts from unbelievers, reports that some workers did not accept anything from the heathen (3 John 7).[1]

SUPPORT-RAISING PRINCIPLES FOLLOWED
BY THE DISCIPLES
In considering the funding methods used by the disciples, first consider their call. Jesus called His disciples away from what they were doing to a new occupation—taking the Gospel to the world. Peter and Andrew were fishermen casting their nets in the sea—working at

their occupation. But then Jesus came to them and said, "Come, follow Me . . . and I will make you fishers of men." At once these two brothers left their nets and followed Him, and from that point on began investing their lives to reach people for Christ (Matthew 4:18-20). Similarly, James and John were mending their nets when Jesus called them (4:21-22). Verse 22 says, "And immediately they left the boat and their father and followed Him." They quit the fishing business and followed Jesus! They left the trade that they had known all their lives to enter a new ministry, or trade. They became fishers of men—investing their time to see people's lives changed.

Luke 5:5-8 tells us that these men fished at night. We might conclude that these disciples ministered during the day with Jesus but still fished at night to provide for their needs. That remains an option until we read verse 11: "They pulled their boats up on shore, left everything and followed Him." So it appears that their fishing at night was prior to their beginning their full-time ministry with Jesus. The Bible does not give us a clear picture of the disciples using fishing skills to support their ministry.

Matthew was sitting in the tax collector's booth when Jesus called him (Matthew 9:9), and he arose and followed Him. Even though tax collecting was a good means of generating a livelihood in those days, there is no indication in Scripture that Matthew went back to collecting taxes.

Consider the instruction that Jesus gave to the disciples, that believers should meet the needs that the disciples had as they were involved in full-time ministry. "Do not take along any gold or silver or copper in your belts; take no bag for the journey, or extra tunic, or sandals or a staff; for the worker is worth his keep. Whatever town or village you enter, search for some worthy person there and stay at his house" (Matthew 10:9-11).

Scripture also shows that support came from both churches and individuals. Acts 4:36-37 tells us of Barnabas, a man of some property, who sold a field, brought the money, and put it at the apostles' feet for their use in the ministry.

In summary, a few patterns can be drawn. The biblical record is unclear as to whether the disciples mixed their skills, trades, or profession with their new occupation. But the implication and principle here is that the provision of support would be provided by God without using their trades or needing an employer. In essence, God became their employer at that point. Additionally, when Jesus called an individual into missionary work, the work was to be full-time with one focus and purpose—helping to fulfill the Great Commission.

Becoming fishers of men implied involvement in an occupation that carried with it that financial support (at least the basic necessities and needs of life) would be provided by or through others. In Luke 22:35 we see that the disciples went out, depending entirely on others to provide their support. When Jesus asked them if they lacked anything when He sent them out without purse, bag, or sandals, the disciples responded exuberantly, "Nothing."

SUPPORT OF JESUS' MINISTRY

There is no record of Jesus using His carpentry skills to support His ministry during the three years of His full-time earthly ministry. Basically, He focused on three main areas: preaching the Gospel, bringing sinners to repentance in an effort to seek and to save the lost, and giving His life a ransom for many.[2] He never mentioned involvement in a commercial trade. His calling from God was the "trade" that consumed His time and attention.

We have historical evidence of this point through Josephus' writings in the antiquities. Josephus wrote that "Jesus was a wise man—if it even be lawful to call Him a man," and that He was "a doer of good works" and "a teacher who drew others to Himself." But nowhere does Josephus state that Jesus was a carpenter.[3]

SUPPORT-RAISING METHODS USED BY JESUS AND HIS DISCIPLES

Other than what has been examined, no other specific passages deal with principles of how Jesus and the disciples raised support, but Scripture does give us an idea of how they handled their finances. Generally, Jesus and His disciples used a pooling method. As they went along, expenses for the group were taken out of the pool to pay for the goods and services they required.

Evidently, followers of Jesus provided private contributions to sustain Him and His ministry, and the ministry of the apostles and other missionaries. Acts 10:1-2 relates that Cornelius, the centurion, gave generously to those in need. Luke 8:1-3 also shows that many others contributed to the disciples' support out of their means.[4]

A conflict in methods may arise when we read Luke 22:36, "But now if you have a purse, take it, and also a bag." It seems that Jesus was saying it was all right to take money along, as opposed to other passages where they were told to take nothing. Yes, different methods do seem to be used, but the principle remains that God would provide as people gave their resources in support of Jesus' ministry.

Hospitality was another means of support. This provision of meals and shelter to a traveler was a custom of the middle and upper class of the day, for it kept them from being at the mercy of greedy innkeepers. Jesus told the disciples that in whatever city they went, whatever village they entered, to inquire who was worthy and then abide with those people while they were in that particular city (Matthew 10:13). It is interesting that those "donors" who provided food and housing had to be "deserving" of the disciples' company.

Often it is easier for people to give monetary gifts than to go to the time and trouble of entertaining people in their homes. But hospitality is a means of giving that should be encouraged, for Scripture records many instances of this type of sharing. In the New Testament record, Martha welcomed Jesus into her home (Luke 10:38); Peter stayed with Simon the tanner for some time (Acts 9:43); Lydia invited the apostles to stay with her (Acts 16:15); the Philippian jailer provided housing to Paul and Silas and gave them food (Acts 16:33-34); and Philip the evangelist provided housing for Paul (Acts 21:8-10). The Old Testament tells us in 1 Kings 17:10-16 that a woman gave provisions of bread and water to Elijah, and that act resulted in her household being able to eat for many days thereafter. Second Kings 4:8-10 shows the Shunamite woman giving Elisha food and lodging. Elisha was also encouraged to return as often as he passed through, and to stay in a room built for him.

The example of Jesus sending out the 70 (Luke 10:1-16) bears a resemblance to some of today's missionary work. The Lord appointed or called 70 to go ahead of Him, sending them out two by two to take the Gospel. The Lord told them to carry no purse, that believers would provide for their support, and that the laborer is worthy of support. This particular example makes no mention of a cashbox, probably because it was easier for a small group of two to find shelter. However, these instructions are similar to those the Lord gave the disciples in Matthew 10:1-15.

Some principles can be drawn from what has been said. First, Jesus gave full time to ministry that was not to be interrupted by secular work. Second, those involved in full-time ministry were to look to God for their provision, which He would provide through His people. We see that Jesus and the disciples depended on the financial gifts and acts of hospitality from their friends, acquaintances, and churches to meet their personal and ministry needs. And, third, as they trusted God for their provision, the disciples' faith was built up.

FUNDING PAUL'S MINISTRY

Acts 18:1-5 is often cited as an indication that Paul funded his ministry through his occupation of tentmaking, but this assumption is questionable. Today the term *tentmaker* has been applied to describe any dedicated Christian worker who is a missionary in terms of commitment, but is fully or partially self-supporting through a secular job. Most often this person lives or works overseas, using secular training or student status to gain entry into a country in order to share the Gospel.

Before going to Corinth, where he stayed with Aquila and Priscilla, Paul was at Athens. While in Athens, Paul gave himself totally to ministry, and two different spheres of witness were opened up: preaching in the synagogue and meeting in the marketplace for discussions with pagan thinkers.[5] But Paul's ministry in Athens was a great disappointment to him, for he had not been successful in the synagogue and had been ridiculed in the marketplace. There was so much indifference and contempt that he was forced to leave Athens.

When Paul arrived in Corinth, he was exhausted, at least emotionally, and somewhat depressed. This is evident, for he later wrote to the Corinthians, "I came to you in weakness and fear, and with much trembling" (1 Corinthians 2:3). Possibly some of this weakness had physical cause, but it seems more likely that it was rooted in his unusual dismissal from Athens.[6]

Also, Paul's colleagues had not returned from Macedonia with the provisions he needed while in Athens. He did not have, therefore, the encouragement and fellowship from others involved in the ministry—not to mention that his funds were probably running short.[7]

In any case, we do see in Acts 18:1-3 that Paul found Aquila and Priscilla and stayed with them. Scripture states that they were working at the tentmaking trade, but it is unclear to whom "they" refers. Some translations indicate that the people working were Aquila, Priscilla, and Paul; others say just Aquila and Priscilla were working, that Paul was only staying with them, perhaps in a time of recuperation.

Verse 4 says specifically, however, that during the period of time Paul was with Aquila and Priscilla, he was involved in ministry once a week, every Sabbath, in the synagogues. When Silas and Timothy came down from Macedonia, he began devoting himself exclusively to preaching and testifying to the Jews that Jesus was the Christ (v. 5). It is not unrealistic to assume that probably only 10 to 20 percent of Paul's ministry was funded by tentmaking, and for the balance of his ministry Paul lived on support from various individuals and churches.

The point here is not to make a case against tentmaking, but to keep this method in proper perspective. There are times when tentmaking might be a biblical means of funding a ministry, but we cannot assume that it was the primary way Paul supported his activities.

Acts 20:33-35 mentions that Paul worked with his hands: "I have not coveted anyone's silver or gold or clothing. You yourselves know that these hands of mine have supplied my own needs and the needs of my companions." Here again, exactly what Paul means is unclear. Is he talking about coveting something another has, or is his point that he was supporting himself?

One explanation is that he was telling them that by this kind of hard work others must help the weak by being an example to them. There is indication that some people were waiting for the Lord's return and, believing it was imminent, they stopped working. This passage might also imply that when Paul was working, it was to help the believers see that they should not just sit and wait, but be actively about their business until the Lord's return. Paul probably worked at tentmaking in this particular situation, because he wanted to make a specific ministry point.

Nevertheless, an obvious conclusion is that receiving personal support allows individuals to devote all their efforts to the ministry to which they have been called. A second point is that when wages are interrupted, the alternative is to work at another job at the cost of ministry.

Another interesting portion of Scripture is 2 Corinthians 11:7-9, where Paul says, "I robbed other churches by receiving support from them so as to serve you." Not many full-time Christian workers would want to admit that they "rob churches" in order to be involved in full-time ministry, but Paul did.

He continues on, giving the reason, "[So that] when I was with you and needed something, I was not a burden to anyone, for the brothers who came from Macedonia supplied what I needed." He then went on to explain that this was the method he used for his ministry and one he planned to continue using. One principle that can be concluded from this is that it is biblical for churches to support individuals in ministry in areas far removed from them.

Paul funded his ministry another way. In the beginning of 1 Corinthians 9 Paul defends his apostleship, but then the chapter turns into a case that can be used as rationale for personal support. In verses 4-6 Paul talks about having the right to eat and drink, to take along a believing wife, to refrain from working but receive pay or support from those that they were serving. In verse 5 he mentions not only himself, but also the other apostles, the brothers of the Lord, and Peter (Cephas).

Paul, however, did not always accept support from those to whom he ministered. *Halley's Bible Handbook* tells us that one of the objections that Paul's critics had against him in this instance was that he had taken no pay for his work. That made them suspicious. Paul explained that he had the right to be supported by the church, and the Lord definitely ordained that those in ministry should be supported (vv. 4-7, 14).[8]

He begins to set out the principle of "return on labor" (vv. 7-11). Full-time Christian workers do the work of the church; therefore, the church should supply or provide their means or wages. Expecting to receive benefits from the fruit of one's labors is customary. The plowman and the thrasher have the hope of sharing in the crop; sowers should reap something at the harvest. This is the basic concept of living on personal support.

But preaching without pay from those he ministered to directly became a life principle for Paul. It wasn't that Paul thought he couldn't or shouldn't accept support, but that he chose not to. He thought this was a privilege he would forego for a specific purpose, to "win as many as possible" (v. 19; see also vv. 12, 15, 18). His reasons were at least two: because of a great personal satisfaction on his part, thinking that he was doing more than what he was commanded to do, and because he did not want his example to be abused by false teachers whose main concern was salary. He says that his reward was that he could preach the Gospel, offering it free of charge, "and so not make use of [his] rights in preaching it" (v. 18).

Besides the support from the Macedonian church which was mentioned earlier, Paul also received support from the church in Philippi. Philippians 4 points out that their gifts were "a fragrant offering, an acceptable sacrifice, pleasing to God" (v. 18). The apostle also enjoyed gifts of hospitality from believers; for when planning his journey to Rome, Paul was anticipating not only enjoying the company of the believers there "for a while," but also receiving financial support from them for his travels into Spain (Romans 15:24).

A DISCIPLESHIP PROCESS

This area of personal support fund-raising needs to be viewed as a discipleship process. When a person is asked to become a partner in a particular ministry, he has to make a decision about what he is going to do with the resources God has entrusted to him. Will he use them for his own pleasure or for expanding the kingdom of God? Paul greatly encouraged the early churches to support people involved in full-time Christian ministries. Second Corinthians 8 and 9 both contain instructions about offerings for the poor saints in Jerusalem, and relate how the churches wholeheartedly entered into this ministry—even the poor were giving. These two chapters lay out four specific directions for donors: give voluntarily, give proportionately, give systematically, and give to those who are worthy and above reproach.

Any consideration of giving raises the issue of whether to give to churches or parachurch organizations. Most references in the New Testament speak of giving to the church, and although the organized church can be the primary receiver of our tithes and offerings, there is also a basis for individuals to give to others involved in ministry through parachurch organizations. Since parachurch organizations exist to augment the ministry of the church, gifts to them are really accomplishing the same purposes as the church.

By way of testimony, this author can personally attest that having lived on a personal support system for over 15 years, my faith is dramatically different today than what it was when I began. It's not just in relationship to finances but in all areas of my life because of this discipleship process I have personally experienced.

Personal support-raising is a viable, exciting opportunity for giving and receiving funds and other assistance for ministry. It is a valid, reasonable concept that has been sanctioned by God, offering increased donor awareness because individuals can be involved vicariously in the work of the one called out for special service. The missionary gains both financial support and prayer support. The cause of missions is promoted, and churches are edified.⁹ Blessings and rewards double as together the Christian worker and his friends who support him "work together for truth" (3 John 8).

H. ANDREW READ is a graduate of both Temple University in Pennsylvania and Pepperdine University in California. He currently serves as the president of the Evangelical Development Ministry headquartered in Dallas, Texas. His prior experience includes serving as the U.S. national director for the Development Association for Christian Institutions (DACI), and as a full-time staff member of Campus Crusade for Christ for twelve years. He has extensive experience in training staff members of several major ministries in successful support raising and maintenance methods from both a philosophical as well as a practical standpoint.

Mr. Read lectures at conferences, training representatives from both national and international ministries in development and management.

The
Climate in Evangelical Fund-Raising

(23)
HERESIES IN EVANGELICAL
FUND-RAISING:
A THEOLOGIAN'S PERSPECTIVE

CARL F.H. HENRY

Heresy is a powerful word that must be used cautiously—particularly by theologians. To apply it unwittingly to certain issues can be presumptuous and problematic. I believe, however, the term is appropriate when it relates to certain policies and procedures that are, unfortunately, typical of some evangelical fund-raising. Christians need to be alert to such distortions or deficiencies in the apprehension and application of biblical truths, and to the overall impact of these heresies on our ministry and witness for Christ.

My observation is that evangelical fund-raising practices, unfortunately, are sometimes more shoddy than those of nonreligious agencies. Some secular agencies maintain a level of integrity in the use of funding techniques that certain religious enterprises may well emulate. Fortunately, however, evangelical scams are relatively few. A religion that prizes truth more than feelings inevitably turns the searchlight on flimflam.

Money—at least a certain amount of it—is indispensable. And raising money to establish, preserve, and enlarge legitimate Christian enterprises is not evil. Yet the danger is ever present that fund-raising will encroach on the spiritual vitality and moral integrity of evangelical efforts. This is true of educational, of evangelistic, and of eleemosynary agencies.

Therefore, some soliciting practices need to be examined and then avoided. Jesus called Satan "the father of lies" (John 8:44). If a fund-raiser thinks the way to promote the Lord's work is by deception,

271

however subtle, he is in the service of false gods. I cite here examples of various approaches—some questionable, some downright unscriptural—and I have placed them under seven general categories. These I call "heresies," orthodoxies that have been twisted by some evangelical fund-raisers in their struggle to reach a monetary goal. I don't want to depict fund-raisers as villains; some current funding strategies and practices are carefully and thoughtfully handled. Many evangelical fund-raisers are credible religious lobbyists; a few are irreligious ones. But all run the risk of watching the bottom line more than God's highest priority.

I want to challenge the supposedly biblical rationale behind some evangelical fund-raising and to suggest potential heresies that need to be avoided.

SUBSTITUTING SLOGANS FOR SCRIPTURES

At the top of my list of concerns is that evangelical fund-raisers need to reaffirm the Bible as their all-sufficient guide to faith and practice and to honestly submit every campaign principle and slogan to biblical scrutiny.

An example of a slogan is "God's work done in God's way will never lack God's supply." That is an acceptable enough statement, *if* it is honestly understood in the light of Jesus' awesome and fearsome warning:

> Not everyone who says to Me, "Lord, Lord," will enter the kingdom of heaven, but only he who does the will of My Father who is in heaven. Many will say to Me on that day, "Lord, Lord, did we not prophesy in Your name and in Your name drive out demons and perform many miracles?" Then I will tell them plainly, "I never knew you. Away from Me, you evildoers!" (Matthew 7:21-23)

He repudiates those who call Him "Lord," who do works like His own and even give Him the credit. God's supply or blessing is, therefore, not based on orthodoxy of profession or on altruism or magnanimity of service, but on obedience to His Word and will. Anyone soliciting funds for Christian work must be fully persuaded that the ministry represented not only is a response to human need or opportunity but preeminently is a response to God's divine mandate.

SUBSTITUTING SUPPOSED PROOF TEXTS FOR INTRINSIC PRINCIPLES

Some evangelical fund-raisers base their principles on isolated Scripture texts, invoking them without regard to other biblical references and molding Scripture to fit a preconceived warped view.

Fund appeals are almost routinely cloaked with some aura of biblical legitimacy, and passages on stewardship are used as bases for unrelated solicitations. Malachi 3:8-10 is frequently invoked to support "storehouse giving." In view of this passage many pastors encourage channeling all contributions through the local church. Yet complex hermeneutical presuppositions underlie an extension of this passage to any and all modern giving. If we evade sound exegesis and open such texts to allegorical meanings, what are the overall implications for Scripture?

Often an appeal letter will begin with a Bible text such as, "Thanks be to God for His indescribable gift!" (2 Corinthians 9:15) Having enlisted Jesus Christ merely as a transitional theme, it will then conclude by soliciting funds for some current project and promising donors the promoter's latest book brimful of unprecedented spiritual blessing. Seldom is the fund-seeker content to mention a need for which he is "looking to the Lord in faith" without the further suggestion that the Lord in turn is looking to the letter's recipient to handle the matter in His absence.

SUBSTITUTING A MOTIVATION OF GIVING FOR A MOTIVATION OF GETTING

Most evangelical agencies, though not all, avoid adducing a "prosperity theology" as a motivation for giving: the more you give, the wealthier you become. Some invoke Luke 6:38, "Give, and it will be given to you," as a reciprocity guarantee, thus obscuring Jesus' teaching cited by the Apostle Paul, "It is more blessed to give than to receive" (Acts 20:35). The spiritual rewards of stewardship are thereby subordinated to material blessing. Successful entrepreneurs who stress that God has been instrumental in the growth of their businesses wittingly or unwittingly reinforce such prosperity theology. The error of the prosperity theme is not its emphasis that God blesses commercial integrity and sacrificial stewardship, nor that business success is attributable to divine providence, but rather its conversion of stewardship into a material prosperity tool, its attachment of giving to the expectation of personal financial benefit, and its correlation of spirituality with material gain. This approach fails to see stewardship first and foremost as a spiritual exercise for the glory of God and the advancement of His goals, one that, when the giving is sacrificial, yields distinctive compensation of character to the donor.

What the Lord pours out on givers is blessedness or happiness, and treasures of the Spirit (see Matthew 7:11). There is no implication in Jesus' commendation of the widow who made the biggest contribution (two mites) at the temple that she would from that moment prosper materially. But she did receive a blessing from the Lord that the "major donors" present that day in the temple would never have (Mark 12:42-44).

Sometimes the appeal for "seed faith" or "seed money" is simply a variation of prosperity theology: funds are solicited with the assurance that God not only will repay the gift materially but will also multiply the donor's cash reserves. Apart from such distortion, however, the notion of seed money has much to commend it as a launchpad for pilot projects.

SUBSTITUTING SECULAR SOURCES FOR SPIRITUAL RESOURCES

The growing evangelical pursuit of funds from nonevangelical or secular foundations, or unbelieving philanthropists, raises vexing problems. Some administrators at evangelical organizations or institutions are inclined to "take all the devil's money" one can get, and put it to godly uses. Others balk at drafting proposals that deliberately downplay specifically biblical convictions in order to shape programs that non-Christian philanthropies are most likely to approve.

To be sure, there may be overlapping moral and scientific concerns of interest to both an evangelical college and a secular foundation. No objection can be mounted if available funding does not oblige the receiving institution to compromise its own principles and does not encourage reliance on secular sources that in time may tempt that institution to deviate from its distinctive commitments. Trustees have been known to moderate an institution's commitments in order to secure outside funding that removes personal financial pressure from themselves. Additionally, the question of acceptance or nonacceptance of federal funds, a subject that falls outside the purview of this discussion, raises many of the same issues and introduces still others. But in any event, evangelical colleges, along with all other evangelical causes and organizations, must be supremely concerned that nothing shall erode their loyalty to God, their devotion to charter objectives, the goodwill of their constituency, and their dependence on prayer for faithful survival.

The miracle of feeding the 5,000 with one boy's loaves and fishes was divine multiplication of limited resources and not—as some imaginative liberals have explained it—a prodding of the crowd's nobler impulses to share their own lunches with each other.

As budgets spiral ever upward, ministries often look for leadership skilled in public relations and in raising funds from large foundations. Sophistication is required in preparing grant proposals, and personal contacts in the financial world are important. All of this tends to treat God as a Peeping Tom in economic affairs, except when deficits so threaten survival that no earthly hope remains but to return to the prayer meeting.

The notion that gifts may be advantageously solicited from wealthy persons irrespective of their basic convictions often leads fund-raisers to conform proposals to the special interest of one or another monied prospect. Helen Bergan's *Where the Money Is: A Fund-Raiser's Guide to the Rich* (Alexandria, Va.: VioGuide Press) then becomes the solicitor's main source book. The Chicago *Tribune*'s biweekly newsletter, *Donor Briefing*, alerts him to who is giving what to whom and why. Yet the fund-raiser may be quite unaware that buying into nonevangelical or subevangelical funding may in the long run do as much harm to a ministry's theological and spiritual orientation as it does good to its present fiscal condition. As a compensation for their gifts, some large donors have expected personal or proxy representation on a board or governing body or other preferences and favors.

Not a few enterprises take their promotional cue from Madison Avenue, and eagerly tailor their appeals to secular approaches. Evangelical ministries need constantly to investigate such dependency on the philosophy of secular professionals. It is understandable that some evangelical administrators readily enlist the expertise of secular fund-raisers and investment agencies. But this practice brings with it great risks. Promotion built on philosophies of the secular world must always be carefully scrutinized; Madison Avenue's most successful commercials, it is said, are those which stretch the truth but do it subtly. In transferring financial activities to professional managers, administrators may unwittingly lose control of an organization's destiny.

SUBSTITUTING MATERIAL INCENTIVE FOR SPIRIT-LED GENEROSITY

The prophet motive and the profit motive are often on a collision course; the prophet offers a free salvation, the profiteer wants to add a commission charge. Some fund-raisers use radio and direct mail to peddle contribution premiums that vary in quality in ratio to the dollars given. They are hucksters of merchandise, indulging in such jargon as "No Christian home should be without one," using valuable air time or expensive brochures to tout the virtues of the "product" which will be sent in return for a donation.

Fund-raising premiums raise serious ethical problems. For one thing, the monetary value of such premiums is often exaggerated. At worst, a special spiritual benefit is attributed to floral sprigs or tiny twigs from the Holy Land, mother-of-pearl crosses from Bethlehem, olive wood amulets from Jerusalem, or cheap jade charms from Hong Kong or Taiwan. Such relics may not carry all the implications of the medieval indulgences, but they are nonetheless reminiscent of them insofar as they are depicted as laden with blessing if not with miracle-power because they have been prayed over or are thought to protect the recipient against evil. If this were merely a religious extension of the cosmetic industry's "free bonus with purchase," it would be bad enough; far worse is the promise not merely of physical enhancement but of spiritual benefits that the almost worthless trinkets are presumed to convey.

Books, magazines, or cassettes are frequently sent as premiums. Donors must deduct their value from any I.R.S. claim for a tax-exempt contribution. The hawker often puts their value not at actual cost but at the publisher's or producer's inflated price. I.R.S. requirements are more murky when gift books are provided by an independent source to help stimulate support for a program. Publishers' closeouts, now and then distributed by evangelical agencies, often do little to enhance organizational goals. Some tax-exempt groups are careful to distribute books that reflect an organization's creative interests and achievements, thereby stimulating larger long-term support. Doctrinally responsible ventures will distribute books of theological integrity that truly promote spiritual life. "Health and wealth" solicitations are often somewhat more ambiguous than are theologically articulate ministries and are sometimes less precise about how contributions will be used. Some theologically indefinite efforts focus constantly on world emergency needs, and alter their appeal goals and even modify their doctrinal tenets when they shift to new crisis concerns.

Much fund-raising links generosity in making charitable gifts primarily to the tax break such gifts bestow on donors. In 1986 many charities advised U.S. citizens how they could benefit taxwise by giving before year's end when the new tax law became effective. The accounting firm of Arthur Anderson & Co. advised nonprofit institutions that opportunity was vanishing for wealthy donors to "get the government to pay as much as one-half the cost of lifetime charitable giving."

Fortunately evangelical appeals seem to have escaped the misleading secular offers of "something for nothing." No evangelical college has yet promoted an alumni lottery offering free tuition for a child or grandchild, or offered the second prize winner an all-expense-paid trip to homecoming weekend for a class reunion.

Peter and John at the gate of the temple did not offer a "premium"; they offered to the lame beggar the power of the name of Jesus. What they themselves got in return was not dollars but a dungeon (Acts 3–4).

SUBSTITUTING METHODOLOGY FOR MINISTRY

Evangelical organizations do not wholly escape the temptation to post fake mailgrams or to dress up junk mail to look like first-class personal correspondence. Evangelistic enterprises and humanitarian agencies routinely imprint their envelopes with "Urgent—Immediate Reply Requested" or "Priority Mail" so that gullible recipients may think the correspondence is selective and private.

A more blatantly offensive device is the first-class letter sent by a stranger who addresses the prospect by first name and signs off on a first-name basis. The correspondence shares supposedly confidential information (usually so intangible that its release could harm no one) and charts new evangelistic opportunities that promise certain success.

A special public relations feature of evangelicals is a vaunted personal interest in the individual as a person uniquely fashioned in God's image and created for distinctive service in the world. But in reality this personal touch is continually jeopardized. Obviously movements with large supportive constituencies cannot maintain personal relationships with all donors, and overstatement readily becomes the first step toward manipulating and exploiting the donors. Computer-generated correspondence that gives the impression of a personal exchange is bad enough. But when the person whose mechanical signature ends the letter guarantees that he will personally pray for all who write expressing their needs—and conveys the impression of a truly significant prayer burden for each respondent—the pitch is unconscionable.

One recent solicitation letter from a religious magazine began with the sender's personal assurance, "Today I have your name before me in prayer." But even the most determined correspondent would never manage 10,000 three-second sound blips like, "O God, remember Carl Henry wherever he is, whatever his need," even if he prayed for eight solid hours without stopping for breath. The writer adds that I am "deeply and strongly on (his) heart" because the American economy may suddenly plummet and seed gifts are needed. The letter proceeds to invert apostolic priorities by saying far more about money than about ministry.

The temptation also arises, on the basis of an evangelical entrepreneur's private faith, to exceed budget prospects by anticipating support which is not really in hand or in view for new and enlarged programs. Some such funding appeals have even blamed God for unfortunate overextension of enterprises. "The Lord has blessed this work so abundantly that now we are really in trouble trying to keep it going." Or again, "Without additional help we must cut back critical programs, but I know that is not God's will for us."

Financially faltering enterprises may suggest a need for Christian cooperation and merger. Personality or cult movements run great risk when leaders become, as Mel Lorentzen, associate director of the Billy Graham Center, phrases it, "builders of personal empires 'in His name' "; rather than serving as "commissioned agents of the heavenly kingdom," they compete with each other for cash from a common constituency. Just as lamentable is the sale and exchange of donor lists by some evangelical or fundamentalist agencies.

The fact that a cause is good does not of itself justify telephone intrusion at any hour of the day or evening. The year-end phona-thon is an unpleasant tactic; the caller is not personally known, often interrupts something the responder considers more important, usually solicits a larger contribution than the responder is disposed to make, and demeans the prospect list into a series of technological statistics. Even worse is the long-distance "person-to-person" call in which the "operator" asks if one has just a minute to listen to an "important personal message" from Big Name Evangelical, in actual-ity a recorded tape. Such an approach is an invasion of a person's time under false pretenses.

Other fund-raisers suggest asking a "volunteer" to make a pitch to someone in his particular peer group. If the potential donor is per-sonally unable or indisposed to give, fund-raisers then invite the recalcitrant prospect to address the most vulnerable of his well-to-do acquaintances.

The appeal to donor ego nullifies the ethical and spiritual gratifi-cation that donors ought to experience in giving. Another question-able device is publishing lists of donors and their gifts, thus making public what ought to be a private matter, namely, the extent of a donor's contribution. This practice exposes contributors to solicita-tion by still other fund-raisers. Moreover, if such tactics are used to send smaller donors on a "guilt trip," they may alienate an important and perhaps even the largest segment of supporters.

SUBSTITUTING FEAR FOR FAITH AS THE MOTIVATION FOR GIVING

Direct mail experts who advise Christian agencies, and in many cases devise their funding campaigns, say, "Create a crisis, press the panic button—people will not give to something successful but only to a salvage operation." How does this cynical philosophy square with

Jesus' teaching in Matthew 16:18, "I will build My church"?

Nowhere does the Bible hint that the Lord needs our finite efforts to bail Him out of a budget crunch. To assume so maligns the faithfulness of God to His servants and His adequacy to run His business.

Yet some direct mail strategists suggest playing on emotions. Conservatively worded direct mail that deals with substantive issues is said to be financially unrewarding; only by feeding on "raw meat"— anxieties over homosexuality, pornography, sexual delinquency, drugs, and so on—will the recipient feel sufficiently moved to respond.

When prospective donors are told that the first $15,000 received will go to meet some dire need, what is often unmentioned is that the first contributions by radio and television audiences usually go toward meeting program overhead expenses. Unless an independent source has underwritten the salaries of an institution's development or stewardship staff, a substantial part of the money raised goes to pay salaries and travel costs, even where solicitation is done on commission. No fund-raising can be done without administrative costs, and few organizations are in a position to devote every cent that is given to the cause for which contributions are intended. Hence the percentage of funds that remain to advance an institution's spiritual and moral vision is crucially important.

Few factors permanently motivate the giving of believers more than a clear, unambiguous definition of objectives enunciated by a leader perceived to be trustworthy. A touch of charisma is an asset, but it will not compensate for a lack of personal integrity or for imprecise formulation of goals or for uncertainty over the intended use of funds. The risk of concentrating the promotion of an enterprise on a single personality is evident, however; not only does such a policy create problems of succession but the leader is sometimes also conceived as being more important than the work; consequently, the temptation arises to perpetuate family dynasties.

IMPETUS FOR CHANGE

It would be somewhat useless to discuss these problems without offering any solutions. Those who know my views understand my strong conviction that evangelicals are in a struggle for the mind and will of our generation. The results of this struggle will determine, among other things, the nature and theology of our fund-raising practices and beliefs.

A critical starting point that can result in change of fund-raising practices lies with the evangelical college and its special academic mission to teach a Christian world-life view. As evangelicals are educated with biblical convictions, Christian colleges can be catalysts in the promulgation of truth and the ongoing practice of faith— which will extend to how we give our money and how we ask for it.

Whatever the evangelical enterprise, fund solicitation is best done by dedicated believers who are assured of the doctrinal, moral, and fiscal integrity of their enterprises and who venture into fund-raising primarily as a divine vocation rather than simply for the commission that represents or augments their salaries. Promotion and funding must be placed conspicuously in the service of preserving, propagating, and vindicating truth. To do this requires an unapologetic statement of doctrinal conviction, a platform of fund-raising principles compatible with those commitments, and a promotional policy that stresses how the institution or agency succeeds in advancing its God-ordained purposes. By hoisting a new standard of promotion and fund-raising, evangelical colleges, churches, and parachurch organizations become nothing more or less than God's trusted guardians of Christian truth and morality.

CARL F.H. HENRY is recognized as a foremost author, educator, lecturer, and theologian. He has taught or lectured on college campuses throughout the United States, and in countries on every continent. He has written or edited more than 40 books, including The Christian Mindset in a Secular Society *and the series* God, Revelation, and Authority.

Dr. Henry served on the founding faculty of Fuller Theological Seminary and was the founding editor of Christianity Today *magazine. He has also served as the editor-at-large of* Christianity Today *and lecturer-at-large for World Vision International.*

(24)
WHAT THE PUBLIC
THINKS ABOUT EVANGELICAL
FUND-RAISING

PAUL H. VIRTS and GEORGE GALLUP, JR.
Questions about fund-raising and the use of money in churches and
other Christian organizations are as old as the church itself. Paul was
so concerned about what people would say about the way he raised
and used money that he set up guidelines for himself and the church
for centuries to come (2 Corinthians 8:18-21). One of Jesus' disciples, Judas, had the reputation of pilfering the purse for Jesus' band
of followers (John 12:6).

It should not surprise us, then, that questions continue to be
raised today about fund-raising by churches and other religious organizations. As long as these groups need money to accomplish their
tasks, they will have to raise and use money and some will be
charged with unethical fund-raising and misuse of funds.

Recent history may become known as the one period of time when
the fund-raising of religious organizations received the greatest attention and raised the most serious questions. Oral Roberts attracted
press attention when he told his supporters that God had threatened
to "call him home" if he didn't raise money to support medical
students who were being trained at his university. He pled with his
contributors to send $8 million to spare his life before the deadline.
As Oral Roberts' deadline approached, the sex and pay-off scandal of
PTL's founder, Jim Bakker, exploded in public. The pay-off was
reportedly made with money raised for PTL's religious activities.
Financial audits also revealed that the Bakkers were paid exhorbitant
salaries while heading the PTL organization.

These events raise a number of important questions for those raising money for religious organizations and for those making financial contributions: What kinds of people contribute to churches and other religious organizations? How much do they contribute? What are their attitudes toward fund-raising by Christian churches and organizations? Two polls conducted by The Gallup Organization ("Religious Fund-Raising" and "Television Evangelists") provide some answers to these important questions. The "Religious Fund-Raising" study was conducted in January 1987 just as the story about Oral Roberts first appeared in the press, but before a great deal of attention was paid to this story. The study on "Television Evangelists" was conducted in mid-April after the Jim Bakker scandal became public knowledge. After providing answers to these questions, we will discuss implications of the findings for Christian fund-raising.

CONTRIBUTORS TO RELIGIOUS ORGANIZATIONS

According to the "Religious Fund-Raising" study, two of every three Americans have made a contribution to a Catholic or Protestant church or other religious (parachurch) organization in the past year. This compares with slightly more than seven in ten who said they made a contribution to a religious charity in a 1984 study conducted by Yankelovich.[1] In the Gallup study, the best predictor of whether a person made a contribution in the past year was whether he or she had attended church. More than eight in ten of those who made a contribution said they had attended church in the past six months. This confirms findings from a previous study on charitable giving which indicated that church attendance was highly correlated with making contributions.[2] Other groups of people in the Gallup study who were most likely to make a contribution included people over 50 years old, those living in all geographical regions of the country except the West, Republicans, women, and those describing themselves as "evangelical."

Contributors expressed a clear preference for their local church or denomination over parachurch organizations. Nearly six out of every ten made a contribution only to their local church or denomination, while only a handful contributed only to a parachurch organization. Nearly four in ten made contributions to both churches and parachurch organizations. As might be expected, those who do not attend church are more likely than church attenders to send money only to parachurch organizations, but were significantly less likely to support both local churches and parachurch organizations.

The single-mindedness of most contributors is evident in other ways. Slightly more than six out of every ten contributors said they donated to only one church or parachurch organization. This finding held true across nearly all demographic groups. Only one in five said they contributed to two or three organizations. When asked how they apportion their giving, nearly six in ten contributors said three-quarters or more of their contributions go to their local churches or denominations. Those most likely to say they give *all* of their religious contributions to their local church include men, people 30-49 years of age, nonevangelicals, and Catholics. At the other end of the spectrum, those most likely to give less than one-quarter of their contributions to the local church include women, people 18-29 years of age, those living in the Midwest, evangelicals, and Protestants.

Previous research indicates that while there is widespread support for religious organizations and other charities among the American public, the depth of that support is somewhat shallow. A Yankelovich, Skelly and White study conducted in 1984 indicated that of all those giving to religious charities, nearly two in three contributed $500 or less each year.[1] The average contribution was $740, nearly 70 percent of which went to religious causes. To look at it another way, those who contribute to religious causes give 2.4 percent of their income to religious charities. People who gave the largest proportion (5 percent) of their total income to religious causes were those who not only attend religious services regularly but also discipline themselves to set aside a specified percentage of their income to religious charities.

Data from the Gallup study on religious fund-raising follows the same pattern as previous research. Six in ten gave $500 or less to Christian causes. These smaller contributors were most likely to be women, people 18-29 years of age, those with less education and income, nonevangelicals, Catholics, and Democrats.

AMOUNT AND MEDIA FOR CHRISTIAN FUND-RAISING
One issue of importance to religious fund-raisers is the extent to which the American public is exposed to fund-raising efforts. It is

safe to say that at no time in history has the public been as bombarded with fund-raising appeals as they are today. Both religious and nonreligious charities conduct annual (if not more frequent) telethons. Hundreds of religious radio stations air programs that solicit funds to pay production and distribution costs. But the tool of modern technology most responsible for increasing charitable fund-raising activities is the computer, which makes it possible to send "personalized" letters to hundreds of thousands of people who have supported one's organization in the past or whose names appear on other mailing lists that can be rented.

How widespread is exposure to religious fund-raising? According to the Gallup study, nearly three in four Americans recall exposure to fund-raising by Christian churches and organizations in the past six months. Those who are most likely to recall exposure to Christian fund-raising include women, people over 30 years of age, those with higher levels of education and income, people living in the South, nonevangelicals, and Republicans.

Those who recalled exposure to Christian fund-raising think there are a fair number of such appeals. Slightly more than one-half recalled seeing, hearing, or reading as many as four appeals in the past month. Nearly one in three recalled exposure to five or more appeals. The people who recall higher exposure to fund-raising include women, people 30 years of age and older, those with higher levels of education and income, and evangelicals.

Predictably, a substantial number of people think there are too many fund-raising appeals by Christian organizations. Nearly one-half of those who were exposed to Christian fund-raising said there were far too many or somewhat too many appeals, while one in three said there was about the right number. Those most disturbed about the number of appeals include men, people over the age of 50, those with incomes of $25,000 or more, and nonevangelicals.

Another strategic issue Christian fund-raisers face is which medium to use. The more saturated a medium is with fund-raising, the less useful it will be in the future. People in the Gallup study were asked where they recalled seeing appeals in the past six months. Television ranked highest with slightly more than two in three people recalling funding requests in that medium. Approximately one-half of the people recalled appeals at church (53 percent) or in newspapers or magazines (47 percent). Direct mail ranked fourth (42 percent) and radio took the fifth spot (32 percent) on the list. Only about one in ten recalled telephone solicitation. Interestingly, only a handful of people (2 percent) recalled another person directly asking them to contribute. Fund-raising appeals on television are more likely to get through to men, people over 50, and evangelicals. On the other hand, solicitation at church is most likely to reach women, people 30-49 years of age, and those with higher levels of income and education. Direct mail is most likely to get through to older donors, those with more education, and nonevangelicals.

Christian fund-raisers have learned well the lessons taught by marketing experts—target people with higher total incomes and those with more discretionary income (people over 50). But these people are much closer than others to reaching the saturation point with fund-raising appeals.

PUBLIC PERCEPTIONS OF FUND-RAISING ETHICS

Communication scholars tell us that one of the most important factors in persuading people to believe or act in a given way is the perceived credibility of the persuader. When the audience believes the speaker has a high level of credibility, it is more likely to be persuaded by that speaker, all other things being equal.

Research has shown that audiences think a person is highly credible if he or she possesses three characteristics: *qualifications* (expertise in the subject at hand), *character* (personal qualities such as honesty and trustworthiness), and *dynamism* (delivery qualities such as enthusiasm and activeness).[4] One of the major purposes of the current research project was to assess the public's perceptions of the character of Christian fund-raisers.

Are the activities of Christian fund-raisers ethical? Nearly one-half of the American public thinks all or most of this fund-raising is ethical, while slightly fewer (four in ten) said only some or very little of it is ethical. A handful would dismiss all Christian fund-raising as unethical. Fund-raising was given the highest marks by people ages 18-29, people living in the East, those with higher levels of education and income, nonevangelicals, and Roman Catholics. The people most likely to challenge the ethics of Christian fund-raising were older people (50+), those with less education, those earning less than $15,000 a year, those living in the South, and Protestants.

In short, upscale people were more positive about Christian fund-raising activities than downscale people were. Part of this difference may be accounted for by differential exposure to types of fund-raising. Upscale people are more likely to recall exposure to local church fund-raising and mail solicitation.

Those people who said most or all of Christian fund-raising is ethical displayed a predictable amount of trust in Christian fund-raisers. Four in ten said fund-raising activities were ethical because fund-raisers were honest people. Those most likely to perceive fund-raisers as honest people included women, people 50 or over, those with less education and lower income, and evangelicals. Other reasons for thinking fund-raising was ethical were expressed. Nearly one in five said they knew where funds were going, while one in five said they thought the cause was a worthy one. A handful said they had seen the results of their donations in the organizations they supported and that they thought little money was spent on administrative costs.

People who expressed partial or complete doubt about the ethics of fund-raising activities gave a variety of reasons for their opinions. Slightly more than one in four felt that Christian organizations or churches misused money, though they didn't say how. Men, and people with higher levels of income and education were more likely than others to give this reason. Nearly one in five said these fund-raisers are dishonest people, while one in ten said fund-raising was too commercialized, especially on television. Less than one in ten mentioned high pressure tactics used in fund-raising, lack of clarity in how funds are used, low credibility of fund-raisers, and excessive amounts of money used for administrative costs.

Overall, people gave more positive than negative reasons for their views on the ethics of fund-raising. For example, based on the total sample, three times as many people said Christian fund-raisers were honest than said they were dishonest. Similarly, three times as many people said they knew how funds were being used or that they had seen results of their contributions than said the use of funds was unclear. However, three times as many people reacted negatively as reacted positively to the amount of money spent on administration.

How these data are interpreted will depend a great deal on whether the interpreter sees a half-full or a half-empty glass. It is impressive that nearly one-half of those questioned gave high marks to Christian fund-raising. It is cause for deep concern, however, that nearly as many people raise serious questions about the ethics of Christian fund-raising. The proportions of people expressing negative attitudes toward Christian fund-raising is of particular concern for fund-raisers in light of the fact that these data were collected *before* the Oral Roberts and Jim Bakker stories received significant press attention. We return to the subject of the public's reaction to religious broadcasters in particular in a later section.

It is one thing to pass judgment on Christian fund-raising in general, but it is quite another to take action based on those attitudes. For all of the negative attitudes toward Christian fund-raising, relatively few people admit terminating contributions because of unethical fund-raising. People who had made a contribution to a Christian cause in the past year were asked if they had stopped supporting a church organization in the past year and why they had done so. Fewer than one in ten contributors had stopped supporting a Christian entity in the past year, and only a handful of all givers (2 percent) stopped their contributions because of fund-raising or questionable use of funds. Again, fewer than one in ten contributors to religious organizations said they had *ever* stopped making contributions because of unethical fund-raising. The three most common reasons for the cutoff in funds was that money was not being used as it should have been, that there was too much pressure to give, and that too much money was spent on administrative costs.

It may well be that many contributors carefully check organizations before they start their support. This explanation is feasible, especially in view of the fact that people are most likely to contribute to their local churches where they can more easily monitor the raising and use of money before they give. It may also be that many people are not aware of unethical fund-raising practices because they support organizations (for example, parachurch organizations) that they do not have easy access to. Or, it may simply be that for all the negative attitudes toward fund-raising by Christian organizations, people are rarely moved to take action.

FUND-RAISING ETHICS BY MEDIUM
One important question for fund-raisers is whether people think the fund-raising on one medium tends to be more or less ethical than

that in other media. A tentative answer to that question is in the affirmative. (We say "tentative" because people were not directly asked this question, but the findings are inferred from responses to other questions.) Of those who attend church, slightly more than one-half recalling exposure to radio fund-raising say all or most fund-raising is ethical, while slightly less than half recalling exposure to telephone fund-raising and television fund-raising say all or most Christian fund-raising is ethical. The difference in the positive ethical rating for newspapers or magazines (58 percent) and television (46 percent) is not large but is statistically significant. These data suggest that telephone and television fund-raising are perceived as less credible than that of other media.

After the news of Jim Bakker's difficulties surfaced in early April 1987, Gallup conducted a study of the public's perceptions of television evangelists and their fund-raising techniques. By that time, people had clearly become negative toward television evangelists. (Gallup did not attempt to assess reactions to fund-raising by other types of religious organizations in this study.) Gallup asked people to indicate how favorable they were to television evangelists and then compared these data to similar findings obtained in 1980. The results were as follows:[5]

TV Evangelist	Awareness Levels		Highly/Mildly Favorable	
	1980	1987	1980	1987
	%	%	%	%
Billy Graham	92	90	76	76
Robert Shuller	19	53	78	61
Rex Humbard	43	50	73	55
Pat Robertson	25	72	65	50
Jimmy Swaggart	23	76	76	44
Jerry Falwell	--	78	--	38
Oral Roberts	83	89	66	28
Jim Bakker	28	78	58	23

Awareness levels for television evangelists increased from 1980 to 1987, while their favorability ratings decreased for everyone except Billy Graham. As we might expect, the public had become more negative toward television evangelists on a number of dimensions related to fund-raising. The number of people who said TV evangelists were honest slipped from slightly more than one-half in 1980 to about one in three in 1987. Those who said TV evangelists were trustworthy with money decreased from four in ten in 1980 to slightly less than one in four in 1987. Those calling for federal government regulation of religious fund-raising increased from slightly more than one in three in 1980 to more than four in ten in 1987.

These data support the tentative conclusion from the Christian fund-raising study that TV fund-raising may suffer from lower levels of credibility. Of course, TV fund-raising has the highest level of visibility and may invite closer scrutiny than other forms.

GENERAL FUND-RAISING GUIDELINES

As already discussed, few donors have ever stopped supporting a Christian cause because of unethical fund-raising. But how much of a consideration is fund-raising methods—or other important factors—in deciding whether to support an organization in the first place? Of a number of qualities of Christian organizations people think are very important in making a decision to contribute, the top-ranked consideration (as rated by nearly nine out of ten contributors) was whether the organization is ethical and honest. (This finding is not surprising—this question was asked after some initial questions about the ethics of Christian fund-raising.) Other qualities of organizations that rated very high include whether the organization is caring and compassionate, gets things done, and has a cause the donor is interested in. The qualities that contributors were less likely to consider as highly important include low administrative costs and the longevity of the organization.

Donors may have high expectations for the ethics of fund-raisers, but they experience trouble articulating exactly what biblical principles or guidelines Christian churches and organizations should follow in raising money. Four in ten in this study could not think of any biblical guidelines. One in four simply said fund-raisers should be honest. One in six said fund-raisers should use money to help people in need. A handful of people suggested the following: The commandment to love God and one's neighbor, free-will offerings, the Golden Rule, the principle "Give and you will receive," and tithing.

RECOMMENDATIONS

These research findings suggest some future directions for Christian fund-raisers.

● In the long run, the best way to raise money for Christian causes may not be to increase fund-raising activities so much as to encourage people to attend church more frequently. In short, leading people to greater maturity in their Christian faith usually increases their sense of responsibility for others. All this points to a cardinal principle of Christian fund-raising: Money follows ministry. People give when they feel their needs are met. But one word of caution is in order. Sooner or later, people will assess the motives behind the ministry. People are most likely to support those organizations whose true motives are to bring people to Christ and to mature them in their Christian faith, not simply to minister for the sake of raising money.

● Another important way of getting people to increase their giving to Christian organizations and churches is to persuade them to volunteer time for the organization. According to a Gallup study conducted in 1985, people who volunteer their time for nonprofit organizations give significantly more to charitable causes than those who do not volunteer time.[6]

● Church and parachurch organizations alike should work together to find ways to teach financial stewardship to the people they serve. American Christians are generally considered to be among the most generous in the world, but they still give a relatively small portion of their income to Christian causes. Whether one uses either the Old Testament concept of tithing 10 percent of one's income or the New Testament concept of giving proportionally (giving as God has prospered—1 Corinthians 16:2) as a standard, the level of giving by churchgoers is relatively low. The Yankelovich study highlights the importance of setting up a systematic program of giving.[7] Those who set up their own systematic program of giving are likely to give more.

● Since much Christian fund-raising is directed at older people and those with higher incomes, and since it is these people who express most concern about the amount of Christian fund-raising, leaders of churches and Christian organizations need to target fund-raising to other segments of the population. Older people are generally more concerned about spiritual matters and usually have more discretionary income. People with higher levels of income also have more discretionary income. For a number of reasons, both of these groups of people are more accessible and, to a certain extent, more susceptible to Christian fund-raising appeals.

Much has been written about the baby boomers and their influence in the marketplace, but this generation is known to be less charitable than others.[8] Many explanations can be offered for this stinginess—they have less discretionary income, they tend to be more skeptical because of the era in which they grew up, and so forth. Fund-raisers need to explore ways to encourage baby boomers to give to Christian causes. Based on some recent research, Cohen suggests that fund-raising directed at this younger generation will have to be different from that directed at the older generation. He suggests the following:

- get them involved in one's organization,
- show them what's in it for them (use social gatherings, appeal to status, etc.),
- provide them with plenty of giving options,
- provide them with information (show how money is used, show tangible results, produce materials with high production values, etc.),
- use spokespersons they relate to,
- make it easy and convenient to give,
- appeal to their focus on children, and
- utilize connections with existing organizations (employer, schools, and colleges, etc.).[9]

Similarly, fund-raising strategies need to be developed for people who are less well off financially. It is a well-documented fact that people who earn less than $20,000 a year give a larger percentage of their incomes to religious causes.[10] We think it is particularly important to encourage these people to contribute, given Jesus' praise for the poor woman who gave all she had (Luke 21:1-4).

● Since people are much more likely to give to local churches than to parachurch ministries, parachurch organizations would do well to tie in their work more closely with local churches. This allows donors to see the results of these ministries firsthand and even to get personally involved. This research suggests that seeing results firsthand will bring about increased levels of support.

● Given the substantial amount of skepticism about the ethics of

Christian fund-raising, leaders of churches and Christian organizations need to take bold steps to bolster public confidence in their fund-raising activities.

Religious fund-raisers should join "watchdog" organizations that have established standards for fund-raising such as the Evangelical Council for Financial Accountability (ECFA), and the Ethics and Financial Integrity Commission of the National Religious Broadcasters. They should seek ways to actively promote these organizations and their standards. Similarly, religious fund-raisers should look for ways to educate the public about acceptable standards of fund-raising in general.

Christian fund-raisers should regularly explain to their publics what standards they follow. This research suggests many of these standards:

   – demonstrate honesty in the raising of and use of money,
   – clearly explain how funds will be used and remain true to that commitment,
   – show donors the results obtained from helping people,
   – clearly explain how much money is used for administrative costs,
   – raise money for people who are truly needy,
   – avoid using high-pressure tactics.

They should also explain fund-raising procedures to donors—for example, how designated gifts are handled, the availability of financial statements upon request, and so forth.

Religious broadcasters and others using TV as a fund-raising medium especially need to demonstrate to the public that they are ethical and honest.

   ● Christian fund-raisers also need to rethink the use of television as a fund-raising tool. People over 50 are most likely to be aware of TV fund-raising and are also most likely to say there is too much fund-raising for Christian causes in general. It may be necessary to shift more fund-raising to other media. For example, given the lack of one-on-one fund-raising and problems with the credibility of fund-raisers, it may be necessary to return to more personalized forms of fund-raising. It may also be necessary to change the ways telethons are produced on TV, such as reducing the length.

The fact that questions will probably always be raised about the raising and use of money by churches and parachurch ministries should not deter Christian leaders from establishing and following the highest of ethical standards.

Religious fund-raisers need to be reminded periodically that the public trust is critical to the survival of nonprofit organizations. A substantial number of people still place a great deal of trust in churches and parachurch organizations, but once that trust is violated it is often difficult to regain.

PAUL H. VIRTS *is the director of marketing research for the Christian Broadcasting Network. He has conducted numerous donor research projects for CBN. He earned a Ph.D. in communication research from the University of Iowa in 1979. Dr. Virts taught at CBN University Graduate School of Communication for five years before joining CBN's broadcasting network.*

GEORGE GALLUP, JR., *is the cochairman of The Gallup Organization and is the president of the Gallup Poll. He is the author of numerous books and articles, and the coauthor of a weekly newspaper column titled "The Gallup Religion Poll."*

(25)
THE EVANGELICAL DONOR
TALKS BACK

JAMES F. ENGEL

The best way to comprehend fund-raising stategies is to understand the people who give—what motivates them, why they give, who they are, etc. This chapter, based on research findings gathered over the past 15 years from nearly 75 Christian organizations, provides answers to many of these concerns.[1] The chapter develops these succinct sections: donor decision processes, the organization's role in partnership, the donor's role in partnership, and building partnership.

DONOR DECISION PROCESSES

It is clear from the research that giving decisions are made in two distinct and different ways, *active reasoning* and *passive reasoning*, and there are many stewardship implications for both the donor and the organizational recipient.

• Active reasoning. John and Sally Riley heard a presentation at their church given by a field representative from a mission they respect. He appealed for scholarships to help support Latin American pastors who are studying new techniques of urban evangelism and church planting. After some discussion John and Sally concluded that they could cut corners a bit and contribute $500. Ever since a visit to Mexico City, they had been concerned about urban evangelism and welcomed this opportunity to participate. Two months later, they pledged another $500 after receipt of a personalized direct mail appeal telling them some of the outcomes of the training project that they supported.

John and Sally are quite interested in this cause; they made their decision on the basis of *active reasoning* and extended the problem-solving in which the options are weighed and evaluated.[2] In other words, thinking led to feeling which led to action (see Figure 1).

Figure 1. **Active Reasoning Versus Passive Reasoning**

Active Reasoning

high awareness ---› thinking ---› feeling ---› action

Passive Reasoning

low-level awareness ---› action ---› thinking ---› feeling

They first became aware of the need and then actively evaluated whether or not they should participate financially. A positive feeling (attitude) toward this cause then led to a decision to give. The act of becoming donors, in turn, was seen in a favorable light because of their commitment to Latin America and the ministry of this mission. Therefore, they are likely to continue as loyal donors. More details on this type of decision process are given in Figure 2.

Figure 2. **The Involved Donor**

1. Personal needs and motives are fulfilled by the act of giving. Hence, the cause is perceived as significant.
2. As information is gathered and processed, there are progressive changes in understanding and awareness, attitude toward the act of giving, intention to act, and ultimate behavior.
3. When asked, donors who are motivated in this way can readily verbalize the benefits received from support.
4. Involvement will vary from one situation to another:
   • It is likely when there is direct ministry to the donor (i.e., television evangelists and teachers).
   • Involvement also can be present when the cause is highly emotional (ministry to children, etc.).
   • Donors over the age of 50 often are highly involved in missions giving because of the central importance of evangelism ingrained from their Christian background.
5. Loyalty and continued giving over time will be maintained as long as the cause is perceived as having relevance and the organization as having credibility.

The Evangelical Donor Talks Back

Active reasoning and donor loyalty is an outcome of high *involve-ment*—the degree of pertinence and relevance to the individual.[3] In the best sense of the word, donors always ask, "What's in it for me?" High involvement exists when one or more of these factors are present:

there is strong interest in the cause;

the organizational spokesperson has high credibility and there is motivation to respond for that reason; and

there is a strong desire to support an individual missionary.

When involvement is high, the donor acts as a rational problem-solver. As Figure 2 shows, information is weighed and evaluated as are various alternatives. Before a final decision is made, the act of support must be seen as offering a true benefit in the context of motives and interests. The outcome is a response which says, in effect, "I believe in you and in what you are doing and it is impor-tant for me to have a part."

This type of donor has a Spirit-motivated need to be a financial contributor and is rewarded by God for obedience.[4] A common ques-tion in donor research asks, "If this organization has a financial need, how do you feel when it is brought to your attention and you are asked to participate?" Almost without fail the replies from com-mitted friends are strongly affirmative. After all, isn't this an essen-tial quality of true partnership and friendship?

A decision based on active reasoning motivated by high involve-ment signifies the donor's desire to become a partner in the cause. Partnership exemplifies mutual participation and equality. To use Phillip Kotler's term, the donor becomes an essential "stakeholder" in the organization and its outcomes.[5] The challenge to the recipient organization is to recognize and exemplify this mutuality in donor relations.

● Passive reasoning. Returning once more to the Riley family, Sally listened to Christian radio and heard an appeal for funds to help relieve a recent drought in Somalia. Although she had never before given to the sponsoring organization, she had heard its name several times. Immediately she sent a check for $25 without much thought and evaluation. She was glad to help in a small way, and a gift of $25 was no sacrifice. In other words, the perceived risk of a wrong decision was quite low.

After a week or so Sally received a nonpersonalized information package in the mail from this organization. She glanced at it and was glad she had given, but she never gave again, in spite of many direct mail appeals.

In this case Sally followed *passive reasoning* diagrammed in Figure 1 in which some low-level organizational awareness triggered a small gift when the need was made known. There was little deliberation prior to decision, and Sally really did not think about it again until she received the information package. Therefore, the act of giving led to thinking which led to attitude or feeling.

Sally's decision-process behavior reflected low involvement (see Figure 3). There was legitimate need mentioned by a credible organization, but her response was one of "Why not?" rather than a thought-through decision. In her eyes, nothing much would be lost, even if the gift were not properly used. In a sense this represents a spur-of-the-moment reaction which is of marginal psychological and spiritual relevance and which may or may not be repeated in the future. A positive attitude after giving is often transient, with the outcome being high donor attrition. It is fair to say that true partnership has not yet been established.

Figure 3. The Noninvolved Donor

1. Awareness of the organization and its ministries is minimal.
2. The most frequently verbalized motivation for giving is some interest in the cause, accompanied by some perceived credibility for the organization and/or its spokesperson. Most find real difficulty in articulating much else.
3. Unless the low level of involvement increases, there is only a sporadic pattern of continuing support. The result is high attrition rates.

It is only recently that we have come to see the fallacy of assuming that all donor decisions are made through use of active reasoning accompanied by evaluation and reflection. Not as many respond on the basis of perceived benefits as some fund-raisers seem to assume. Growing numbers make their decision by saying, in effect, "It is no big thing—try it and see."

THE ORGANIZATION'S ROLE IN PARTNERSHIP
Partnership thrives when there is frequent and relevant communication. The donor's strong interest usually will motivate a willingness

to take the time to read and process newsletters, appeal letters, and other forms of relevant information. Slick or sensationalized devices are usually not required to attract attention. Within bounds, *what is said is far more important than how it is said.* Also, donors are willing to participate meaningfully in organizational ministry through financial contribution, prayer, and service if given the opportunity.

• A segmentation strategy. It is not uncommon for an active or potential donor to receive 10 to 15 or more pieces of direct mail in a given week. The majority of these will have the salutation "Dear Friend" and are not personalized unless the recipient happens to be a major donor (usually defined as $500 or more contributed in a given year). What kind of response is expected when thousands receive exactly the same nonpersonalized appeal? The returns are increasingly meager from such an undifferentiated strategy.

A cardinal principle of communication strategy is *segmentation.* The audience is partitioned into homogeneous groupings or segments based on commonality of background, interest, and motivations. It then is possible to design varying messages for each segment to capitalize on these differences. When this principle is applied properly in fund-raising and embodies personalization by name, the results almost invariably are higher giving and greater donor loyalty.

Ideally, each donor would be contacted personally. Although this is difficult to do, many are finding the telephone to be a good substitute along with banquets and other types of meetings. Whenever possible, two-way communication is worth the effort.

• The principle of relevancy. Those on a mailing list also are the recipients of magazines, newsletters, and informational items from other organizations. While donors are far more prone to read and respond than their nondonor counterparts, research has consistently shown that readership of magazine articles seldom exceeds 25 to 30 percent even among donors.[6] This is far below secular readership norms and results in minimal or even negative return on investment.

Part of the problem lies in irrelevant content. It is surprising how seldom editors and writers attempt to speak to reader interests and motivations. Those articles that feature changed lives of both ministry recipients and staff invariably elicit more positive response because they speak directly to donor motivation. The primary purpose of giving is usually to help achieve these outcomes, and there is interest in discovering what has happened.

Contrast the changed-life emphasis with these titles: "The Hermeneutical Implication of Contextualization," "New Building Is Dedicated in Cancun," "Pastor X Joins Board." The usual response is
"Who cares?" If the material presented is not seen to be relevant and
of personal interest, it is ignored. No amount of writing or design
skill (even four-color printing) can reverse this outcome.

It also is often forgotten that fewer people in today's hectic world
have much time to read. Therefore, short newsletters are more effective in stimulating readership than magazines.

• A willingness to ask for money. The Apostle Paul exemplified
three fund-raising strategies: asking only God, tentmaking, and direct appeal to Christians. There is a mistaken belief in some Christian circles that only the first two strategies are biblical; but this is
not the case at all. Any of these can be used, legitimately following
Paul's example.

The issue of asking takes on a new light when it is viewed from
the donor's perspective. Already mentioned is the frequency with
which donors voice a desire to hear of need and an equally strong
willingness to give. If a loyal donor partner is not given opportunity
to participate in this way, then the concept of partnership is stripped
of much of its meaning.

The real issue in raising funds is a fear of rejection. This is understandable but difficult to justify in terms of donor willingness. Here
is the key: *If true partnership is established based on commitment
and accountability, donors will feel a legitimate need to participate financially.*

• Accountability. A donor partner has both the need and the
right to know how his or her financial investment is being used. The
importance of financial accountability has long been stressed by such
watchdog groups as the Evangelical Council for Financial Accountability (ECFA).

Accountability, however, goes far beyond the financial books and
encompasses all phases of ministry. Donors have a right to know the
extent to which ministry goals (if they even exist) have been met.
Such blanket terms as "God blessed richly" are too often spiritual
smokescreens to conceal the absence of strategic planning and ministry evaluation. When such information is not provided, the discerning donor has no basis to assess his or her stewardship in the use of
money. It is small wonder that many cease being active givers.

THE DONOR'S ROLE IN PARTNERSHIP

Because we are using the term *donor*, there is obvious presumption that the individual has given financially or in some other way; however, there are additional dimensions to partnership.

• Prayer. This gives rise to a perplexing issue. All Christian organizations when asked for their needs always mention prayer as being most important. Yet, donor profiles reveal inconsistent response to this need. Some pray, but most do not do so with any regularity with the exception of prayer for individuals who are the object of support.

Does this sporadic pattern indicate donor indifference? This may be the case, but we think the root of the problem lies with the organization. Donors frequently indicate that they are not motivated by long lists of prayer needs encompassing unknown people and unknown ministries. The failure to pray consistently is understandable in this context. They will show a different response, however, when the need is with a known individual or ministry in which they are vitally interested.

On the other hand, donors must move beyond financial support and see giving as only part of what is expected from true partners. Not praying consistently reflects a weak commitment and poor stewardship.

• Discernment. Extended problem-solving which accompanies high involvement behavior quickly gives way to a routinized giving in response to the requests from a highly credible source. Routines always are needed if we are to cope with life demands, and giving then becomes almost automatic.

While routinized giving is good in many ways, it can have the negative consequence of loss of discernment. Continued giving is justified only by true organization accountability. We are appalled by the virtual herd instinct shown by some supporters of television evangelists in particular. "If Rev. Y asks, we don't have any questions at all and we give him what he needs." This is a common response in some quarters.

It is almost as if the donor absolves the organization of any accountability whatsoever. No wonder abuses occur. The problem is that no one really forces the leadership to justify what it does. Pious words are a poor substitute for true accountability.

The donor must be encouraged to see his or her role as an organizational stakeholder. This does not imply an unjustified veto power which occasionally is exercised by large donors under the threat of withdrawal of giving, if certain actions are not taken. The reference here is to a conscientious evaluation of information on performance accompanied by an ongoing review before the Lord as to whether or not continued support is justified. The spirit is a distinctly positive one of responsible partnership.

ORGANIZATIONAL RESPONSIBILITY TO BUILD PARTNERSHIP

When there is low involvement, potential donors are attracted more on the basis of *how it is said,* as opposed to *what is said.*[7] A sensationalized appeal, graphic and pictorial interest, or other dramatic and unusual means may be needed to attract attention. The reason is that there is low felt need and a consequent indifference to appeals unless they somehow stand out in the crowd. Television may be an ideal medium to facilitate the needed dramatic impact.

"Reason why" appeals mostly will fall on deaf ears because of the absence of strong motivation to respond. All the prospect needs to see is urgency or need, general credibility of the organization, and ease and simplicity of response.

While some initial response can be generated this way, low involvement does not often lead to sustained giving. For loyalty to be generated, involvement levels must be raised through *immediate personalized follow-up.* Sally Riley received only a "Dear Friend" package. What she needed was a vivid introduction to the organization and its cause along with clear evidence continued giving will have ministry impact. Face-to-face follow-up is frequently an unattainable ideal, but a telephone call can have beneficial results.

It also is important to establish a general level of organizational awareness, because the low-involvement donor will not respond to an unknown entity. This cannot be built by public relations confined to the Christian media which reach only a miniscule proportion of potential Christian givers.

THE DONOR'S RESPONSIBILITY

Donors must realize that financial giving is a significant measure of their stewardship as Christians. A low-involvement, spur-of-the-moment decision may or may not represent wise action. We hope that giving is not viewed the same way as purchasing a new soft drink. Greater discernment is expected both before and after the decision.

Stewardship demands evaluation and sensitivity to the Holy Spirit. When these are absent, the giver is an easy pawn for manipulation through exaggerated or distorted appeals. Here is the underlying principle: *Because not every cause is worthy of support, financial stewardship requires reflection and discernment.*

Each family or giving unit must establish priorities. "What are we most interested in?" "Why do we feel this way?" "What is the Lord trying to say to us?" In short, low involvement should give way to a greater involvement leading to true partnership.

BUILDING DONOR PARTNERSHIP

Too many fund-raisers view their profession from a sales perspective. The focus is on short-term financial gain, and in some quarters it seems as if anything goes as long as the dollars keep rolling in. Organizational marketing, on the other hand, moves beyond initial giving to establishment of partnership and loyalty based on an understanding of motivations and decision processes. Competition for the donor dollar is increasing every day, and the surviving organizations must be cognizant of two fundamental imperatives, establishing credibility and strengthening donor partnership and involvement.

• Establishing credibility. Given the plethora of competing causes, donor indifference is likely to increase. This is especially probable among the baby boomers who mostly are in their 30s and 40s. Their motivations and interests differ sharply from their older counterparts.[8]

Evangelical donors in their middle 50s and beyond tend to have a worldview shaped by the profound influences of the Great Depression and World War II. Here are the kinds of values which the majority of them embrace:

– Patriotism
– Economic security and wealth
– Maintenance of tradition as a defense against a rapidly changing environment
– Individual achievement

– A traditional evangelicalism based on an earlier fundamentalism versus liberalism controversy
– Support of Christian causes manifesting these values and reflecting a more traditional "romance of missions."

Credibility among this older evangelical segment often requires avoidance of emphasis on such debatable strategies as contextualization, holistic witness, and body life. Greatest appreciation is expressed for those ministries that faithfully proclaim the Gospel in more familiar ways. Many of these organizations have been old friends since childhood and loyalty is strong.

Baby boomers have a different outlook. They were born after World War II, have not known large-scale economic deprivation, and assume a certain level of affluence. They have always felt the threat of nuclear annihilation and hence place greater focus on the "here and now." Here are some values and motivations that affect their perceived credibility and willingness to support Christian causes:

– Life is to be lived now. Therefore, Christian experience is not just something for a distant future.

– There is a premium on biblical koinonia that reflects close interpersonal relations and ministry to one another.

– Economic and political injustice are not tolerated. There is appreciation for the need to "set the captives free."

– There is growing suspicion of institutions of all types, and the church and its agencies are not exempt. Accountability is expected and demanded.

– There is distrust of outreach that focuses only on man's soul to the exclusion of his whole being.

What this means is that an organization perceived as credible by an older donor might be perceived in an opposite fashion by the Christian baby boomer. The dilemma enters because most evangelical donors are beyond the age of 50. While some are wealthy and generous, their numbers are small to begin with and are decreasing. Few organizations can survive for long without making inroads with younger Christians who have different expectations. How can one segment be attracted without alienating the other?

The answer starts with organizational ministry. It goes without saying that today's strategies must be sharply different from those undertaken in earlier decades. Foreign missions, for example, must take account of contextualization and nationalization if they are to be relevant at all. When it can be demonstrated that the ministry has a genuine cutting edge, ways can be found to communicate with differing segments without alienation.

Older donors can be reassured that their legitimate concerns over doctrinal purity and evangelistic emphasis are still maintained, even though forms of ministry are different. Their younger counterparts, in turn, can be attracted by new forms of contemporary ministries that build on a true commitment to organizational mission. This is what we mean by a segmented strategy.

The key to perceived credibility is rigorous accountability. In other words, *credibility must be earned and not assumed on the basis of the past.* Notice that accountability goes far beyond financial considerations. As Peter Drucker puts it, every organization must demonstrate that its mission is being carried out with excellence and impact, its people are productive and fulfilled, and the general aims of society are enhanced.⁹

Donor stewardship, in turn, should demand this accountability and not be satisfied if it is not forthcoming. God is not honored when unjustified loyalty takes the place of Christian discernment.

• Building involvement and partnership. Fund-raising is a ministry, not a sales activity. To be productive, a partnership must be established in which both participants receive value. A donor motivated by low involvement is not yet a true partner. Involvement must be built and strengthened by frequent, relevant communication and demonstration of how organizational ministries fulfill and extend the contributor's values and interests.

The days of nonpersonalized mass communication with donors are past for the reasons mentioned throughout this chapter. Responsible Christians should not condone hucksterism. Their model always must be the ministry of the Apostle Paul in Thessalonica:

> For the appeal we make does not spring from error or impure motives, nor are we trying to trick you. On the contrary, we speak as men approved by God to be entrusted with the Gospel. We are not trying to please men but God, who tests our hearts. You know we never used flattery, nor did we put on a mask to cover up greed—God is our witness. We were not looking for praise from men, not from you or anyone else (1 Thessalonians 2:3-6).

JAMES F. ENGEL, *cofounder and senior vice president of Management Development Associates, is also professor of communications research at Wheaton College Graduate School (Illinois). He was formerly on the faculties of marketing at the University of Michigan and Ohio State University, and has been honored internationally as "founder of the field" of consumer behavior research.*

Dr. Engel is senior author of the standard business school texts Consumer Behavior *(Dryden) and* Promotional Strategy *(Irwin). He has consulted with well over 100 Christian organizations worldwide.*

(26)
ETHICAL ATTITUDES
AND BELIEFS OF
EVANGELICAL FUND-RAISERS

LINDA A. KEENER

George Gallup has stated that "unethical fund-raising is offensive to God and undercuts legitimate fund-raising efforts. Abusive practices have given Christianity a bad name."[1] The majority of evangelical fund-raisers have strong negative attitudes toward the exposed fund-raising abuses of certain highly visible groups such as broadcast and relief organizations.

In early 1987 a survey was conducted among approximately 2,500 evangelical fund-raisers to determine ethical beliefs in fund-raising within Christian organizations. These organizations included evangelical missions, relief organizations, youth ministries, camps, colleges and seminaries, broadcasters, evangelists, consultants, family/social ministries, and Bible/literacy agencies. All of the surveyed fund-raisers recognized that there is ethical abuse of fund-raising and one-quarter felt that *most* Christian organizations are guilty of abuse.[2]

ATTITUDES TOWARD FUND-RAISING

Several prevalent attitudes toward fund-raising form filters through which fund-raisers view and judge the rightness or wrongness of specific practices. Although dealt with in much greater depth in other chapters, we will look at them briefly here as various approaches to fund-raising.

• Ask no one but God. The first is sometimes found in the faith missions—those holding to the ask-no-one-but-God approach to fund-raising often associated with George Mueller and Hudson Taylor. This approach does have scriptural foundation, and God has blessed the faith of several organizations who have used this method. (For an expanded perspective on George Mueller, see chapter 19.) An extreme version of this view, however, assumes that asking for funds from God's people is *always* due to a lack of faith and is only self-serving.

This attitude has penetrated many evangelical organizations, so that top leadership and sometimes even professional fund-raisers feel embarrassed, guilty, or apologetic in asking for funds. The attitude that "asking is wrong," while often unstated, is the underlying reason for uneasiness over specific practices.

• "They owe us support." Tending toward the opposite extreme, is a second attitude that "those people out there owe it to us to support us." This attitude, again at times very subtle, views the donor as an unrelated object which must be acted upon to reach a desired result. The organization or the cause has become the single focus, and God's overall work in the church has slipped out of view. The building up of individual believers and the impressions made on a watching world are not as important to them as the furthering of the organization's cause; therefore, the rightness or wrongness of fund-raising choices is not considered.

• A positive relationship. A third attitude toward fund-raising is one that balances the previous two. Based on scriptural teaching about stewardship, it views the fund-raising process as a positive relationship which benefits both parties. The organization is responsible and accountable to the donors and seeks to serve them. In a 1985 survey, 20 percent of evangelical fund-raisers saw their work including the serving of donors in fostering biblical principles of stewardship.' This attitude seems to be growing by its recurring appearance as a topic for articles and seminars. When the donor is viewed as a partner to be served, the ethical questions take on a new importance. If benefiting the donor is right, then anything which misleads or in any way takes advantage of the donor is intrinsically wrong.

• Do what works. A final attitude toward fund-raising in general is a cultural one which has infiltrated every fund-raiser's thinking to some degree. Pragmatism, or doing what works, in itself is not bad;

but it must constantly be balanced with stronger purposes. Every fund-raiser is put under the pressure of meeting crying financial needs and achieving goals. Good stewardship demands a return on investment in fund-raising. If a fund-raiser does not bring in the needed money, his job is probably not too secure.

A recent *Harvard Business Review* article pointed out that unethical behavior often involves top management's goals and middle management's efforts to interpret those aims.[4] Top management must set the example and establish a code of ethics which is well above any questionable practices. Almost one-half of evangelical fund-raisers have income goals set by the president or board, and most others have board input into the goals.[5] Under pressure to achieve goals and deadlines, they are tempted to allow pragmatic considerations to overpower sound biblical principles.

Another fact is that donors do respond to certain tactics, some of which are questionable. Theologian Carl F.H. Henry states it plainly, "But fund-raisers are merely responding to what the people want. Sound, conservatively worded appeals don't work."[6] When another Christian organization has great success with a particular method, there is a strong temptation to use that method without examining any biblical implications. The "everybody's doing it" mentality causes some fund-raisers to ignore inner reservations.

ATTITUDES TOWARD PRACTICES
In the 1987 survey of evangelical fund-raisers, a number of practices that contained possible ethical issues were presented through nine scenarios to which the fund-raisers were asked to respond.[7] They were asked if they would recommend or oppose the practice, if any scriptural principles applied, and if any ethical issues were raised.

Deception/truthfulness was the major ethical issue illustrated by the scenarios. Pragmatic considerations and unsubstantiated opinion were more common responses than Scripture-based reasoning. Most respondents could not provide scriptural principles or references except in the cases of deception or favoritism. This uncertainty indicates not so much an absence of values as a failure to have thought through the issues in light of Scripture.

• Use of banquets for major donors. Banquets for major donors who have given over a certain dollar amount are common among

Christian organizations. Half of the respondents use this approach, yet only 36 percent recommend it and 64 percent voiced reservations or opposition. Colleges were most positive and camps were strongly opposed.

Those who oppose this practice most commonly stated it was favoring the rich and cited James 2:1-9:

> My brothers . . . don't show favoritism. Suppose a man comes into your meeting wearing a gold ring and fine clothes, and a poor man in shabby clothes also comes in. If you show special attention to the man wearing fine clothes . . . have you not discriminated among yourselves and become judges with evil thoughts? . . . But if you show favoritism, you sin and are convicted by the law as lawbreakers.

Those who favor banquets see no scriptural/ethical problems and use them because they work. They also mentioned "honoring those who deserve honor" in support of this practice.

• Offer of premiums as incentives. The use of premiums as an incentive is common, specifically to those who give over a certain dollar amount. One-third of the respondents used this practice in the past year. Only one-fourth were opposed, these primarily again because of favoritism to those who can give large amounts.

A smaller number were opposed to premiums themselves because they provide an improper motivation for people to give. This "give to get" motivation raises legal questions regarding receipting for the gift and deducting for the value of the premium.

Most do not feel that scriptural or ethical issues are involved, and recommend incentives because they succeed in raising more money. When the premium is a ministry tool such as a book or Bible, it is also seen as a legitimate way to minister to the donor.

A related ethical issue not dealt with in the survey, but of expressed concern, is the promise of intangible personal gain in exchange for a donation. The promise of prayer, blessing, healing, or other personal benefit, is a common and effective appeal. It raises ethical concerns, however, both in fulfillment of the promise and in use as a motivation for giving.

• Use of a signature machine. Although only a handful use this strategy, over half are in favor of it, largely for pragmatic reasons (it saves time and money) and do not view it as being deceptive or misleading. A little less than half either have reservations or are opposed because they feel truthfulness and integrity are violated. The underlying concern is that donors may be deceived by what appears to be a legitimate signature. Only a very few voiced any specific biblical references.

• High frequency of mailings. Although highly frequent appeals are a complaint among donors, it does not appear to be an ethical issue to fund-raisers. Ninety percent of Christian organizations send six or fewer appeals a year.[8] While the majority oppose a strategy of very high frequency, only one-fourth gave violation of ethics or scriptural principles as their reason, with very few able to back this up with scriptural references or principles. Pragmatic concerns of "donor wear-out" were a much more frequent reason for opposition.

• Misrepresentation. In this scenario a ministry focused all its fund-raising appeals on a small area of its ministry because this area pulled the most responses. Most (86 percent) opposed this strategy as deceitful. Nearly all based their conviction on biblical passages prohibiting false witness.

Ethical concern has recently been expressed over two other practices, that although more subtle, deal with the same issue of misrepresenting how funds are to be used.[9] These are the overstating of what a donation will actually accomplish and the skimming off of an inappropriate percentage for administration. In both cases the donor is not aware of how the donation is being used.

• Altered use of funds without donor notification. When a certain project is oversubscribed, funds are sometimes channeled into other areas without informing the donors. There is strong opposition to this practice, and the near unanimous agreement that donors should be notified and given the choice of having the gift returned or directed to a different project. The most commonly cited Scripture was 2 Corinthians 8:19-21: "We want to avoid any criticism of the way we administer this liberal gift. For we are taking pains to do what is right, not only in the eyes of the Lord but also in the eyes of men."

• Distortion of truth about ministry needs. Often what is left unsaid is more misleading than what is said. The work of other religious groups in a certain field is left unmentioned, implying that a particular ministry is the *only* Gospel witness in this scenario. As would be expected, the vast majority opposed this strategy. More than one-half were strongly opposed, citing over fifty different scriptural references that focus on lying and false witness. There was agreement that organizations should not intentionally withhold pertinent information. A few recognized, however, that there can be some very fine lines in this area.

• Use of "urgent" teaser copy. This very common practice of an "Urgent" message printed on the envelope is wholeheartedly recommended by only 20 percent, whereas another 29 percent recommend it with reservations. The primary concern is that the urgency message overstates the true situation, and is therefore untruthful. One-third feel this practice raises ethical issues. A secondary concern is a pragmatic one that if used too often, the "urgency" copy will lose effectiveness, even when truthful.

• Regular financial crisis appeals. While 86 percent of those surveyed oppose this approach of regularly making needs known by stating a financial crisis, 28 percent used a crisis appeal at least once during the past year. About two-thirds have ethical concerns about consistent use of this tactic, and back their opinions with scriptural principles. The bottom line here is a concern over false witness and violation of truthfulness. A number also noted that an organization which has consistent financial crises is probably poorly managed and may not be worthy of donor support.

Crisis appeals, for both organizational and ministry needs, raise pragmatic issues as well as ethical. Arthur Borden, ECFA Executive Director, concurs: "It really concerns me to see so many crises portrayed by Christian organizations, especially crises of physical hunger and suffering. True, the crisis may exist, but we seem too eager to play it up. Eventually, it inoculates donors against compassion."[10]

Those regularly using such appeals are caught in a negative cycle in which each crisis must be more desperate than the previous one in order to maintain response levels. Crises do exist, always have, and until the Prince of Peace reigns in power on earth, always will. But individual crises need to be put into the context of the whole.

• Emotional appeals. When ethical concerns are discussed, *emotional appeal* is inevitably mentioned. To define this commonly used term, fund-raisers most frequently gave these answers:

  – a manipulative action to cover up a lack of legitimate, rational reasons for giving to a cause

– a heartrending story (starving children) without support of underlying facts

– overstatement of results of giving.

The term *emotional appeal* has taken on a negative meaning to a large number of fund-raisers. All three of the definitions given above include a deliberate distortion of facts. A distinction is noted by some, however, between legitimate use of emotion (a vital God-given human capacity) and abuse of emotion. An appeal may be totally truthful and still be very emotional.

All fund-raisers recognize that some organizations abuse emotional appeals. Over 80 percent feel that some, most, or all Christian organizations are involved in such abuse. Excessive appeals to emotion, often guilt or fear, become manipulative and encourage people to act against their better judgment.

Although not dealt with in the 1987 survey, another area of expressed ethical concern in Christian fund-raising is the exploitation of senior citizens, often through the use of strong emotional appeals and biased counsel in estate planning. As our senior citizen population grows, this problem will become more prevalent. ECFA standards warn against accepting gifts which put a hardship on the donor or his family.

CONCLUSION

Some of the above practices touch on clear-cut ethical issues; others enter into gray areas in which motive and specific situations become important factors. All, however, are practices encountered in fund-raising, and every evangelical fund-raiser needs to have a well thought out ethical/scriptural rationale for his or her convictions. There seems to be a real lack of this type of clear thinking.

While not all fund-raisers will agree on every method, the main abuses would be eliminated if all evangelical fund-raisers would honestly seek to apply God's principles. While virtually all would claim belief in the standards of God's Word, professed belief and attitude do not always affect practice. Some simply have not taken the time and effort to apply scriptural principles to specific situations.

Standards such as those set out by ECFA will help, but offending groups will continue to do as they see fit apart from the self-monitoring groups, unless perhaps government begins to enforce some standards of its own. A balance of method with dependency upon God and an awareness of personal accountability to God is the answer . . . but that is another chapter.

LINDA A. KEENER *has been an account executive with Keener Marketing, a full-service advertising agency, since 1981. She has worked closely with many Christian organizations in the areas of fund-raising and marketing. In 1987 she received her master's in communications/marketing and research from Wheaton Graduate School.*

In the fall of 1986, Miss Keener was one of a five-member team to conduct research for the Funding the Christian Challenge conference. This research forms the foundation for this chapter. Other research conducted by Miss Keener includes a study done of evangelists at Amsterdam '86 for the Billy Graham Evangelistic Association.

(27)
HISTORICAL PERSPECTIVES ON EVANGELICAL FUND-RAISING

LAWRENCE M. WEBER

Giving is one of life's most pragmatic events in which the Christian exercises a tangible expression of the inward faith. Through past centuries, as well as today, giving and getting money for God's work have been vivid testimony of Christian belief and God's provision. This chapter is a brief overview of some of the more important historical practices, beginning with the Old Testament, and philosophical trends that have brought us as Christians to where we are today in our stewardship.

The Bible contains penetrating commentary on money, including warnings and caution about its use. The predominate theme of Scripture as it relates to money and possessions is that all our resources are God's and our responsibility is to be good stewards of those resources. Holding something in trust for someone else is vastly different from handling something that we view as ours. But resources are given to multiply and enlarge, to preserve and protect, and to use and to spend for His glory. The Old Testament picks up on this theme.

THE OLD TESTAMENT

Adam and Eve were given dominion over the earth, but they acted as though it were theirs, and subsequently lost it all. Long after they were cast out of the Garden of Eden, a nomadic agribusinessman moving about to find the place where God was leading him had a skirmish or two with the local squatters. He won. Afterward, he met a mysterious priest-king, Melchizedek of Salem. Abraham, "very wealthy in livestock and in silver and gold" (Genesis 13:2), gave him a tenth of his spoil from battle. In a manner similar to the pattern of earlier sacrifices Abraham gave to God the firstfruits of his labor. He gave the profits of his labor to the rightful owner. (See Genesis 13.)

His son, Isaac, and grandson, Jacob, and Jacob's sons became the nation God promised to Abraham, and God proclaimed that they were not just stewards of His world but were His people in a special sense. For His chosen people, the Israelites, God gave the law which prescribed the tithe. The law required a tenth given to the priests, annually; the festival tithe, another tenth each year; and every third year a tenth for the poor. Together with the jubilee tithe, the obligation to the theocracy approached 30 percent.

David, a man after God's own heart, went substantially beyond the law when he gave strong personal support to build the temple, and then organized this little tribal nation to give proportionately as appropriate to his example. Even more astounding, they loved it.

Volunteers were enlisted to keep records and publish the gifts, which are recorded in 1 Chronicles 29.

Some years later Nehemiah took on a thankless task with significant opposition, as he rebuilt the wall of Jerusalem in record time. He organized the people to give their time and money. More interestingly, as a result of their work and gifts they returned to worship and giving the tithes which had been neglected.

It was many more years after David's remarkable fund-raising program that these people who belonged to God again neglected the tithe, and a prophet named Malachi declared they were robbing God.

The Old Testament clearly warns of misplaced trust in money. While Solomon who had great riches knew the proverb, "The blessing of the Lord brings wealth" (Proverbs 10:22), he also knew the psalm of his father, King David, who declared the judgment of God on "the man who did not make God his stronghold but trusted in his great wealth" (Psalm 52:7).

THE NEW TESTAMENT
With the dawn of the New Testament, "the worries of life and the deceitfulness of wealth" were seen as "choking" the Word of God

(Matthew 13:22). Jesus Christ angrily tossed out those who were commercializing the temple sacrifices. Ananias and Sapphira became another negative example. They had the option of keeping their property, but chose to give it to the church. While the choice to give part of the proceeds rightfully belonged to them, they lied and said that they were giving it all, and fell victim to one of the harshest judgments in Scripture.

After the time of Christ, in the apostolic years of the church, a new teaching of stewardship not only went beyond the law, but fulfilled the law. The example was established by the Lord Jesus Christ Himself: "For you know the grace of our Lord Jesus Christ, that though He was rich, yet for your sakes He became poor, so that you through His poverty might become rich" (2 Corinthians 8:9).

Our attitude toward money has the potential to be destructive, and Paul wrote that "the love of money is a root of all kinds of evil. Some people, eager for money, have wandered from the faith and pierced themselves with many griefs" (1 Timothy 6:10-11). A special admonition was reserved for the wealthy believer; they were not "to be arrogant nor to put their hope in wealth . . . but . . . to be rich in good deeds, and to be generous and willing to share" (vv. 17-18). On the other hand, the poor widow who gave all received the commendation of the Lord Jesus Himself. Money is a gift from God, but it is not to be a god in itself. The Bible is not ascetic; poverty is not inherently virtuous, nor is wealth sinful. But true wealth, the Bible teaches us, is spiritual, not material.[1]

As an apostle, Paul urged Christians to give. The specifics of how money was to be raised are omitted, but the inferences of Scripture and the historical traditions enable the thoughtful Christian fund-raising professional to construct a consistent practice which is honoring to God.

Paul held up the Macedonians as his prime example of New Testament stewardship at its best, as he wrote to the church of Corinth, directing them in their giving. In careful examination of 2 Corinthians 8 and 9, we see proportionate, disciplined, voluntary, specific, generous giving related to the indescribable gift of God.

Scripture provides little support for emotional response to appeal after appeal. Nor does the Bible suggest that it is wrong to ask. On the contrary, both Old and New Testaments have examples of one person making an appeal to another for a specific cause. The passage from 2 Corinthians 8 and 9 includes a request by Paul and his colleagues who asked for gifts on behalf of others, not themselves.

Jesus placed Himself where He could see the specific gifts of those in the temple. One of the great principles of teaching is example, and how can we show an example of giving unless it is visible to others?

The most important element in giving principles outlined in 2 Corinthians 8 is not the planning, the proportionate generosity, the liberal grace out of poverty, or the exhortation to advance in giving. The underlying fact is that the Macedonians "gave themselves first to the Lord." From this perspective, gifts to God are the pragmatic works of heavenly faith. Faith without works is dead; love without giving is empty. The Lord loves a cheerful giver. Giving is a joy. Giving is exhilarating.

The key is love. Love makes sacrifice and total denial an hilarious election rather than a reluctant compulsion. Only with the example of the Lord Jesus Christ emptied out . . . made poor . . . so that we might be rich . . . can we know the joy of giving.

CHURCH PRACTICE IN FUND-RAISING
Little is known about the first two or three centuries of church fund-raising. We can assume that it followed the pattern of 2 Corinthians 8 and 9, but it changed radically in the fourth century when Christianity moved from the catacombs, upper rooms, and other secret hiding places into the highest councils of respectability and legitimacy. By A.D. 313, Constantine declared Christianity acceptable, and "before the end of the same century Christianity had become the only legal religion of the Empire."[2]

Until the adoption of Christianity by Constantine, this new faith existed as a voluntary, unpopular movement, and entailed significant personal risk and sacrifice for its followers. "To be a Christian prior to the year 313 was to opt for a life outside the pale of respectability and against the stream of the dominant culture."[3] After embrace of Christianity by the empire, Christians began moving into the ruling class.

The historical fiat of Constantinople altered the future of the Christian establishment, and we deal with these implications today. During the worldwide development of the church, Christians have exhibited a strong desire to retain the supposed benefits of establishment. The church that evolved from the Constantine era became *self-serving;* stewardship, in its full meaning, is *self-giving.*

Beginning in the fourth century, a person could become a Christian automatically, as one would enroll in a school or begin employment, without any change of heart or repentance. One was born into a Christian family or nation with little or no personal commitment. The state was willing to sustain the church's material needs, so the necessity of sharing money with God or with the poor or persecuted gradually diminished.

"The Christian view of stewardship begins with the stewardship of the One who did not grasp at equality with God, but was obedient to the cross (Philippians 2). It is *His* stewardship in which we participate."[4] The basic concept of giving all to God (money is just one aspect) was nearly lost. In A.D. 585, the Second Council of Mascon enacted the tithe as official law in the Roman church.

Upon the establishment of religion, the church built a body of laws for giving, complete with coercion and power of taxation to raise money. The theology of buying salvation and spiritual position was propagated. Threat of excommunication was used to enforce mandatory gifts. The medieval church developed indulgences (escape from punishment) and sold church offices to the highest bidder.[5] The insatiable appetite for more resources ran headlong into negative response and unwillingness to give, which spawned even more ingenious schemes to raise funds.

The pre-Reformation church of Rome forcibly took money and land; subsequently, most Protestant denominations retained the church-state alliance with its coercive methods of fund-raising. During these eras there is scant evidence of purely voluntary, love-motivated, proportionate stewardship, except among the Anabaptists, the Brethren, and later the Methodists.

THE GREAT AWAKENING

In the American colonies, the Great Awakening of 1733-1744 laid the groundwork for voluntary support of the church in the New World. Believers outside the "established" Church of England committed themselves to support their beliefs in the manner that first and second century Christians did. They voluntarily and generously gave as did the American patriots a few decades later who pledged "their lives, their fortunes and their sacred honor" to "self-evident" truths. (All but one signer of the Declaration of Independence died in poverty and/or violent death for their pledge. As with many believers outside the established church, it cost them everything.)

The fund-raising practices which survived the American Revolution retained the complex linkage of works and reward designed to forcibly raise money from unwilling followers. The persecution of separatists leaped across the Atlantic Ocean. While proclaiming religious liberty the new colonies enacted mandatory giving laws enforced by civil authority. Compulsory giving died a slow death.

Lotteries were common in American and European churches. Subscription lists were circulated to embarrass and shame recalcitrant members into giving. Commercial enterprises persist even today (raffles, bingo, sales of pies and books, real estate ventures, etc.). The vitality of the Great Awakening and Methodism, with its concomitant social awareness, was accompanied by dramatic examples of faith ministries most vividly illustrated by George Mueller's refusal to make his needs public much less appeal openly for funds.

The impact that Mueller has had on "faith missions" has been enormous. He renounced any salary, and with his wife and staff refused any direct appeals for money except in prayer to God. His steadfast refusal to answer about his needs was legendary, and the practice is followed in some measure today.

Other influences moved the church slowly toward voluntary giving. A countermovement on the new continent was awareness of the freedom not to be religious at all. Secularism provided a background which forced churches to appeal to individual faith and responsibility to support the work of the church. That support could no longer be counted on as a matter of course; people had a respectable alternative. This proved to be the beginning of a disestablishment that struck at the very foundation of beliefs and organizational structures of church and society.

CURRENT PATTERNS

In our secular society we still hold on to the *King James* word for love, *charity*, to describe our philanthropic activity and institutions. The religious roots of philanthrophy are also confirmed in a recent

Rockefeller Brothers Fund study which suggests that the single most consistent thread among donors is regular church attendance.

This national survey on the charitable behavior of Americans was published by Independent Sector. It states that 89 percent of Americans give a yearly average of $650 to charities, and there is "a clear relationship between regular attendance at religious services and giving to religious charities."[6]

More than that, "Those who pledged a certain dollar amount each week . . . on average gave almost twice as much . . . compared to those who did not pledge."[7]

The most dramatic giving comes from those who purposefully try to give a certain percentage of their income to their church or synagogue each year. All of this is confirmed in the comparative analysis: "The most generous giver to a church is one who attends nearly every week and pledges a proportion of his or her income to the church."[8]

The patterns of giving confirmed in this report are quite broad; for our purposes the implication is that considered, purposeful, disciplined and systematic giving produces greater generosity. Giving is habitual and it is elastic. The historical evidences of Christian fund raising also support this thesis.

In both giving and asking the Christian will grow in love and grace. Giving belongs at the core of the Christian life. Investment in eternal values assures that the Christian will grow in interest and involvement—for where our treasure is, there will our hearts be also.

LAWRENCE M. WEBER, president of Ketchum, Inc., joined the firm in February 1969 after a 12-year career in the radio-television field. He is involved in several professional organizations including the American Association of Fund-Raising Counsel, the National Society of Fund-Raising Executives, the National Association for Hospital Development, and the Council for Advancement and Support of Education. He is a board member of the AAFRC Trust for Philanthropy.

Mr. Weber is a frequent speaker at professional development conferences, and at church and church-related fund-raising programs. He has provided counsel to the Foreign Mission Board, Southern Baptist Convention, and the Presbyterian Church, U.S.A. He also counsels colleges and universities, including church-related institutions.

(28)
DOES IT PAY
TO PRAY?

MELVIN E. LORENTZEN

Fund-raisers often favor euphemisms. They call their direct mail solicitations for money "prayer letters," and the donors who respond with cash contributions "prayer partners." But moral and ethical scandals among evangelical empire builders, shades of Elmer Gantry revisited, breed public skepticism and even cynicism about such terminology.

Do Christian financial consultants and development officers secretly think that George Mueller's philosophy of fund-raising through prayer alone is possible today? Or, even if his approach was not normative for all religious enterprises, as he himself insisted, do they really believe in the priority of prayer as the ultimate support base for ministry? Their answers are not in their professional claims but in their personal practices, as James pointed out: "You see that a man is justified by what he does and not by faith alone" (2:24).

When it comes to rallying people to pray and give, Christian fund-raisers need to be exemplars. The motto "Prayer changes things" makes an inspiring plaque to hang on the office wall, but it needs to represent a discipline as well as an axiom. If response to a funding appeal is low or slow, do we assume that the pressure was inadequate? Or do we admit that prayer might have been inadequate?

Adequate prayer has more to do with kind than amount. It is not that insufficient prayers are offered; it may be that the praying that is done is of inferior quality. James commented on this too: "When you ask, you do not receive, because you ask with wrong motives, that you may spend what you get on your pleasures" (4:3). It is obvious that only "right asking" in prayer is sure to bring the desired results.

It is equally obvious that the *what* of prayer is not the issue. Jesus repeatedly said, "You may ask Me for anything in My name, and I will do it" (John 14:14; 15:16; 16:23). "Anything" includes money, certainly. At stake is not the *what*, but the *how* to pray.

In this, as in all other matters of belief and behavior, the Scriptures are the authoritative guide. Fortunately, they illustrate as well as instruct, so that there need be no misunderstanding.

It's one thing to expound the Bible's prayer *promises*, but it is another to comprehend its *premises* for the quality of praying that counts with God. Whether giving or raising funds for the Lord's work, prayer must be *right*.

RIGHT PRAYER IS RESPONSIVE TO SCRIPTURE

The disciples of Jesus Christ—who was the Word of God in the flesh—watched Him and listened to Him before they asked Him to teach them to pray. It was not an idea which originated with them; they took their cue from their Master. What they observed of the incarnate Word prompted their curiosity and concern to know more, because they had witnessed the evidence that whenever Jesus prayed things were never the same again.

Reading the Bible thoughtfully, therefore, is prerequisite to prayer that pays. A self-inventory might be uncomfortable, but it is necessary to ask a few pointed questions.

• When do I read the Bible? Some people read the Scriptures only in spurts of devotion or desperation. Others do a periodic nostalgic replay of favorite passages, or occasionally leaf through for nebulous inspiration. The habit of "following along" in Sunday School class or a weekly church service suffices for many. Several may do a daily dip into its pages at random when convenient. Probably the fewest pursue a daily reading program with a set time and system.

Few realize that Bible reading is essential to right praying. If they knew that, their answer to the second question might be quite different.

• How do I read the Bible? As with their aerobics or jogging, some believers read their "daily dozen" of chapters or verses as a painful but vaguely beneficial duty. Others play hopscotch with Scriptures, skipping over the "begats" and any of the supposedly irrelevant or difficult passages. Some like to focus on "stories" in both Testaments. Old favorites like Psalms, Proverbs, or the Gospels draw their fans for return visits. The more studious may use "helps" like a devotional guide, or a commentary, or a concordance—materials unfamiliar to the casual reader, and more about Scripture than Bible-centered. Again, the fewest practice meditation on through-the-Bible comparison of passages to get the grand sweep of God's revelation, accompanied by intensive reflection on the connections.

While methods of reading may vary, the constant factor that makes a difference is regularity. Alternately gorging or starving oneself when it comes to nurturing one's spirit from the Scriptures is unhealthy to the soul. Bible reading is not to be an isolated ritual, but is to be linked with other vital activities.

• Why do I read the Bible? Bible reading can stem from no more than a sense of religious duty, or the need to fulfill an assignment for a class or a public presentation. It can also be limited to the search for answers to questions and problems. At a better level, Christians derive a lifting of their spirits from biblical precepts, and satisfy their curiosity about many marvels in nature and in human society. But the noblest reason for spending extensive time with God's Word is to make the most of the privilege of communion with the Author.

If the Bible were like any other book, its words would lie on its pages with more or less objective impact, depending on one's mood or need of the moment. But since the Holy Spirit who authored it through such a diversity of human personalities is with each reader to interpret it as well, reading the Bible becomes a perennially fresh adventure of discovery. The diligent reader is repeatedly surprised by new flashes of insight or new surges of reaction while reading even the best-known passages. The Bible is a living book, and the Spirit of God creates a connection between it and the spirit of the reader.

A Christian is well advised to listen to the voice of the Lord as it is recorded in Holy Scripture before presuming to pray to the Almighty for a blessing.

Meditation on the Scriptures is a springboard to prayer. While it is a breach of royal etiquette not to wait on the King or to let Him speak first, it is equally insulting not to reply when He does speak.

RIGHT PRAYER IS REPENTANT

When the King has spoken, how does one reply? Not flippantly, because it is awe-inspiring to be in His presence and to be addressed by Him personally. And not brazenly, of course, because the power He represents is so absolute that there is no human prerogative that can compare with it.

Humility is the proper attitude in responding to the Lord God, whose holiness blazes with such glory that it cannot be looked at with human eyes, as Moses discovered (Exodus 24:17; 33:20).

When we reflect on the inspired Word that reveals God's holiness, wisdom, authority, and love—what can we say? Daniel, who cut no mean figure himself in the fashions of the court of Darius, nevertheless could only begin his prayer with the words, "We have sinned" (9:5). This faithful man had passed every spiritual test with flying colors; and yet in identifying with his own people he had to admit "in fasting, and in sackcloth and ashes," "WE have sinned and done wrong," "WE have been wicked and have rebelled," and "WE have sinned against you" (9:3, 5, 8).

As Christians and with a fuller disclosure of God's viewpoint than Daniel ever enjoyed, we are cautioned by the Apostle John, "If we claim to be without sin, we deceive ourselves and the truth is not in us" (1 John 1:8). The Apostle Paul wrote to the believers living in Rome, "All have sinned and fall short of the glory of God" (Romans 3:23).

Confession of sin, of falling short, of missing the mark, is a tougher order than we might think, despite our sometimes casual recital of the petition Jesus included early in the pattern prayer He gave His disciples: "Forgive us our sins" (Luke 11:4).

Again, it helps to crystallize this attitude of humility by some pointed questions.

● How do I define sin? The famous psychologist Karl Menninger raised a profound question in the title of one of his books: *What Ever Happened to Sin?* In this permissive age of situation ethics, people have become too accustomed to excusing and rationalizing their flaws and faults. Sometimes that descends to the level of popular song lyrics, "It feels so good it can't be wrong," or the even more widespread notion that misbehavior can be justified because "everybody is doing it," or, "it's the only way you can survive."

In Scripture, the Lord makes it clear that attitude and motive are

325

at the core of evil (Matthew 7:21-23). It is not only what we do, but why we do it, that comes under divine judgment. And until sin is confessed, God's goodness is blocked from flowing to us even in response to our most earnest asking.

Nowhere is this underscored better than by the Prophet Isaiah as he delivers a one-two punch about God's ability to save and man's disqualification of himself for that divine mercy: "Surely the arm of the Lord is not too short to save, nor His ear too dull to hear. But your iniquities have separated you from your God; your sins have hidden His face from you, so that He will not hear" (59:1-2).

• How do I deal with sin? "The devil made me do it" is a favorite cop-out on personal responsibility for sin. Once having recognized the reality of sin, people elect various options for handling it.

Beyond blaming the devil or someone else, people may minimize sin's seriousness on a scale of 1 to 10; or rationalize it as a standard practice in their particular profession (even fund-raising); or defend it on the grounds of the end justifying the means (a "worthy cause" is served); or assume immunity from judgment for it under the perceived terms of salvation—which is presumption, not trust.

God deals with sin through His Son, the Lord Jesus Christ. We cannot expect Him to overlook our wrongdoing, but we do not need to beg Him to forgive it. All the forgiveness He could possibly provide is already in place through the Cross, and His grace is greater than our sin. What is required of us is the humbling of our pride to submit to the divine mercy, in recognition that we cannot set things right ourselves. Pride says, "I will atone in my own way." Humility says, "I will accept what God has done for me."

• What is my attitude toward other sinners? This might seem a strange question to raise. After all, personal responsibility is crucial; we cannot assume responsibility for everyone else.

That leads to a variety of ways to cope with others when they do wrong. One can blacklist them from any future relationship; or assume that whatever punishment they get is coming to them; or reprimand them and withdraw from association; or even excuse them for simply doing "what comes naturally."

The biblical approach is to intercede on their behalf for God's forgiveness, and to do everything possible to help them get straightened out. When people make "honest mistakes," that course is not so hard to follow. But when they seem to have erred in a deliberate and calculated way, having a charitable spirit toward them is difficult.

In the competition between Christian organizations to draw on the limited resources of common or overlapping constituencies, it is easy to condemn the methods others use and to gloat over any misfortune that might come to them. That attitude is sin, and it will hinder one's own ministry, both in support and in impact. Enough religious chicanery has been exposed before the world's eyes to make Christian workers, personally guilty or not, hang their heads in shame. Prayer that pleases God is repentant, not only for one's own sins, but for those of the brothers and sisters.

RIGHT PRAYER IS REVERENT

To urge respect for God in prayer might seem to belabor the obvious. Is it conceivable that anyone would pray irreverently?

There is a major booby trap lurking for Christian fund-raisers in this area, what Dr. Karl Olsson once called the "posture of perfection." Because they represent Christian enterprises, they face the double temptation of projecting a personal image of saintliness and an organizational image of flawless and endless triumphs for the kingdom. After all, with so many groups going after dollars from the same prospect pool, a fund-raiser has to come across as several notches above the competition. In the process, the truth is not always well served and integrity can get a little wrinkled and torn.

Reverence in prayer is a matter of motivation. Is the *why* of our prayers a *my* or a *Thy?* Again, three pointed questions will sharpen perspective where it is acutely needed.

• What motivates fund-raising solicitations? The crass realities of the industry generate ulterior motives that can infect even a Christian: the development department quota system; the ego satisfaction of being Number One among professional colleagues; the fiscal crisis in an organization that prompts repeated pushing of the panic button in appealing for money.

Up a step from those motives are two that are more altruistic. First, the need for donors to be guided in their giving is a legitimate reason for presenting stewardship opportunities. With excessive demands on their limited resources, they must be selective. As a minimum, therefore, they are entitled to know how each contributed dollar is disbursed as well as the rate of spiritual return on that dollar. Surely the kingdom of heaven should operate on at least as high a scale of integrity as earthly business.

The second commendable motive for seeking support is the opportunity for expansion of ministry. Everyone wants to see the Lord's work prosper. But numerous pitfalls threaten the fund-raiser here simply in definition of terms: What is "ministry"? What is "the Lord's work"? Flagrant violation of acceptable standards by a few prominent Christian personalities has raised suspicion in the minds of thoughtful givers about self-serving enterprises. Is every expansion proposal necessarily God's will?

If one motivation should be judged worthy above the others, it is the magnifying of the Lord's reputation for wonder-working. The hallowing of God's name was Jesus' first concern, the performing of God's will on earth to reflect what goes on in heaven (Matthew 6:9-10). The prayer concludes where it began: *"Thine* is the glory" (v. 13).

Only when the motivation issue is resolved can a fund-raiser really proceed to the next two questions.

• What influences the choice of funding appeal methods? Sorting out the ways to get people to give can range from the comfort zone for one's own personality type to industry statistics on successful tactics. In between are questionable leverages such as tax advantages to the donor (a fringe benefit, perhaps, but not the reason for stewardship), or scare techniques that actually predict disaster for the organization or hint at potential loss to the donor (an insult to God's credibility and power).

Heresy is truth distorted. There are two ways for Christians to keep on guard against the deceptions of Satan and to be preserved from slipping into error. First, they need to be thoroughly familiar with biblical principles and precedents regarding stewardship. Jesus taught on many occasions that wealth is a trust to be invested, not squandered, and that the *attitude of the giver* outweighs the *amount of the gift* in God's estimation. Those who appeal for funding, therefore, need to communicate such truths to prospective donors.

Second, once securely established in general biblical principles, fund-raisers can seek and receive specific guidance from the Holy Spirit for each individual case. God's ways are dynamic, not static or mechanical, and they are always exactly suited to the situation. Jesus approached pious Nicodemus, the Samaritan adulteress, and Zacchaeus the tax collector very differently, yet with the same intent for each of them—their redemption.

Praying for instruction over an open Bible and praying for the Spirit's prompting in front of an open door are the fund-raiser's most reliable sources of wisdom for choosing the right method.

• What will help most to improve fund-raising skills? Again, carnal considerations—the world's way of doing things—confront Christian fund-raisers who want to be competent and productive. If they are kept in proper perspective on the scale of values, some of them might be useful, such as attendance at conferences and seminars, better psychological understanding of donor mentality, and improved verbal or written communications skills.

On a more personal level, improvement could come through affirmation of one's ability from a supervisor, or from stronger confidence in the organization's commitment to its mission.

However, given all the spiritual directions described previously, there is probably no more certain route to improvement than through closer personal communion with Christ in His Word and in prayer.

Suppose Daniel had stopped short of that. He was not a fund-raiser in the modern sense, of course, but he carried a lifelong burden for the dream of a reconstructed *city of God,* Jerusalem, where the *people of God* would carry forward the *work of God* to bring honor to the *name of God* among the pagan nations. In the midst of a heathen power structure alien to his cherished convictions, he stood against any compromise of his righteous heritage, even though by bucking the system he risked not only his livelihood but his life.

Three things sustained the prophet in Babylon: a few friends who understood; diligent reflection on the Scriptures; and persistent prayer to the God who could and did deliver him.

Today's special-assignment emissaries of God—those who plead with people to support the ongoing of His purpose to redeem lost men and women and to restore a blighted universe—need to pray, and to be prayed for, on several fronts:

– Personal spiritual growth, inasmuch as hearts are inseparable from treasure (Matthew 6:21).

– Equipping for presentation, because the truth is to be served under all circumstances (John 8:31-32).

329

– Selection of prospects, to identify those whom the Spirit has prepared to respond (Matthew 8:10).

– Ministry to prospects, considering that serving, not being served, is Christlike conduct (Mark 10:45).

– Fellowships with colleagues, affirming, not discrediting, the worthy works of other Christians (Luke 9:49-50).

– Institutional accountability, recognizing that employment by someone else brings inevitable reckoning (Matthew 25:19-21).

Does it pay to pray? In other words, when all the conditions are met for effective praying, does God come through with the desired blessing? No less a celestial personage than the Archangel Gabriel flew to Daniel from the presence of God in heaven while the prophet was still at prayer. He said, "Daniel, I have now come to give you insight and understanding. As soon as you began to pray, an answer was given, which I have come to tell you, for you are highly esteemed. Therefore, consider the message and understand the vision" (9:22-23).

The word and vision of the apocalyptic seventy weeks follow as the specific response to Daniel's prayer, far more than he had bargained for when he asked simply for the restoration of Jerusalem. His inward eyes were opened to behold the plan of God right on to the end of time.

Each of us will get a different answer when we pray, sent by God in a different way, but meant for us personally within our given circumstances. The principles in the salutation of Gabriel, however, are eternally operative, and they bring God's encouragement to all of us today.

First, God will open up and light up our understanding. Where we were puzzled, confused, or questioning, we will be gifted with insight.

Second, God starts answering the moment we start praying, not waiting until we are finished so the Trinity can hold a consultation, but sending His Word of reply on its way the moment we are responsive to His voice in the Scripture with our own voice in repentant and reverent prayer.

Third, God does this for us because He loves us—not because we merit it, not because we are always right in our prayers or in our lives, not because He owes us anything—but purely because He loves us.

330

Does it pay to pray? With right prayer, you can't miss.

MELVIN E. LORENTZEN, associate director of the Billy Graham Center, and member of the faculty at Wheaton College since 1958, served for a time as assistant to Wheaton's vice president for development. He has lectured on grant proposal writing for the Development Association for Christian Institutions (DACI), and has drafted varieties of fund-raising materials, from letters to brochures. He directed the first three Faith/Learning institutes for the Christian College Consortium, and was founding editor of the Consortium newspaper, Universitas.

An ordained American Baptist minister, Dr. Lorentzen holds degrees from Wheaton College, The Johns Hopkins University, and Northern Baptist Theological Seminary.

(29)
NO COMPETITION
IN THE KINGDOM

GORDON D. LOUX

"You've played hardball politics in the White House," I said to Chuck Colson—once known as President Richard Nixon's "hatchet man."[1] "But you haven't seen anything yet; wait until you see church politics!" Colson was just out of prison, where he served time for his Watergate-related offense, and we were talking about his vision for a prison ministry.

What he'd seen behind bars he couldn't forget—prisoners rotting in bleak, dreary cells. His own life had radically changed after trusting Jesus Christ as Lord. He felt a call to offer the hope of the Gospel to the inmates whose plight seemed so hopeless. When Colson challenged me to help him realize his vision, I accepted. But not before we'd talked about competition.

In 1976, when Prison Fellowship began, we hosted discipleship training classes in Washington, D.C. These classes were for Christian inmates who then returned to their prisons as skilled leaders. But Norman Carlson, then head of the Federal Bureau of Prisons, encouraged us to extend our thinking. He suggested we train and place Prison Fellowship chaplains inside the institutions.

The idea was appealing. We would place an "elder brother" in an institution to live among the inmates. He'd be a man from the same background as the inmates who could empathize with them. At Carlson's request, we stationed two such chaplains in the Memphis Federal Prison.

Almost immediately we began to feel repercussions. Unwittingly, we were stepping on toes. We were new to prison ministry, and others were suspicious of our program and motives. We received flack from both Protestants and Catholics who favored government-paid chaplains; they didn't like us "cutting in."

"We found ourselves plunged headlong into encounters with critical church bureaucracies," recalls Colson. "Accusations were hurled at us: we were not part of *the* church; we were another cult; we favored only evangelicals and wouldn't minister to others; we would endanger prison security."[2]

Eventually, God led us into additional areas of ministry. Today we have a wonderful relationship with most chaplains who wholeheartedly welcome Prison Fellowship programs and volunteers. This story serves as an apt example; we had entered unexplored territory; we hadn't thought things through as well as we should have. Capable people were already doing the job, and our niche would be found in working alongside them in cooperation, not competition. Our short-lived experiment with Prison Fellowship chaplains proved a hard-learned lesson about competing interests in kingdom work.

WHERE DID THE PROBLEM COME FROM?

Competition among believers is nothing new. It seems to have been at the heart of Cain and Abel's conflict. The disciples often argued about who would be the greatest.

> An argument started among the disciples as to which of them would be the greatest. Jesus, knowing their thoughts, took a little child and had him stand beside Him. Then He said to them, "Whoever welcomes this little child in My name welcomes Me; and whoever welcomes Me welcomes the One who sent Me. For he who is least among you all—he is the greatest" (Luke 9:46-48).

In *Church and Parachurch: An Uneasy Marriage,* Jerry White addresses the issue of competition among believers. "Conflict and division have been dishearteningly present in every century up to the present day," notes White. "Both internal and external conflict have been the norm." He adds, "Doctrine, structure, and authority have always been a major point of conflict."[3]

Although it's a universal problem, in the United States we seem to have a special bent toward competition. We *love* competition. Our whole society is designed around it—in sports, business, education, and politics. We think we can build things bigger, better, and faster than anybody else.

Competiton and individualism have marked America since its founding. Our forebears came to this land to escape religious persecution, to be. free to worship as they wished. But by the time the colonies were united as one country, the entrepreneurial spirit seemed nearly as strong as the religious fervor. As our land grew and thrived, those two motivating forces wove together into what has not always been a healthy alliance.

In the past 35 years, church denominations and parachurch endeavors have grown rapidly. Today over 20,800 denominations exist. In addition, says White, parachurches number "between 5,000 and 10,000, and that number is increasing daily. Some estimates run as high as 20,000."[4] Why are there so many different Christian entities?

Some people say the American religious institutions are particularly factional as a result of our tradition of injecting the principle of competition and free enterprise into every situation—opting for pluralism. Other analysts consider the individuals who founded and head Christian organizations to be people with a frontier mentality toward ministry. Self-reliant and infatuated with anything new, they have little respect for tradition.

Still other church watchers believe that God has raised up so many denominations and parachurch organizations as part of His strategy for this age.

Whatever the reason, one thing is clear: all too often we Americans compete in our efforts for Christ rather than cooperate. We are like two people riding a bicycle-built-for-two up a hill. When they reach the top, the first, gasping for air, exclaims, "I thought we'd never make it!" And the second replies, "We wouldn't have if I hadn't kept the brakes on to keep us from rolling back down!"

Competition in Christ's kingdom has led to the weakened influence of His church in the world. Nonbelievers are wary of a Gospel message preached by Christians who can't even worship together or cooperate in a common concern. Many prison inmates say they've had about all the "religion" they can stand. What they need is someone who will come in with the Gospel as one beggar telling another beggar where to find bread. If we are downgrading others in order to make ourselves look better, we are hurting the influence of the life-changing message we say we have.

WHY THE COMPETITION?

Jerry White, whose extensive research gives credibility to his work, considers how the church and parachurch view each other.[5] Many pastors believe parachurch ministries take responsibilities that belong to the church, and often drain the church of its resources.

On the other hand, White says, many involved in parachurch ministries hold that they reach a segment of the population otherwise unreachable. They see churches as being "too program- and building-oriented," too "brand" conscious, "too parochial and narrow in viewpoint and concern."[6]

There are reasons why competition is so prevalent in the kingdom. One involves the need for financial support. Without money, each program would be unable to stay afloat. A second is the need for workers. From leadership to grassroots support, church and parachurch alike need people who offer their special God-given gifts and talents to the tasks at hand.

But these first two reasons are founded on a third premise—the need for power and control among leaders to build an empire. Richard Foster's *Money, Sex, and Power* addresses particularly the desire within our hearts to assert control over resources and people.

"You're just out after *my* money and *my* people," says the church pastor to the parachurch leader. "You're after the best of them for *your* efforts. What about *my* programs, *my* vision?" Note the emphasis. Says Foster, "Our headstrong determination to do it our way makes God's voice distant and His word hard to hear."[7] Christian leaders would do well to pay attention to these words from Scripture.

If you have any encouragement from being united with Christ, if any comfort from His love, if any fellowship with the Spirit, if any tenderness and compassion, then make my joy complete by being like-minded, having the same love, being one in spirit and purpose. Do nothing out of selfish ambition or vain conceit, but in humility consider others better than yourselves (Philippians 2:1-3).

335

Humility produces unity, whereas selfish ambition—listed in Galatians 5:20 as an "obvious" act of the sinful nature—produces discord. We are not to indulge the sinful nature, but "to serve one another in love" (Galatians 5:13). Indeed, we have strayed. A problem we face in society today—if we allow ourselves to acknowledge it—is the desire for power or control. We suffer from the competitiveness of personality cults. Each leader raises his own funds and emphasizes his own distinctiveness.

Cheryl Forbes, in her penetrating book *The Religion of Power*, notes that "no follower of Christ should think about his status, position, or place. Service is to be the mark of a Christian. Jesus washed His disciples' feet—in those days the ultimate symbol of a servant."[8]

I am an ordained Baptist preacher, so it made me a bit uneasy when I heard about a young revival preacher who got offtrack and quit preaching from the Word and started pushing his own denomination—Baptist.

He shouted, "How many of you here tonight are Baptists?" All stood except for one gray-haired woman in front. The preacher looked at her with mild scorn. "And what, may I ask, are you, Ma'am?"

"Methodist," she replied.

"Why?" he questioned.

"Because my grandfather and father were Methodists, so I'm a Methodist."

The young preacher smirked. "Suppose your grandfather was a fool, and your father a fool," he persisted; "what would you be?"

She replied coolly, "Then I guess I would be a Baptist."

Sometimes we hold too tightly to our particular ministries, thinking that we have the only message and the only way of doing things. By adopting "exclusive labels," we further insulate and distance ourselves from each other. Remember the disciples' squabble in Luke 9:49-50? Jesus' response still applies today.

> "Master," said John, "we saw a man driving out demons in Your name and we tried to stop him, because he is not one of us."
> "Do not stop him," Jesus said, "for whoever is not against you is for you."

REPRESENTING JESUS CHRIST?

After the initial rocky introduction with the prison chaplains, Prison Fellowship discovered it could better work alongside them. One thing they told us was that they were exhausted. They pointed to the coterie of individuals coming into their institutions—in the name of Christianity.

But these people were not leading Bible studies or sharing what God had done in their lives so much as they were trying to make everyone conform to their denominational tenets. They were not declaring, "We come as representatives of Jesus Christ. We will work together to do what God has called us to accomplish."

The sad fact is that many voices in the Christian church would rather "major in the minors" than affirm our unity in the sovereign Lord; we lack the humility necessary to admit that the task is much greater than ourselves. Our tunnel vision regarding God's agenda for today can lead us to discredit the ministry efforts of others.

This truth is exemplified in a story I once heard. More than a century ago in London, the Archbishop of Canterbury offered the head of the Catholic church in England, Cardinal Hensley, a ride in his carriage. The archbishop said to the cardinal, "After all, we both are engaged in God's work." The cardinal agreed. "Yes," he said, "you in your way, and I in *His!*"

Our competition in the work of Christ has led to duplication and waste of resources. Research shows that many churches and parachurch organizations are too small to do much more than survive. But if there were greater cooperation in the kingdom, needless duplication of fund-raising and administrative expenses would not exist.

FRONTLINE MENTALITY

Christian leaders must be drawn together under the unifying power of a common cause, as soldiers on the front line of battle. During wartime, often the soldiers behind the lines of battle griped about the chow, the uniforms, the duty roster, and the like. Racial and cultural differences erupted in fights, causing general confusion and despondency.

But once they were transferred to the front to engage the enemy, these same soldiers were unified in a common cause. No longer did they fight among themselves or gripe about their petty differences or inconveniences. They developed a frontline mentality. They were fused together by a common mission.

We need to develop this same kind of frontline mentality, both in our churches and in parachurch groups. Our focus must always be on the larger objective that unifies us in cooperative service rather than on the doctrinal issues or "personal callings" that set us apart from each other. We must transcend our differences so that Jesus Christ may be glorified. As Bishop Brent once said, "The world is too strong for a divided church."

A good example of this "frontline mentality" in action is the Institute for Prison Ministries, one of the ministries of the Billy Graham Center in Wheaton, Illinois. Many prison ministries joined this cooperative program from its inception.

The Institute is quickly becoming a valuable resource for both professionals and volunteers involved in prison ministry. It offers graduate-level courses and internships, maintains an extensive library of resources, administers a scholarship fund for ex-offenders to attend Wheaton College in Wheaton, Illinois, and publishes a national directory of prison ministries. In pulling together various parachurch ministries involved in prison ministry, it's also a great unifying force.

As Christian leaders draw together, they also need to clarify the visions and missions of their organizations. In 1 Corinthians 12, the Apostle Paul reminds us that we Christians are all a part of the body of Christ—"many parts, but one body."

One sign of a healthy body is that its members function as intended. So it is with the body of Christ. Not all are called to perform the same function: "If the whole body were an eye, where would the sense of hearing be? If the whole body were an ear, where would the sense of smell be?" (1 Corinthians 12:17) God intends for us to work together in unity.

> For by the grace given me I say to every one of you: Do not think of yourself more highly than you ought, but rather think of yourself with sober judgment, in accordance with the measure of faith God has given you. Just as each of us has one body with many members, and these members do not all have the same function, so in Christ we who are many form one body, and each member belongs to all the others (Romans 12:3-5).

As we come to a better understanding of our particular role in the greater mission of Christian service, we begin to see how our efforts might dovetail with the efforts of others. In prison ministry, for example, some, like Chaplain Ray, have a vision for the wide distribution of Christian literature; others, such as Bill Glass, for evangelism. Still others, like the Good News Jail and Prison Ministry, for providing trained, well-qualified chaplains. We must understand and focus our energies on what we do well.

THE BROADER PERSPECTIVE
Looking at the broader perspective, parachurch organizations need to clarify their roles in relation to the church, since *para* means "alongside." The mission of parachurch groups ought to include assisting as well as equipping the church for effective ministry in modern society.

When Long Island Youth Guidance was established in 1981, the leadership recognized the tremendous potential that lay in the church to reach troubled youth. Hurting kids needed consistent caring adult role models whose lives would reflect the Good News of Jesus Christ. Area churches were filled with concerned Christians, but very little was happening.

Long Island Youth Guidance recognized its unique role. The outreach would pull community churches together into working relationships, providing both the expertise and time necessary to mobilize and train lay volunteers to work with troubled youth and their families.

Because of this clear sense of mission of Youth Guidance, over 60 local churches have now formed four regional coalitions that work closely together in reaching hundreds of hurting families. This group has proved that we can work together—interdependently.

STRENGTH IN UNITY
Two are better than one, because they have a good return for their work: If one falls down, his friend can help him up. But pity the man who falls and has no one to help him up! . . . Though one may be overpowered, two can defend themselves. A cord of three strands is not quickly broken (Ecclesiastes 4:9-12).

We are stronger when we are together, and we are weak when we act like lone rangers. We Christians must cooperate with one another in ministry, keeping in mind that cooperation does not mean compromising on the Gospel. Two really are better than one. Jesus demonstrated this principle when He sent out His disciples two-by-two.

Indeed, when we identify our resources, organizational strengths, and vision, we then begin to see how we can effectively and jointly work with other Christian organizations.

A recent visit to Iowa drove this point home to me. There, staff members of Prison Fellowship Ministries were working hand in hand with World Vision, Teen Challenge, Habitat for Humanity, and local churches on a Community Service Project (CSP).

The Prison Fellowship CSP is a program that offers Christian inmates a chance to leave prison for purposes of restitution and Christian witness. Nonviolent offenders provide restitution to the community by restoring the homes of the needy and performing other community service.

Each participant working at the joint CSP in Iowa served a particular part in the project, and it had a profound impact on the entire community. At the end of the CSP, all four parachurch groups participated in one church service.

TAKING THE INITIATIVE
As Christian leaders, it is time we raise the white flag and agree to stop shooting at each other. We mustn't say, "I will if you will." Rather, "I will!"

Individuals, not organizations, break down barriers and foster cooperation. We've got to take the initiative. This will take place when people are willing to sublimate their personal egos and desires to control for the greater good.

Leaders should not seek power and control. "Truth and power cannot exist side by side," Forbes reminds us. "If our work is true, power will kill it. By deciding for truth and against power, by what may seem to us like dying, we will find our life."[10]

Our lives should be models of the Master. The question on our lips should be, "How can we serve?" The Apostle Paul wrote, "Let us therefore make every effort to do what leads to peace and to mutual edification" (Romans 14:19). We must look for opportunities to cooperate rather than occasions to compete.

WINNING WITH COOPERATION

In the 1984 Olympics in Los Angeles, the U.S. men's gymnastics team did what was considered the impossible by beating China for the gold medal on team competition—the first time since 1904. The Americans had worked together as a team since the 1981 World Championships.

"This year they overcame their instincts to compete against each other," team member Bart Conner said. "We've all had our individual moments. But nothing matches the feeling of winning as a team. It's six times the emotion, six times the success."

When we Christians cooperate in furthering the kingdom of God, it is a win-win situation in which we all come out ahead. We move forward with integrity in furthering the Gospel of Jesus Christ in a dying world.

During the U.S. Army's heroic defense of the Bataan Peninsula in the Philippines in World War II, a company commander lined up his men and asked for a volunteer for a dangerous mission. Anyone willing to serve was asked to take two paces forward. He glanced down at a memorandum in his hand, and when he looked back up, the line was unbroken. "What," he said, "not a single man?" An aide at his side interrupted, "You don't understand, Sir; the whole line stepped forward two paces." Paul wrote to Christians in Philippi:

"Whatever happens, conduct yourselves in a manner worthy of the Gospel of Christ. Then, whether I come and see you or only hear about you in my absence, I will know that you stand firm in one spirit, contending as one man for the faith of the Gospel" (1:27).

We need to work together where we can and also to encourage each other. There are going to be times when, for one reason or another, we will not be able to work together. At that point we need to pray for one another. We must strive together in eliminating competition in the kingdom of God. Like the heroic soldiers who defended the Bataan Peninsula in the Philippines in World War II, we ought to take two paces forward, contending together for the faith of the Gospel in our work for Jesus Christ. There ought to be no competition in the kingdom of God; there is too much work to be done.

GORDON D. LOUX has more than twenty years of management experience. From 1976–1988, he was president and chief executive officer of Prison Fellowship Ministries, which he helped to found. He is currently the president and CEO of International Students, based in Colorado Springs.

Mr. Loux has been a national spokesman for integrity in fund-raising and is one of the founders of the Evangelical Council for Financial Accountability, of which he is currently chairman. He holds the master of divinity degree from Northern Baptist Theological Seminary, and a master's degree in management from the National College of Education.

Section
Five

A
Bibliography
of Funding the
Evangelical Enterprise

(30)
A BIBLIOGRAPHY
OF FUNDING THE
EVANGELICAL ENTERPRISE

JANIS W. SOKOLOSKI

The bibliography which follows has been compiled as a resource for those wishing to do additional reading on the subject of funding the evangelical challenge. For ease in use, titles have been categorized under the following headings:

- Understanding and exercising biblical stewardship.
- Stewardship and the local church.
- Ethical concerns and public perceptions related to fund-raising.
- The fund-raising climate, who gives, and why.
- Relevant newsletters and periodical for evangelical fund-raisers.

When approaching this bibliography, the reader should be aware of two items. First, several secular books and articles have been included based on the assumption that some of the information is relevant to the evangelical. Secondly, by design, titles having to do with the mechanics and techniques of *doing* fund-raising (e.g., how to write direct mail, how to secure foundation monies, etc.) have been excluded. Rather, the primary focus of this chapter, consistent with the body of the book, is the responsibility of the donor, the integrity of the Christian organization, the profile of the Christian donor public, and the atmosphere in which fund-raising among evangelicals is being conducted.

UNDERSTANDING AND EXERCISING
BIBLICAL STEWARDSHIP

Agar, F.A. *The Stewardship of Life.* New York: Fleming H. Revell, 1920.

Anderson, H. George. "Stewardship of Life." *Currents in Theology and Mission* 8 (Fall 1981):31–34.

Azariah, V.S. *Christian Giving.* New York: Association Press, 1955.

Babbs, Arthur V. *The Law of the Tithe.* New York: Fleming H. Revell, 1912.

Bair, Ray and Lillian. *God's Managers.* Scottdale, Pennsylvania: Herald Press, 1981.

Baldwin, Stanley G. *Your Money Matters.* Minneapolis: Bethany House, 1977.

Barnett, Jake. *Wealth and Wisdom: A Biblical Perspective on Possessions.* Colorado Springs: NavPress, 1987.

Barringer, Paul G. "Stewardship: More Than Giving." *Fundamentalist Journal* 4 (September 1985):56.

Berner, Carl W., Sr. *The Power of Pure Stewardship.* St. Louis: Concordia Publishing House, 1970.

————. "The Power of Pure Stewardship." *Concordia Journal* 7 (November 1981):229–233.

Biddle, Perry H. "The Eternal Money Problem: Suggestions for Improving Stewardship and Fund-Raising Programs." *Ministry* (November 1984): 5–7.

Blue, Ron. *Master Your Money: A Step-by-Step Plan for Financial Freedom.* Nashville: Thomas Nelson Publishers, 1986.

Brattgard, Helge. *God's Stewards: A Theological Study of the Principles and Practices of Stewardship.* Minneapolis: Augsburg, 1963.

Brazell, George. *This Is Stewardship.* Springfield, Missouri: Gospel Publishing House, 1962.

Briggs, Edwin. *Theological Perspectives on Stewardship.* New York: McGraw-Hill Book Co., 1969.

Burkett, Larry. *Answers to Your Family's Financial Questions.* Pomona, California: Focus on the Family, 1987.

————. *Your Finances in Changing Times,* rev. ed. Chicago: Moody Press, 1982.

Burroughs, P.E. *The Grace of Giving.* Nashville: Sunday School Board of the Southern Baptist Church, 1934.

Calkins, Harvey Reeves. *Stewardship Starting Points.* New York: The Methodist Book Concern, 1916.

Carroll, Lenard R. *Stewardship: Total Life Commitment.* Cleveland, Tennessee: Pathway Press, 1967.

Clinard, Turner N. *Responding to God: The Life of Stewardship.* Philadelphia: Westminster Press, 1980.

Conrad, Alphin Carl. *The Divine Economy: A Study in Stewardship.* Grand Rapids: William B. Eerdmans, 1954.

Cook, Charles A. *Stewardship and Mission.* Philadelphia: Judson Press, 1908.

Crawford, John R. *A Christian and His Money.* Nashville: Abingdon, 1967.

Crawford, Julies Earl. *The Call to Christian Stewardship.* Nashville: Publishing House of the Methodist Episcopal Church, 1924.

Cunningham, Richard B. *Creative Stewardship.* Nashville: Abingdon, 1979.

Cushman, Ralph S. *Dealing Squarely With God.* Cincinnati: Abingdon, 1927.

————. *The Message of Stewardship,* rev. ed. Nashville: Abingdon-Cokesbury, 1946.

————. *The New Christian Studies in Stewardship,* rev. New York: Interchurch World Movement, 1919.

————. *Will a Man Rob God?* New York: Abingdon-Cokesbury, 1942.

Davis, Lee E. *In Charge: Managing Money for Christian Living*. Nashville: Broadman, 1984.

Dayton, Howard L., Jr. *Your Money: Frustration or Freedom*. Wheaton, Illinois: Tyndale House, 1979.

Dillard, J.E. *Bible Stewardship*. Nashville: Executive Committee for the Southern Baptist Convention, 1947.

————. *Good Stewards*. Nashville: Broadman, 1953.

Dollar, Truman. *How to Carry Out God's Stewardship Plan*. Nashville: Thomas Nelson, 1974.

Duncan, John Wesley. *Our Christian Stewardship*. Cincinnati: Jennings and Graham, 1909.

Evangelical Council for Financial Accountability. *ECFA's Seven Standards of Responsible Stewardship*, rev. ed. Washington, D.C.: Evangelical Council for Financial Accountability, 1987.

————. *The Giver's Guide*, rev. ed. Washington, D.C.: Evangelical Council for Financial Accountability, 1987.

Fagan, A.R. *What the Bible Says about Stewardship*. Nashville: Convention Press, 1976.

Fisher, Wallace E. *All the Good Gifts: On Doing Biblical Stewardship*. Minneapolis: Augsburg, 1979.

Ford, George L. *All the Money You Need*. Waco, Texas: Word Books, 1976.

"Gallery of Church Fathers and Their Thoughts on Wealth." *Christian History* (6:2):10–11, 35.

Habecker, Eugene B. "Biblical Guidelines for Asking and Giving." *Christianity Today* (May 1987):32–34.

————. "The Leader as Fund-Raiser." In *The Other Side of Leadership*. Wheaton, Illinois: Victor Books, 1987.

Hales, Edward J., and Youngren, J. Alan. *Your Money, Their Ministry: A Guide to Responsible Christian Giving*. Grand Rapids: William B. Eerdmans, 1981.

Hall, Douglas John. *The Steward: A Christian Symbol Come of Age*. New York: Friendship Press, 1982.

Harrell, Costen J. *Stewardship and the Tithe*. Nashville: Abingdon, 1954.

Hembree, Ron. *You and Your Money: A Guide from God's Word.* Grand Rapids: Baker, 1980.

Hendricks, William L. *Resource Unlimited.* Nashville: Stewardship Commission of the Southern Baptist Church, 1972.

Hensey, James A. *Storehouse Tithing or Stewardship Up-To-Date.* New York: Fleming H. Revell, 1922.

Hitchings, B. "What Americans Give to Charity: Survey by Rockefeller Brothers Fund." *U.S. News & World Report* (28 April 1986):80.

Howell, Roy Wilbur. *Saved to Serve: Accent on Stewardship.* Grand Rapids: Baker, 1965.

"The Institute Talks to Fund-Raisers." *Christianity Today* (15 May 1987):35–39.

Jeremiah, David. *Biblical Stewardship.* Winona Lake, Indiana: BMH Books, 1978.

Johnson, Douglas W. *The Tithe.* Nashville: Abingdon, 1984.

Jones, Joseph F. *Studies in Christian Stewardship.* Austin, Texas: Sweet Publishing Co., 1968.

Kantonen, Taito Almar. *A Theology for Christian Stewardship.* Philadelphia: Fortress Press, 1956.

Katz, Harvey. *Give! Who Gets Your Charity Dollars?* Garden City, New Jersey: Anchor Books, Doubleday, 1974.

Kauffman, Milo. *Stewards of God.* Scottdale, Pennsylvania: Herald Press, 1975.

Kendall, R.T. *Tithing: A Call to Serious Biblical Giving.* Grand Rapids: Zondervan, 1983.

Knudsen, Raymond B. *New Models for Creative Giving.* New York: Association Press, 1976.

Lewis, Graegory. *Is God for Sale?* Wheaton, Illinois: Tyndale House, 1979.

Long, Roswell C. *More Stewardship Parables.* Nashville: Abingdon-Cokesbury, 1947.

———. *Stewardship Parables of Jesus.* Nashville: Cokesbury, 1931.

Luccock, George N. *The Meaning of Stewardship.* Philadelphia: The Board of Education of the Presbyterian Church, 1923.

MacArthur, John F., Jr. *Giving: God's Way*. Wheaton, Illinois: Tyndale House, 1978.

―――. *God's Plan for Giving*. Panorama City, California: Word of Grace Communications, 1979.

McConoughy, David. *Church Stewardship*. Philadelphia: The Presbyterian Board of Publications, 1919.

McKay, Arthur R. *Servants and Stewards*. Philadelphia: Geneva Press, 1963.

McQuaid, Elwood. "You're Passing the Bucks." *Moody Monthly* (May 1986):19–22.

Martin, Alfred. *Not My Own*. Chicago: Moody Press, 1968.

May, Lynn E., Jr. "The Stewardship Heritage of the Southern Baptists." *Baptist History and Heritage* (21 January 1986):1–56.

Mennonite Board of Missions. *Giving—From the Heart, with the Head*. Elkhart, Indiana: Mennonite Board of Missions, 1978.

"Money in Christian History." *Christian History* (6:2):1–40.

Morro, William Charles. *Stewardship*. St. Louis: Bethany Press, 1932.

Muether, John R. "Money and the Bible." *Christian History* (6:2):6–9.

Muncy, W.L. *Fellowship with God through Christian Stewardship*. Kansas City: Central Seminary Press, 1949.

Murray, Andrew. *Money: Thoughts for God's Stewards*. New York: Fleming H. Revell, 1897.

Olford, Stephen. *The Grace of Giving: Thoughts on Financial Stewardship*. Grand Rapids: Zondervan, 1972.

O'Nan, Lawrence W. *Giving Yourself Away*. San Bernardino, California: Here's Life, 1984.

Piper, Otto A. *The Christian Meaning of Money*. Englewood Cliffs, New Jersey: Prentice-Hall, 1965.

Powell, Luther P. "Stewardship in the History of the Christian Church." In *Stewardship in the Contemporary Life*. New York: Association Press, 1960.

Powell, Timothy M. *You've Got to Hand It to God: An Approach to Good Stewardship*. Springfield, Missouri. Gospel Publishing House, 1985.

Ray, Cecil A. *How to Specialize in Christian Living: What the Bible Says About Christian Stewardship*. Nashville: Convention Press, 1982.

―――. *Living the Responsible Life*. Nashville: Convention Press, 1974

Reid, Russ. "How to Spread the Joy of Giving. *Religious Broadcasting* (December 1982):18–20.

Reinert, Paul C. "The Spiritual Dimensions of Giving and Getting." *Momentum* (16 September 1985):6–9.

Rice, John R. *All about Christian Giving.* Wheaton: Sword of the Lord, 1953.

Salstrand, George A.E. *History of Stewardship in the United States.* Grand Rapids: Baker, 1956.

Sharpe, Robert F. *Before You Give Another Dime.* Nashville: Thomas Nelson, 1979.

Sider, Ronald J. *Rich Christians in an Age of Hunger.* Downers Grove, Illinois: InterVarsity Press, 1977.

Siemans, Peter. *The New Testament Conception of Stewardship.* Unpublished thesis, Northern Baptist Theological Seminary, Chicago, 1952.

Smith, Fred. "The Four Faces of Stewardship." *Leadership* 5 (Spring 1984): 109–114.

Smith, Ken. "The Stewardship of Money." *Crux: A Quarterly Journal of Christian Thought and Opinion* 20 (March 1984):16–21.

————. "The Stewardship of Money." *Fundamentalist Journal* 4 (April 1985):31–33.

Sorensen, Charles M. *Stewardship Upside Down.* New York: Hawthorn Books, 1975.

Speer, William. *God's Rule for Christian Giving.* Philadelphia: The Presbyterian Board of Publication, 1875.

Stafford, Bill. *The Adventure of Giving.* 1965 Reprint. Wheaton, Illinois: Tyndale House, 1986.

Steps to Success in Stewardship. Neibauer Press. Available through the Stewardship Commission of the National Association of Evangelicals, Wheaton, Illinois.

Stewart, E.B. *The Tithe.* Chicago: Winona Publishing Co., 1903.

Strang, D.W.P. *Studies in Christian Stewardship.* Glasgow: The International Association for Church Finance and Organization, 1931.

Taylor, J.R. *God's Miraculous Plan of Economy.* Nashville: Broadman, 1975.

Thomas, Winburn T., ed. *Stewardship in Mission.* Englewood Cliffs, New Jersey: Prentice-Hall, 1964.

Thompson, Thomas K., ed. *Stewardship in Contemporary Life.* New York: Association Press, 1965.

_____. *Stewardship in Contemporary Theology.* New York: Association Press, 1960.

Van Benschoten, A.Q., Jr. *What the Bible Says About Stewardship.* Valley Forge, Pennsylvania: Judson Press, 1983.

Vander Lugt, Herbert, and Smith, Carl H. *As the Ushers Come Forward: The Christian and His Money.* Grand Rapids: Radio Bible Class, 1976.

Ward, Hiley H. *Creative Giving.* New York: Macmillan, 1958.

Watson, Tom, Jr. "The Art of Intelligent Giving." *Moody Monthly* (March 1972):20.

Watts, Wayne. *The Gift of Giving.* Colorado Springs: NavPress, 1982.

Webley, Simon. *How to Give Away Your Money.* Downers Grove, Illinois: InterVarsity Press, 1978.

Werning, Waldo J. *Supply-Side Stewardship: A Call to Biblical Priorities.* St. Louis: Concordia, 1986.

_____. *The Stewardship Call.* St. Louis: Concordia, 1965.

White, John. *The Golden Cow: Materialism in the Twentieth Century Church.* Downers Grove, Illinois: InterVarsity Press, 1979.

Young, Samuel. *Giving and Living: Foundations for Christian Stewardship.* Grand Rapids: Baker, 1974.

THE LOCAL CHURCH
AND STEWARDSHIP

Ashcraft, Morris, ed. *Mission Unlimited.* Nashville: The Stewardship Commission of the Southern Baptist Convention, 1976.

Bassett, William, and Huizing, Peter. *The Finances of the Church.* New York: Seabury, 1979.

Bayne, H. Raymond. *Before the Offering: Mini-Messages on Giving.* Grand Rapids: Baker, 1976.

Bleick, Roy H. *Much More Than Giving: Resources for Preaching Christian Stewardship.* St. Louis: Concordia, 1985.

Byfield, Richard, and Shaw, James P. *Your Money and Your Church.* New York: Doubleday, 1959.

Cassell, Fred W. *Major Fund Campaigns and Their Impact on the Financial Giving Pattern of the Local Church.* D.Min. dissertation, San Francisco Theological Seminary, 1984.

Crowe, Charles M. *Stewardship Sermons.* Nashville: Abingdon, 1960.

Davenport, Arthur, ed. *The Ten Best Stewardship Sermons.* Oklahoma City, Oklahoma: Arthur Davenport Associates, 1963.

Ferenback, Campbell. *Preaching Stewardship.* Laurinburg, North Carolina: St. Andrews Press, 1967

Gravrock, Mark. *Stewardship Preaching, Series B.* Minneapolis: Augsburg, 1984.

Grindstaff, W.E. *Principles of Stewardship Development.* Nashville: Convention Press, 1967.

353

Grindstaff, W.E. *Developing a Giving Church*. New York: Fleming H. Revell, 1954.

Hess, Bartlet L., and Hess, Margaret J. *How to Have a Giving Church*. Nashville: Abingdon, 1974.

Holck, Manferd, Jr. *Church Finance in a Complex Economy*. Nashville: Abingdon, 1983.

————. *Money and Your Church*. New Canaan, Connecticut: Keats Publishing, 1974.

Johnson, Douglas W. *Finance in Your Church*. Nashville: Abingdon, 1986.

King, Julius. *Successful Fund-Raising Sermons*. New York: Funk and Wagnalls, 1953.

Knudsen, Raymond B. *Developing Dynamic Stewardship: Fifteen Sermons on Commitment and Giving*. Nashville: Abingdon, 1978.

————. *New Models for Financing the Local Church*. New York: Association Press, 1974.

McDermet, Wiliam W. "Making Ministry Meaningful: Churches Ought to Provide Opportunities for Members to Express and Experience Christian Stewardship." *Christian Ministry* (July 1983):8–9.

Pappenheim, Eugene. *Stewardship without Failure*. Milwaukee: Agape Publishers, Inc., 1974.

Parrott, Roger. "A Time to Raise Funds: Making Your Denominational Affiliation an Asset." *CASE Currents* (November–December 1985): 17–18.

Pendleton, Othniel A. *New Techniques for Church Fund-Raising*. New York: McGraw-Hill Co., 1955.

Petry, Ronald D. *Partners in Creation: Stewardship for Pastor and People*. Elgin, Illinois: The Brethren Press, 1980.

Poovey, W.A. "Preaching about Money." *Christian Ministry* (July 1983): 4–7.

Powell, Luther P. *Money and the Church*. New York: Association Press, 1962.

Rolston, Holmes. *Stewardship in the New Testament Church*. Richmond, Virginia: John Knox Press, 1959.

Shedd, Charlie W. *How to Develop a Tithing Church*. Nashville: Abingdon, 1961.

Sullivan, Daniel J. "Stewardship: A Future Direction for Catholic Fund-Raising?" *Fund-Raising Management* 18 (July 1987):76–81.

Swanson, Stephen O. *Stewardship Preaching, Series A.* Minneapolis: Augsburg, 1983.

Walker, Joe W. *Money in the Church.* Nashville: Abingdon, 1982.

ETHICAL CONCERNS AND PUBLIC PERCEPTIONS RELATED TO FUND-RAISING

"Accountability in Fund-Raising Today." *Christianity Today* (6 April 1979): 10.

Bakal, Carl. *Charity U.S.A.: An Investigation Into the Hidden World of the Multi-billion Dollar Charity Industry.* New York: Times Books, 1979.

Black, Larry. "A Price Tag on Salvation." *Maclean's* (2 March 1987):43.

Borden, Arthur C. "The Issue Is Credibility." *Fund-Raising Management* 18 (July 1987):86–90.

Burkholder, Alvin. "Funds and People." *United Evangelical ACTION* (Winter 1976):14–15.

"Chuck Colson Interview: Speaking Out on Fund-Raising Heresy." *Christian Advertising Forum* (April–May 1983):6–13.

"Contributors Misled." *Christian Century* (2 April 1986):321.

Cryderman, Lyn. "Why Do Americans Mistrust Christian Fund-Raisers?" *Christianity Today* (17 April 87):38.

Dingfelder, William. "Non-Profits Must Consider Ethics in Soliciting Gifts." *Fund-Raising Management* 13 (December 1982):36–37.

"Donors Are Told How to Identify Improper Fund-Raising Tactics." *Christianity Today.* (20 April 1984):45.

Dulaney, William. "Financial Accounting for Non-Profit Organizations." *Fund-Raising Management* 16 (December 1985):18–22.

"ECFA: Putting Prestige into Financial Disclosure." *Christianity Today* (6 November 1981):21–22.

Engle, James F., and Wheaton Graduate School Research Team. *A Survey of Ethical Beliefs and Practices Used in Fund-Raising for the Christian Organization.* Research report, Wheaton College Graduate School, 1987.

Evangelical Council for Financial Accountability. *ECFA Member List.* Washington, D.C.: Evangelical Council for Financial Accountability, 1988.

————. *ECFA Standards for Fund-Raising,* rev. ed. Washington, D.C.: Evangelical Council for Financial Accountability, 1987.

Fagar, Chuck. "A Recipe for Financial Trust." *Christian Century* (24 November 1982):1202–1203.

"Falwell Says Media Ministries Need More Accountability." *Christianity Today* (10 July 1987):42.

Flanagan, William G. "Some Dare Call It Charity." *Forbes* 132 (Fall 1983): 240–246.

Frame, Randall L. "Did Oral Roberts Go Too Far?" *Christianity Today* (20 February 1987):43–45.

————. "Policing Its Ranks." *Christianity Today* (16 October 1987):44.

————. "The State of Christian Broadcasting." *Christianity Today* (20 March 1987):48–50.

————. "Trying to Tighten the Belt of Financial Accountability." *Christianity Today* (20 November 1987):50–51.

Genet, Harry. "The New Watchdog on the Block Enlarges Its Turf." *Christianity Today* (29 May 1981):38–42.

"God and Money." *Newsweek* (6 April 1987):16–23.

"God and Money." *Time* (3 August 1987):48–55.

Griffin, Emory A. *The Mind Changers: The Art of Christian Persuasion.* Wheaton, Illinois: Tyndale, 1976.

"Heaven Can Wait." *Newsweek* (8 June 1987):58–62.

Holloway, George T. "Accountability and Ethics: A Priority for All Fund-Raisers." *Fund-Raising Management* 18 (July 1987):82–85.

"Holy Hoaxers?" *U.S. News & World Report* (23 March 1987):10.

Hopkins, Bruce R. "Tax Exempt Status Threatened by Fund-Raising?" *Fund-Raising Management* 14 (October 1983):94–95.

Huntsinger, Jerry. "Ethics and Fund-Raising Letters: Ten Suggestions." *Fund-Raising Management* 16 (May 1985):106–107.

"The Institute Talks to Fund-Raisers." *Christianity Today* (15 May 1987): 35–39.

"Is Christian Fund-Raising Ethical?" *Fund-Raising Management* 18 (May 1987):68–70.

King, Roland. "Painting the Wrong Picture." *Currents* 13 (January 1987):26–30.

McKenna, David L. "Financing the Great Commission." *Christianity Today* (15 May 1987):26–31.

Mason, T., and Ticer, S. "The Gospel According to Free Market." *Business Week* (6 April 1987):43–44.

Maust, John. "The Good Housekeeping Seal of Approval." *Christianity Today* (6 April 1979):48–49.

Melvin, Billy. "The Scandal of Evangelical Giving." *United Evangelical ACTION* (Winter 1976):11–13.

Nicholas, Dan. "How to Get Cash Without Compromising Ethics." *Fund-Raising Management* 18 (July 1987):30–34.

O'Connor, William P. "Supporting a Global Mission." *Fund-Raising Management* 18 (July 1987):94–98.

Ostling, Richard N. "Of God and Greed." *Time* (8 June 1987):70–72.

———. "Your Money or His Life." *Time* (26 January 1987):63.

"Praise the Lord and Pass the Loot." *Economist* (May 1987):23.

Press, Aric. "Will Those Cards and Letters Keep Coming?" *Newsweek* (11 May 1987):72.

"Questioning Tactics." *Time* (30 March 1987):70.

Ross, Lanson. "The Cross in Crisis." *Fund-Raising Management* 18 (July 1987):70–74.

Schmidt, J. David. "Where Does the Money Go?" *Fund-Raising Management* 18 (July 1987):66–69.

Smith, Joel P. "Professionals in Development: Dignity or Disdain." *CASE Currents* 7 (March 1981):10–13.

Spring, Beth. "Interaid Activities Provoke a Federal Investigation: National

Media Focuses on Allegations of Mishandled Donations." *Christianity Today* (1 March 1985):36–39.

_____. "TV Ministries and Taxation." *Christianity Today* (6 November 1987):36–42.

Staecker, Delmar. "For-Profit Activities in the Nonprofit World—Where Do We Draw the Line?" *Nonprofit World* (March–April 1987):31–32.

Tarr, Leslie K. "Better Business Bureaus Warn against Humbard's Fund-Raising Letters." *Christianity Today* (21 September 1984):70–71.

_____. "Senior Citizens Chide Oral Roberts over His Fund Appeals." *Christianity Today* (15 March 1985):44.

"Test Your Ethics." *Currents* 13 (January 1987):8–11.

Virts, Paul H. "Public Perceptions of Christian Fund-Raising Ethics." *Fund-Raising Management* 18 (July 1987):36–46.

"What Will Oral Roberts Do Next?" *U.S. News & World Report* (9 March 1987):25.

Willmer, Wesley K. "Seeking a Godly Perspective for Fund-Raisers." *Fund-Raising Management* 18 (July 1987):60–65.

_____. "Impact of Scandals on Giving." *Fund-Raising Management* (November 1988):32–40.

THE FUND-RAISING CLIMATE,
WHO GIVES,
AND WHY

Andrews, Frank Emerson. *Attitudes toward Giving.* New York: Russell Sage Foundation, 1953.

Barna, George. "Profile Attitudes of Christian Parachurch Group Donors." *Fund-Raising Management* 15 (February 1985):52–55.

————. "An Examination of Direct Mail Fund-Raising." *Christian Marketing Perspective* (September–October 1986):2–4.

————. "Raising Money for Ministry." *Christian Marketing Perspective,* (May–June 1986):1–2.

Briley, Gaylord. "Religious Fund-Raising Awaits a New Millenium." *Fund-Raising Management* 18 (July 1987):92–93.

Brooks, Elton H. "Charitable Giving—A Viable Market?" *Manager's Magazine* 59 (December 1984):4–10.

Carlson, Martin E. *Why People Give.* New York: Morehouse-Barlow Co., 1973.

Cohen, Robert. "A Social Climate Perspective on Charitable Giving." Paper delivered at National Society of Fund-Raising Executives Convention, Chicago, February 1987.

Edmondson, Brad. "Who Gives to Charity?" *American Demographics* (8 November 1986):45–49.

Engel, James F. *Averting the Financial Crisis in Christian Organizations: Insights from a Decade of Donor Research.* Wheaton, Illinois: Management Development Associates, 1983.

_____. "What Motivates Giving to Christian Organizations?" *Fund-Raising Management* 18 (July 1987):48–52.

Engel, James F., and Wheaton Graduate School Research Team. *Survey of Development Programs of Nonprofit Organizations.* Research report, Wheaton College Graduate School, 1985.

Fisher, Wallace E. *A New Climate for Stewardship.* Nashville: Abingdon, 1976.

Gibson, E. Burr. "Why People Do and Don't Give to Religious Causes." *Christian Ministry* 11 (September 1980):5–10.

Hodgkinson, Virginia, and Weitzman, Murray. *The Charitable Behavior of Americans: Findings From a National Study.* Research conducted by Yankelovich, Skelly and White, Inc. and commissioned by the Rockefeller Brothers Fund. Washington, D.C.: Independent Sector, 1986.

Hopkins, Bruce. "Awesome Clashes Seen in Religion, Fund-Raising." *Fund-Raising Management* 11 (June 1980):46–48.

"Is Christian Fund-Raising Ethical?" *Fund-Raising Management* 18 (May 1987):68–70.

Jones, Landon Y. "The Baby-Boom Consumer." *American Demographics* (February 1981):28.

Katz, Harvey. *Who Gets Your Charity Dollar?* Garden City, New Jersey: Doubleday, 1974.

Kauffmann, Duane; Kauffman, Kenten; Zimmerly, Terry; and Harder, Kathy. "Religious Salience and Contributions to a Charitable Organization." *Journal of Psychology and Christianity* 4 (Spring 1985):56–61.

Kerr, Baine. "Responsible Corporate Giving from Donor's Viewpoint." *Fund-Raising Management* 14 (September 1983):62–65.

Lant, Jeffrey. *Development Today: A Fund-Raising Guide for Nonprofit Organizations.* 3rd ed. Cambridge, Massachusetts: JLA Publications, 1986.

Lausanne Committee for World Evangelization. "Hindrances to Cooperation—The Suspicion about Finances." In *Cooperating in World Evangelization: A Handbook on Church/Parachurch Relationships.* No. 24 in Lausanne Occasional Papers, pp. 57–82. Wheaton, Illinois: Lausanne Committee for World Evangelization, 1983.

Lindenmann, Walter K. "Who Makes Donations? National Survey Provides New Data." *CASE Currents* 9 (February 1983):18–19.

McAuley, John. "Giving and Getting: A Study of Charitable Contributions." *School Business Affairs* 50 (February 1984):26.

Markam, Ray. "Little Things Mean a Lot—Especially in Fund-Raising." *Fund-Raising Management* 17 (November 1986):64–68.

Naisbitt, John. *Megatrends: Ten New Directions Transforming Our Lives.* New York: Warner Books, 1982.

Olberding, Greg. "Personal Touch Establishes Relationship with Donors." *Fund-Raising Management* 11 (December 1980):20–27.

Reece, William S. "Charitable Contributions: New Evidence on Household Behavior." *American Economic Review* 69 (March 1979):142–151.

Religion in America—1987. Princeton, New Jersey: Princeton Religion Research Center, 1987.

Roel, Raymond. "Striking the Right Balance Between Mission and Premiums." *Fund-Raising Management* 15 (February 1985):26–36.

Rust, Brian, and McLeish, Barry. *The Support-Raising Handbook.* Downers Grove, Illinois: InterVarsity Press, 1984.

"Shift in Society Will Impact Fund-Raising." *Fund-Raising Management* 13 (July 1982):40–41.

Stocker, Leslie E. "Market Research Points Out Donor Perceptions." *Fund-Raising Management* 13 (September 1982):28–33.

Willmer, Wesley K. *Friends, Funds, and Freshmen for Christian Colleges: A Manager's Guide to Advancing Resource Development.* Washington, D.C.: Christian College Coalition, 1987.

"You Are Always Asking for Money." *Christianity Today* (11 December 1981):13.

RELEVANT NEWSLETTERS AND PERIODICALS FOR EVANGELICAL FUND-RAISERS

The following list was compiled based on conversations with development professionals from select Christian organizations. While the majority of these newsletters and periodicals are not directed at the evangelical fund-raiser per se, their contents are often applicable.

Christian Management Report. Christian Ministries Management Association, P.O. Box 4638, Diamond Bar, California 91765. Bimonthly. Service to CMMA members; subscriptions for nonmembers.

Christian Marketing Perspective. Barna Research Group, 529 Hahn Ave., Glendale, California 91203. Quarterly.

Direction. Ketchum, Inc., Ketchum Center, 1030 Fifth Ave., Pittsburgh, Pennsylvania 15219. Quarterly.

Emerging Trends. Princeton Religion Research Center, P.O. Box 628, Princeton, New Jersey 08542. Published 10 times/yr.

Foundation News. Foundation News Fulfillment Service, P.O. Box 501, Martinsville, New Jersey 08836. Bimonthly.

Friday Report. Hoke Communications, Inc., 224 Seventh St., Garden City, New York 11530. Weekly.

FRI Monthly Portfolio. Includes *FRI Newsletter, FRI Bulletin,* and *FRI Letter Clinic.* The Fund-Raising Institute, Box 365, Ambler, Pennsylvania 19002. Monthly.

Fund-Raising Management. Hoke Communications, Inc., 224 Seventh St., Garden City, New York 11530. Monthly.

Fund-Raising Management Weekly (FRM Weekly). Hoke Communications, Inc., 224 Seventh St., Garden City, New York 11530. Weekly.

Give & Take: News and Ideas for Development Executives of Nonprofit Institutions. Robert Sharpe and Co., 5050 Poplar Ave., Memphis, Tennessee 38157. Monthly.

Grantsmanship Center News. The Grantsmanship Center, 1031 South Grand Ave., Los Angeles, California 90015. Bimonthly.

Journal of Stewardship. Commission on Stewardship, National Council of the Churches of Christ in the U.S.A., New York, New York 10015. Annually.

The Public Pulse. Roper Organization, 205 E. 42nd St., New York, New York 10017. Monthly.

Reid Report. Russ Reid Company, 2 North Lake Ave., Pasadena, California 91101. Quarterly.

Research Alert. 30-87 37th St., Long Island City, New York 11103. Biweekly.

A wide range of fund-raising resources are also available from:

PUBLIC SERVICE MATERIALS CENTER
111 N. Central Ave.
Hartsdale, New York 10530

THE TAFT GROUP
5130 MacArthur Blvd., NW
Washington, DC 20016

JANIS W. SOKOLOSKI was a member of the senior staff of Management Development Associates from 1982 to 1987. This full-service agency serves Christian organizations worldwide in the areas of fund-raising, research, and management consulting and training. As vice president of MDA's research division, she spearheaded the design and implementation of both quantitative and qualitative market research projects for over 50 Christian organizations.

Mrs. Sokoloski continues to provide marketing and research services to Christian organizations as an independent consultant. In additon, she writes and produces fund appeals, newsletters, and other donor and member communications.

She holds an M.A. in communications from Wheaton College Graduate School and did her undergraduate work at Pennsylvania State University.

NOTES

CHAPTER 1
1. Gordon MacDonald, "Developing Spiritually Sensitive Fund-Raising Practices for Your Organization," speech delivered at Funding the Christian Challenge conference, March 1987, Kansas City, Missouri. Co-sponsored by the Billy Graham Center and the Christian Stewardship Council.
2. Carl F.H. Henry, *Such as I Have: The Stewardship of Talent* (Nashville: Abingdon-Cokesbury Press, 1946).
3. Charles Colson, "Speaking Out on Fund-Raising Heresy," *Christian Advertising Forum*, April/May 1983, 6.
4. Ibid.
5. Jerold Panas, *Mega Gifts* (Chicago: Pluribus Press, Inc., 1984), 35.
6. Harold J. Seymour, *Designs for Fund-Raising* (New York: McGraw-Hill, Inc., 1966), 16.

CHAPTER 3
1. From a pamphlet published by the Mennonite Board of Missions, 1973.
2. Harold J. Seymour, *Designs for Fund-Raising* (New York: McGraw-Hill Book Company), 29.
3. Admirable as this strength of commitment may be, a legal note is appropriate here. If the individual worker being supported joins an organization which the steward finds wanting and would not otherwise support, that steward should be aware of this IRS rule: contributions which are termed "fully designated"—gifts which the donor insists go only to the support of the designee—are *not* tax deductible. In addition, should the designee's support be oversubscribed, the donor will then, in effect, be supporting the organization itself, and with a nondeductible gift.

CHAPTER 7
1. The basic principles of this chapter can also be found in the book by Lawrence W. O'Nan, *Giving Yourself Away* (San Bernardino, California: Here's Life Publishers, Inc.), 1984.
2. William R. Bright, *How to Be Filled with the Holy Spirit* (booklet) (San Bernardino, California: Campus Crusade for Christ, Inc.), 1971.

CHAPTER 8
1. Ray Stedman, *Body Life* (Glendale, California: G/L Regal Books, 1972), 1–2.
2. Richard Byfield and James Shaw, *Your Money and Your Church* (New York: Doubleday & Co.), 26–27.
3. Truman Dollar, *How to Carry out God's Stewardship Plan* (Nashville: Thomas Nelson, Inc.), 67.

CHAPTER 10
1. Jeremy Rifkin, *Algeny* (New York: The Viking Press, 1983), 72–73.
2. Ibid., 74.
3. Ibid., 79.
4. John White, *The Golden Cow* (Downers Grove, Illinois: InterVarsity Press, 1979), 112–113.
5. Rifkin, *Algeny*, 83.
6. Ibid., 82.
7. Ibid., 82.
8. Ibid., 91.
9. John H. Yoder, *He Came Preaching Peace* (Scottsdale, Pennsylvania: Herald Press, 1985), 52.
10. Cheryl Forbes, *The Religion of Power* (Grand Rapids: Zondervan Publishing House, 1983), 29.
11. Rifkin, *Algeny*, 103.
12. Charles Colson, *Who Speaks for God?* (Westchester, Illinois: Crossway Books, 1985), 27–29.
13. E.M. Bounds, *Power Through Prayer* (Grand Rapids: Baker Book House, 1972), 60, 125.
14. Ibid., 125.
15. Ibid.
16. Rifkin, *Algeny*, 254.
17. Bounds, *Power Through Prayer*, 114.

CHAPTER 11
1. Ron Wilson, "How to Read a Fund-Raising Letter," *Christian Herald*, July/August 1986.

CHAPTER 12
1. Ben Armstrong, *The Electronic Church* (Thomas Nelson Company, Nashville, 1979).
2. Some useful books on the topic are:
   Peter Elvy, *Buying Time* (Mystic, Connecticut: Twenty-Third Publications, 1986).
   John Steward, *Holy War: An Inside Account of the Battle of PTL* (Enid, Oklahoma: Fireside Publishing and Communications, 1987).
   John W. Bachman, *Media: Wasteland or Wonderland* (Minneapolis: Augsburg, 1984).
   George Gerbner, *Religion and Television* (Philadelphia: Annenberg School of Communications, 1984).
   Peter G. Horsfield, *Religious Television* (New York: Longman, 1984).
   Razelle Frankl, *Televangelism: The Marketing of Popular Religion* (Carbondale, Illinois: Southern Illinois University Press, 1986).
   William Fore, *Television and Religion: The Shaping of Faith, Values and Culture* (Minneapolis: Augsburg, 1987).
3. Charles E. Swann, "The Electronic Church," *Presbyterian Survey* (May 1979), pp. 9–16.
   James Montgomery, "Religious Broadcasting Becomes Big Business," *The Wall Street Journal* (19 May 1978), p. 1.
   William F. Fore, "Religion and Television: Report on the Research," *The Christian Century* (18 July 1984), pp. 710–718.
   Thomas C. Oden, "Truth or Consequences," *Christianity Today* (18 March 1988).
4. Jeffrey K. Hadden, "Soul Saving Via Video," *The Christian Century* (28 May 1980), p. 612.
5. *Religion and Television*, (1984: The Annenburg School of Communications and The Gallup Organization, Inc.), p. 10.
6. Martin E. Marty, "The Invisible Religion," *Presbyterian Survey* (May 1979), p. 13.
   Swann, pp. 9–12, 14–16.
   William F. Fore, "Commentary: 'There Is No Such Thing as a TV Pastor,' " *TV Guide* (19 July 1980), pp. 15–18.
7. *Religion and Television*, p. 10.
8. *Religion and Television*, p. 5.
9. *A Viewership and Donor Study of THE 700 CLUB* (1983, CBN).
10. *1986 Non-renewing Donor Study* (CBN) pp. 5, 9.
11. *The Christian Marketplace*, (1980, American Research Corporation).
12. Ben Armstrong, "The Critics Have Misrepresented Religious Broadcasting," *Religious Broadcasting* (December 1987).

CHAPTER 13

1. Jerry Huntsinger, "Prediction for 1987: A Year of Intense Change," *Fund-Raising Management* (December 1986), 56.

CHAPTER 14

1. *British Statute of Charitable Uses 1601*, 43 Eliz. 1, C4. See generally, *The Exemption of Nonprofit Organizations from Federal Income Taxation*, Bittker and Rahdert, 85 *Yale Law Journal* 299, 301 (1976); Reiling, *Federal Taxation: What Is a Charitable Organization?*, 44 A.B.A.J. 525, 526 (1958); 50 Cong. Rec. 1306 (1913) (discusses state constitutional exemptions of religious, scientific, and benevolent organizations from property taxation).

2. Act of August 27, 1984, Ch. 349, Sec. 32, 28 Stat. 556. There was even an earlier recognition of exemption for "literary, scientific, or other charitable institutions" in the short-lived federal income tax imposed during the Civil War. G.P. Boutwell, *A Manual of the Direct and Excise Tax System of the United States*, 275 (1863). These charitable and religious exemptions were reinacted in the corporation income tax of 1909 (Act of August 9, 1909, Ch. 6, Sec. 38, 36 Stat. 112) and the Revenue Act of 1913 (Act of October 3, 1913, Ch. 16, Sec. 2(G), 38 Stat. 172).

3. Shortly after ratification of the 16th Amendment on February 3, 1913, Representative Cordell Hull, author of the Revenue Act of 1913, argued against the enlargement of the Act's exemption clauses to embrace "benevolent" and "scientific" organizations on the ground that the Statute's reference to "net income" automatically excluded all nonprofit organizations. 50 Cong. Rec. 1306 (1913).

4. The doctrine of granting religious and other charitable organizations qualified if not complete immunity for the negligence of agents and employees was common into the early part of this century. It was based on the view that the funds of religious and other charitable organizations are held in trust for charitable purposes and may not be diverted to the payment of damages. Further, it was perceived that the misconduct of an employee should not be imputed to a charitable organization when the services of the employee are for the benefit of humanity and not for the economic gain of the charitable employer. See generally, E. Fisch, D. Freed, and E. Schachter, *Charities and Charitable Foundations*, Ch. 25 (1974 and Suppl. 1982–83); R. Hammar, *Pastor, Church and Law*, 285 (1983). Only Arkansas and Maine presently grant complete charitable immunity.

5. Alexis Charles Henry Maurice Clerel, 1805–1859, French statesman and author as quoted in A. Knopf, *Democracy in America* (NY 1945).

6. The YMCA movement, launched in London in 1844 by a group of salesmen, was transplanted to Boston in 1851. The Salvation Army, which, like the YMCA, had its roots in England, came to this country in 1880. The American Red Cross, which was a branch of the International Red Cross Movement that grew out of a conference in Geneva, Switzerland, in 1863, was formed in this country as the American Association of the Red Cross in 1881. C. Bakal, *Charity U.S.A.*, pp. 28–29 (NY 1979).

7. The most fundamental duty of a trustee to a beneficiary is the duty of loyalty which means that the assets and funds received in trust must be administered solely in the interest of the beneficiaries, that is, the public. The trustee may not place himself in a position where he could personally benefit from the trust assets. The trustee also has a duty to protect and perserve the trust property by administering it in a business-like manner in full compliance with the law, making the trust property productive, and defending the trust against attack. Scott, *Law of Trust*, Sec. 169, 170 (3rd ed.).

8. The common law trust concept permits the revocation of property transfers or the undoing of other transactions brought about by undue influence or fraudulent misrepresentation. See *Ambassador College v. Geotzke*, 244 GA 322, 260 S.E.2d 27 (1979), *cert. denied*, 444 U.S. 1079 (1980); *Nelson v. Dodge*, 68 A.2d 51 (Ri.1949); *Brown v. Father Divine*, 298 N.Y.S. 642 (NY 1937), *aff'd.*, 4 N.Y.S.2d 89 (1938). See, e.g., *Stern v. Lucy Webb, Hayes National Training School for Deaconesses and Missionaries*, 381 F. Supp. 1003 (D.C. 1974).

9. The Uniform Trust Act, Sec. 5 forbids a trustee from directly or indirectly buying or selling any property from the trust, from or to himself, or from or to any relative, employee, partner, or other business associate. Sec. 379 prohibits any act of self-dealing. *See* Restatement (Second) of Torts Secs. 525 to 549 for a discussion of the cases charging fraud in the acquisition of control of church funds or property; Taylor, *Diversion of Church Funds to Personal Use: State, Federal, and Private Sanctions*, 73 J. Crim. L. & Criminology 1204 (1982); Oaks, *Trust Doctrines in Church Controversies*, 1981 B.Y.U.L. Rev. 805. *Hendrix v. People's United Church*, 42 Wash. 336, 84 P. 1123 (Wa. 1906) is illustrative of the court's refusing to let the First Amendment be used as a cloak for concealing fraud that is not even arguably in furtherance of a religious purpose. As the Washington Supreme Court said there:

> [The] bald question here is, can a man or set of men, or a majority of the church organization, by chicanery, deceit and fraud, divert the property of a church organization to a purpose entirely foreign to the purposes of the organization, for their own selfish benefit, whether

369

by the expulsion of members or in any other fraudulent manner? Neither the law nor public policy will sustain such a rule. (*Id.* at 346, 84 P. at 1127)

10. *Worldwide Church of God, Inc., et. al.,* 623 F.2d 613 (AR 9th 1980).

11. The term "security" contained in the Federal Securities law as well as the Uniform Securities Act which has been adopted either in whole or in significant part by nearly 40 states is defined broadly enough to include many instruments utilized in church fund-raising efforts. There are limited exemptions for securities offered by any entity "organized and operated not-for-private but exclusively for religious . . . purposes" (Sec. 3(a)(4) of the Federal Securities Act of 1933 and Sec. 402 of the Uniform Securities Act). However, it is important to note that some states provide no exemption for the securities of religious organizations, while many require an application for exemption before any securities are issued. Moreover, all securities laws subject churches and other religious organizations to the antifraud requirements. For example, in *Securities and Exchange Commission v. World Radio Mission, Inc.,* 544 F.2d 535 (1st Cir. 1976), the church and its leader were prosecuted for violating the antifraud provisions of the Securities Act of 1933 because of soliciting funds through an investment plan consisting essentially of the sale of interest-bearing notes to the general public. The notes were promoted through advertisements extolling the soundness of this investment as contrasted with the "floundering world economy," when, in fact, the church's operating deficit had jumped from $42,000 to $204,000 in the preceding three years. In rejecting the church's First Amendment defenses, the court observed "defendants constantly emphasize that they are engaged in 'God's work.' No court has ever found that conduct, by being so described, is automatically immunized from all regulation in the public interest." *Id.* at 539 n. 7. The court quoted with approval the U.S. Supreme Court's earlier observation that "[nothing] we have said is intended even remotely to imply that, under the cloak of religion, persons may, with impunity, commit frauds upon the public." *Id.* at 537 n.3, *quoting Cantwell v. Connecticut,* 310 U.S. 296, 306 (1940). Also see *Order of Florida Comptroller,* No. 78-1-DOS (2/17/78) (minister found guilty of fraudulent practices in failing to disclose to investors of church securities that he had $116,000 of unsatisfied debts and that he had incurred $700,000 in unsatisfied debts on behalf of a previous church through the sale of securities); *People v. Life Science Church,* 450 N.Y.S.2d 664 (1982) (church found guilty of fraudulent practices in conducting a pyramid marketing scheme for ministerial credentials). As is typical with most laws, neither good faith, nor the innocent intentions of the seller are defenses to viola-

tions. See *Moerman v. Zipco, Inc.*, 302 F. Supp. 439 (E.D.N.Y. 1969), *aff'd.*, 422 F.2d 871 (2d Cir. 1970).

12. The following 33 jurisdictions have some form of registration or licensing laws for charitable organizations soliciting funds from residents of their states: AR, CA, CT, DC, FL, GA, HI, IL, KS, ME, MD, MA, MI, MN, NE, NH, NJ, NM, NY, NC, ND, OH, OK, OR, PA, RI, SC, TN, VA, WA, WV, and WI. In addition, IN, KY, and NV, while not having registration laws for charitable organizations, do require registration for outside fund-raising counsel. Source: *Fund-Raising Review*, published by the American Association of Fund-Raising Counsel (12/86).

13. In *Schumburg v. Citizens for Better Environment*, 444 U.S. 620, 100 S. Ct. 826 (1980), the Supreme Court ruled that a charitable organization cannot be denied the right to solicit based upon its fund-raising costs. In 1984, the Supreme Court ruled in *Maryland v. Munson*, 467 U.S. 947, 104 S. Ct. 2839 (1984), that the percentage caps on fund-raising costs restrict free speech in violation of the Constitution. Subsequently, Arkansas' 25 percent limit and Kentucky's 15 percent limit on the amounts of total contributions that could be spent for fund-raising were removed. In 1984, Florida, Maryland, and New York eliminated their fund-raising cost caps. In 1985, West Virginia and Hawaii took similar actions. Other states have subsequently reported that while they retained the cost limitation proviso, only cases involving flagrant violations are being enforced. Massachusetts regulators, for example, were not enforcing a 50 percent solicitation ceiling but were continuing to require compliance with a 15 percent cap applicable to fees paid to professional solicitors. In March of 1986, a District Court held that five sections of North Carolina's Charitable Solicitation Act were unconstitutional, including the disclosure of the net proceeds received by charities after expenses paid to fund-raisers. On June 12, 1986, the Maine State Superior Court held that its state laws disclosure requirements were unconstitutional. Subsequently, a Minnesota court enjoined the 30 percent limitation on fund-raising costs.

14. The Mode Charitable Solicitation law was adopted by the National Association of Attorney Generals in December 1986 and is in the process of being considered by various states. Among its more controversial provisions are requirements that: (1) point of solicitation disclosure be made of the percentage received by paid solicitors; (2) there be no exemption for solicitation of members only; (3) the small organization exemption be limited to ten or fewer donors and no paid staff; (4) a church may not be exempt if it has unrelated business income; (5) there is no grace period for filing fund-raising contracts; (6) it does not

adequately relieve the burden of multistate filing; and (7) it gives the government the power of injunction for even minor violations of the statute. Further information can be obtained from, and concerns expressed to, Joseph I. Liberman, Chairman, NAAG Committee on Trust and Solicitation, Office of the Attorney General, 30 Trinity Street, Hartford, CT 06106.

15. See B. Hopkins, *Journal of College and University Law (Vol. 2, No. 4)* at 306 ff.

16. Van Deerlin Bill-H.R. 1199, 93rd Cong., 2d Sess.; reintroduced as H.R. 1123, 94th Cong., 1st Sess. (1975); hearings held 1/14/75. See also Lehman Bill-H.R. 478, 96th Cong., 1st Sess. (required distribution of at least 50 percent of gross revenue for charitable purposes). Mondale Bill, S. 1153, 93rd Cong., 1st Sess.; hearings held 2/4–6, and 3/12/74.

17. According to allegations brought in federal court, only approximately $1 million of some $20 million collected in support for foreign missions was used for those purposes. Most of the balance went to fund-raising costs, with some diverted to such unrelated purposes as financing the divorce of a state governor, a loan to an associate of a former Vice President of the United States, and to various real estate investments made by this Baltimore Catholic charity.

18. Wilson Bill-H.R. 825, 96th Cong., 1st Sess. The bill would have given the Postal Service access to all financial records, including contributions and expenses and would have required annual disclosure of various financial information.

19. The Revenue Act of 1987 (H.R. 3545) signed by the President on 12/22/87 provides that (1) all tax-exempt organizations receiving in excess of $100,000 per year must conspicuously disclose the fact that gifts to the organization are not deductible as charitable contributions; (2) all tax-exempt organizations must maintain for public inspection a copy of their three most recent Annual Information Returns (IRS Form 990); (3) the Annual 990 Report must disclose direct and indirect transactions between any tax-exempt organization and certain lobbying groups or political organizations; (4) excise taxes are imposed on political expenditures by charitable organizations.

20. On 10/6/87, six well-known TV evangelists and spokespersons for the Evangelical Council for Financial Accountability (ECFA) and the National Religious Broadcasters' (NRB) newly created Ethics and Financial Integrity Commission (EFICOM), plus representatives of the IRS and others, testified before Chairman J.J. Pickle and members of the House Ways and Means Oversight Subcommittee. In June 1987, Chairman Pickle led his Subcommittee in several days of hearings

investigating unrelated business income activity by nonprofits. In March 1987, the Committee held 2 days of hearings to determine the growth in lobbying and political activity by tax-exempt organizations. New UBIT legislation is expected, but probably not until after results are received from a new taxpayer compliance audit program, that the IRS launched in the fall of 1987.

21. In August 1987, Congressman Mickey Leland (D-TX) announced that he is initiating a Congressional fact-finding study into the fund-raising practices of certain religious organizations. He asked the General Accounting Office and his Subcommittee staff to conduct a comprehensive examination into the mailing activities of eight religious organizations. Among the questions asked are: (1) What printed items are mailed under the organization's third-class mail permit? (2) How many items per year are mailed by each organization? and (3) How many times per year are mailings made?

22. Since a tax-exempt entity must be operated substantially for tax-exempt purposes, the conduct of more than an insubstantial amount of unrelated business would jeopardize its tax-exempt status. Furthermore, Section 511 of the Code imposes a tax on unrelated business taxable income which is defined in Section 512 as "the gross income derived by any organization from any unrelated trade or business regularly carried on by it." This concept has pertinence to a charity's fund-raising activities because increasingly charities are turning to more creative means of producing income, including the sale of goods at a church bazaar, talent shows, garage or rummage sales, bingo games, sales of cookbooks, contracting staff to businesses to collate and stuff envelopes, operating recycling centers, theater benefits, parking lot rentals, sale of greeting cards, sale of printing services, and so on. All of these have the potential of generating unrelated business income. Examples of more spectacular entrepreneurial activity include (1) the Nonprofit Children's Television Workshop netting $8 million in 1983 by marketing miniature versions of Kermit the Frog, Big Bird, and other Sesame Street characters; (2) Chicago's Lincoln Park Zoo earning $10,000 per week on the sale of stuffed animals, jewelry, and souvenirs; and (3) the New York Museum of Modern Art selling air rights above the Manhattan Museum to a developer for $17 million. The developer erected a 44-story condo and sold units to private individuals who pay no property taxes. Instead, they pay fees to a tax-exempt trust for the benefit of the museum.

23. Entrepreneurial investment partnerships are partnerships between nonprofits and individuals or business entities. Such partnerships can further charitable goals while offering investors a return on their

money. Investor funds channeled into charitable activities have become increasingly important in achieving nonprofit goals. By examining the numerous IRS rulings in this area, the following guidelines can be extracted: (1) such partnerships must have a charitable objective; (2) the partnership agreement must permit the exempt entity to act primarily to further its own exempt purposes and not primarily to benefit the investor/limited partners; (3) the investor benefits must be incidental to the charitable purposes of the partnership; (4) the investor's return must be reasonable and must be capped to prevent windfalls; (5) the scope of the charitable achievement should be commensurate with the resources used; (6) the partnership must be structured to avert conflicts between the organization's charitable purposes and its duty to protect the financial interests of its investors; (7) the exempt organization should not profit at the expense of the charitable class that it is seeking to serve; and (8) the organization's resources should not underwrite the investments of the private investors.

24. See, e.g., *Miller v. Commissioner*, No. 862090 (4th Cir. 9/18/87) (Church of Scientology member's payments for religious counseling were not deductible gifts but were payment for services); *Graham v. Commissioner*, 83 TC 575 (1984) (same). But see *Staples v. Commissioner*, 821 F.2d 1324 (8th Cir. 1987).

25. The substantiation rules for gifts of noncash property are detailed in IRS Reg. Secs. 1.170A-1 and 1.170A-13 and Temp. Reg. Sec. 1.170A-13T. Though the substantiation rules were passed primarily to curb donor abuse, they directly impact all nonprofit organizations receiving contributions from the general public. To date, however, these rules have probably been honored more in the breach than in the keeping, largely because of lack of information.

26. IRS Sec. 4942(a)(2) subjects charitable remainder unitrusts to the same self-dealing rules applicable to private foundation. Thus, in the context of an exempt organization's deferred giving program, it could inadvertently stumble over the self-dealing prohibitions and be subject to the 5 percent excise tax assessed against disqualified persons and the 2-1/2 percent excise tax on the foundation manager or trustee [IRS Reg. Sec. 53.4941(f)(-1)]. There is also a 200 percent penalty if the self-dealing is not corrected within 90 days of IRS notification.

27. The FTC has been trying to carve out a slice of the religious exemption area by promoting legislation that would modify the FTC governing statute so as to define corporations subject to the FTC's jurisdiction as including not-for-profit organizations. See *Community Blood Bank of the Kansas City Area, Inc. v. FTC*, 405 F.2d 1011 (8th Cir. 1969).

28. In *PTL of Heritage Village Church and Missionary Fellowship, Inc.*, et. al.,

54 R.R.2d 824 (FCC 1983), the Commission summarized its action as follows: "By Order, FCC 79-210, released 4/5/79, the Commission established a nonpublic inquiry pursuant to Section 403 of the Communications Act of 1934, as amended [to investigate whether] WJAN (TV) may have operated contrary to the public interest [by making] . . . misrepresentations or false, misleading or deceptive statements . . . over the station in connection with broadcast announcements concerning fund raising for particular projects or purposes." Because PTL subsequently applied to transfer its TV station to another entity, the Commission decided to grant the transfer and dismiss the proceeding while forwarding relevant information obtained in the inquiry to the Justice Department.

In a decision involving the controversial Dr. Eugene Scott, President and Pastor of Faith Center Church and President of Faith Center, Inc., licensee of various television and radio stations in California and elsewhere, the Ninth Circuit held that "when Scott and the Church decided to acquire television and radio stations, they availed themselves of facilities which, under Congressional mandate, must be operated in the public interest" [47 U.S.C. Secs. 307(a), 309(a)]. "[An] allegation of fraud, even if not sufficiently specific or reliable generally to justify inquiry into solicitations made by a congregation and church, may nevertheless be sufficient to justify inquiry into broadcast solicitations." *Scott v. Rosenburg*, et al., 53 R.R.2d 127, 137 (9th Cir. 1983). See also *Faith Center, Inc.*, 69 F.C.C.2d 1123, 1127, 43 R.R.2d 401 (1978), where the Commission warned Faith Center of the consequences of refusing to provide documents requested to investigate allegations of misuse of funds solicited through the use of its broadcast facilities.

29. Charles W. Colson, *Kingdoms in Conflict* (Grand Rapids: William Morrow and Zondervan Publishing House, 1987), 227.

30. For an illuminating discussion of the duty of loyalty, see Scott, *Law of Trust*, Sec. 348.2 at 2780 (3d Ed.) and Phelan, *Nonprofit Enterprises*, Sec. 4:05; Fletcher Encylopedia of Corporations, Sec. 861.1. For a good discussion on the duty of care, see Henn & Alexander, *Law of Corporations*, Sec. 234 (3d Ed.); Phelan, *Nonprofit Enterprises*, Sec. 4:08. Scripturally the Parable of the Shrewd Manager in Luke 16:1-12 clearly portrays the duty of loyalty when Jesus announces that the standard for promotion is faithfulness in the little. The duty of care which is inherent in the master commending the shrewdness of his manager is clearly portrayed in the Parable of the Ten Talents where the servant who did not use ordinary care in investing the funds of his master was condemned as a "wicked servant" (Luke 19:11-27).

31. For example, though ECFA has seven primary standards, it has identified 14 key criteria for the purposes of making standard comparisons between itself and other financial certifying agencies, and 25 separate questions must be answered to complete its application.
32. This avoidance attitude is seen, for example, in the small numbers of tax-exempt organizations that have taken the necessary steps to comply with the multiple-state charitable solicitation requirements. A number of organizations seem to have taken the attitude that because the laws are complex, nonuniform, and in some cases constitutionally suspect, they will take few if any steps to comply, but rather adopt a reactive approach—for example, waiting for the posse to come to the door. This avoidance strategy may ultimately be vindicated, but the point is that it would not likely occur with an effective self-regulation. Either the rule would be enforced or it would be changed.
33. See Malvern J. Gross, Jr., and William Warshauer, Jr., *Financial and Accounting Guide for Nonprofit Organizations* (3d Ed.) (NY 1983); Price Waterhouse, *Effective Internal Accounting Control for Nonprofit Organizations* (1982); Rev. Manferd Holck, Jr., and Manferd Holck, Sr., *Complete Handbook of Church Accounting* (Englewood Cliffs, NJ 1978).

CHAPTER 16
1. Guy Greenfield, *We Need Each Other* (Grand Rapids: Baker Book House, 1984).
2. Paul Tournier, *The Person Reborn* (New York: Harper and Row, 1966).

CHAPTER 17
1. *Christianity Today*, November 6, 1987, 28–31.
2. Holy Trinity House of God, Macon, Georgia: "How to Have More Money" (direct mail flyer).
3. *EP News Service*, May 23, 1986, 2–3.
4. See also Jeffrey K. Hadden and Charles E. Swann, *Prime Time Preachers: The Rising Power of Televangelism* (Reading, Massachusetts: Addison-Wesley, 1981).
5. Release form from PTL.
6. Letter from Bob Seiple dated November 25, 1986.

CHAPTER 18
1. Parker J. Palmer, *The Company of Strangers* (New York: Crossroads Press, 1983), 130.
2. Laurent A. Daloz, *Effective Teaching and Mentoring* (San Francisco: Jossey-Bass Publishers, 1987), 14.
3. Parker J. Palmer, *To Know As We Are Known: A Spirituality of Education*

(San Francisco: Harper & Row Publishers, 1983), 63.
4. Northrup Frye, *The Great Code: The Bible and Literature* (Toronto: Academic Press Canada, 1982), 159.
5. Martin Buber, *I and Thou.* Translated by Walter Kaufmann. (New York: Charles Scribner's Sons, 1970), 158.

CHAPTER 19
1. *A Narrative of Some of the Lord's Dealings with George Mueller, Written by Himself* (London: J. Nisbet & Co., 1869), B. Also cited in the *Autobiography of George Mueller* (London: Pickering & Inglis, 1929), 1.
2. *Narrative*, 4. *Autobiography*, 3.
3. *Narrative*, 2. *Autobiography*, 2.
4. Ibid.
5. Ibid.
6. *Narrative*, 4. *Autobiography*, 3–4.
7. *Narrative*, 12. *Autobiography*, 10.
8. *Narrative*, 44. *Autobiography*, 32.
9. *Narrative*, 50–51. *Autobiography*, 36.
10. *Narrative*, 111–13. *Autobiography*, 64–66.
11. *Narrative*, 321–22. *Autobiography*, 134.
12. G. Fred. Bergin, compiler, *Ten Years After: A Sequel to the Autobiography of George Mueller* (London: J. Nisbet & Co., 1909), 11.
13. *Narrative*, 239–245
14. Philippians 2:9-11 is a classic treatment of this theme of Christ's lordship. Hebrews 2:6-10, wherein it is said of Christ, "God left nothing that is not subject to Him," is another clear reference to His Lordship. Further, the whole of Scripture revolves around the concept that God is Lord of all—as its Creator and Sustainer.
15. Philippians 4:17. In this chapter the Apostle Paul makes some very interesting points about the benefit to the donor being greater than the benefit to the recipient. For a most rewarding study, pursue Paul's argument further.

CHAPTER 20
1. Philip Kotler, *Marketing for Nonprofit Organizations* (Englewood Cliffs, New Jersey: Prentice-Hall, 1982), 83.
2. Ibid.
3. This definition is my own and is selective rather than comprehensive.
4. Tony Campolo, in address, "Setting an Agenda for Evangelicals," Winnipeg '85 conference.
5. Stephen Isaac and William B. Michael, *Handbook in Research and Evaluation for Education and the Behavioral Sciences* (San Diego: Edits Publishers, 1982), 13.

6. These pitfalls are my adaptations to the marketing context of thoughts on culture originally put forth by Os Guiness in *The Gravedigger File* (Downers Grove, Illinois: InterVarsity Press, 1983), 25.

7. John White, *The Golden Cow: Materialism in the Twentieth-Century Church* (Downers Grove, Illinois: InterVarsity Press, 1979), 100.

8. Guiness, *The Gravedigger File*, 131.

9. Ibid., 27.

10. Adapted from Louis A. Allen's definition of the "key objective." *Making Managerial Planning More Effective* (New York: McGraw-Hill, 1982).

11. Robert R. Blake and Jane S. Mouton, *The New Managerial Grid* (Houston: Gulf Publishing Company, 1978), 11.

CHAPTER 22

1. Brian Rust and Barry McLeish, *The Support-Raising Handbook* (Downers Grove, Illinois: InterVarsity Press, 1984), 14.

2. Merrill C. Tenney, *New Testament Survey* (Grand Rapids: William B. Eerdmans Publishing Company), 225.

3. Philip Schaff, "Josephus, The Antiquities XVIII, iii, 3," *History of the Christian Church, Volume 1* (Grand Rapids: William B. Eerdmans Publishing Company), 92ff.

4. Henry H. Halley, *Halley's Bible Handbook* (Minneapolis: Zondervan Publishing House for the Grason Company), 408.

5. Tenney, *New Testament Survey*, 285.

6. Ibid., 287.

7. Ibid., 289.

8. Ibid., 491.

9. Walter L. Liefeld, "Can Deputation Be Defended Biblically?" *Evangelical Missions Quarterly*, October 1986, 360.

CHAPTER 24

1. Virginia Hodgkinson and Murray Weitzman, *The Charitable Behavior of Americans* (Washington: Independent Sector, 1986), 29. Study conducted by Yankelovich, Skelly, and White and funded by the Rockefeller Brothers Fund.

2. Ibid., 32.

3. Ibid., 3.

4. Emory Griffin, *The Mind Changers: The Art of Christian Persuasion.* (Wheaton, Illinois: Tyndale House Publishers, 1976), 122.

5. *Religion in America.* The Gallup Report, Report No. 259. (Princeton, New Jersey: Gallup Organization, April 1987), 57–71.

6. Hodgkinson, *Charitable Behavior*, 33.

7. Ibid., 10.

8. Robert Cohen, "A Social Climate Perspective on Charitable Giving." Paper delivered at National Society of Fund-Raising Executives convention, Chicago, February 1987, 12–13.
9. *Americans Volunteer 1985*. (Washington, DC: Independent Sector, 1986), 16–17.
10. Hodgkinson, *Charitable Behavior*, 5.

CHAPTER 25
1. For a summary of donor research through 1983, see James F. Engel, *Averting the Financial Crisis in Christian Organizations* (Wheaton, Illinois: Management Development Associates, 1983). Also see James F. Engel, "What Motivates Giving to Christian Organizations?" *Fund-Raising Management* (July 1987), 49–52. Figures 1–3 were reproduced from this article by special permission from Hoke Communications, Inc.
2. For a background on decision-process models, see James F. Engel, Roger D. Blackwell, and Paul W. Miniard, *Consumer Behavior*, 5th ed. (Hinsdale, Illinois: Dryden Press, 1986) and Icek Ajzen and Martin Fishbein, *Understanding Attitudes and Predicting Social Behavior* (Englewood Cliffs, New Jersey: Prentice-Hall, 1980).
3. See Engel, Blackwell, and Miniard, *Consumer Behavior*, chapter 2.
4. For more discussion of the biblical rationale, see *Giving Yourself Away*, by Lawrence O'Nan.
5. For a more extended discussion of the stakeholder concept, see Philip Kotler, *Marketing for Nonprofit Organizations*, 2nd ed. (Englewood Cliffs, New Jersey: Prentice-Hall, 1982).
6. See Engel, *Averting the Financial Crisis*, 20–24.
7. For further discussion see Richard E. Perry and John T. Cacioppo, *Attitudes and Persuasion: Classic and Contemporary Approaches* (Dubuque, Iowa: William C. Brown, 1981).
8. Engel, *Averting the Financial Crisis*, 7–9.
9. Peter F. Drucker, *An Introductory View of Management* (New York: Harper & Row, 1977).

CHAPTER 26
1. *Christianity Today*, 17 April 1987, 38.
2. James F. Engel and Wheaton Graduate School Research Team, *A Survey of Ethical Beliefs and Practices Used in Fund-Raising for the Christian Organization* (Wheaton, Illinois, 1987).
3. James F. Engel and Wheaton Graduate School Research Team, *Survey of Development Programs of Non-Profit Organizations* (Wheaton, Illinois, February 1985).
4. *Harvard Business Review*, 89.

---

5. Engel, *Survey of Development Programs*, 1985.
6. *Christianity Today*, 38.
7. Engel, *Survey of Ethical Beliefs*, 1987.
8. Engel, *Survey of Development Programs*, 1985.
9. David L. McKenna, "Financing the Great Commission," *Christianity Today*, 15 May 1987, 26.
10. *Christianity Today*, 15 May 1987, 38.

CHAPTER 27
1. *Christian History*, Vol. VI, Number 2 (Worchester, Pennsylvania), 7.
2. Douglas John Hall, *The Steward, A Biblical Symbol Come of Age* (New York: Friendship Press), 35.
3. Ibid.
4. Ibid., 25.
5. A vivid description of such practices is included in *Christian History*, Vol. VI, number 2, by Randy Petersen, "Selling Forgiveness Sparked the Protestant Reformation."
6. *The Charitable Behavior of Americans* (Washington, DC: Independent Sector, 1986), 1.
7. Ibid., 2.
8. Ibid., 34.

CHAPTER 29
1. Charles W. Colson's first of several best-sellers, *Born Again*, recounts his life before and immediately after his conversion to Christianity. Today, Colson is chairman of Prison Fellowship Ministries.
2. Charles W. Colson, *Life Sentence* (Lincoln, Virginia: Chosen Books, 1979), chapter 21.
3. Jerry White, *Church and Parachurch: An Uneasy Marriage* (Portland, Oregon: Multnomah Press, 1983), 55.
4. Ibid., 35.
5. Ibid., chap. 1.
6. Ibid., 32.
7. Richard J. Foster, *Money, Sex and Power* (San Francisco: Harper & Row, 1985), 176.
8. Cheryl Forbes, *The Religion of Power* (Grand Rapids: Zondervan Publishing House, 1983), 117.
9. " 'Battle of Evangelists' Casts Shadow on TV Ministries, Evangelical Movement," The Gallup Poll, 14 May 1987, 1.
10. Forbes, *The Religion of Power*, 159.